SharePoint® 2007 and 2010 Customization for the Site Owner

Michael T. Smith

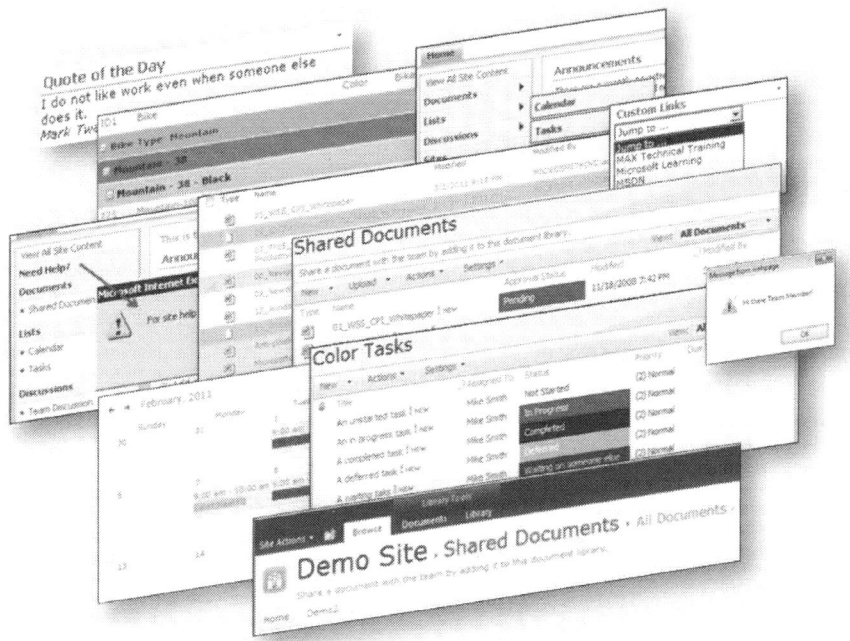

Read Me First

AUTHOR

Michael T. Smith

COPYRIGHT

© 2011 Microsmith, Inc. All Rights Reserved. This book, its support web site and any sample files are copyrighted with all rights reserved. No part of this publication may be reproduced, transmitted, transcribed, stored in a retrieval system or translated into any language in any form by any means without the written permission of the author.

The scanning, uploading, and distribution of this book via the Internet or by any other means without the permission of the author is illegal and punishable by law. Please purchase only authorized printed or electronic editions and do not participate in or encourage electronic piracy of copyrighted materials. We appreciate your support of the author's rights.

TRADEMARKS

Brand names, company names and product names used herein are trademarks or registered trademarks of their respective companies.

ISBN 9780982899205

About the Author

Mike Smith is currently a Senior Instructor at MAX Technical Training in Cincinnati Ohio. He has worn many IT hats over the last thirty years as a business owner, developer, tech writer, trainer, DBA and consultant. He is a SharePoint MVP for 2010 and 2011 and a Microsoft Certified Trainer (MCT). He specializes in SharePoint, SQL Server and .NET development. Mike is a member of the Cincinnati SharePoint User Group leadership team and when time permits, speaks at SharePoint user groups, SharePoint Saturday events and other SharePoint events. Mike has written over 120 training and technical manuals, and now a book!

You can contact the author through the book's web site. http://www.microsmithinc.com/books

Acknowledgments

A book like this one owes a lot to many people. Here's just a few...

- My wife Kathy and my four sons - for their never ending patience with my working way too much.
- Denise Bartick and the MAX Technical Training team - for giving me the opportunity to focus on SharePoint training over the last five years, and for putting up with my idiosyncrasies.
- Microsoft - for creating such an amazing product as SharePoint!
- All of those who have attended my classes and have asked some of the most interesting questions - many of which led to customizations in this book.
- Everyone in the MSDN and TechNet Forums - who both ask the questions to test my knowledge of SharePoint and answer many of my dumb questions.

Preface

None needed! Turn to chapter 1 and get started!

Table of Contents

About the Author iii
Acknowledgments iii
Preface iii

1. **Read Me First** 11
    Sample Files and Resources 12
    The Three C's of SharePoint Customization 12
    What can a site owner customize? 13
    What's not in this book? 13
    Are you a Site Collection Administrator or a Site Owner? 13
    Are we doing Site Branding? 14
    Can I Damage My SharePoint Site? 14
    Tools and Skills Needed 14
    SharePoint Versions 15
    What won't work? 16
    Useless SharePoint Trivia 16

2. **An HTML Primer** 17
    Do you need this chapter? 17
    HTML in SharePoint 18
    Basic HTML – HyperText Markup Language 19
    What is DHTML? 30
    References 32
    Useless Trivia! 32

3. **A CSS Primer** 33
    Do you need this chapter? 33
    What is CSS? 34
    In the beginning… 34
    And then there was CSS… 34
    CSS Syntax 37
    CSS Selectors 37
    Style Classes 38
    One style per ID 38
    Comments 39
    Positioning 39
    Using Styles to Control Visibility 39
    Inline Styles 40
    Overriding Inline Styles 40
    Adding CSS to SharePoint 41
    Using a Different Style when Printing 42

	Style Resources	44
	Useless Trivia!	44
4.	**A JavaScript Primer**	45
	Do you need this chapter?	45
	JavaScript	46
	Where can you use JavaScript in SharePoint?	46
	JavaScript Basics	46
	Key parts of a script	47
	JavaScript Variables	50
	JavaScript Functions	51
	Browser Detection	52
	Finding HTML Elements	52
	JavaScript IF blocks and FOR loops	61
	Accessing the URL's Query String from JavaScript	64
	Is That All?	65
	jQuery	65
	What's next?	70
	Important Tips for JavaScript in SharePoint	71
	When will my scripts run?	71
	JavaScript and SharePoint Dates	72
	Useless Trivia!	74
5.	**Hacking Tips!**	75
	Do you need this chapter?	75
	HTML Detective Tools	76
	How to Find a Web Part in Code	78
	Controlling when JavaScript Runs	81
	SharePoint Version Detection	84
6.	**SharePoint Designer**	93
	Do you need this chapter?	93
	Can I Even Use SharePoint Designer?	94
	Customizing / Un-ghosting a Page	95
	Editing a SharePoint master page	97
	Editing a SharePoint Site Page	100
7.	**Security Tricks**	105
	Do you need this chapter?	105
	Identify the Current Logged In User	106
	SharePoint Permissions	113
	How to Hide "View All Site Content" for Selected Users	114
	Customizing the People and Groups Views	115

8. Web Part Must Knows 119
Do you need this chapter? 119
Does this page have web parts? 120
My page won't load… how do I delete a "bad" web part? 120
Exporting, Importing and Reusing Web Parts 121
Using "Static" web parts 122
SharePoint 2010, the Content Editor Web Part, and Broken Views… 122
Prevent the Closing of web parts 125

9. The Content Editor Web Part 128
Do you need this chapter? 128
A Gift to Customizers! 129
What about the Form Web Part and the Page Viewer Web Part? 129
What about direct page edits using SharePoint Designer? 130
The CEWP in SharePoint 2007 131
The CEWP in SharePoint 2010 132
Reusing a Content Editor Web Part Customization 135
Best Practices 136

10. User Interface Customization 137
Do you need this chapter? 137
Some of the customizations in this chapter: 138
Add a message at the top or bottom of a page 139
Add a message at the top of every page using SharePoint Designer 142
Site Title and Icon (2007) - Change the Font Size, Face or Hide It 145
Site Title and Icon (2010) - Change the Font Size, Face or Hide It 148
A Redesign of the SharePoint 2010 Site Title and Crumb Trail 152
Hide the SharePoint 2010 Ribbon from Visitors and Anonymous Users 156
Hide Menu Options (2007) 158
Hide Menu Options (2010) 162
Hide Menu Options for Selected Users (2007 and 2010) 164
Hide Disabled Ribbon Options (2010) 165
Quick Launch and Top Link Bar Tricks - Add Message Pop-ups (2007 and 2010) 166
Quick Launch and Top Link Bar Tricks - Confirm Site Exit (2007 and 2010) 167
Quick Launch Pop outs (2007 and 2010) 169
Quick Launch Accordions 175
Quick Launch Accordions (2007) 176
Quick Launch Accordions (2010) 177
Add Quick Launch Back Into Basic Pages and Web Part Pages (2007) 179
Cleaning up the Basic Page (2007) 181
Cleaning up the Basic Page (2010) 187
Remove Quick Launch from a Basic Page (2010) 188
How to hide the right web part column (2007) 189
Setting the Web Part Zones to 50% and 50% 191

Modify / Add / remove web part zones (2007 and 2010) 192
Change or Hide the Bullet Image in Quick Launch (2007) 194
Customizing the Tree View (2007 and 2010) 196
Add Dropdown Menus to the Top Link Bar (2007) 203
Add Dropdown Menus to the Top Link Bar (2010) 211
Create Your Own Custom Menus 212
Change or Replace Your Home Page 216
Add Colors, Borders and Fonts to Web Parts 218
Don't forget Links lists! 234

11. List and Library Customization 235

Do you need this chapter? 235
Before you get started 236
What's in this chapter? 236
Color coded lists 237
Customizing the "New" button 244
Group By on more than 2 columns in a view 250
Group By on more than 2 columns in a view (2007) 253
Group By on more than 2 columns in a view (2010) 261
Quote of the Day / Tip of the Day 270
Removing View Group Headings and Group Counts 276
Web Part Customizations 280
Create a "What's New" web part for a library or list (2007 and 2010) 280
Add a web part to display a document library folder 281
Hide a web part with zero rows 283
Change the "No Items" message in a discussion web part (2007 & 2010) 289
Change the "Add New" message for a web part 292
Adding hyperlinks to document libraries 295
Add hyperlinks for special URLs 296
How to truncate a Multiline column and add a "More" link (2007 & 2010) 298
How do to add columns (metadata) to SharePoint folders (2007 & 2010) 302
Hiding the Checked Out icon from anonymous users (2007 & 2010) 303
One library, multiple sites! 305
Rotating Pictures, Random Pictures 309
The List, the Whole List, Nothing but the List 321

12. Surveys 327

Do you need this chapter? 327
Surveys 328
Survey Pages 328
Survey Tips 329
You can create custom views! (2007 only) 331
A better Yes/No field for surveys and lists 334

Adding a Welcome or Instructions Message to the Overview page 335
Adding a Welcome, Thank You or Instructions Message to a Survey 336
Adding Color, Fonts and HTML to Surveys... 339
Add Instructions and Color!.. 339
Adding Color, Fonts and HTML to Rating Sub Questions 340
Hide the "Save" button.. 342
Hide survey bars where not needed! 346
Modifying the "Respond to this Survey" prompt... 348
Reuse Your Custom Surveys 352

13. Links Lists 353

Do you need this chapter?... 353
The Links List... 354
Adding Pop-ups to Link lists (open in new window) 354
Add a "You are leaving this site" message 356
Add a "You are leaving this site" message to a links list with confirmation! 357
Convert a Links list to a Dropdown list 357
Convert a Links list into a dropdown list that opens in a new window 360
Convert a Links list to a dropdown list that opens in a different web part................................... 361

14. Task Lists 362

Do you need this chapter?... 362
Color Coding Task Lists 363
Project Tasks / Gantt Chart (2007 only) 367
Prevent editing of completed tasks 368
Color Code Past Due / Late Tasks in a Task List 370

15. Calendars... 379

Do you need this chapter?... 379
Color Coded Calendars... 380
Strike Out Canceled Events in the Calendar 384
Create a Calendar View without Hyperlinks (2007).. 388
Create a Calendar View without Hyperlinks (2010).. 389
Using the Calendar to Schedule Meeting Rooms (multiple fields in a month view) 392

16. Bonus Content 393

What's on the web site 393

1. Read Me First

Work on this book started with the creation of my blog site in 2007. Or maybe it started in 2006 with the students in my SharePoint classes when they asked questions about how to do things with SharePoint that just could not be done out of the box. As I did the research to answer their questions I started to see all kinds of ways that SharePoint could be easily changed. Most of these solutions became articles on the blog site, some as detailed articles and some as quick tips. As I looked back over these I thought it would be a good idea to revisit these and include a lot more detail. Late last year I had a couple weeks open and thought I would just sit down and whip out a book. Little did I know just how much I would end up writing, testing and rewriting to get this thing done! Eight months later and it's finally done!

This book is designed to get you started with customizing your SharePoint site with the tools you have readily at hand. It has complete copy and paste solutions, and it also shows how each solution was crafted and how it works. After working through a few of the customizations and picking up some basic skills you will see how SharePoint has been put together and will be able to start creating your own customizations.

The book is for the SharePoint site owner and the SharePoint power user. It's also for the developer who does not want to "reinvent the wheel" to create a complex solution when a simpler one is available. It's also for the SharePoint administrator who is always asked to do the impossible!

The solutions in this book take advantage of SharePoint's web based design by using HTML, JavaScript and Cascading Style Sheets to create some very easy and useful SharePoint customizations.

In this chapter:

- Sample Files and Resources (*Make sure you read this!*)
- The Three C's of SharePoint Customization
- Are we doing Site Branding?
- Can I Damage My SharePoint Site
- Tools and Skills Needed
- SharePoint Versions
- Useless SharePoint Trivia!

Sample Files and Resources

The web is dynamic. Web sites and URLs change, and sometimes even go away. To help keep the book's web resource links up-to-date and working, this book will list links in the book text as "Link: 1234". To find these links you can go to URLs listed below.

To see if there are updates or news for the book:

Go to http://www.microsmithinc.com/books and click the **Microsmith Book Blog** link)

To Register:

Go to http://www.microsmithinc.com/books, click the book title and register. All you need to provide is a user name and password and answer a question about the book.

To see all of the resource links or sample code:

1. Go to the book's web site: http://www.microsmithinc.com/books
2. Click the book's link (SharePoint® 2007 and 2010 Customization for the Site Owner)
3. Click **Updates, Code and Links**

Note: Anything can happen on the web! If any of the addresses above change or no longer work, go to http://www.microsmithinc.com to check for updated links.

You can stay up to date with what I am doing with SharePoint by visiting my blog site at http://TechTrainingNotes.blogspot.com.

The Three C's of SharePoint Customization

So where can you change SharePoint? And what tools, permissions and skills do you need? There are three different levels of SharePoint customizations:

- Configuration
- Customization
- Custom Development

Configuration is everything you can do with SharePoint "out of the box" by using web parts and options from Site Actions, Site Settings and from a list's Settings menu.

Customization is everything you can do without access to the SharePoint web servers and includes using SharePoint Designer and creating web part "tricks" with HTML, JavaScript and Cascading Style Sheets.

Custom Development includes anything that requires access to the SharePoint servers. This includes custom themes, web parts, custom ASPX pages and advanced workflows.

What can a site owner customize?

Site Owners can customize SharePoint using the first two "C's", Configuration and Customization. Some of the kinds of customizations that you can do without needing access to the SharePoint Servers include:

- Changing fonts and colors in a single page or the entire site
- Hiding or resizing the site title
- Creating simple charts
- Adding color, and especially, conditional color, to lists and libraries
- Customizing the appearance of surveys

What can't a site owner customize?

- Most of the administrative pages, in particular those with "_LAYOUTS" in the URL. As an example you cannot modify the Site Actions, Site Settings page. (http://...../_layouts/settings.aspx)
- In SharePoint 2007 you cannot upload or edit SharePoint Themes, but you can override the CSS used with SharePoint themes. (see the CSS chapter)

What's not in this book?

This book does not cover any SharePoint customization that requires developer skills or administrator access to the servers. This includes:

- Needing Visual Studio or programming in languages like C# and VB.NET
- Requiring any direct access to the SharePoint servers
- Requiring links from your site to anything on the internet
- Needing to purchase any additional software
- Needing advanced development skills such as the SharePoint 2010 Client API, web services or AJAX (developers should explore all of these...)

Are you a Site Collection Administrator or a Site Owner?

Your organization may have its own name for a Site Owner, such as Site Administrator or SharePoint Site Manager. In this book we will use the SharePoint terms "Site Owner" and "Site Collection Administrator".

The Site Owner:

- has Full Control permissions to their sites
- is responsible for a site or subsite and all of the subsites below their site
- is in charge of site security
- owns all of the lists and libraries and their content

- is responsible for making the site useful to their users
- has rights to use SharePoint Designer to access and modify their sites

A Site Collection Administrator is responsible for the top level site of a site collection and in addition to the responsibilities of the site owner also has:

- access to the web part, list template and site template galleries
- access to site collection reports
- access to all subsites and all content
- the ability to limit the permissions of other Site Owners in the same site collection

Almost all of the customizations in this book require at least Site Owner permissions.

Are we doing Site Branding?

Site branding is the redesign of a site with the goal of creating a complete new look and feel to a site, typically to make the site look like "anything but SharePoint". Site branding is a big topic worthy of another book or two and is not the focus of this book. Here we focus on all of the little things that can make a site more useful and functional. Along the way we will explore topics that border on branding or could be used in the branding process.

Can I Damage My SharePoint Site?

Yes, but only in ways that can be quickly fixed! Everything we do in this book can be undone, either by deleting a web part or by resetting the design of a file.

Tools and Skills Needed

Microsoft designed SharePoint from of a basket full of standard web technologies. Each of these are pretty simple to get started with, but also can take years to fully master. You will be working with a small core set of features from each of the technologies listed below and for most of the customizations in the book you can start with a simple copy and paste of the sample code, and as you have time and interest, dive in as deep as you like.

- SharePoint Designer
- HTML / DHTML
- JavaScript
- Cascading Style Sheets (CCS)

SharePoint Versions

SharePoint comes in a number of flavors and it will be important to know which you are using as you implement the tricks in this book. Unless noted otherwise, the customizations in the book work for both SharePoint 2007 and SharePoint 2010 and for each of the editions. In some cases there are two versions of a customization, one for 2007 and one for 2010.

Before you start on any customization you will need to know:

Which SharePoint do you have?

This book only covers these two "generations" of SharePoint:

- SharePoint 2007
- SharePoint 2010

Which Edition do you have?

The customizations in the book should work fine with all of these editions, unless noted otherwise:

- 2007
    - WSS - Windows SharePoint Services 3.0
    - MOSS - Microsoft Office SharePoint Server 2007
    - MOSS Enterprise - Microsoft Office SharePoint Server 2007 Enterprise Edition
- 2010
    - SharePoint Foundation 2010
    - SharePoint Server 2010
    - SharePoint Server 2010 Enterprise Edition
- Internet Editions?
    - SharePoint 2007 is available as a hosted service from a number of vendors on the internet and as a service from Microsoft known as "BPOS". Everything in this book marked as "WSS" should work.
    - SharePoint 2010 "in the cloud" (Office 365) will be announced shortly after this book goes to press, but everything in the book should work there also. Any exceptions will be posted on the book's web site.

Version Detection

If you are writing JavaScript code that will run almost identically in SharePoint 2007 and in SharePoint 2010 then you may want to include some code to test the version and deal with the version differences with an IF statement. A few techniques are documented in chapter 5.

Site Templates

SharePoint is supplied with a number of site templates. Some of the customizations in the book may only work with certain templates. Templates generally fall into these broad categories:

- non-publishing templates (Example: Team Site)
- publishing templates
- and in 2010, both publishing and non-publishing, and somewhere in between… the "wiki page" templates like the Team Site

What won't work?

If your site has been extensively rebranded with custom style sheets, or with major changes in the master pages, then some of the customizations in the book may not work or will have to be adjusted to work. Each customization includes an explanation of how it works and you should be able to figure out what you will need to change.

Useless SharePoint Trivia

- "In the beginning…" SharePoint was called Tahoe
- "Before the beginning…" was the Digital Dash Board, which is where the idea of web parts came from
- The first version of SharePoint released in 2001 was called "SharePoint Portal Server" (Those three letters "SPS" are still found throughout SharePoint)
- OWS stands for Office Web Server - those three letters are scattered throughout SharePoint
- Windows SharePoint Services 2.0 (WSS) and SharePoint Portal Server 2003 were introduced in… well… 2003
- WSS is not free, it is licensed as part of Windows Server, but at no extra cost beyond the server license
- SharePoint 2003's internal version number is 6, SharePoint 2007's version number was bumped to 12 to match Microsoft Office 2007's version number
- SharePoint 2010's version number is 14 (13 is unlucky?)
- For a really crazy chart of SharePoint's history see Link 103
- SharePoint 2001 stored it's documents on disk drives, SharePoint 2003 and later stored documents in a SQL Server database
- For more see the Microsoft SharePoint team's blog history of SharePoint (see Link 104)

2. An HTML Primer

Do you need this chapter?

If you already have decent HTML skills, or you have a good HTML book, then you can skip most of this chapter. You should still skim it for both a review and a few details about HTML and SharePoint.

In this chapter:

- HTML in SharePoint
- Basic HTML
- What is DHTML
- Useless HTML trivia!

HTML in SharePoint

No matter how a web application builds a web page, the end result is always HTML plus JavaScript, plus Cascading Style Sheets. In addition to basic HTML, SharePoint takes advantage of many ASP.NET features along with a number of custom SharePoint controls. When you are looking at a page or a master page in SharePoint Designer you may find a lot of tags that are not part of HTML. These tags are ASP.Net and SharePoint "controls." These controls will always be converted into HTML plus JavaScript plus Cascading Style Sheets when the server builds the final page. Bottom line, most of the customizations in this book will be working with the final rendered HTML. This is the HTML that you can see with your browser's "View Source" option.

A typical SharePoint page is built like this:
1. You enter a URL: http://myserver/sites/mysite/default.aspx
2. SharePoint loads the following into the server's memory:
    - default.aspx
    - default.master or v4.master (the SharePoint master page)
    - CORE.CSS or corev4.css (the primary SharePoint style sheet)
    - an optional theme style sheet
    - a number of custom SharePoint controls such as the search box and the navigation controls
    - a number of JavaScript libraries
    - navigation data for the Top Link Bar and for Quick Launch
    - all of the content need for the web parts
3. SharePoint converts the controls and web parts into HTML and then sends the HTML, CSS and JavaScript back to your browser (where we can apply our customizations!)

SharePoint 2010 also frequently includes Silverlight controls in the final page.

Basic HTML – HyperText Markup Language

For more detailed information on HTML see Links 201 and 202.

Tags

Originally HTML was used to "mark up" text to make it computer readable. A tag like <H1> was used to indicate the top level of a table of contents. For example, <H1> might be a chapter title and <H2> might be a chapter section. As a result, there are now a number of almost never used tags such as <ADDRESS> and <AUTHOR>. The browser manufactures decided to add formatting to the tagged text to make the marked up documents more human readable. So <H1> now also defines formatting and causes <H1> text to be displayed as large and bold text. As display formatting was not part of the HTML standard, each browser vendor picked their own fonts, sizes and margins. This is one reason we now have Cascading Style Sheets! Today we use HTML tags and CSS to control the appearance of text and images on a web page.

For example, the following HTML:

Welcome to <b>Mike's <i>SharePoint</i> Test</b> site.

displays the text like this:

Welcome to **Mike's *SharePoint* Test** site.

The <b> tag starts the display of bold text and the </b> ends the bold text. The same applies to the italics tag <i>. When using SharePoint Designer you may also see <strong> used in place of <b> and <em> used in place of <i>.

Welcome to <strong>Mike's <em>SharePoint<em> Test</strong> site.

The <strong> and <em> tags display the text exactly the same as <b> and <i> tags:

Welcome to **Mike's *SharePoint* Test** site.

Page Tags

Tags are also used to mark sections of the entire page. For example:

```
<html>
<head>
 <title>Mike's SharePoint Site</title>
 …. Non-display tags: scripts, metatags, CSS ….
</head>
<body>
 Welcome to my web page
</body>
</html>
```

The tags used above:

<html>	Marks the beginning and end of the page. Each page has exactly one of these.
<head>	Marks the beginning and end of the page header. The page header can contain the page title, CSS code, JavaScript functions, links to external files containing CSS and scripts, and instructions to search engines (META tags). Content in the <head> tag is never displayed in the page, but may impact how the page is displayed. Each page has exactly one of these.
<title>	Used to supply the title text to display in the title bar of the browser and is the default text for bookmarks. This does not display anywhere in the page. Each page has exactly zero or one of these.
<body>	Marks the beginning and end of the displayed portion of the page. All text and HTML to format the page goes here. Each page has exactly one of these.

Most tags are used in pairs

Most tags are used in pairs with the end tag starting with a slash:

        <html>   </html>
        <b>   </b>

An HTML Primer

Some tags do not have end tags

Some tags such as
 (line break) and <hr> (horizontal line) do not have matching end tags. While these can generally be typed without anything to mark the end, proper formatting includes a "/" to self close the tag.

    <hr />
    <input type="text" name="username" bgcolor="yellow" />

 Some tags may not have content, but still must have a closing tag. One of these is the <script> tag when it is used to link to a script file.

    <script src="http:// ..."></script>

Tags are nested

Correct:

    this is bold italic text

Incorrect:

    this is bold italic text

 Although out of order tags are technically incorrect, most browsers can still display the text correctly, *but this is not a good practice!*

Attributes

Many HTML tags can be modified by adding attributes.

    <body bgcolor="green">
    <table width="100%">

Attribute values should be enclosed in either single or double quotes. (Note: SharePoint generated HTML frequently does not use quotes.)

Colors

Colors can be represented by using names or hexadecimal numbers. The numbers represent colors by specifying the amount of red, green and blue using hexadecimal values 00-FF (0-255 decimal) prefixed with "#".

 Something to think about... 256 reds times 256 greens times 256 blues equals 16,777,216 different colors!

An HTML Primer

Here are a few common colors:

Black =	#000000	Green =	#008000
Silver =	#C0C0C0	Lime =	#00FF00
Gray =	#808080	Olive =	#808000
White =	#FFFFFF	Yellow =	#FFFF00
Maroon =	#800000	Navy =	#000080
Red =	#FF0000	Blue =	#0000FF
Purple =	#800080	Teal =	#008080
Fuchsia =	#FF00FF	Aqua =	#00FFFF

For a color list see: Link 210

Formatting Text

Formatting tags are always used in pairs ("<b>some text</b>"). Here is a sampling of the formatting tags:

<b> <strong>	Bold
<i> <em>	Italics
<u>	Underline
<sub>	Subscript
<sup>	Superscript
<font>	Font name, size and color

For a more complete list see Link 211

Line breaks and spaces

HTML generally ignores line breaks, extra spaces and tabs. For example, all of the following produce the same results:

```
        Text text        text
```

```
        Text
        text
        text
```

```
        Text text text
```

Results for all of the above:

Text text text

Controlling breaks and spaces:

Browsers ignore line breaks and extra white space in HTML. To control line breaks you will need to use BR, P and DIV tags. When you need to force white space you can use the   HTML entity code.

 	New line
<p> …. </p>	New paragraph
	Non-breaking space – use to add additional white space and to keep two related words on the same line. "Computer training" could be split across two lines "Computer training" will never be split across two lines

IDs

If any code (client side JavaScript or server side .Net) will be interacting with an HTML element, the element will need a name in the form of "id=".

```
<input type="text" id="usernamebox" name="username" value="Cincinnati"/>
<button onclick="javascript:usernamebox.value='Dayton'">Change City</button>
```

Note the use of quotes. When you need quoted text inside of quoted text you can alternate single and double quotes.

```
onclick="javascript:usernamebox.value='Dayton' "
```

Names

Elements that submit data back to the server may have a Name attribute. These tags include **INPUT**, **SELECT**, and **TEXTAREA**. Most SharePoint elements that have a name also have an ID attribute. When both are available your JavaScript should use the ID.

Sample:

```
<input name="ctl00$PlaceHolderSearchArea$ctl01$S6AE27B38_InputKeywords"
       type="text"
```

An HTML Primer

```
maxlength="200"
id="ctl00_PlaceHolderSearchArea_ctl01_S6AE27B38_InputKeywords"
accesskey="S"
...
```

Name vs. ID

While you should do a web search on "HTML name vs ID" for better information, here are the differences in a nutshell:

Name:

- A name does not have to be unique - example: grouped checkboxes share the same name (Note the "s" in **getElementsByName** that is not in **getElementById**)
- Names are used inside of <form> tags for post backs to the server - so names are needed for server side code to ready data from the page

IDs

- IDs can be used on most HTML elements (except for a few like **HEAD, HTML, BODY**) to uniquely identify the single use of the element
- CSS styles can be applied to elements using IDs, but not to Names (by using the "#" prefix)
- IDs are typically used for interacting with the DOM with JavaScript

Lists

HTML list tags are the quickest way to list data that does not need a full table structure. HTML list items can also auto number items using numbers, letters and Roman numerals.

HTML has two kinds of lists, Ordered and Unordered:

Unordered List:
 	
`<ul>`
`<li>item 1`
`<li>item 2`
`<li>item 3`
`<li>item 4`
`</ul>`
	• item 1
	• item 2
	• item 3
	• item 4

Ordered List:
 	
`<ol>`
`<li>item 1`
`<li>item 2`
`<li>item 3`
`<li>item 4`
`</ol>`
	1. item 1
	2. item 2
	3. item 3
	4. item 4

An HTML Primer

Ordered lists can also include a type: A, a, I, i, or 1 (default)
 	
`<ol type="A">`
`<li>item 1`
`<li>item 2`
`<li>item 3`
`<li>item 4`
`</ol>`
 	
`<ol type="I">`
`<li>item 1`
`<li>item 2`
`<li>item 3`
`<li>item 4`
`</ol>`
	A. item 1
	B. item 2
	C. item 3
	D. item 4
	
	I. item 1
	II. item 2
	III. item 3
	IV. item 4

Entities

Some characters cannot be represented in HTML just by typing them. These include spaces, "<", ">", "@" and others. These need to be typed as HTML entities.

A list of frequently used HTML entities:

<	&lt;	Less than
>	&gt;	Greater than
&	&amp;	Ampersand
©	&copy;	Copyright
™	™ or ™	trademark
		Non-breaking space (or a hard space)

See this site for a partial list of HTML entities: Link 212

An HTML Primer

Tables

Tables can be used to display any tabular data and are often used to layout the overall design of a page. While page layout using tables is no longer recommended for page design, tables are used extensively for this in SharePoint 2007.

Table tags:

- Each **table** will have one pair of <table> tags.
- Each **row** will have one pair of <tr> tags.
- Each **cell** will have one pair of <td> tags.

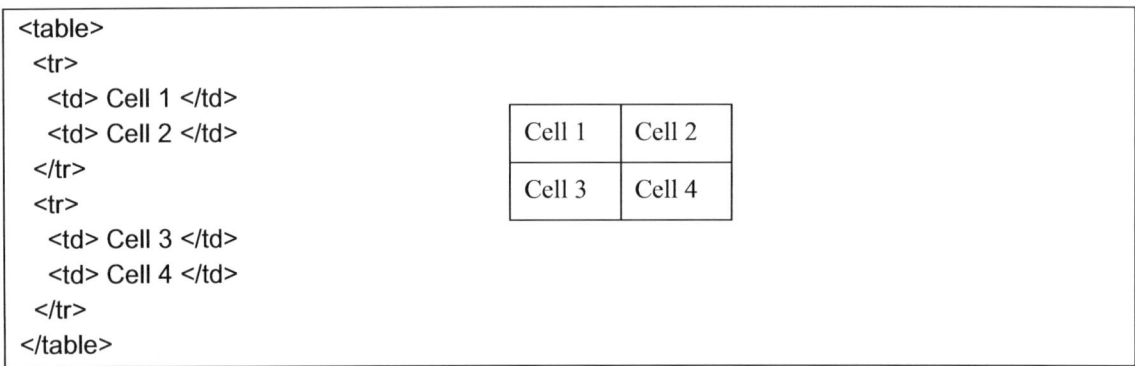

```
<table>
 <tr>
  <td> Cell 1 </td>
  <td> Cell 2 </td>
 </tr>
 <tr>
  <td> Cell 3 </td>
  <td> Cell 4 </td>
 </tr>
</table>
```

| Cell 1 | Cell 2 |
| Cell 3 | Cell 4 |

Table cells can be merged, both within a row (colspan) or a column (rowspan):

```
<table>
 <tr>
  <td colspan="2"> Cell 1  </td>
 </tr>
 <tr>
  <td> Cell 3 </td>
  <td> Cell 4 </td>
 </tr>
</table>
```

| Cell 1 | |
| Cell 3 | Cell 4 |

> Remember that HTML ignores line breaks and excess spaces. The following is also valid HTML for the table above:

```
<table><tr><td colspan="2">Cell 1</td></tr><tr><td>Cell 3</td><td>Cell 4</td></tr></table>
```

Table, row and cell tags have attributes. Here are a few samples:

```
<table border="1" width="100%" height="200px" bgcolor="green">

<tr bgcolor="yellow">

<td colspan="2" valign="top" align="center" cellpadding="5">
```

✎ Formatting attributes have been generally replaced with CSS. To learn about CSS see the next chapter.

Links and Anchor

HTML uses the <A> to link to another web page, link to a location in the current page and to mark (anchor) a location in the current page.

Link to another web page:

```
<a href="http://www.microsoft.com" > Microsoft </a>
```

Link to another web page and open it in a new browser window:

```
<a href="http://www.microsoft.com" target="somename" > Microsoft </a>
```

Anchors can also be used to scroll up or down to a predefined location in a page. The destination is marked with an <A> with a name attribute and the link includes an HREF with "#" prefix and the name.

Insert an anchor in the current page:

```
<a name="pricing" >Pricing as of 4/1/2008 follows:</a>
```

Anchors do not impact the display in the page, i.e. the "Pricing…" text above will display no hints that it is an anchor. For that matter the anchor tag does not need to enclose text to work. The following produces the same result.

```
<a name="pricing" ></a>Pricing as of 4/1/2008 follows:
```

An HTML Primer

Link to a location (anchor) in the current page:

> `<a href="`**`#pricing`**`" >` see our current pricing `</a>`

When a user clicks the above link the browser will scroll up or down to the anchor spot.

Link to a location (anchor) in another page:

> `<a href="http://www.somewebsite.com/products.htm`**`#pricing`**`" >` see our current pricing `</a>`

When a user clicks the above link the browser open the new page and then will scroll up or down to the anchor spot.

Defining blocks of text – DIV and SPAN

DIV and SPAN are used to group blocks of HTML and text. SPAN is an inline element while DIV is generally rendered with a line break before and after.

SPANs are often used for:

- applying a style to an area of text
- as a place holder for text that will be added or changed using scripting

  ✎   SPANs cannot include block level tags such as P and TABLE

DIVs are often used for:

- floating blocks of text (pop-ups, help boxes, etc)
- an alternate to tables to layout a page design

  ✎   DIVs can include block level tags such as P and TABLE

`<span>` example:

> Some text `<span style="font-style: italic">` some more text `</span>` and even more text

Result:

> Some text *some more text* and even more text

`<div>` example:

> Some text **<div style="font-style: italic">** some more text **</div>** and even more text

Result:

> Some text
> *some more text*
> and even more text

Note that the DIV starts a new block of text and moves the enclosed text to a new line.

ASP.Net tags

SharePoint pages will also include non-HTML tags within the HTML. ASP.Net includes controls that are processed on the server and converted into HTML for use in a browser. These controls will be frequently seen when using SharePoint Designer to edit a page. ASP controls range from simple button controls to complex controls like the Calendar control. Many ASP controls, such as the web part zone control, add functionally to a page without generating HTML.

Examples of ASP controls:

```
<% ......... %>
<asp:... >
<asp:Calendar... >
<WebPartPages:...
```

> ASP tags and custom SharePoint tags that contain **"runat='server'"** can be added to site pages and master pages using SharePoint Designer, but will not work if added to a Content Editor Web part.

SharePoint and other custom tags

Developers can create their own server side tags for ASP.NET applications. SharePoint includes its own collection of custom ASP controls. Like the ASP.Net controls, these controls are always processed on the server and generally return HTML back to the browser. SharePoint controls start with the prefix "sharepoint":

    <sharepoint:...

All SharePoint server controls must be added to ASPX web server installed files (in the LAYOUTS directory) or to site pages (using SharePoint Designer). They will not work if added to a Content Editor Web Part.

As an example of a useful SharePoint control, consider the Security Trimmed Control . This control does not render any HTML of its own, but rather controls if a block of HTML is displayed or not. It does this based on a user's permissions. As an example, if you only wanted to display a message to site owners (who have the ManageWeb permission) you could set **PermissionsString** to **"ManageWeb"**.

An HTML Primer

```
<SharePoint:SPSecurityTrimmedControl runat="server" PermissionsString="ManageWeb">
   Your HTML, CSS or JavaScript for site owners only here…
</SharePoint:SPSecurityTrimmedControl>
```

📖 For more on permissions and the SharePoint Security Trimmed control see chapter 7.

📖 Tags that contain **runat='server'** can be added to site pages and master pages using SharePoint Designer, but will not work if added to a Content Editor Web Part.

What is DHTML?

HTML stands for Hyper Text Markup Language. The "D" in DHTML adds "Dynamic" to the name. DHTML is HTML plus CSS, JavaScript and other technologies that can change HTML after it has been downloaded to the user's browser.

Here is a very simple example that dynamically changes the formatting of an HTML table by using CSS and JavaScript when the user clicks a button:

```html
<button onclick="myJSfunctionStyle()"> Change styles </button> <br/>
<button onclick="myJSfunctionWidth('+')"> Change width + </button> <br/>
<button onclick="myJSfunctionWidth('-')"> Change width - </button> <br/>
<br/>
A plain ordinary table:
<br/>
<table width="300" border="1" id="mytable">
  <tr>
    <td>text goes here</td><td>text goes here</td><td>text goes here</td>
  </tr>
</table>
<br/>

<script type="text/javascript">

  function myJSfunctionStyle()
  {
    var doc = document.getElementById("mytable");
    doc.style.color='red';
    doc.style.fontSize='24pt';
    doc.style.fontFamily='Comic Sans MS';
  }
```

```
function myJSfunctionWidth(direction)
{
  var doc = document.getElementById("mytable");
  if (direction == "+")
    doc.width=parseInt(doc.width) + 100;
  else
    doc.width=parseInt(doc.width) - 100;
}
</script>
```

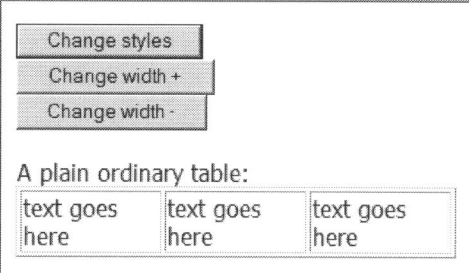

References

- DHTML at W3Schools.com (Link: 231)
- Microsoft's DHTML reference (Link: 232)
- DHTML examples from W3Schools.com (Link: 233)
- DHTML samples (Link: 234)
- A brief history of HTML (Link: 235)
- Fun stuff: Snowflakes! (Link: 236)
- Fun stuff: Butterflies! (Link: 237)

Useless Trivia!

- HTML, and therefore the web as we know it, started at the European Laboratory for Particle Physics in Geneva, Switzerland (CERN) in 1989 as a way for researchers to electronically exchange documents.
- HTML 2 was introduced in 1994, HTML 3 in 1995, HTML 3.2 in 1997, HTML 4 in 1998, and HTML 5 in 2008.
- HTML is based on SGML (Standard Generalized Mark-up Language).
- The earliest browsers were text only.
- NCSA Mosaic was released in 1993, Netscape in 1994, Internet Explorer in 1995, Opera in 1996, Safari in 2003, Firefox in 2004, and Chrome in 2008.
- Firefox has had several names: Phoenix, Firebird, and then Mozilla Firefox.
- The internal code name for Netscape was Mozilla. Mozilla is now part of almost every browser's user agent string - IE 6 indentifies itself as: "Mozilla/4.0 (compatible; MSIE 6.0; ..."
- Now go search the web and find out what "Mozilla" means!

3. A CSS Primer

Do you need this chapter?

If you already have decent HTML and CSS skills, or you have a good CSS book, then you can skip most of this chapter, except for the section about CSS in SharePoint.

What's in this chapter?

- What is CSS
- CSS Syntax
- CSS Selectors
- Style Classes
- Comments
- Positioning
- Controlling visibility
- Inline Styles
- Adding CSS to SharePoint
- Using a Different Style when Printing
- Style Resources
- Useless Trivia!

What is CSS?

Cascading Style Sheets are used in a web page to control the use of fonts and colors of text, and the height, width, color, background images and visibility of sections of a page. The power of CSS to SharePoint customizers is how CSS "cascades". We do not need to replace or edit the CSS supplied with SharePoint, all we need to do is to supply "add-on" CSS to override the SharePoint CSS. This is easy to do as our CSS only needs to occur on the page somewhere after where the SharePoint CSS is loaded. As the core CSS is loaded at the very top of the page, we can add our CSS anywhere after that, including in Content Editor Web Parts, at the bottom of a page or at the bottom of a master page.

In the beginning...

Before CSS, web pages were formatted using embedded HTML tags such as:

- <FONT SIZE="4" FACE="arial" COLOR="red">some text </FONT>
- <CENTER>some text</CENTER>
- <TABLE BORDER="2" WIDTH="100%" ...

The problems with this:

- The tags must be repeated over and over again - for example, to change the color or size of text in a table the <FONT> tag must be repeated in every cell
- There is no single place to make a single change to update formatting of a particular tag
- There is no way to store the formatting external to the HTML file

And then there was CSS...

CSS is:

- a way to store all formatting information separate from the HTML, either in <STYLE> tags or in an external file
- a way to build styling in modules that "cascade"
- cascadable - a second style sheet will append to and override a previously defined style sheet
- powerful - a few lines of CSS can change the appearance hundreds of HTML tags

CSS can change:

- fonts (font family and attributes like bold and italic, size)
- color (text, background, borders)

- images (backgrounds, bullets…)
- borders (around tables, DIVs, images…)
- location and visibility

Adding styles:

Styles can be stored:

- **in separate files**, usually with a name ending with ".CSS" and linked from the web page with:
  `<link type="text/CSS" href="mystylesheet.CSS" />`

- **in a style block in a page,** usually in the <HEAD> section:
  ```
  <style type="text/css">
    style details…
  </style>
  ```

- **in individual tags:**
  `<span style="color:red; font-size:24px"> some text </span>`

Example: An HTML table with blue text:

The following does not work! The only text that will be blue is the text outside of the table.

```
<font color="blue" size="3">

Text outside of the table

<table width="300" bgcolor="gray">
  <tr>
    <td>text goes here</td>
    <td>text goes here</td>
    <td>text goes here</td>
  </tr>
  <tr>
    <td colspan="2">
      <a href="abc">click me</a>
    </td>
  </tr>
</table>

</font>
```

The following does work, but it's very repetitive, and any change of color or size requires a very careful search and replace.

Text outside of the table

```html
<table width="300" bgcolor="gray">
  <tr>
    <td><font color="blue" size=3>text goes here</font></td>
    <td><font color="blue" size=3>text goes here</font></td>
    <td><font color="blue" size=3>text goes here</font></td>
  </tr>
  <tr>
    <td colspan="2">
      <a href="abc"><font color="blue" size=2>click me </font></a>
    </td>
  </tr>
</table>
```

By using CSS we can style all the <TD> tags without all of the copy and paste work, and we can update everything with a single edit. We also now have precise control over font sizes and other attributes. In the example below, the text outside of the table is displayed in the default colors of the page and the table cell text is now blue. Notice that the HTML no longer has any embedded formatting!

```html
<style type="text/css">
  td {
    color:blue; font-size:12pt;
  }
  table {
    background-color:gray;
    width:300px;
  }
</style>

Text outside of the table
<table>
  <tr>
    <td>text goes here</td>
    <td>text goes here</td>
    <td>text goes here</td>
  </tr>
  <tr>
    <td colspan="2">
      <a href="abc">click me</a>
    </td>
  </tr>
</table>
```

The text inside of the anchor tag (<A>) can formatted with another color with this quick style sheet change.

```html
<style type="text/css">
  td {
```

```
    color:blue; font-size:12pt;
  }
  td a {
    color:red;
  }
  table {
    background-color:gray;
    width:300px;
  }
</style>
```

The change above only impacts <A> tags inside of <TD> tags.

The entire style sheet can be moved out of the page into its own file and then shared across many pages by using a <LINK> tag. You can then edit the one style sheet file and update all of the pages that link to it.

```
<link rel="stylesheet" type="text/css" href="mystyles.css" />
```

CSS Syntax

A single CSS definition has a selector and one or more pairs of a property and a value.

```
selector { property: value }

selector {
  property: value;
  property: value;
  property: value;
}
```

CSS Selectors

A selector can be a simple HTML tag name.

To make all tables 100 pixels wide:

```
table { width: 100px }
```

To make all text within P (paragraph) tags blue:

```
p { color: blue }
```

Groups of tag styles can be defined with one style entry by listing the tags separated with commas:

```
h1, h2, h3 { color: blue }
```

A CSS Primer

Selectors can be used to select tags by ID and styles by class name (details follow):

```
#myTagId  { color: blue }
```
```
     .myClassName  { color: blue }
```

Selectors can be nested and grouped in many ways. Example: to make only bold (<b>) tags inside of a table cell (<td>) blue:

```
td b { color: blue }
```

Style Classes

A selector can be a "class name" that only impacts tags marked with the class name:

The style definition:

```
p.bigtext { font-size: 24px }
```

The tag with a class attribute:

```
<p class="bigtext"> some text that needs to be big </p>
```

Multiple styles can be selected with a class attribute:

```
<p class="bigtext boldtext"> some text that needs to be big </p>
```

To create a style class that can be applied to any tag name the class starting with a period:

```
.bigredtext { font-size: 24px; color: red }
```

The above style used on a table cell:

```
<td class="bigredtext"> some text that needs to be big </td>
```

One style per ID

Styles can be defined for a single instance of a tag by using the tag's ID:

```
    #companyname { font-size: 24px; color: blue }
```

The CSS above will only apply to this one tag:

```
<span id="companyname"> XYX Corp. </span>
```

Comments

Comments can be added to styles for documentation purposes:

```
/* this make all tables have the same fixed width */
table { width: 100px }
```

Positioning

Styles can be used to position DIVs by setting X and Y coordinates.

```
.popuphelp
{
  position:absolute;
  left:300;
  top:50;
  height:200;
  width:200;
}
```

```
<div class="popuphelp">To submit your order just…</div>
```

Using Styles to Control Visibility

Styles can be used to hide content that will later be exposed using scripting.

```
<style type="text/css">
 .hiddentext
 { display:none }
</style>

<span class="hiddentext"> Order completed! </span>
<button onclick="javascript:block1.style='display:inline' ">Buy it!</button>
```

Inline Styles

Styling can be added directly to a tag using the "style=" attribute.

```
<span style="color:red; font-size:24px"> some text </span>
```

Overriding Inline Styles

Styles defined in a tag using "style=" will override styles set at any other level, with one exception. Inline styles can be overridden by adding "**! important**" to the style.

Example: Override the font size in Quick Launch

Quick Launch has the font size and border options hardcoded in the <A> tag used for the link. If you want to override font size or border you will need to add "!important" to your style.

An inline style found in Quick Launch:

```
<a class="zz2_QuickLaunchMenu_1 ms-navitem zz2_QuickLaunchMenu_5"
 href="/sites/Demo/Demo2/Lists/Calendar/calendar.aspx"
 style="border-style:none;font-size:1em;"
>Calendar</a>
```

Style needed to change the font-size:

>   font-size:24px **!important**;

To override the hardcoded font size your style would have to be declared as "!important ":

```
<style type="text/css">
 .ms-navitem a
 {
   font-size:24pt !important;
 }
</style>
```

All of the following will work:

```
font-size:24pt!important;
font-size:24pt !important;
font-size:24pt ! important;
```

Adding CSS to SharePoint

CSS "cascades", so the order CSS is added to the page is important. Your CSS must follow any CSS already loaded in the page by SharePoint. In SharePoint most of the CSS is loaded from one or more linked CSS files, the most important being CORE.CSS (corev4.css in 2010). These are loaded in the <HEAD> section of the master page using custom SharePoint controls. The first is used to load CORE.CSS and the second is used to load the theme's CSS, if one has been selected:

```
<SharePoint:CssLink runat="server"/>
<SharePoint:Theme runat="server"/>
```

CSS can be added directly to the master page using SharePoint Designer. While it can be added anywhere after the SharePoint CSS, it is often added in the <HEAD> section just after the SharePoint CSS controls. When added directly to a page, the CSS is enclosed in a pair of HTML <STYLE> tags.

```
<SharePoint:CssLink runat="server"/>
<SharePoint:Theme runat="server"/>
<!—the following overrides the SharePoint ms-sitietile Core CSS class -->
<style type="text/css">
  .ms-sitetitle
  {
    color:blue;
  }
</style>
```

CSS can also be linked from an external text file. This makes updates and reuse across multiple pages and sites a lot easier. If you have access to the web servers, your custom CSS file can be stored in the "12 hive" (2007) or the "14 hive" (2010). Site owners will typically store their CSS files in a SharePoint library. You do not use the <STYLE> start and end tags when storing CSS in an external file that is linked using a <LINK> tag.

Adding a linked CSS file to a master page:

existing master page tags:

```
<SharePoint:CssLink runat="server"/>
<SharePoint:Theme runat="server"/>
```

new tag:

```
<link rel="stylesheet" type="text/css"
    href="/sites/training/shared documents/mycustom.css" />
```

A CSS Primer

CSS can be added to a single page by using a Content Editor Web Part (CEWP). For SharePoint 2007, just add the web part, click **Edit, Modify Shared Web Part** and click the **Source Editor** button. SharePoint 2010 Content Editor Web Part users will generally want to link to a text file stored in a library.

Just add the CSS between HTML <STYLE> start and end tags.

```
<style type="text/css">
  .ms-sitetitle
  {
    color:blue;
  }
</style>
```

Using a Different Style when Printing

As a teaser I'm going to give you a few hints for improving the printed view of a SharePoint page. For more details and ideas you should do a web search for "@media print" and for "link media=print".

Try this: print the homepage of a SharePoint site and compare the printed copy to what you see on the screen. (This example is for SP 2007, but is also true for SP 2010.)

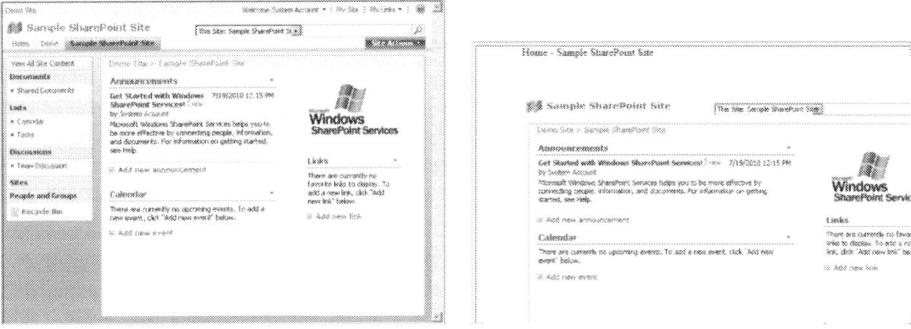

Notice what has changed, and what has disappeared:

- Quick Launch and the Top Link Bar are gone
- The top bar with the Welcome menu and the help button is gone

But…

- The search box is still there
- The site logo, which might be quite large, is still there
- The font colors have not changed, and could be a problem when printed

What made these changes?

Open CORE.css (or corev4.css for SharePoint 2010)
(http://yourservername/sites/yoursitename/_layouts/1033/styles/core.css) and search for "@media print".
Here's what it looks like:

```
@media print
{
  .ms-leftareacell,.ms-globallinks,.ms-siteaction,.ms-areaseparatorleft,
  .ms-rightareacell,.ms-areaseparatorright,.ms-areaseparatorcorner,
  .ms-titlearealeft,.ms-titlearearight,.ms-searchform,.ms-banner,
  .ms-buttonheightwidth,.ms-buttonheightwidth2
  {
  display:none;
  }
}
```

Nice clean and simple! This is just a list of all of the CSS classes to hide when printing. Just add to this section your choices of CSS classes to hide, change color, change font, or even relocate.

Some ideas:

- Hide the entire site image, site title and search box area by adding ", .ms-globalTitleArea" to the list of classes for "**display:none**"
- Hide just the image by adding ", #GlobalTitleAreaImage"
- Hide just the site title by adding ", .ms-sitetitle a"
- Hide just the search boxes by adding ", .ms-sbrow" or ", #SRSB"

Remember, as a site owner you do not have access to the CORE.CSS file stored on the server so you will need to find a way to add these changes to your master page. Here are three ways:

- In the master page, just below where SharePoint loads its style sheets, add your own **@media** section:

```
<Title ID=onetidTitle><asp:ContentPlaceHolder   ...

<SharePoint:CssLink runat="server"/>
<SharePoint:Theme runat="server"/>

<style type="text/css">
@media print
{
  .ms-sbrow, #GlobalTitleAreaImage
  {
```

```
    display:none;
  }
}
</style>
```

- In the master page add a LINK tag to link to a file that contains your **@media** section - this sample links to a file stored in a site library named **CustomizationFiles**:

```
<Title ID=onetidTitle><asp:ContentPlaceHolder   …
<SharePoint:CssLink runat="server"/>
<SharePoint:Theme runat="server"/>

<link rel="stylesheet" type="text/css"
    href="/sites/Demo/Demo2/CustomizationFiles/customPrint.css" />

<SharePoint:ScriptLink language="javascript" name="core.js"   …
<SharePoint:CustomJSUrl runat="server"/>
```

- A third technique is not to use an **@media** section, but instead create a standard CSS file and link it with a <link> tag with an added "media" element:

```
<link rel="stylesheet" type="text/css" media="print"
href="x/sites/Demo/Demo2/CustomizationFiles/customCoreForPrint.css" />
```

If you want to change all of the fonts or colors when the page is printed, you'll want to download a copy of CORE.css, (corev4.css for SharePoint 2010) search and replace the styles as needed, upload to a library and then link to it.

Style Resources

For more on styles see: (Link 301)

Useless Trivia!

- CSS1 was introduced in 1996 and Internet Explorer 3 was the first to implement it.
- CSS2 is the current standard and was introduced in 1998.
- CSS also stands for Content Scramble System and Committee for State Security (KGB in Russian), neither of which have much to do with HTML.

4. A JavaScript Primer

Do you need this chapter?

If you already have decent JavaScript programming skills, or you have a good JavaScript book, then you can skip most of this chapter, except for the section about JavaScript in SharePoint and the section on jQuery.

While this chapter does not include everything you need to know about JavaScript, it does include the JavaScript features used in the book's sample code. To move beyond the basics, go get a good JavaScript book, find a good JavaScript tutorial site or go to a JavaScript class! (Link: 401)

What's in this chapter?

- JavaScript
- Where can you use JavaScript in SharePoint?
- Important Tips for JavaScript in SharePoint
- When will my scripts run?
- JavaScript Basics
- jQuery

JavaScript

SharePoint uses JavaScript throughout the product to build menus, populate data and to respond to user clicks. In fact, much of SharePoint will not work if JavaScript has been disabled. By using JavaScript you can interact with much of the SharePoint user interface, including adding and removing menu items, adding color to lists and libraries, and hiding and showing parts of the page.

Many people think of JavaScript as a trivial scripting language while in fact it is a full featured programming language. But don't panic, most of the work you do in JavaScript to customize SharePoint can be done with a small subset of JavaScript. The first skill needed for some of the easier customization is Copy and Paste! (from the book's web site -- see chapter 1) A lot of the cool things you can do are available on the web, and you can simply copy and paste the JavaScript code into a web part or into SharePoint Designer.

Where can you use JavaScript in SharePoint?

JavaScript can be used in:

- Content Editor Web Parts
- SharePoint Master Pages[1]
- Customized list Display, New and Edit pages[1]
- Customized pages [1]
- Custom pages displayed in Page Viewer Web Parts

   (1) Using SharePoint Designer

JavaScript Basics

JavaScript is a rich programming environment. One chapter cannot do it justice, so you should also be looking for good JavaScript books or tutorial web sites. (See Link 401) In this chapter you will find key features of JavaScript that you will need to know to understand the examples in this book.

For the JavaScript examples in this book you will need to know how to:

- write and call a JavaScript function
- find HTML elements in a web page
- change properties of HTML elements
- write loops
- test strings and values (IF statements)

Key parts of a script

Basic JavaScript Syntax

JavaScript is written inside of <script> tags. This example displays a popup message:

```
<script type="text/javascript">
  alert('hello!');
</script>
```

JavaScript can also be directly called from tag events: ("onclick" is an event)

```
<button onclick="javascript:alert('hello');">Click me</button>
```

JavaScript is written as a series of statements separated by semicolons:

```
var x = 3;
var y = 5;
var z = x * y;
alert(z);
```

JavaScript is "case sensitive"

These examples would fail:

```
Alert('hello');
ALERT('hello');
document.GETELEMENTBYID('test');
document.GetElementById('test');
```

These examples work:

```
alert('hello');
document.getElementById('test');
```

Comments

The two toughest coding things you will have to do is figure out someone else's code, or six months after you have written it, figure out your own code. So document your work. Add comments to explain what you did, or where you borrowed the code from.

Add a comment as a single line:

```
// this code from Mike Smith's book!
var allTables = document.getElementsByTagName('table');
```

Add a comment to the end of a line:

```
var x;  // this holds the counter
var y;  // this is the row number - I should have used better names!
```

Add a block of comments between "/*" and "*/":

```
/*
  the follow routine is used to color code
  task lists by looking for key words in cells
  and then changing the color of the row
*/
```

Blocks

JavaScript works with blocks of code that are enclosed with curly brackets. Most of the JavaScript blocks you will find in the examples in this book are for IF, FOR and FUNCTION statements. Here's an example of using a FOR loop to repeat a block of code for each TD element found in the page:

```
var allTDs = document.getElementsByTagName("TD");    // find all of the TDs

for (var i=0; i< allTDs.length; i++ )  // loop through all of the TDs
{   // for block starts here

  if (allTDs[i].className=="ms-vb2")  //find the TDs styled for lists
  {  // if block starts here

    if (allTDs[i].innerHTML=="In Progress")
    {  // nested if block ends here
      alert("found a cell containing 'In Progress' ");
    }  // nested if block ends here
```

```
    }    // if block ends here
}        // for block ends here
```

While the brackets are required when the block has more than one line of code, they are optional if the block only has one line. Your code will be easier to understand if you always add the brackets.

This works without the brackets:

```
for ( var i=0; i<10; i++ )
  alert( "This is loop # " + i);
alert( "all done" );
```

But this is easier to understand as the brackets show which lines of code are used with the FOR:

```
for ( var i=0; i<10; i++ )
{
  alert( "This is loop # " + i);
}
alert( "all done" );
```

Spaces, line breaks and semicolons

While JavaScript generally does not need line breaks, indents or extra spaces, these will make the code much easier for humans to read. Semicolons are the "official" end of line punctuation, but code will still work if the line of code ends with a line break. Semicolons are not needed after closing curly brackets (}).

The follow works as one long line of code, but is hard to read and debug:

```
var allTDs = document.getElementsByTagName("TD"); for (var i=0; i< allTDs.length; i++ ) ; { if (allTDs[i].className=="ms-vb2") { if (allTDs[i].innerHTML=="In Progress") { alert("found a cell containing 'In Progress' "); } } }
```

This code is much easier to read, and you can easily see if you are missing a bracket somewhere:

```
var allTDs = document.getElementsByTagName("TD");   // find all of the TDs

for (var i=0; i< allTDs.length; i++ )   // loop through all of the TDs
{          // for block starts here

  if (allTDs[i].className=="ms-vb2")   //find the TDs styled for lists
  {
```

49

```
      if (allTDs[i].innerHTML=="In Progress")
      {
        alert("found a cell containing 'In Progress' ");
      }

    }
  }          // for block ends here
```

Some JavaScript libraries do look like the first example. By removing the excess characters and comments you can shrink the file size and reduce download time, but at the expense of readability. If you do this, keep in mind that end of line semicolons are required and that while block comments (/* ... */) will work, "//" comments will not.

JavaScript Variables

Variables are not assigned data types when they are created as in C# or VB.NET.

```
var a;
var b;
a = 5;
b = "abc";
```

Variables can store simple data types such as strings and numbers. A variable can also store an object such as an HTML element (tag). This example finds a table with an ID of "table1" and stores in a variable named "atable":

```
var atable = document.getElementById('table1');
atable.width = "100px";
```

Variables can store arrays, including arrays of HTML elements:

```
var allTableCells = document.getElemenstByTagName('td');
alert('there are ' + allTableCells.length + ' TDs in this page');
```

Individual array elements are addressed by using an indexer ([*index*]) that starts with zero:

```
var allTableCells = document.getElemenstByTagName('td');
alert( 'The first cell contains: ' + allTableCells[0].innerHTML);
alert( 'The second cell contains: ' + allTableCells[1].innerHTML);
alert( 'The last cell contains: ' + allTableCells[ allTableCells.length - 1 ].innerHTML);
```

Arrays can be created in code by adding new items to the end of the array:

```
var carArray = new Array();
carArray[0] = "Chevy";
carArray[1] = "Ford";
carArray[2] = "Jeep";
```

Arrays can also be created by defining a list of items between square brackets:

```
var carArray = ["Chevy","Ford","Jeep"];
```

Arrays are often accessed using a FOR loop:

```
for ( var x=0; x<carArray.length; x++)
  {
  document.write(carArray[x] + "<br />");
  }
```

JavaScript Functions

Functions are "reusable blocks of code" that you can write once and then call one or many times from other code.

A function declaration can be as simple as:

```
function myfunctionname()
{
  // my code here
}
```

Functions can also have parameters so you can pass different data to the function each time it is called.

```
function annoyUser(msg)
{
   alert(msg);
}

annoyUser("hello!");
annoyUser("JavaScript is fun");
annoyUser("do you like popups?");
```

A JavaScript Primer

Browser Detection

No two browser brands work exactly the same, display HTML the same way or have the same set of JavaScript features. As a result you will often need to know which browser brand and version is being used, or more often, the general type of browser being used.

As an example, Firefox does not support the **innerText** property while Internet Explorer does. Firefox instead has a **textContent** property that does the same thing. So, one property works in Firefox and the other in Internet Explorer, and neither works in the other! One way to test for a browser feature is to check for the feature's existence with an IF statement. Here is an example that tests for an Internet Explorer unique feature (**document.all**) and then chooses to use the IE or Firefox compatible option.

```
if (document.all)     // is IE
   {var username = document.getElementById("someID").innerText;}
else                  // is Firefox or other
   {var username = document.getElementById("someID").textContent;}
```

For additional information on browser detection, and an even better approach called object detection, see: Links 402, 403 and 404.

Finding HTML Elements

The complete HTML of a web page can be accessed using the Document Object Model (the DOM). The primary DOM object is simply called "**document**". The document object can be searched in a number of ways including by ID, Name, Tag Name and CSS Class Name:

- document.getElementById('*id*')   <table id='*idname*'...
- document.getElementsByName('*name*')   <table name='*name*'...
- document.getElementsByTagName('*tagname*')   *tagname* = TABLE, TD, etc
- document.getElementsByClassName('*classname*')   <table class='*classname*' ...

Finding HTML elements by ID

document.getElementById('id')

HTML tags that have an ID defined are the easiest to find and interact with. IDs are (or are at least supposed to be) unique and therefore a search by ID will never find more than one object. **getElementById** will return a null if the element is not found.

As an example of searching by ID, let's find the site image in a SharePoint 2007 Team Site page. As you can see in the following HTML fragment from the page, the Site Image is inside of a TD that has an ID of

"GlobalTitleAreaImage". Knowing this ID we can use JavaScript to hide, replace or reformat the Site Image.

```html
<td class="ms-globalTitleArea">
  <table width=100% cellpadding=0 cellspacing=0 border=0>
    <tr>
      <td id="GlobalTitleAreaImage" class="ms-titleimagearea">
        <img id="ctl00_onetidHeadbnnr0" src="/_layouts/images/titlegraphic.gif"
             alt="" style="border-width:0px;" />
      </td>
      <td class="ms-sitetitle" width=100%>
        <h1 class="ms-sitetitle">
          <a id="ctl00_PlaceHolderSiteName_onetidProjectPropertyTitle"
             href="/sites/training/"> Training Site
          </a>
        </h1>
      </td>
```

The JavaScript to change the image's border might look like this:

```javascript
var siteImage = document.getElementById('GlobalTitleAreaImage');
if (siteImage != null)
{
  siteImage.style.border = 'dashed';
}
```

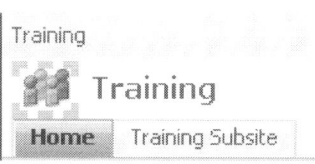

- You may also see **document.all** used to find elements by their ID. **document.all** was created in the days of Internet Explorer 4 and before **document.getElementById** became the standard for all browsers. In general, "document.all" should not be used. (For one exception see "Browser Detection" earlier in this chapter.)

- Also see how to find items by ID using jQuery later in this chapter.

Finding HTML elements by Name

document.getElementsByName('*name*')

A JavaScript Primer

Finding HTML elements by name is identical to finding elements by ID, except we are looking for the "name" attribute instead of the "id" attribute. Where possible you will want to access an element by ID as the ID should be unique in the page. In the following example we are searching for all of the elements (tags) named "somename" and then displaying the HTML between the start and end tags.

```
// look for tags like   <td name="somename"> <b>this is text</b> </td>
//
var items = document.getElementsByName('somename')
if ( items.length > 0}
{
  //do something with the items...
  for (var i=0; i < items.length; i++)
  {
    alert( "the contents of element " + i + " is " + items[i].innerHTML);
  }
}
```

Note that the "items" variable above is an array containing zero or more items that match the name. If you know that there is only one element with that name, you can directly access the first item in the array (item zero) and immediately use it. I.e. to display the HTML of the element: **alert(items[0].innerHTML)**

   Also see how to find items by Name using jQuery later in this chapter.

Name vs. ID?

While you should do a web search on "HTML name vs. ID" for detailed information, here are the differences a nutshell:

Name:

- A name does not have to be unique - for example: grouped checkboxes share the same name (Note the "s" in **getElementsByName** that is not in **getElementById**)
- Names are used for elements inside of **<form>** tags - names are needed for server side code to read data from the page

IDs

- IDs can be used on any HTML element (except for a few such as HEAD, HTML, BODY) to uniquely identify the single use of the element in a page
- CSS styles can be applied to elements using IDs (by using "#" prefix), but not those using names
- IDs are typically used for interacting with the DOM with JavaScript

Many SharePoint elements that have a name also have an ID. When both are available your JavaScript code should use the ID.

Sample SharePoint tag with both a name and an ID:

```
<input name="ctl00$PlaceHolderSearchArea$ctl01$S6AE27B38_InputKeywords"
       type="text"
       maxlength="200"
       id="ctl00_PlaceHolderSearchArea_ctl01_S6AE27B38_InputKeywords"
       accesskey="S"
       ...
```

Finding HTML elements by Tag Name

document.getElementsByTagName('tagname')

If you are looking for all <table> or all <td> tags you can use getElementsByTagName. This will return an array of tags with zero to many items.

As an example, to find all of the tables on the page and add a border around them:

```
var tables = document.getElementsByTagName("TABLE");
if ( tables.length > 0 )
{
  for (var i=0; i<tables.length; i++)
  {
    tables[i].style.border="solid red 2px";
  }
}
```

🖎 Also see how to find items by tag name using jQuery later in this chapter.

Finding HTML elements by CSS Class Name

"getElementsByClassName" is a very needed and useful function, but it is not supported by all browsers. You can use the following routine to test a browser for this feature:

```
if ( document.getElementsByClassName )
{
  alert('this browser supports getElementsByClassName');
}
else
{
  alert('this browser DOES NOT support getElementsByClassName');
}
```

A JavaScript Primer

As this function is not supported in Internet Explorer until IE 9, you will have to find your own way to duplicate the function. Here's one way that I've tested with IE 6, 7, 8 and Firefox:

```javascript
<script type="text/javascript">

if ( ! document.getElementsByClassName )
{
  // this browser does not support getElementsByClassName, so add our own...
  document.getElementsByClassName = function(classToFind)
  {
    var elementArray = [];
    // create a Regular Expression to search for a class name
    var regExpForClass= new RegExp('\\b' + classToFind + '\\b');

    // get all tags
    var alltags = this.getElementsByTagName('*');

    // check them all for a match
    for (var i = 0; i < alltags.length; i++)
    {
      if (regExpForClass.test(alltags[i].className))
      {
        // match found, so add it to the array
        elementArray.push(alltags[i]);
      }
    }

    // return the results
    return elementArray;
  }
}


// This is a test to see if the above works… (hides Quick Launch)
var x = document.getElementsByClassName('ms-nav');
x[0].style.display='none';

</script>
```

While the above works nicely, it loops through all of the tags in the page. Most of the examples in this book that might use getElementsByClassName implement a similar solution, but one that is more targeted to just the tags we need. For example, the following finds only the <td> tags, and then checks all of the <td> tags for tags with a style class of "ms-vb2". (Note: The "ms-vb2" class is used in most SharePoint web parts that display rows of data from lists.) So instead of checking all tags for the class name we are now only checking a subset, in this case just the <td> tags.

```
var x = document.getElementsByTagName("TD");  // find all of the TDs
for (var i=0; i<x.length; i++)
{
  if (x[i].className == "ms-vb2")   //find the TDs styled for lists
  {
    // now do something with "ms-vb2" tags…
  }
}
```

If we choose to use the **getElementsByClassName** function then the above would look like:

```
var x = document.getElementsByClassName("ms-vb2");
for (var i=0; i<x.length; i++)
{
    // now do something with "ms-vb2" tags…
}
```

Also see how to find items by class name using jQuery later in this chapter.

Finding nearby elements using "parentNode"

Often in SharePoint pages you will need to get access to a tag that does not have an ID, a unique class name or a unique tag name. If you study the HTML in the page you will often find a useful tag somewhere above or below the tag you need. As an example, in a task list we would like to highlight a row with a new color when the text "In Progress" appears in a cell.

New ▼	Actions ▼	Settings ▼		
	Title		Assigned To	Status
	Task 1 ! NEW		Sam Conklin	Not Started
	Task 2 ! NEW		Sam Conklin	In Progress
	Task 3 ! NEW		Sam Conklin	Completed

A JavaScript Primer

Using the browser's View Source option and then doing a search for "In Progress" you will find this HTML:

```
<TD Class="ms-vb2">In Progress</TD>
```

Finding this cell using JavaScript is not too hard. First find all of the TDs by using getElementsByTagName, then loop through the TDs to find those styled as "ms-vb2", then look for any with data (innerHTML) equal to "In Progress". Here's the code:

```
<script type="text/javascript">
  var x = document.getElementsByTagName("TD") // find all of the TDs

  for (var i=0; i<x.length; i++)   // loop through all of the TDs
  {
    if (x[i].className == "ms-vb2")  //find the TDs styled for lists
    {
      if (x[i].innerHTML == "In Progress")
      {
      // add code here to set the color of the entire row
      }

    }
  }
</script>
```

The code above found the cell containing "In Progress", but that's not the element we want to change. We want to change the color of the entire row, which is the parent or the container of the <td> we found.

JavaScript supplies a number of options to drill up or down in the HTML tree. To explore this, let's start with a sample table. This table has the structure shown in the simple example below. Note that the parent of our <td> is a <tr> element.

```
<table>
  <tr>
    <td>some data</td>
    <td>some data</td>
    <td>some data</td>
    <td>In Progress</td>
    <td>some data</td>
```

58

```
    </tr>
  </table>
```

To access the parent <tr> all we need to use is "*element*.parentNode". Or to complete the sample code seen earlier you would need this code:

```
x[i].parentNode.style.backgroundColor = 'aqua';  // set the color
```

"x[i]" is the current node selected by the for loop and is a <td>, "parentNode" is the <tr>, and "style.backgroundColor" is a property of the row element.

Here's the result:

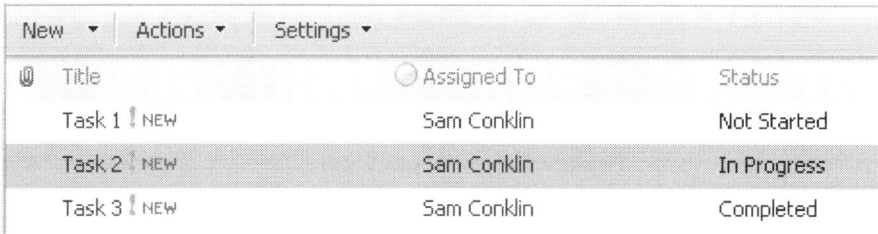

How would you select the entire table?

Be careful guessing the node hierarchy! If we got to the row element with the cell's **parentNode** you might be thinking that the parent of a row is the <table> element. Even if your HTML does not include all of the typical HTML for a table, the browser internally creates a full table structure including another element named <tbody>. From the example table above the browser actually creates the following HTML:

```
<table>
  <tbody>
    <tr>
      <td>some data</td>
      <td>some data</td>
      <td>some data</td>
      <td>In Progress</td>
      <td>some data</td>
    </tr>
  </tbody>
</table>
```

As a result, to get the <table> element from the cell element requires going up three levels:

```
cellelement.parentNode.parentNode.parentNode
```

So if you want to put a border around any table that has a cell that contains "In Progress" you would need:

```
x[i].parentNode.parentNode.parentNode.border = '1';
```

Finding nearby elements using "childNodes"

Drilling down the HTML tree uses the concept of "child nodes". Accessing a "**childNodes**" object will always return an array, even if there are no child nodes or if there is only one child node. As an example, a <tr> tag contains one child node for each <td>. If you have a variable named "x" representing the row then x.childNodes[0] is the first <td> in the row and x.childNodes[x.childNodes.length-1] is the last <td> in the row.

Using the example JavaScript for the **parentNode** example, if you wanted to change the color of the third cell of any row that had "In Progress" in any other cell you could use:

```
x[i].parentNode.childNodes[2].style.backgroundColor = 'aqua';
```

Here "x[i]" is the cell containing "In Progress", "**parentNode**" is the row (<tr>) and "**childNodes[2]**" is the third cell. (JavaScript always counts from zero, so "**childNodes[2]**" is the third cell.)

Finding nearby elements using "previousSibling" and "nextSibling"

In HTML structures such as tables and lists (<ol> or <ul>) you can select the previous and next nodes using **previousSibling** and **nextSibling**. To change the color of the cell to the left of the current cell you would use:

```
x[i].previousSibling.style.backgroundColor = 'aqua';
```

So in summary:

Starting with the "In Progress" cell of the table:

<table>	← parentNode.parentNode.parentNode
<tbody>	← parentNode.parentNode
<tr>	← parentNode
<td>some data</td>	← previousSibling.previousSibling.previousSibling
<td>some data</td>	← previousSibling.previousSibling
<td>some data</td>	← previousSibling (or parentNode.childNodes[2])
<td>In Progress</td>	← **the element we started with**
<td>some data</td>	← nextSibling

```
  </tr>
 </tbody>
</table>
```

🖎 Also see how to find nearby items using jQuery later in this chapter.

JavaScript IF blocks and FOR loops

Looping through an array

Many of the selectors such as **getElementsByTagName** return an array of HTML elements. Once you have the HTML elements you want to work with stored in an array, you can then loop through them with a "FOR" loop. JavaScript's FOR statement has three parameters: the initial value of the indexer (typically 0), the test for loop completion (typically when the indexer exceeds the number of items in the array), and how the indexer is incremented (typically by 1). Here's an example that displays an alert 10 times (i = 0 through 9):

```
for ( var i=0; i<10; i++ )
{
  alert( "This is loop # " + i);
}
```

If your FOR loop always loops through all the items in an array then you can use this version:

```
var someitems = ["apples","oranges","pears"];
for ( var i=0; i<someitems.length; i++ )
{
  alert( "This is item " + someitems[i]);
}
```

Or you could use this shorter FOR - IN version:

```
var someitems = ["apples","oranges","pears"];
for ( var i in someitems )      // i will equal 0 through the number of items - 1
{
  alert( "This is item " + someitems[i]);
}
```

A JavaScript Primer

 Although this second example using FOR...IN is easier to type, it is generally recommended that you use the more traditional FOR with your own counter. For more on FOR...IN see Link 405.

We have mentioned blocks before, but now is a good time for a review. Note that FOR is a block structure and that the start and the end of the block is marked with curly brackets. The brackets are optional if there is only one line of code in the block. The following is identical to the previous example:

```
for ( var i=0; i<10; i++ )
  alert( "This is loop # " + i);
```

JavaScript does not care about line breaks, so both of the following are also identical to the previous example:

```
for ( var i=0; i<10; i++ ) {  alert( "This is loop # " + i); }
```

```
for ( var i=0; i<10; i++ ) alert( "This is loop # " + i);
```

Blank lines, spaces and tabs are free! So use them to improve readability. Here's a more complete and nicely formatted example:

```
var x = document.getElementsByTagName("TD");   // find all of the TDs

for (var i=0; i<x.length; i++ )  // loop through all of the TDs
{
  if (x[i].className=="ms-vb2") //find the TDs styled for lists
  {
    if (x[i].innerHTML=="In Progress")
    {
      alert("found a cell containing 'In Progress' ");
    }

  }
}
```

Testing values - IF

JavaScript's IF statement is used to conditionally run a block of code. The most common mistake made by new JavaScript developers is typing just one equal sign when doing comparisons.

Example - if A equals B then display an alert:

```
var a = 5;
var b = 6;
if ( a == b ) { alert("it's a match!") }
```

> Note in this example the single equal sign for assignments (a = 5) and the double equal signs for equality (a == b).

Example - if A is greater than B then display an alert else display a different alert:

```
var a = 5;
var b = 6;
if ( a > b )
{
  alert("A is greater than B");
}
else
{
  alert("B is greater than or equal to A");
}
```

Example - if A and B are not equal then display an alert:

```
var a = 5;
var b = 6;
if ( a != b ) { alert("it's not a match!") }
```

JavaScript Comparison Operators

==	is equal to
===	is exactly equal to (value and type)
!=	is not equal to
>	is greater than
<	is less than
>=	is greater than or equal to
<=	is less than or equal to

A JavaScript Primer

Accessing the URL's Query String from JavaScript

Data can be passed from page A to page B by adding a query string to the linking URL. The query string is basically everything after the "?" in a URL. In the following example the query string includes two parameters, color and width:

http://yourserver/sites/yoursite/shared documents/mywebpartpage.aspx**?color=red&width=100**

Parameters are separated by an ampersand ("&") and are in the form of "**keyword=value**". Reading these values in JavaScript requires just a little more work than expected as JavaScript can only retrieve the entire query string. You will need to take this string apart with a little code.

```
<script type="text/javascript">

// window.location       returns the URL
// window.location.search     returns the query string starting with the "?"
// window.location.search.substring(1)    returns the query string starting without the "?"

var querystring = window.location.search.substring(1);

// querystring now contains something like color=red&width=100
// so split the string into an array of parameters

var parameters = querystring.split("&");

// now take the array of parameters and copy to an array of names and values

var QueryString = Array();
for (var i=0;i<parameters.length;i++)
{
  QueryString[parameters[i].split("=")[0]] = parameters[i].split("=")[1];
}

// and let's test by retrieving one of the parameters
alert(QueryString["color"]);

</script>
```

Is That All?

By no means, but this chapter does introduce most of the basic JavaScript that is used in the examples in this book. Now go find a good book on JavaScript and read on...

jQuery

A lot of the coding work you will do with JavaScript to customize SharePoint will be to first find a fragment of HTML and then manipulate that HTML. Often all we are doing is some searching, or querying, of the HTML and then doing a quick update. jQuery is ideal for this.

First the negatives:

- jQuery is not part of JavaScript or part of SharePoint - you will either download the jQuery library from the web and upload it to a SharePoint library, or you will directly link to a copy of the library on the web
- The library is not large, but it will add to page load time, at least the first time a user visits a page - after the first visit the user's browser will use a local cached copy of the library
- If you share web parts you create that include jQuery with other site owners, then they will also need access to the library in their sites

And then the positives:

- jQuery can create some very compact solutions, often with just one line of code
- jQuery is just a function call into a library so it can be intermixed with regular JavaScript - in fact all of jQuery is just one big JavaScript function named jQuery() or $()
- There are a lot of web resources for both jQuery and jQuery used with SharePoint

What follows is a very, very, brief overview of jQuery along with a few notes on using jQuery in SharePoint. For more on jQuery see:

- jquery.com - the official web site for jQuery
- Many resource links for JavaScript and jQuery (See Link 401)
- "jQuery: Novice to Ninja" by Earle Castledine and Craig Sharkie (See Link 401)

Downloading the library

Downloading your own copy of the library is often the preferred method of accessing the library, especially if you are not supporting internet users. You will then know the library is where you need it, will still be there when you need it, and that it will not change. (For downloading jQuery see Link 406)

As you customize SharePoint you will start collecting an assortment of files such as icons, JavaScript libraries and documentation about your customizations. To keep these organized you will want to add a

A JavaScript Primer

library to your top level site for these files. One of the more obvious names, "Site Files", is one you should not use as it is a reserved library name in SharePoint 2010. So pick a name such as "CustomizationFiles" or something short like "cfiles". Remember that all of your users will need at least "View" permissions to this library.

 Tip! Rename the downloaded jQuery library from its full name (jquery-1.4.2.min.js) to just jquery.js so when you download updated versions you won't have to edit all of your scripts.

Linking to the library

Here's an example of a link to a jQuery library stored in a SharePoint library:

```
<script src="/sites/demo/CustomizationFiles/jquery-1.4.2.min.js" type="text/javascript"></script>
```

or if you follow the renaming tip above:

```
<script src="/sites/demo/CustomizationFiles/jquery.js" type="text/javascript"></script>
```

This link can be used in each page or web part as needed, or loaded once from a master page. If you are going to be using jQuery in a number of pages then it is best to load it from your master page.

Linking to an external library

If you don't want a local copy of the library or to have multiple copies in various sites and site collections then you can link to a file stored in a common location on the internet. You can take advantage of Content Delivery Networks (CDNs) as public locations for commonly used files such as jQuery. Be aware that if you go this route that your users will always need access to the internet while accessing your site. While this may be a disadvantage for users on your local network, this can reduce load on your web servers when supporting thousands of internet users. But also consider that these remote sites are outside of your control and could be changed, compromised or deleted at any time. Here's a sample of loading the library from Microsoft's AJAX CDN site (Link: 407):

```
<script src="http://ajax.microsoft.com/ajax/jquery/jquery-1.4.2.min.js" type="text/javascript"></script>
```

Where should you put the link to the library?

If you only need the library "here and there" then only load it as needed in the page or the Content Editor Web Part where you added your jQuery code. If you will be using jQuery in many pages then consider adding the library link to the site's master page. You will need SharePoint Designer to do this. Whichever you do, don't do both or you will get errors.

To add the library in a Content Editor Web Part, add the script link just before your script area:

```
<script src="/sites/demo /CustomizationFiles/jquery-1.4.2.min.js"
type="text/javascript"></script>

<script type="text/javascript">
  //your code here
</script>
```

To add the library in the master page, just add the script link somewhere in the <HEAD> section of the page.

Want to see it work?

If you are impatient and want to see some jQuery in action then consider how you would discover and highlight all of the tables in a SharePoint page. You could write a JavaScript routine to loop through all of the tables and then turn on borders and set the width and color:

```
var tables = document.getElementsByTagName("TABLE")
for (i=0;i<tables.length;i++)
{
  tables[i].style.border="solid red 2px";
}
```

First the code has to get the collection of tables into an array, then it has to loop through all of those tables and then finally set the style for each table.

Here's the jQuery to do the same:

```
$("table").css("border","solid red 2px");
```

The "$" is a shortcut for "jQuery". Typing "jQuery" in place of the "$" will also work. Basically the above says find all "table" elements (tags) and set their CSS border property.

To test this:

1. Upload the jQuery library file to a SharePoint library
2. Add a Content Editor Web Part to a SharePoint page
3. Edit the web part and use the Source Editor (2007) to add the following script - For 2010, add this script to a text file, upload it to a library and then enter the path to the text file to the Content Editor Web Part's Content Link property

```
<script type="text/javascript">
```

A JavaScript Primer

```
var tables = document.getElementsByTagName("TABLE")
for (i=0;i<tables.length;i++)
{
  tables[i].style.border="solid red 2px";
}
</script>
```

4. Save your changes and you should see a lot of red lines!
5. Edit the CEWP again and replace the script with jQuery as follows:

```
<script src="/sites/demo /CustomizationFiles/jquery-1.4.2.min.js" type="text/javascript"></script>
<!-- change this to the path to your copy of jQuery -->

<script type="text/javascript">
  $("table").css("border","solid blue 2px");
</script>
```

6. Edit the path for the jQuery library to match your library location library file name
7. Save your changes and you should see a lot of blue lines!

By the way… not every table is outlined in red. Only the tables in the page that were defined in the HTML from the start of the page down to our CEWP have been updated. JavaScript is run as the page is loaded unless you do something to delay it. Below is an example that ensures our code runs after the entire page has been loaded. (See "When will my scripts run" later in this chapter.)

```
<script src="/sites/demo /CustomizationFiles/jquery-1.4.2.min.js" type="text/javascript"></script>
<!-- change this to the path to your copy of jQuery -->

<script type="text/javascript">
  function ColorfulTables()
  {
    $("table").css("border","solid red 2px");
  }

  _spBodyOnLoadFunctionNames.push("ColorfulTables"); // wait for page load

</script>
```

Selecting Elements using jQuery

jQuery is a query tool, and searching for and retrieving HTML objects is what jQuery is best at. When searching for tags based on CSS properties jQuery uses the same notation as CSS to select elements: "." for classes, "#" for IDs etc.

- Tags are selected by adding the tag in quotes:
  $("table")
- Tags with IDs are selected using "#":
  $("#someID")
- Tags assigned to a CSS class are selected using ".":
  $(".someClassName")
- Tags can be selected with combinations of selectors just like in CSS:
  $(".ms-sitetitle A")
  (This selects all anchor tags inside of elements assigned the class named **ms-sitetitle**)

Using the data returned by jQuery

jQuery will return an array of all of the matched HTML elements. You can store the results of a "query" in a variable or directly update all of the objects found in a single step.

For example, both of the following produce the same result. The example first finds all tables and applies CSS formatting to all of the found elements. The second example finds all tables, stores the result as an array of tables, and then loops through the array to apply CSS properties to the tables.

```
$("table").css("border","solid red 2px")
```

```
var tables = $("table")
for (var i=0; i<tables.length; i++)
{
  tables[i].style.border="solid red 2px"
}
```

Setting CSS properties

To set a single property:

```
$( selector ).css("propertyName","propertyValue")
```

```
$("table").css("border","solid blue 2px")
```

69

A JavaScript Primer

To set multiple properties (note the curly brackets and the colons):

```
$( selector ).css( { "propertyName" : "propertyValue" , "propertyName" : "propertyValue" , "propertyName" : "propertyValue" } )
```

```
$("table").css( { "border-style":"solid", "border-color":"blue", "border-width":"2px" } )
```

Running a function against the return set

jQuery does not have a built in function for everything you can think of. For example, if you need to do a double search and replace ("<" and ">" in the example here) you might write a function like this one:

```
$('.ms-gridT1').html(function(index,oldhtml) {
   return oldhtml.replace(/&lt;/g,'<').replace(/&gt;/g,'>')
})
```

or with a little better formatting:

```
$('.ms-gridT1').html(
    function(index,oldhtml)
    {
       return oldhtml.replace(/&lt;/g,'<').replace(/&gt;/g,'>')
    }
)
```

If you do a search at jQuery.com for ".html" you will find that it can be called using a function:

.html(function(index, oldhtml))

Here "index" is the position of the item in the return set and "oldhtml" is the original value of the HTML in the element in the returned item in the set.

What's next?

The JavaScript and the jQuery coverage in this chapter is only the bare minimum needed to understand the examples in the book. To master these tools will require a lot more than you have seen here. So go visit Link 401 for a list of tutorial sites, recommended books and videos.

Important Tips for JavaScript in SharePoint

Where to put your JavaScript

Where you put the JavaScript largely depends on what it does and if it needs to interact with a single list, a single page or an entire site. Here are some possibilities:

- **Content Editor Web Part** - Use a CEWP when you want to add JavaScript to a single web page that is also a web part page. (See the Web Part chapter for ways to see if a page is a web part page)
  Features:
    - Easy to use (Source Editor)
    - Easy to reuse (Export - see the Web Part Must Knows chapter for details)
    - Can be placed directly in the web part page that needs the JavaScript
    - JavaScript can be added using the Source Editor or by linking to a JavaScript file stored in a SharePoint library
- **Directly in a page** - Use SharePoint Designer when you want to directly edit a Basic Page, Web Part page or a site page. You can add the JavaScript inside of <SCRIPT> tags or link to a file that contains the JavaScript.
- **Master Page** - Use SharePoint Designer to add code to a master page when you want to code to be available on every page in a site. You can add the JavaScript inside of <SCRIPT> tags or link to a file that contains the JavaScript.

When will my scripts run?

A simple embedded script like the following will run as soon as the browser loads it.

```
<script type="text/javascript">
  alert('hello world!');
</script>
```

If the script is in the middle of the page, like it would be when loaded using a Content Editor Web Part, then the script will run before the page has been fully created by the browser. Most JavaScript for SharePoint projects will need to run after the HTML that it's going to interact with has been fully loaded, and quite often, after the entire page as been loaded.

To see how to deal with JavaScript running at the wrong time in SharePoint see chapter 5's section on "Controlling when JavaScript Runs".

A JavaScript Primer

JavaScript and SharePoint Dates

How does your SharePoint site display a date? The answer is… "it depends." Create a new task and schedule it for January 3rd, 2012. Now display the task list and see how the date is displayed.

Do you see this 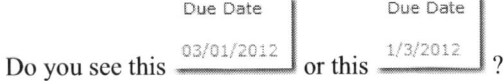 ?

You would see the first if you had your SharePoint preferences (Regional Settings) set to a country where they enter dates as dd/mm/yyyy, such as France. To play with the regional settings, click the Welcome menu at the top right of a SharePoint page and click My Settings. Then click My Regional Settings, un-checkmark "Always follow web settings" and pick a locale.

So what's the problem?

If you are writing JavaScript code that needs to work with the date you may get the wrong date! As an example, if you wrote some JavaScript to read the Due Date from a task and changed the color or font for past due tasks you would probably use the Date.parse method to test the date:

72

```
var colDueDate = 7;    // list column with Due Date
if (d.getTime() >= Date.parse(row[i].parentNode.childNodes[colDueDate].childNodes[0].innerHTML) )
{
  row[i].parentNode.style.backgroundColor='red'; // set the color
}
```

In this example, if today's date is February 15th 2012 and the Due Date is March 1st 2012 then Date.parse would show the task as past due for the French users and not past due for the United States users.

📖   JavaScript date references: See Link 1401 and Link 1402

The fix? Display the date in a format that Date.parse likes. JavaScript first attempts to parse the date as an ISO formatted date. It then tries a few other rules, but none of those support dd/mm/yyyy. What we need to do then is deliver a date in the SharePoint list that will always work with JavaScript, and one that always works is yyyy/mm/dd. You could just pick a locale that uses that format, but your users are not likely to be happy with that.

What works is to add a calculated column to the list that generates a date with a yyyy/mm/dd format, hide that column in the display (view or web part) and use that column for the JavaScript date math.

Steps:

1. Add a new column to your list and give it a name like DueDateYYYYMMDD
2. Add a formula:
   =YEAR([Due Date]) & "/" & MONTH([Due Date]) & "/" & DAY([Due Date])

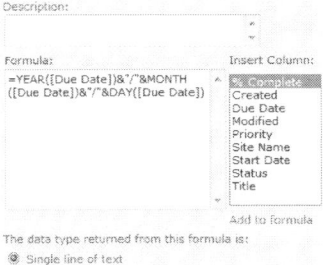

3. Save your changes
4. Add this new column to your view
5. Add some tasks with a due date and verify that both Due Date and DueDateYYYYMMDD have the same dates, just formatted differently
6. Go to your Welcome menu, click My Settings, My Regional Settings and change your locale to France and confirm that while the Due Date column has changed, the DueDateYYYYMMDD is still the same

📖   To see this in use see chapter 14: "Color Code Past Due / Late Tasks".

Useless Trivia!

- JavaScript was first called "Mocha" and when first released with Netscape 2.0 in September 1995 JavaScript was called "LiveScript".
- LiveScript was renamed to JavaScript in December of 1995 as part of a partnership with Sun to integrate Java applets into LiveScript and Netscape.
- Microsoft added JavaScript to Internet Explorer 3.0, but called it JScript
- In November of 1996 JavaScript became formalized into an international standard named ECMAScript
- According to builtwith.com, over 900,000 web sites are now using jQuery

5. Hacking Tips!

Do you need this chapter?

Absolutely! This chapter is about the tools, tips and tricks needed to create your own SharePoint customizations.

What's in this chapter?

- HTML Detective Tools
- How to Find a Web Part in Code
- Controlling When JavaScript Runs
- SharePoint Version Detection

Hacking Tips!

HTML Detective Tools

Almost everything in this book modifies the HTML created by SharePoint. The only exceptions are a few of the modifications made using SharePoint Designer to SharePoint master pages and site pages. As site owners we cannot change how SharePoint creates most of the HTML in the page. All we can do is "tweak" the HTML by using CSS and JavaScript. A lot of your work will be as a detective. You will be in navigating the generated HTML, figuring out how it works and finding out how to get a "handle" on the piece you want to change. So let's take a look at a few tools that will help you with your detective work.

View Source

All browsers have a "View Source" option that lets you see the HTML that was sent to the browser by the web server.

- Internet Explorer - From the menu select "View" and "Source" or right-click the page and select "View Source"

- Firefox - From the menu select "View" and "Page Source" or right-click the page and select "View Page Source"

Internet Explorer 6 and 7 displays the HTML in Notepad while Internet Explorer 8 and Firefox displays the HTML in a custom window. Neither is very good for detective work. As the raw HTML is, well, quite a mess, you will find this source code much easier to work with if you copy and paste it into a real HTML editor.

> The HMTL you see with View Source is the HTML delivered to the browser before any changes made by your JavaScript code and SharePoint's JavaScript code. Much of the HTML in

SharePoint is modified by JavaScript as, and after, the page is loaded. To see this HTML you will need to use the browser developer toolbars and add-ins described later in this chapter.

HTML Editors

HTML editors supply HTML auto-completion, color coding, reformatting options and other tools to help in the reading and customizing of HTML.

Useful editors include:

- SharePoint Designer (free) (Link 501 and Link 502)
- FrontPage (not free, but you may already have it - only use FrontPage for basic HTML editing, it is not a replacement for SharePoint Designer or suitable for directly editing SharePoint pages)
- Visual Studio (not free)
- Visual Studio Express (free) (Link 503)
- and many others

Using SharePoint Designer to study code:

1. Copy the text from the browser's "View Source" option or from the HTML captured by a browser developer toolbar or add-in
2. In SharePoint Designer click **File, New,** and **HTML** to create a temporary file
3. Delete the default text in the page and paste the copied source
4. Right-click anywhere in the HTML code and select **"Reformat HTML"** to fix the indention and layout of the HTML code

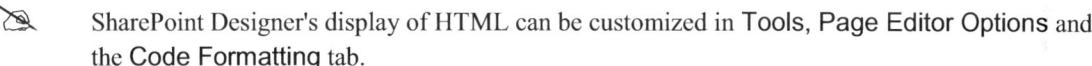 SharePoint Designer's display of HTML can be customized in **Tools, Page Editor Options** and the **Code Formatting** tab.

Using Visual Studio to study code:

1. Copy the text from the browser's "View Source" option
2. In Visual Studio click **File, New, File** and select **HTML Page**
3. Delete the default text in the page and paste the copied source
4. From the **Edit** menu select **Advanced** and **Format Document** to fix the indention and layout of the HTML code (SharePoint Designer does a better job of reformatting the HTML!)

 Visual Studio's display of HTML can be customized in **Tools, Options**. See Link 505 for details.

Browser Developer Toolbars and Add-ins.

Developer toolbars are add-ins or built-in features available for most browsers. These let you search and browse the HTML and CSS in a page, both as delivered from the server and after being updated by JavaScript code. When considering these tools remember that SharePoint 2007 only fully supports Internet Explorer 6 and 7, and that SharePoint 2010 supports Internet Explorer 7 and later (not 6!) and Firefox as the preferred browsers.

- Internet Explorer 6 and 7 developer toolbar - Download from Microsoft [Link 506]
- Internet Explorer 8 and 9 developer toolbar - Built in! No download needed. Help can be found at Microsoft: [Link 507]
- Firefox - There are a number of add-in tools for Firefox that can be found by clicking **Tools, Add-ons, Get Add-ons** and then clicking the **Browse All Add-ons** link. On that page click **Web Development**. (I have used "Firebug" and "Web Developer".) [Link: 508]

How to Find a Web Part in Code

Web parts are rendered as HTML tables and have a fairly predictable structure. This structure can help you find the web part so you can modify it. Finding a way to uniquely identify a single web part can be a challenge. Here are some of the ways:

Look for the "title" attribute in one of the TD tags

If the web part's **Chrome** option is set to display the title, then the web part will include a <TD> tag with a title attribute with the web part's name.

> <td **title="Links - Use the Links list for links to Web pages that your team members will find interesting or useful."** id="WebPartTitleWPQ3" class="ms-WPHeaderTd">

Note that the "title" attribute is built from two pieces of data. The first part is from the Title found in the web part's properties panel. The second is from the list's description found in the list's settings in the "Title, description and navigation" page.

Pros:
- Obvious!

Cons:
- Renaming the web part or changing the list's description will break your code
- Only works if the title is displayed - changing the web part's "**Chrome**" to "**Border only**" or "**None**" will break your code

List Web Parts have a "summary" Attribute

List web parts are easy to find as they have an attribute in one of the <TD> tags named "summary". This is not a standard HTML attribute for a <TD>, but rather a Microsoft created attribute. The "summary" attribute is built from two pieces of data. The first part is from the Title found in the web part's properties panel. The second is from the list's description found in the list's **Settings** page in the **Title, description and navigation** section.

You can create your own attributes for any tag. The browser ignores these, but they are accessible to JavaScript. SharePoint uses many custom attributes in its HTML.

2007:

```
<table summary="Links" ... >
```

2010:

```
<table summary="Links Use the Links list for links to Web pages that your team members will find interesting or useful." ... >
```

Pros:

- Obvious!
- Closer to the rows of data in the web part

Cons:

- Renaming the web part or changing the list's description will break your code
- Changing the web part's **Chrome** to **Border only** or **None** will break your code
- Different in 2007 and 2010 - 2007 only uses the title, 2010 uses the title and description
- The "summary" attribute is not included in the web part when there is no data to display in the list's view
- Only list web parts have a "summary" attribute

This code will find a links list web part:

```
// Change the following to your links list name
var linksListSummaryName = "Links Use the ... (your list summary name here!) ..."

// Find the links list
var x = document.getElementsByTagName("TABLE");    // find all of the Tables
for (var i=0; i<x.length; i++)
{
  if ( x[i].summary == linksListSummaryName )
  {
    //your code to work on the list goes here
  }
}
</script>
```

Hacking Tips!

Look for a unique piece of data in the web part

Neither of the two approaches above will work for web parts like the Image Web Part as they do not have a "summary" attribute and typically do not have the title displayed (**Chrome** is set to **None** or **Border only**). For these web parts you will need to look for a key piece of data such as the URL to the image:

```
<img border="0" id="MSOImageWebPart_WebPartWPQ4"
src="http://yourserver/sites/yoursite/_layouts/images/siteIcon.png" alt="" />
```

JavaScript sample to find an Image web part:

```
var IMGs = document.getElementsByTagName("img");
for (var i=0; i<IMGs.length; i++)
{
  if (IMGs[i].src == "http://pathtoimage...")
  {
    // code to work with the image web part  (IMGs[i])
  }
}
```

JQuery sample to find an Image web part:

```
$("img[src='http://pathtoimage']").yourJQueryCodeHere
```

Look for an ID Pattern

In the case of the image web part, you might also look for a pattern of HTML common to that web part, such as the fact that the IMG tag always has an ID that starts with "**MSOImageWebPart_**". This would be useful when looking for all Image Web Parts on a page.

```
<img border="0" id="MSOImageWebPart_WebPartWPQ4"
        src="http://yourserver/sites/yoursite/_layouts/images/siteIcon.png" alt="" /></td>
```

As the getElementById() function only works with complete ID names you will need to get all of the tags similar to the one you are looking for and then do a check for a name match using a JavaScript function like indexOf.

```
var IMGs = document.getElementsByTagName("img");
for (var i=0; i<IMGs.length; i++)
{
  if ( IMGs[i].id.indexOf('MSOImageWebPart_') > -1 )
  {
```

```
  // code to work with the image web part…   (IMGs[i])
 }
}
```

Controlling when JavaScript Runs

A simple embedded script like the following will run as soon as the browser loads it.

```
<script type="text/javascript">
  alert('hello world!');
</script>
```

If the script is in the middle of the page, like it would be when loaded using a Content Editor Web Part, then the script will run before the page has been fully created by the browser. Most JavaScript code for SharePoint customizations needs to run after the HTML that it's going to interact with has been fully loaded, and quite often, after the entire page as been loaded.

There are several possible solutions:

- Put your script in a Content Editor Web Part and move it below all of the web parts that the script is changing
- Put all of your scripts at or near the end of the page, but in SharePoint this would mean that they would have to be at the end of the master page
- Wrap your code inside of a function and then run it with a JavaScript timer. But how do you know how long is not long enough and how long is too long?

```
function DoSomethingCool()
 {
    alert('message displayed after 5 seconds');
 }
setTimeout("DoSomethingCool()",5000);   // wait five seconds
```

- Wrap your code inside of a function and then run it from the <BODY> tag's **onload** event - this works but again, this would need to be done from the master page

The best solutions:

The best way to run your JavaScript code is to insure that it runs after SharePoint has delivered all of its content to the browser. Here are several ways to do this:

- Wrap your code inside of a function and then run it from SharePoint's own "script queue" (this is usually the best solution):

Hacking Tips!

```
function DoSomethingCool()
 {
   alert('page has loaded');
 }
_spBodyOnLoadFunctionNames.push("DoSomethingCool");
```

- Wrap your code inside of a jQuery "$(document).ready" function (this works, but the above is probably a better choice as the .ready function does not wait until all of the SharePoint code runs):

```
$(document).ready( function() {   alert('page has loaded');   } )
```

The _spBodyOnLoadFunctionNames Array:

"_spBodyOnLoadFunctionNames" is a JavaScript array created in the SharePoint master page and ".push" is a JavaScript method to add a new item to the end of the array. When a SharePoint page is loaded by a browser each function listed in this array is called in the order they were added, but only after the browser has completely loaded the page and run all of the SharePoint JavaScript.

Notes:

- Your function cannot use parameters - the following is not allowed: mycoolfunction(**'abc'**)
- The _spBodyOnLoadFunctionNames feature may change or go away in future versions of SharePoint, but works just fine in 2007 and 2010
- The code that processes _spBodyOnLoadFunctionNames calls the functions in the order they are added; first in, first run
- The jQuery "$(document).ready" will run your code as soon as all of the HTML has loaded, but without waiting for images and other linked files to load and may run the code before some of the SharePoint content has been loaded

What about 2010?

A few things have changed in 2010 that impact "_spBodyOnLoadFunctionNames". As an example of this we will look at the calendar and how it loads its data. In 2010 the data for the calendar is loaded using a JavaScript function placed at the end of the page. That function's name is also added to the "_spBodyOnLoadFunctionNames" array at the end of the page. That means that the data we want to change is not yet in the browser when our JavaScript is loaded and run from our Content Editor Web Part earlier in the page. If we just add our function to the array in the Content Editor Web Part, then our code would be in the array before, and run before, their code.

The work arounds?

- Find a SharePoint library function and intercept it
- Add a "Run Me Last" routine in your master page

Find a SharePoint library function and intercept it

The 2010 calendar uses a delayed (asynchronous) load of the calendar items. Normal techniques to delay the running of scripts are not reliable with the new calendar. After the calendar items have been loaded SharePoint calls a function to display a "loading" message. You can intercept this and run your code before or after this built-in function. The biggest challenge here is to discover the built-in function to intercept! You can usually find these kind of things using one of the browser developer toolbars. The function we can use for the calendar pages example is named "SP.UI.ApplicationPages.CalendarNotify.$4a".

The first step is to write a function to copy the built-in function to a new variable, and the second step is to create a new function that calls the copy and then calls your function. The example below works for calendars.

```
// hook into the existing SharePoint calendar notify function
function hideCalendarEventLinkIntercept()
{
  // save the old function to " OldCalendarNotify4a"
  var OldCalendarNotify4a = SP.UI.ApplicationPages.CalendarNotify.$4a;

  // replace the old function with a little function that calls the old function
  // and then calls your custom code
  SP.UI.ApplicationPages.CalendarNotify.$4a = function ()
   {
     // call the old function
     OldCalendarNotify4a();

     // call our custom code function (or just add the custom code here)
     hideCalendarEventLinks();
   }
}
```

Add a "Run Me Last" routine in your master page

If the previous approach does not work for your project, or you can't find a suitable built-in SharePoint function to intercept, then you can create your own "Run Me Last" feature. The trick is to get our function added to the existing "_spBodyOnLoadFunctionNames" array after SharePoint's functions have been added to the array (such as the calendar update function). One way is to add our calendar customization JavaScript to the master page and write the code so it only impacts calendars. But that's a bad workaround as we would then have JavaScript that's only needed for calendars added to every page, not just calendar pages.

Hacking Tips!

So here's a workaround... Add a bit of JavaScript at the bottom of the master page just before the </body> tag that checks for an array of function names that we need to have run. (Just like how _spBodyOnLoadFunctionNames works...) If there's no array, then do nothing, otherwise copy our function list into the end of the SharePoint "_spBodyOnLoadFunctionNames" list.

```
<script type="text/javascript">
  if (window.runMeLast)  // does the array exist?
  {
    for ( var i=0; i < runMeLast.length; i++ )
    {
      _spBodyOnLoadFunctionNames.push(runMeLast[i]);
    }
  }
</script>
```

To run our code after all the SharePoint code has been run, create a custom function in a Content Editor Web Part, web page or where ever you added your JavaScript, and add it to our "Run Me Last" array.

```
function DoSomethingCool()
{
  // code here
}

if (!window. runMeLast)
{
  runMeLast = new Array();  // create runMeLast array if it does not exist
}
runMeLast[runMeLast.length] = "DoSomethingCool";   //add our function
```

SharePoint Version Detection

It seems like such a simple question: "I'm writing some JavaScript code that will run almost identically in SharePoint 2007 and SharePoint 2010. How can I write an IF statement to test the version?"

So far I have found no perfect answer, but I have found a few that work. Each has an "if" or a "risk", so pick one that works for you. If you know a better way, please post it at the book's web site. Any updates that I find will be at Link 509.

I propose four methods:

- Method 1: Check for the "_fV4UI" variable
- Method 2: Check for an element with "V4" or "s4" in its ID or style name

- Method 3: Get the EXACT (almost) version number
- Method 4: Call a SharePoint 2010 ECMAScript Class Library Object method

SharePoint Versions: (at least those that we currently are interested in)

- 2007, also called 3.0 or V3, also called version 12 (includes BPOS)
- 2010, also called 4.0 or V4, also called version 14 (includes Office 365)
- and one day 201x, called 5.0 or V5 and version 15?

It would be nice if:

- something in the page had the version number? (14.xxx) (I can't find it)
- there was a JavaScript function in one of the core libraries somewhere? (there is in 2010)

Solution requirements:

- Must be available in all site pages, and ideally in all application pages
- Must be available in all templates
- Must still be there after major master page branding surgery

A few quick ideas:

As a SharePoint customizer you look for patterns, so here's where we might start:

- Look for one of the many controls with a tag with "V4" embedded in its ID, or one of the CSS class names with "V4" or "s4" embedded. (Risk? Minimal, but site branders who have heavily modified the master page or the styles could mess this up.)
- Look for a unique JavaScript variable (see _fV4UI below). (Risk? Minimal, but a web search for "_fV4UI" finds a number of articles on branding that mention deleting this from the master pages.)

Solutions

I have found at least four solutions that do what we need. My preference? Right now it is method 1; check the "_fV4UI" variable. While it's simple and light weight, just remember that the variable initialization could get deleted by someone branding the master page.

Method 1: Check the "_fV4UI" variable

SharePoint 2010 pages have a JavaScript variable named "_fV4UI" that indicates if the page is using the "V4" navigation (the ribbon). After an initial upgrade from SP 2007 this variable will be set to "false". When the user interface is later upgraded to the 2010 interface this will then be set to "true".

So:

- if _fV4UI does not exist we probably have SP 2007
- if _fV4UI does exist we probably have SP 2010
- will there be a _fV5UI in the next version? (we can only wait and see)

Hacking Tips!

The code:

```
<script type="text/javascript">
  if ( typeof _fV4UI == "undefined" )
  {
    // 2007 code here
  }
  else
  {
    // 2010 code here
  }
</script>
```

Pros:

- Probably the easiest test to do
- Very simple code
- Can even be reduced to one line:

  ```
          var SPversion = (typeof _fV4UI == "undefined") ? "12" : "14";
  or
          var SPversion = (typeof _fV4UI == "undefined") ? "2007" : "2010";
  ```
- The then in all of your code you can just write:

  ```
          if (SPverion == "2010") { code for only 2010 }
  ```

Cons:

- Your code must be placed after where SharePoint initializes this variable. Be aware that a number of blog articles mention removing the first instance listed below.

  Here is where I found it in a Team Site:
  - Line 13 in the <HEAD> section (this is the only one you will see in the master page)
  - Line 100 in the <BODY> section (auto generated by a control)
  - Line 1033 near the end of the page (auto generated by a control)

- We don't know if it will be supported in the next version.

Method 2: Check for an element with "V4" or "s4" in its ID or style

The challenge here is, which element do you check? You will need to pick an element that will reliably exist in all branded and unbranded pages. Just about everything in the master page is up for grabs when custom branded. (Yes, I have seen branded sites without a title, Quick Launch, Tabs, Search, View All Files or Recycle Bin!) The control you pick needs to be towards the top of the page and most likely left behind in a branded master page. So let's pick one... (let me know if there is a better one) Both SP 2007 and SP 2010 have a hidden <SPAN> or <DIV> named **TurnOnAccessibility**. In 2010 this DIV has a style named **s4-notdlg**, which SP 2007 will never have, so let's test for that.

The code:

```
<script type="text/javascript">
  if ( document.getElementById("TurnOnAccessibility").className == "s4-notdlg" )
  {
    // 2010 (and maybe later) code here
  }
  else
  {
    // 2007 code here
  }
</script>
```

Pros:

- Easy to test
- The tag we are testing is at the very top of the page, therefore it will be loaded before any of our custom code

Cons:

- This will probably be one of the first things a brander will remove (mostly as they have no idea what it is for) - so search your branded page for a tag that has an ID or style name that starts with "v4" or "s4"

 What is **TurnOnAccessibility** for? The dropdown menus in SharePoint, such as the **Welcome** menu or **Site Actions**, are dynamically generated and are somewhat meaningless to a user with vision problems who is using a screen reading program. When "more accessible mode" is enabled, clicking what usually is a dropdown menu will open a popup window with all of the menu options listed.

Method 3: Getting the EXACT (almost) version number

Now this is what I really want, and it is sent by SharePoint for every page request, but it is sent as part of the HTTP Header. And there's a problem... most of what's in that header is not available to JavaScript.

Here's what's sent from SharePoint 2010 in the header:

Hacking Tips!

```
Cache-Control: private, max-age=0
Content-Type: text/html; charset=utf-8
Expires: Wed, 01 Dec 2010 01:22:00 GMT
Last-Modified: Thu, 16 Dec 2010 01:22:00 GMT
Server: Microsoft-IIS/7.5
SPRequestGuid: 87996dec-9ac0-4b5a-bf19-8cda86dc5407
Set-Cookie:
WSS_KeepSessionAuthenticated={5c492918-43f9-4265-bf2b-30e
0f31311bf}; path=/
X-SharePointHealthScore: 3
Set-Cookie:
WSS_KeepSessionAuthenticated={5c492918-43f9-4265-bf2b-30e
0f31311bf}; path=/
X-AspNet-Version: 2.0.50727
Set-Cookie:
http%3A%2F%2Fmaxsp2010f%2Fsites%2FTraining%2FDiscover
y=WorkspaceSiteName=VHJhaW5pbmc=&WorkspaceSiteUrl=aHR
0cDovL21heHNwMjAxMGYvc2l0ZXMvVHJhaW5pbmc=&Workspace
SiteTime=MjAxMC0xMi0xNlQwMToyMjowMA==; expires=Sat,
15-Jan-2011 01:22:00 GMT; path=/_vti_bin/Discovery.asmx
Persistent-Auth: true
X-Powered-By: ASP.NET
MicrosoftSharePointTeamServices: 14.0.0.4762
Date: Thu, 16 Dec 2010 01:22:00 GMT
```

Is that version number right?

14.0.0.4762 is reported in the header

14.0.4763.1000 is reported in Central Admin for SharePoint

14.0.4763.1000 is also reported in Central Admin as the database schema version

This number (14.0.0.4762) is what is found in IIS under HTTP Response Headers.

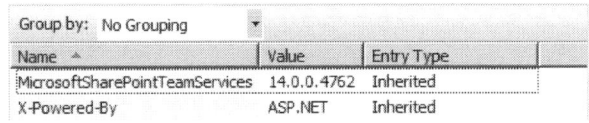

Anyone know why it does not match any other SP 2010 version number?

Ok, the number is not the correct version, but it is close!

SharePoint 2007 reports:

```
Cache-Control: private, max-age=0
Content-Length: 283095
Content-Type: text/html; charset=utf-8
Expires: Wed, 01 Dec 2010 01:36:47 GMT
Last-Modified: Thu, 16 Dec 2010 01:36:47 GMT
Server: Microsoft-IIS/6.0
X-Powered-By: ASP.NET
MicrosoftSharePointTeamServices: 12.0.0.6219
X-AspNet-Version: 2.0.50727
Set-Cookie: WSS_KeepSessionAuthenticated=80; path=/
Set-Cookie: MSOWebPartPage_AnonymousAccessCookie=80; expires=
```

At least this is the correct version!

So if JavaScript code cannot read this header value, how do we get it? It depends on which browser you are using, so you also have to detect the browser version. Here I'm using a routine from an MSDN article to deal with the browser version.

The code:

```
<script type="text/javascript">

 /*
   The following copied from:
   http://msdn.microsoft.com/en-us/library/ms537505(v=vs.85).aspx
 */
 var xmlHttp = null;
 if (window.XMLHttpRequest) {
   // If IE7, Mozilla, Safari, and so on: Use native object.
   xmlHttp = new XMLHttpRequest();
 }
 else
 {
   if (window.ActiveXObject) {
     // ...otherwise, use the ActiveX control for IE5.x and IE6.
     xmlHttp = new ActiveXObject('MSXML2.XMLHTTP.3.0');
   }
 }
 /*
   end copy
 */

 xmlHttp.open('HEAD', location.href, false);
 xmlHttp.send();
 var headers =  xmlHttp.getAllResponseHeaders();
 var SPVersion = xmlHttp.getResponseHeader("MicrosoftSharePointTeamServices");

 if ( SPVersion.substring(0,2) == "12"  )
```

```
{
  // 2007 code here
}
else
if ( SPVersion.substring(0,2) == "14" )
{
  // 2010 code here
}
else
{
  // next version of SharePoint?  Or maybe SP 2003
}
</script>
```

Note: The XMLHttpRequest call is usually setup with an asynchronous callback as the URL called is usually not the same URL that contains the calling JavaScript. The example above does not seem to need this as it appears the header is read from the current in memory copy of the page ("location.href"). Test this in your environment!

It would be a good idea to wrap this code as a function that just returns the major version number and add this to a custom JavaScript library that you would load in the master page. You can then call it as needed from other routines.

```
function getSharePointMajorVersion()
{
// The following copied from: http://msdn.microsoft.com/en-us/library/ms537505(v=vs.85).aspx
  var xmlHttp = null;
  if (window.XMLHttpRequest) {
    // If IE7, Mozilla, Safari, and so on: Use native object.
    xmlHttp = new XMLHttpRequest();
  }
  else {
    if (window.ActiveXObject) {
      // ...otherwise, use the ActiveX control for IE5.x and IE6.
      xmlHttp = new ActiveXObject('MSXML2.XMLHTTP.3.0');
    }
  }
  // end copy
```

```
xmlHttp.open('HEAD', location.href, false);
xmlHttp.send();
var SPVersion = xmlHttp.getResponseHeader("MicrosoftSharePointTeamServices");

return  SPVersion.substring(0,2)
}
```

Pros:

- Gets the version number, so should also work with the "next version" of SharePoint (15?)
- Should work regardless of "branded" master page changes
- Works with the browsers I have tested with: IE6, IE7, IE8 and Firefox 3.5.10

Cons:

- A lot of code for a just to see if we are in 2007 or 2010
- The version number returned is stored in the IIS settings and could get changed independent of SharePoint (I don't know if service packs update this)
- The SharePoint 2010 version returned is not 100% correct (but the major version "14" is correct)

Method 4: Call a SharePoint 2010 ECMAScript Class Library Object Method

SharePoint 2010 supports a JavaScript client object model that can access lists, libraries and other content. One of the classes is called **SP.ClientSchemaVersions** and it has a property called **currentVersion** that returns a version number. This number is not the version of SharePoint itself, but appears to be the version of the library as it returns "14.0.0.0" only.

So:

- if SP.ClientSchemaVersions.currentVersion does not exist we probably have SP 2007
- if SP.ClientSchemaVersions.currentVersion does exist and starts with "14" then we probably have SharePoint 2010
- And... if we are lucky, SP.ClientSchemaVersions.currentVersion will return "15.something" for the next version.

The Code:

```
<script type="text/javascript">

function SampleFunction()
{
  var SPversion = "12";
```

```
try { SPversion = SP.ClientSchemaVersions.currentVersion.substring(0,2) }
catch (e) {}

if (SPversion == "12")
{
   // 2007 code here
}
else
{
   // 2010 (and later) code here
}
}

ExecuteOrDelayUntilScriptLoaded( SampleFunction, "sp.js" );

</script>
```

Pros:

- Gets the version number, so should also work with the "next version" of SharePoint (15?)
- Should work regardless of "branded" master page changes
- Works with the browsers I have tested with: IE6, IE7, IE8 and Firefox 3.5.10

Cons:

- A lot of code for a just to see if we are in 2007 or 2010
- The version number returned is for the script library, not SharePoint (but that should be OK)
- Our code can only be run after the page is fully loaded and the "sp.js" library has been loaded (that's why we need the ExecuteOrDelayUntilScriptLoaded call)
- Our code must be wrapped up in a JavaScript function (SampleFunction in the example above) so it can be loaded using ExecuteOrDelayUntilScriptLoaded

6. SharePoint Designer

Do you need this chapter?

If you are a SharePoint Designer power user, then move on to the next chapter. If you have never edited a SharePoint page or master page, then read on…

What's in this chapter?

- Can I Even Use SharePoint Designer?
- Customizing / Un-ghosting a Page
- Editing a SharePoint Master Page
- Editing a SharePoint Page

SharePoint Designer

SharePoint Designer is a free tool to customize and administer SharePoint sites and is a required tool for almost all SharePoint customizers. This chapter is not an "everything you need to know about SharePoint Designer" resource. Nowhere close! All you will find here is what you need to know to support the customizations in this book.

SharePoint Designer Resources:

List of resources for SharePoint Designer: Link 601
Download link for SharePoint Designer 2007: Link 602
Download link for SharePoint Designer 2010: Link 603

Can I Even Use SharePoint Designer?

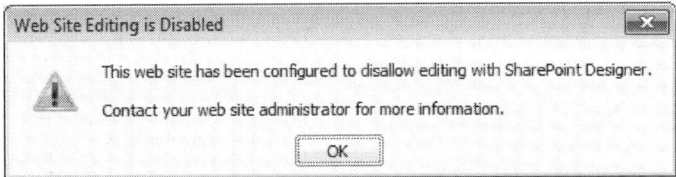

You may find that you cannot edit your site using SharePoint Designer as this tool can be locked down by your administrators to block selected features or even block any use of the tool. Designer can be locked down using user permissions, settings in Central Administration and in Designer itself. For details see:

SharePoint 2007: Link 604, Link 605

SharePoint 2010: Link 606

Here's an example of some of the lock down options in SharePoint 2010 that can be set in Central Administration by your SharePoint server administrators:

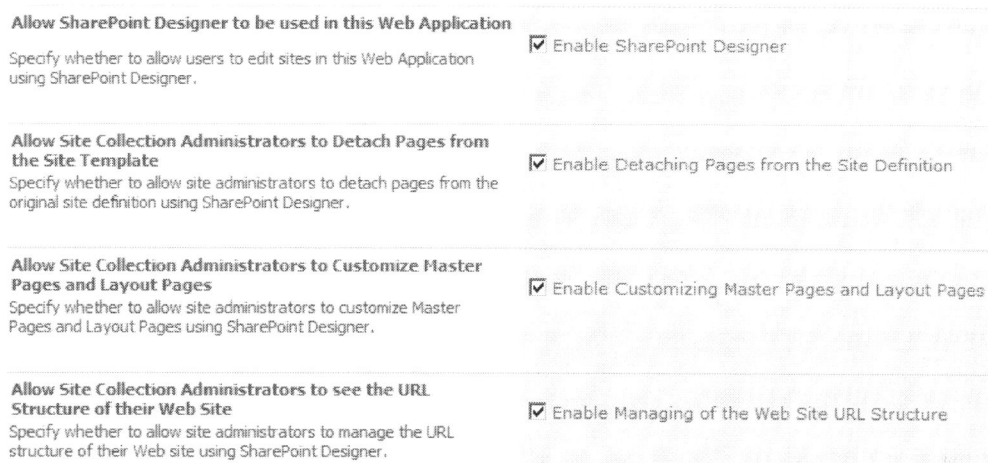

Customizing / Un-ghosting a Page

Somewhere along the way someone is going to say "but SharePoint Designer un-ghosts a page" and they make it sound like a terrible thing. Un-ghosting a page in SharePoint 2003 had a major impact on performance. In 2007 and later the impact is quite minor. So just in case someone asks, here's a little background on the topic.

When you create a new SharePoint site you start by selecting a template, such as the Team Site template. This template "provisions" into SQL Server a list of pages, lists, libraries and features need to build the site. Most of the "pages" in your new site are just pointers to a master copy of the page stored on the SharePoint servers. This use of a common shared page lets SharePoint, via ASP.NET, to cache one master copy of the page in the SharePoint server's memory. With caching SharePoint only needs to load a single copy of a page into memory and then deliver that single copy to thousands of users accessing your hundreds of sites. This is very fast and efficient. When a page is in this state it is called "un-customized", or using a SharePoint 2003 term, "ghosted". When you edit a page using SharePoint Designer, SharePoint saves a unique copy of the page back to SQL Server. When your users visit that page, SharePoint must make an additional request to SQL to retrieve that page. This is clearly not as efficient as the un-customized page. When a page is in this state is called "customized", or using a SharePoint 2003 term, "un-ghosted".

When you first save a page with SharePoint Designer you will be warned that the page is about to be customized:

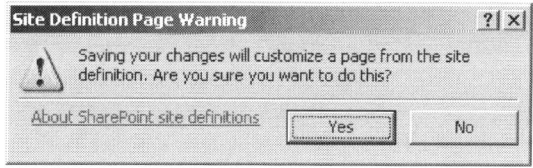

Risks?

Yes there are few. Customizing a page will have a minor impact on performance, but typically not enough to worry about. Customized pages may not properly upgrade when you upgrade your SharePoint farm from 2007 to 2010 or from 2010 to 20*next*.

 Document all of your customizations! Create a Word document and store it in a "customizations" library in your site. You, or the next person who inherits your site, will need this!

Finding Customized Pages

If you have inherited a site from someone else, or your site is just about to be upgraded to the next SharePoint version, you will probably want to find out which pages have been customized. SharePoint Designer makes this easy as it marks customized pages with blue circle ( ).

Resetting / Undoing Customizations

Any customized page can be reset to its original design (its Site Definition). If this reset is done in SharePoint Designer, a backup of the customized page will also be created.

- In SharePoint Designer 2007 right-click the file with the blue icon in the **Folder List** and select **Reset to Site Definition**

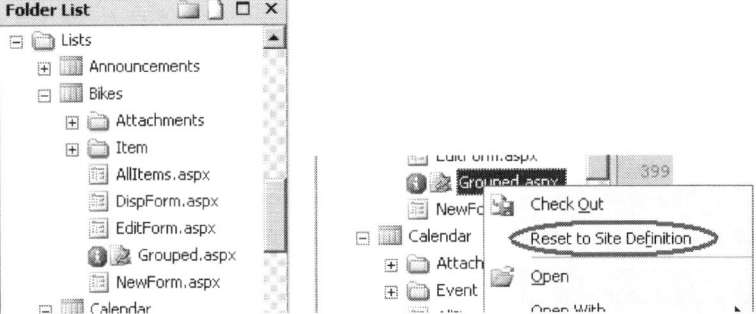

- In SharePoint Designer 2010 in the **Site Objects** pane click the push pin icon in the **All Files** bar, expand folders as needed, right-click the file with the blue icon in the **All Files** list and select **Reset to Site Definition**

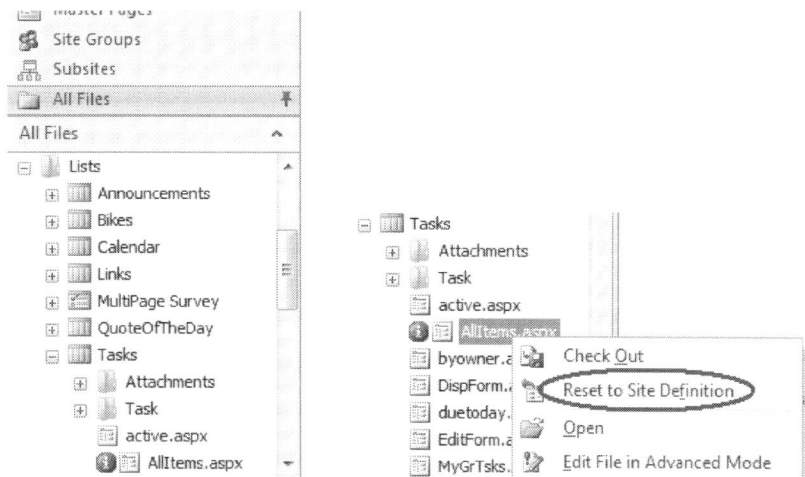

- In a web browser click Site Actions, Site Settings, Reset to site definition

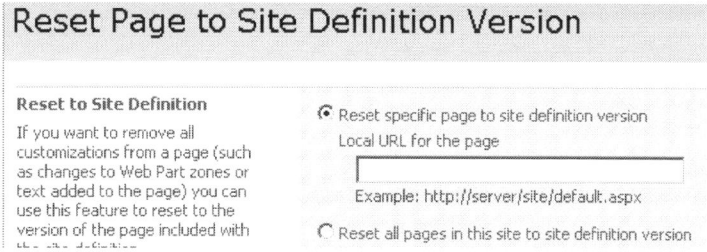

Here you can reset a single page or all pages in the site.

Editing a SharePoint master page

What is a master page?

Master Pages are used by SharePoint to manage the overall design of your web site. The master page defines the parts of a page that are common to every page. When you look at SharePoint pages you see a common pattern that includes overall layout, fonts, colors, and features like Quick Launch and Search. All of these features are defined in the master page. Master pages have names like **default.master** and **v4.master** and cannot be directly displayed in a browser. Master pages are merged with content pages (site pages or application pages in SharePoint) that only have the web parts or list data. The combination is then sent to the browser for display. As the master page has the majority of the HTML, the content page is typically quite small and only has a few **ASP:CONTENT** tags and the code for web parts.

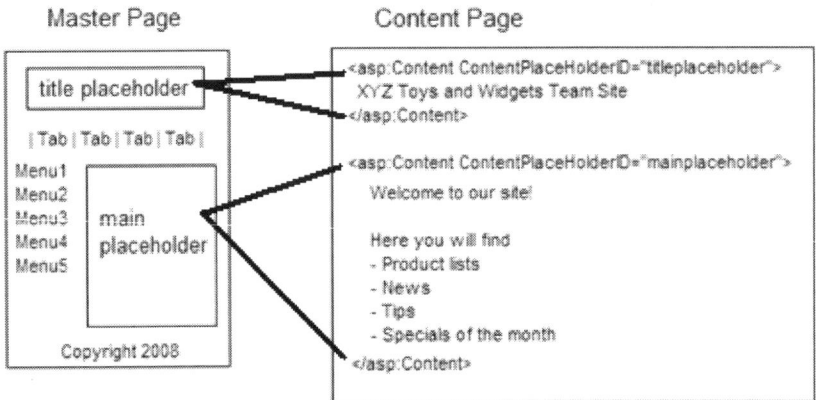

Master Page basics:

- A master page can never be displayed by itself; it is always used in combination with a content page.
- A master page has the primary page layout HTML including the <HTML>. <HEAD>, <BODY> and all layout HTML needed for the page along with any CSS and JavaScript shared by all the content pages.
- A master page has <ASP:ContentPlaceHolder> tags to mark where the content pages can insert their content.
- A content page has no HTML outside of the <ASP:Content> tags.
- Site pages use a shared master page that can be customized for each site or site collection.

Important SharePoint Master Page Notes

- In SharePoint Designer the master pages are found in the _catalogs\masterpage folder
- The Master Page Gallery (Site Actions, Site Settings, Master Page Gallery) is a library and includes most library options such as versioning and permissions
- If Publishing features are enabled, then the Master Page Gallery has **Required Check Out** enabled (A common error is to forget to check in your customized master page. If left checked out you will see the changes, but your users will not.)
- Versioning is enabled on the Master Page Gallery and you can view the version history from the Master Page Gallery or from SharePoint Designer
- Each site has its own Master Page Gallery and customizations to a master page in one site are not automatically copied to another site (see next bullet)
- If your top level site has Publishing features enabled (i.e. the top level site was created from a publishing template, or you manually enabled the publishing features), then you can copy a modified master page to subsites (Site Actions, Site Settings, Look and Feel, Master Page, **Reset all subsites to inherit this Site Master Page** setting)

Editing a master page (2007)

1. Open SharePoint Designer 2007
2. Open your site: **File, Open Site** and enter your URL (http://servername/sites/sitename)
3. In the Folder List expand **_catalogs** and expand the **masterpage (Master Page)** folder

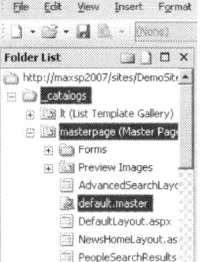

4. Double-click your master page (for non-publishing sites this will usually be default.master)
5. Most of the JavaScript or CSS customizations in this book that impact the entire site can be added to the end of the page just before the **</BODY>** tag

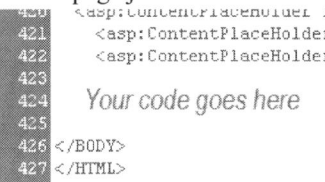

6. If this site has publishing features enabled, remember to Check In your changes (from either SharePoint Designer or the Master Page Gallery in the site)

Editing a master page (2010)

1. Open SharePoint Designer 2010
2. Open your site: Click **Open Site** and enter your URL (http://servername/sites/sitename)
3. In the **Site Objects** pane click **Master Pages**
4. Double-click your master page (most likely v4.master)
5. In the **Customization** section click **Edit File**
6. Most of the JavaScript or CSS customizations in this book that impact the entire site can be added to the end of the page just before the **</BODY>** tag

7. If this site has publishing features enabled, remember to Check In and Approve your changes (from either SharePoint Designer or the Master Page Gallery in Site Actions, Site Settings)

Editing a SharePoint Site Page

SharePoint Designer can be used to edit some, but not all, SharePoint pages.

Types of SharePoint pages:

- **Application pages or "_LAYOUTS" pages** - These are primarily administrative pages like the Site Actions, Site Settings page. LAYOUTS pages cannot be edited with SharePoint Designer and cannot be uniquely customized for a single site. They are stored on the SharePoint web servers and are shared by all sites. Layout pages can always be identified by "_layouts" in their URL:

    http://*yourservername*/sites/*yoursitename*/**_layouts**/settings.aspx

- **Site Pages** - These pages are stored in the SQL database and can be customized in one site without impacting other sites.

Examples of Site Page Edits:

- Add a security or policy message to the "New" page:

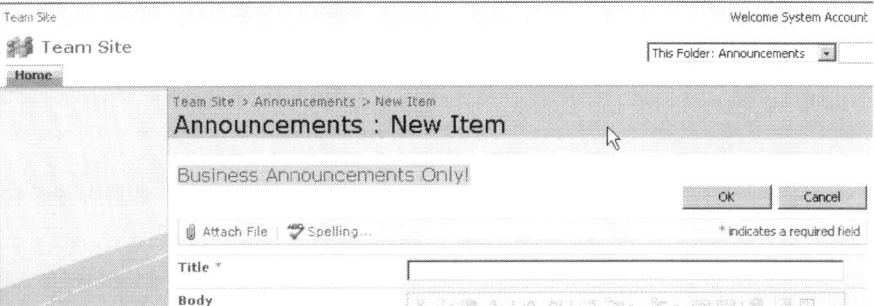

- Adding JavaScript code to a view page, perhaps to color code a list:

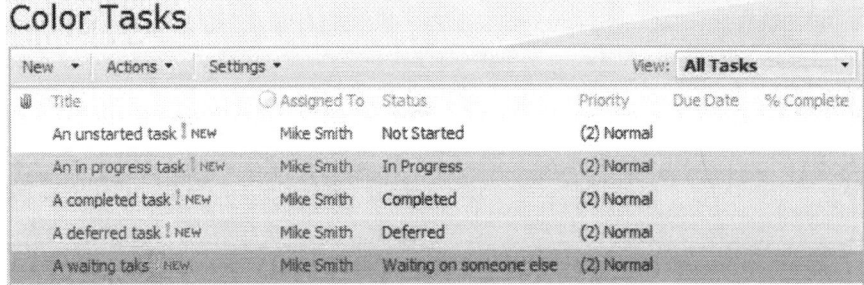

- Convert a list web part into a DataView web part to add functionality not normally available in views, such as grouping on more than two levels:

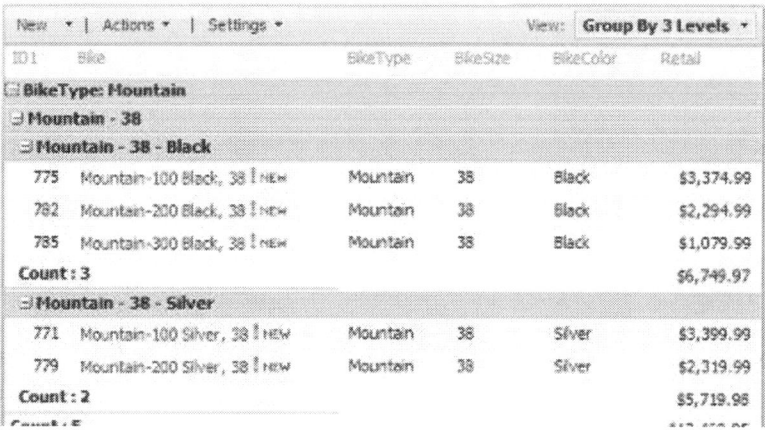

Edit a Site Page (2007)

1. Open SharePoint Designer 2007
2. Open your site: Click **File**, **Open Site**, enter your URL (http://servername/sites/sitename) and click **Open**
   Note: Do not enter the names of pages or libraries when opening a site, i.e. don't enter:
   http://servername/sites/sitename/*default.aspx*

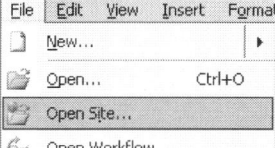

3. In the Folder List:
   - to edit the home page of a Team Site double click **default.aspx**
   - to edit a publishing site home page, or any page added with **Site Actions**, **Create Page**, expand the **Pages** library, click **Edit Page Layout** and then check out the file
   - to edit the "New Item" page (NewForm.aspx), expand Lists, expand your list, double-click **NewForm.aspx**
   - to edit a basic page or a web part page stored in a library expand the library and double-click the page

SharePoint Designer

The Folder List:

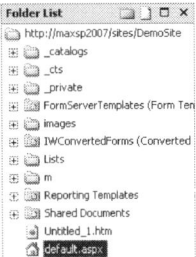

4. After completing your edits, save your work - you will be warned that you have customized your page:

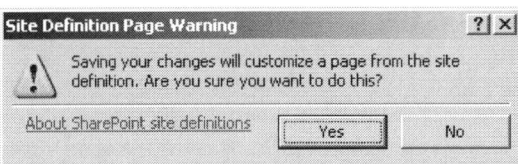

5. Remember to check in your file if you are working with a Publishing page (Pages folder) or a page stored in a library with Required Check Out enabled

Edit a Site Page (2010)

1. Open SharePoint Designer 2010
2. Open your site: Click **Open Site**, enter your URL (http://servername/sites/sitename) and click **Open** - Note: Do not enter the names of pages or libraries when opening a site, i.e. don't enter: http://servername/sites/sitename/*default.aspx*

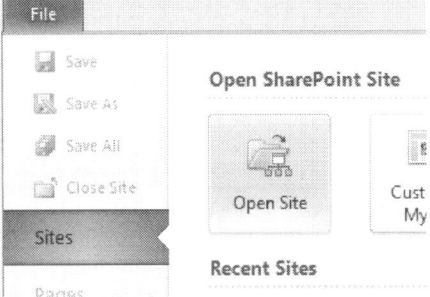

3. In the **Site Objects** pane:

   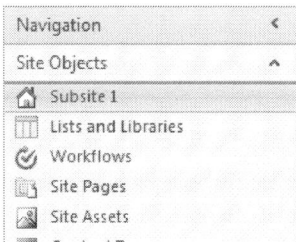

   - to edit the home page of a Team Site click **Site Pages** and double click **home.aspx** (you don't normally want to edit the default.aspx page in the root of **All Files** - this is a left over from 2007)
   - to edit the "New Item" page (NewForm.aspx), expand **Lists and Libraries**, click your list, double-click **NewForm.aspx**
   - to edit any page added with **Site Actions, New Page**, a basic page or a web part page, click **All Files**, click the "push pin" to expand the list of files, expand the **Site Pages** library, and double-click your file

   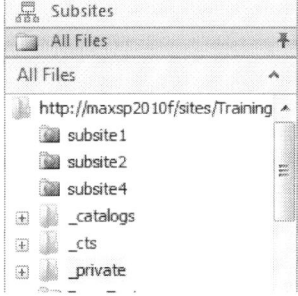

4. In most pages you open you will find most of the code has a shaded background and is not editable. Click **Advanced Mode** in the ribbon (Advanced Mode) to be able to edit the entire page.

   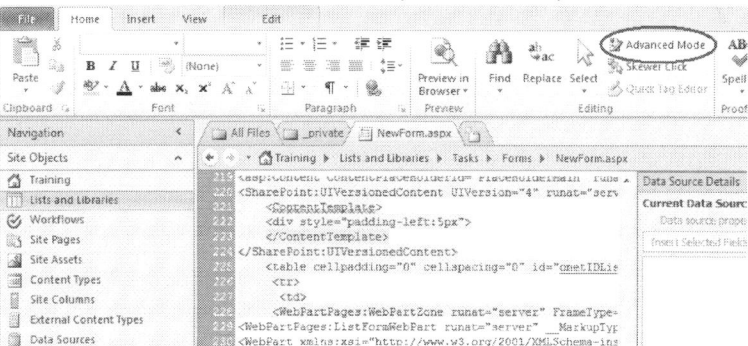

SharePoint Designer

5. After completing your edits, save your work - you will be warned that you have customized your page:

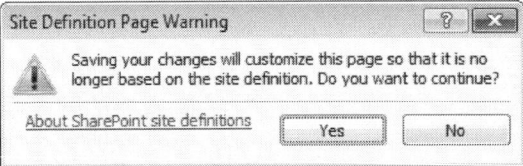

6. Remember to check in your file if you are working with a Publishing page (Pages folder) or a page stored in a library with Required Check Out enabled

"The current page has been customized from its template. Revert to template"

After editing a SharePoint 2010 page you may get this annoying error message at the top of the page:

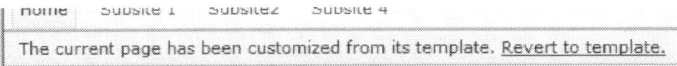

This message is only displayed for users with Design or Site Owner rights, but is still annoying!

To fix this:

1. Go back to SharePoint Designer and scroll to the end of the page
2. Just before the end tag for **PlaceHolderMain** add this style block

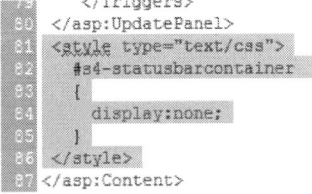

3. Save and test the page

7. Security Tricks

Do you need this chapter?

This chapter deals with identifying who the current user is, filtering content by user and customizing security pages. Many SharePoint customizations need to be seen only by selected users and this can be a challenge as SharePoint page HTML does not give us clean and simple information about the user or their permissions. By exploring the HTML of a SharePoint page, and using a few tricks, we can probably still get what we need.

What's in this chapter?

- Identify the Current Logged In User
- SharePoint Permissions
- How to Hide View All Site Content for Selected Users
- Customizing the People and Groups Views

Security Tricks

Identify the Current Logged In User

You may have times when you want to display messages or content based on who is currently viewing the page. There are several techniques to do this, some more useful than others, none ideal.

- Read the JavaScript variable _spUserId
- Read the text of the user's name from the Welcome menu
- Identify a user by group membership (MOSS 2007 or Server 2010 only)
- Identify the user by the permissions they have: **ManageLists** or maybe **EditItems**

The JavaScript variable "_spUserId"

Any page that displays the Welcome menu also initializes a JavaScript variable named _spUserId. To see this variable visit a page (home page is OK), right-click the page, select the browser's view source command and search for the variable.

The _spUserId variable:

- is a simple number - i.e. 1, 2, 3, etc.
- is a sequential number - the first person granted permissions to the site collection is #1, the next is #2, ...
- is unique to a site collection - i.e. "Mike Smith" might be number 12 in http://yourserver/sites/sales and number 345 in http://yourserver/sites/training
- Is consistent within a site collection - i.e. "Mike Smith" will always be #12 in any site within a single site collection

How to discover the _spUserId of a user:

- Log in as the user, view the source of the page and search for "_spUserId", or
- Add the **ID** column to any of the **People and Group** views (see "Customizing the People and Groups Views" later in this chapter)

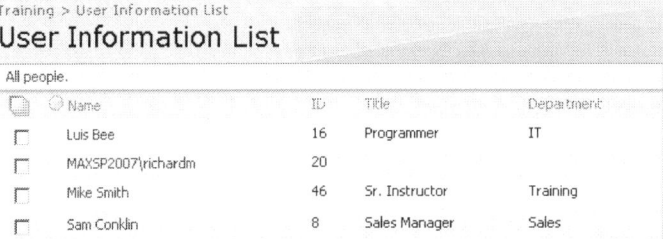

Using the _spUserId of a user:

106

```
<script type="text/javascript">
  if ( _spUserId == 8 )   // for Sam Conklin in the list above
  {
   // add JS code here...
   alert("you are special!");
  }
</script>
```

The ways you can take advantage of this ID are a bit limited as you must know the ID of a user and hard code that into your JavaScript routines, so read further for more ideas.

Read the text of the user's name from the Welcome menu

If your site has not been custom branded and has not had the welcome menu removed, the user's name will be displayed at the top of each site page.

2007:   2010:

Welcome Sam Conklin ▼   Sam Conklin ▼

With a little JavaScript you can extract the user's name and use it your code.

The Code:

```
var Atags = document.getElementsByTagName("A");

for (var i=0; i<Atags.length; i++)
{
  if (Atags[i].onfocus && Atags[i].onfocus.toString().indexOf("PersonalActionMenu") >-1 )
  {
    if (document.all)   // is IE
     {var username = Atags[i].innerText;}
    else           // is Firefox or other
     {var username = Atags[i].textContent;}

    //  2007 also includes the word "Welcome"
    if (username.indexOf("Welcome ") == 0)
      username = username.substring(8);

    // your JS code goes here - alert for demo only
    alert("Hi there '" + username +"'");
```

Security Tricks

```
        break;
    }
}
```

Code Notes:

- The code searches for all <A> tags then checks for a tag with an **"onfocus"** event that includes the text "PersonalActionMenu"
- It then reads the user's name using **innerText** for Internet Explorer or **textContent** for Firefox
- (SP 2007 only) It then checks to see if the word "Welcome" is in the text and then retrieves the user name from just after the Welcome text.

Identify a user by group membership

MOSS 2007 and SharePoint Server 2010 both have a feature called "Audiences" that can be used to hide content from all users except for the members of the audience. This feature is not available in WSS or SharePoint Foundation. An audience is defined in three ways:

- Global Audiences - defined in Central Administration by SharePoint server administrators - provides a way to dynamically assign users to an audience based on their user profile properties
- Distribution / Security Groups - Active Directory groups
- SharePoint Groups

We will use a SharePoint group based Audience and a web part that will be displayed only for that audience to test group membership. The basic steps are:

- Add a Content Editor Web Part with invisible content (maybe a SPAN with an ID)
- Turn off the "Chrome" of the web part to help hide it
- Control if the web part is displayed by using an Audience based on a SharePoint group
- Write some JavaScript code to see if the web part is displayed on the page

Steps:

Create the invisible, audience controlled, web part:

1. Add a Content Editor Web Part to the page
2. Edit the web part and set the **Chrome Type** to **None** (in the **Appearance** section)

    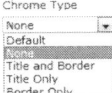

3. Add an empty SPAN to the web part
    a. SharePoint 2007: In the properties panel click the **Source Editor** button and type
       `<span id="isTeamMember"></span>`
       and close the editor

Security Tricks

    b.   SharePoint 2010: Click the "**click here to add content**" link, in the Ribbon click "**HTML**", "**Edit HTML Source**", type
        `<span id="isTeamMember"></span>`
    and close the editor

    Note: Just for testing, you may want to add a little test message so you will know that the audience feature is really working.
        `<span id="isTeamMember"></span>`
        This is the "invisible web part" that only members can "see"

4. In the web part's properties panel, expand the **Advanced** section and scroll to the bottom to find **Target Audiences**

5. Click the **Browse** button
6. From the **Find** dropdown list, select **SharePoint Groups** and search for a group (or just click the search button to display all the groups)
7. Double-click your group and click **OK**

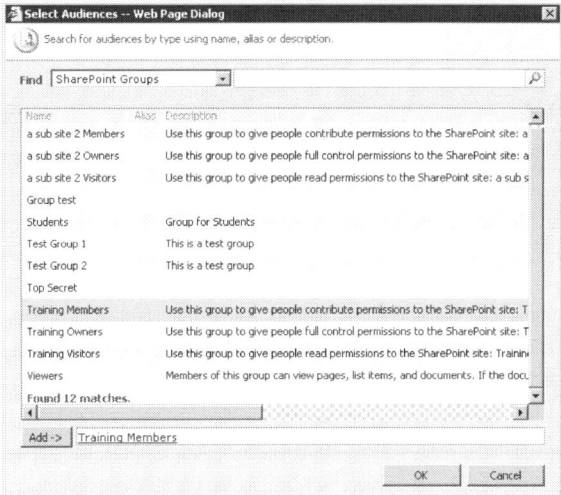

8. Click the **OK** button at the bottom of the **Properties** panel
9. In 2007 click **Exit Edit Mode** or in 2010 click **Save and Close** in the ribbon

You now have the "invisible" audience control web part.

Add JavaScript to test if the web part is on the page:

The JavaScript you write will depend on what action you want to take. In this example we will just display a message to the user.

Security Tricks

```
<script type="text/javascript">
if (document.getElementById("isTeamMember"))
{
  alert("Hi there Team Member!");
}
</script>
```

Users who are members of the "Training Members" group will then see this popup:

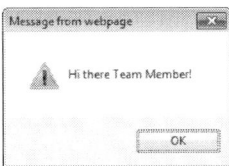

This script block can go anywhere in the page after where the "invisible" web part was placed. You can add the code to another Content Editor Web Part or in the master page somewhere after the **PlaceHolderMain** content placeholder.

Identify the user by their permissions

Users are granted rights to sites and site content by being assigned one or more Permission Levels. These levels can be granted directly to the user or granted by adding a user to a SharePoint group having those permissions. Permission Levels consist of one or more permissions. SharePoint 2007 and 2010 define 32 permissions. As an example you can identify Site Owners and Site Collection Administrators by looking for users who have the "Manage Web Site" permission. To identify users by a permission we can use a SharePoint web control, the SPSecurityTrimmedControl, that can be used to hide or show parts of a page based on a user's permissions.

 The SPSecurityTrimmedControl cannot be used inside of a Content Editor Web Part as it must be processed on the web servers. You must add this control directly to an ASPX page or to the master page using SharePoint Designer.

As an example, you might edit the NewItem.aspx page for the Announcements list and display a message about acceptable use of the announcements list. You might want to display one message for all users and an additional message for site owners. Here's what the HTML might look like:

```
<!-- text for all users -->
The announcements list is only for team announcements. Do not add personal, for sale, or free items as announcements.

<!-- text for users who have the ManageWeb permission -->
<SharePoint:SPSecurityTrimmedControl runat="server" PermissionsString="ManageWeb">
Site Owners may add announcements about site changes and site availability.
```

```
</SharePoint:SPSecurityTrimmedControl>
```

Team members (other than site owners) would see this when they add new announcements:

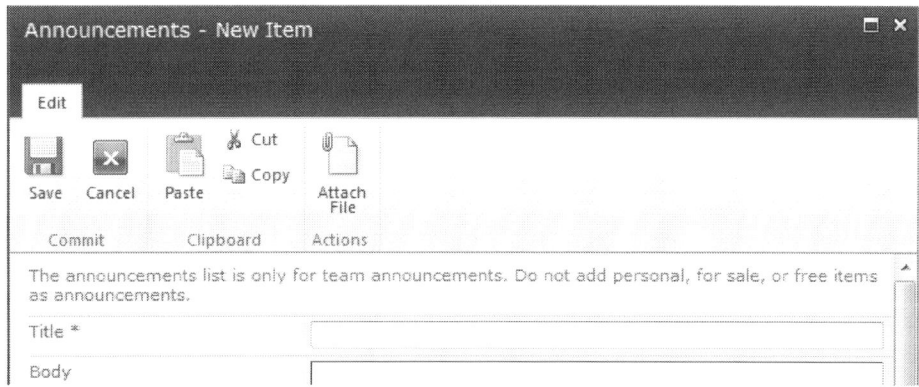

Site owners would see this when they add new announcements:

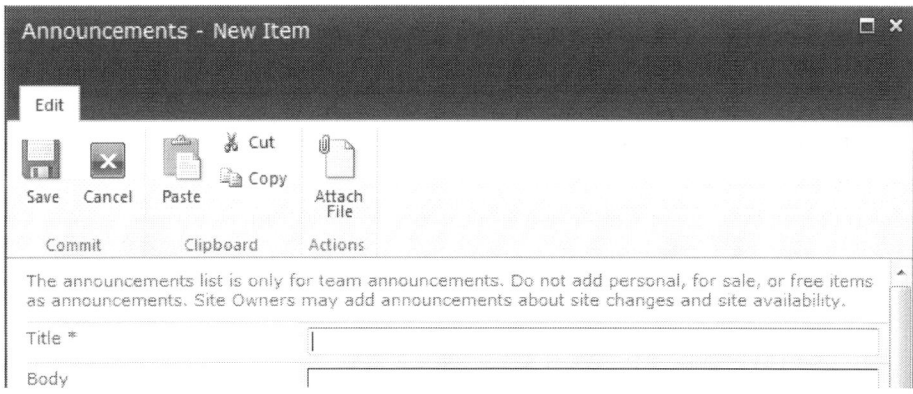

The SPSecurityTrimmedControl is good for only showing content to selected users. What if you want to show content to all except for a selected group of users?

The following will display a message only to Site Owners (who have the ManageWeb permission):

```
<SharePoint:SPSecurityTrimmedControl runat="server" PermissionsString="ManageWeb">
    Welcome Site Owner! (you have the manage web permission)
</SharePoint:SPSecurityTrimmedControl>
```

The following will display a message to everyone except Site Owners:

```
<style type="text/css">
  #allbutowners { display:inline; }
```

Security Tricks

```
</style>
<SharePoint:SPSecurityTrimmedControl runat="server" PermissionsString="ManageWeb">
  <style type="text/css">
   #allbutowners { display:none; }
  </style>
</SharePoint:SPSecurityTrimmedControl>
<span class="allbutowners">
  Welcome Site Visitor or Member! (you don't have the manage web permission)
</span>
```

The above code first adds a style to hide the text, then adds a SPSecurityTrimmedControl to set a second style to hide the text (but only if the user is an owner) and finally adds a SPAN with the message for non-owners. This same technique can be used to run JavaScript one way for users with a particular permission and another way for all other users. The following is how you might use the SPSecurityTrimmedControl in a JavaScript application:

```
<script type="text/javascript">
 var UserHasManageWebPermissions=false;
</script>

<SharePoint:SPSecurityTrimmedControl runat="server" PermissionsString="ManageWeb">
  <script type="text/javascript">
    UserHasManageWebPermissions=true;
  </script>
</SharePoint:SPSecurityTrimmedControl>

<script type="text/javascript">
// do something based on permissions
if ( UserHasManageWebPermissions )
{
  // add your code here
  alert("ALERT from SecurityTrimmedControl (you have the manage web permission!)");
}
</script>
```

The first script block defines a variable and defaults it to false. The SPSecurityTrimmedControl is then used to change this variable if the user has the desired permission. The third script block then runs code based on the user's permissions.

You may want to add several of these tests to your master page so you can then have a collection of variables predefined and available for other code in your pages. These might include **UserHasWebPermissions, UserHasDeletePermissions, UserHasXYZPermissions**, etc.

> For more info on SPSecurityTrimmedControl see Link 701.

SharePoint Permissions

Below is a table showing the 32 SharePoint permissions and how they are assigned to the out of the box permission levels.

Permissions

> R = default permissions for Visitors / Readers
> C = default permissions for Contributors / Team Members
> D = default permissions for Designers
> FC = default permissions for Full Control / Site Owners

Group	Permission Name	Description	R	C	D	FC
List	ManageLists	Create and delete lists, add or remove columns in a list, and add or remove public views of a list.				X
List	CancelCheckout	Discard or check in a document which is checked out to another user.			X	X
List	AddListItems	Add items to lists, add documents to document libraries, and add Web discussion comments.		X	X	X
List	EditListItems	Edit items in lists, edit documents in document libraries, edit Web discussion comments in documents, and customize Web Part Pages in document libraries.		X	X	X
List	DeleteListItems	Delete items from a list, documents from a document library, and Web discussion comments in documents.		X	X	X
List	ViewListItems	View items in lists, documents in document libraries, and view Web discussion comments.	X	X	X	X
List	ApproveItems	Approve a minor version of a list item or document.			X	X
List	OpenItems	View the source of documents with server-side file handlers.	X	X	X	X
List	ViewVersions	View past versions of a list item or document.	X	X	X	X
List	DeleteVersions	Delete past versions of a list item or document.		X	X	X
List	CreateAlerts	Create e-mail alerts.	X	X	X	X
List	ViewFormPages	View forms, views, and application pages, and enumerate lists.	X	X	X	X
Site	ManagePermissions	Create and change permission levels on the Web site and assign permissions to users and groups.				X
Site	ViewUsageData	View reports on Web site usage.				X

Security Tricks

Site	ManageSubwebs	Create subsites such as team sites, Meeting Workspace sites, and Document Workspace sites.				X
Site	ManageWeb	Grant the ability to perform all administration tasks for the Web site as well as manage content.				X
Site	AddAndCustomizePages	Add, change, or delete HTML pages or Web Part Pages, and edit the Web site using a Windows SharePoint Services–compatible editor (SharePoint Designer).			X	X
Site	ApplyThemeAndBorder	Apply a theme or borders to the entire Web site.			X	X
Site	ApplyStyleSheets	Apply a style sheet (.css file) to the Web site.			X	X
Site	CreateGroups	Create a group of users that can be used anywhere within the site collection.				X
Site	BrowseDirectories	Enumerate files and folders in a Web site using Microsoft Office SharePoint Designer 2007 and WebDAV interfaces.		X	X	X
Site	CreateSSCSite	Create a Web site using Self-Service Site Creation.				
Site	ViewPages	View pages in a Web site.	X	X	X	X
Site	EnumeratePermissions	Enumerate permissions on the Web site, list, folder, document, or list item.				X
Site	BrowseUserInfo	View information about users of the Web site.	X	X	X	X
Site	ManageAlerts	Manage alerts for all users of the Web site.				X
Site	UseRemoteAPIs	Use SOAP, WebDAV, or Microsoft Office SharePoint Designer 2007 interfaces to access the Web site.	X	X	X	X
Site	UseClientIntegration	Use features that launch client applications; otherwise, users must work on documents locally and upload changes.	X	X	X	X
Site	Open	Allow users to open a Web site, list, or folder to access items inside that container.	X	X	X	X
Site	EditMyUserInfo	Allows a user to change his or her user information, such as adding a picture.		X	X	X
Personal	ManagePersonalViews	Create, change, and delete personal views of lists.		X	X	X
Personal	AddDelPrivateWebParts	Add or remove personal Web Parts on a Web Part Page.		X	X	X
Personal	UpdatePersonalWebParts	Update Web Parts to display personalized information.		X	X	X

How to Hide "View All Site Content" for Selected Users

As an example of using the SPSecurityTrimmedControl let's take a look at how SharePoint already uses this control. If you open the master page in SharePoint Designer and search for **idNavLinkViewAll** you will find the code to display **View All Site Content**. Notice that it is wrapped in a SPSecurityTrimmedControl configured to display the content for any user with the **ViewFormPages** permission. If you check the chart above you will find that this basically lets everyone see View All Site Content.

```
<SharePoint:SPSecurityTrimmedControl runat="server"
  PermissionsString="ViewFormPages">
  <div class="ms-quicklaunchheader">
    <SharePoint:SPLinkButton id="idNavLinkViewAll" runat="server"
      NavigateUrl="~site/_layouts/viewlsts.aspx"
      Text="<%$Resources:wss,quiklnch_allcontent%>"
      AccessKey="<%$Resources:wss,quiklnch_allcontent_AK%>"/>
  </div>
</SharePoint:SPSecurityTrimmedControl>
```

Hide from all but site owners

The View All Site Content control is very useful for site owners, often useful for site members and something you don't want most visitors to see. If you want to display the All Site Content link to just Site Owners and hide it from Site Members just change the **PermissionsString** to **ManageWeb**.

 If you move this View All Site Content in your redesign of a master page you should also move the SPSecurityTrimmedControl with it.

The Tree View has its own "All Site Content" link

Hiding the "View All Site Content" link may not be enough to hide lists, libraries and subsites not needed by your site users. The Tree View has its own "All Site Content" link that is labeled "Site Hierarchy". Search the master page for **Site Hierarchy** or for **idNavLinkSiteHierarchy** and wrap the SPLinkButton in its own SPSecurityTrimmedControl.

Customizing the People and Groups Views

And now for a very special list... the People and Groups lists. You've always heard that everything in SharePoint is a list. While that's generally true, all of the list options are not available to a few special lists. To get to these options all you need to know is a trick or two. As an example, SharePoint's **All People and Group** views are a bit light weight. If you want to know someone's phone number or ID you have to click their name and wait for another page to load, or to see if they are a Site Collection Administrator you have to visit another screen. Normally to customize a view we would just click the **View** dropdown and click **Modify View** or **Create View**, but in this list the **View** menu only has:

Security Tricks

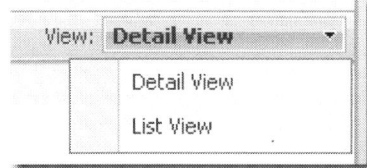

Create New View and Modify this view are missing for this list! Wouldn't it be nice if you could add more columns or even group, sort or filter the list of users? It turns out that you can create your own views of People and choose from 35 fields including both SharePoint and user profile data fields.

Fields available for People and Group views:

About me	Is Site Admin	Responsibilities
Account	Last name	Selection Checkbox
Attachment	Modified	(checkboxes)
Content Type	Modified By	SIP Address
Content Type	Name	Title
Create	Name (linked to item with edit menu)	Type (icon linked to document)
Created By		User name
Deleted	Name (linked to item)	Version
Department	Name (with picture and details)	Web site
Edit (Edit)	Name (with picture)	Work e-mail
Edit (link to edit item)	Name (with presence)	Work phone
First name	Office	
ID	Picture	SharePoint 2010 adds: Mobile Phone

This is the default "Details" view:

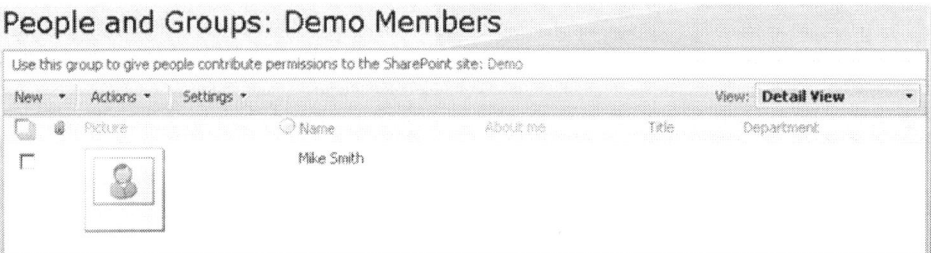

To customize People and Group views:

1. Go to the top level site in the site collection (important!)
2. Go to **People and Groups** (or **Site Actions, Site Permissions** in 2010) and click on any group, including **All People** (they all share the same views)
3. Go to **Settings, List Settings** and scroll down to the **Views** section.

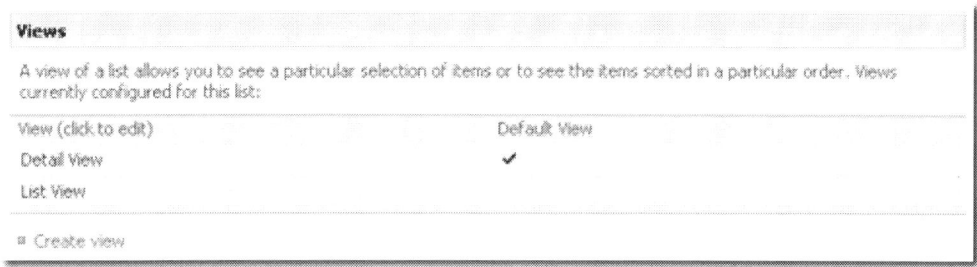

4. Click **Create View** (Rather than changing the exiting views it may be a better idea to create a new view)
5. Select your view options like any other view
6. Optional: set sort, group, filter and other View options
7. Save the changes

Note: This will leave you in the new view, but the View dropdown will not be displayed (bug?), so return to **People and Groups** (or **Site Actions**, **Site Permissions** in 2010) and the view dropdown will be displayed correctly.

Here is a customized view with several additional columns displayed:

And now the View dropdown now has your new view:

Here's a SharePoint 2010 example with grouping by department:

Security Tricks

8. Web Part Must Knows

Do you need this chapter?

If you already are a master of web parts, then just browse through this chapter to see if there's anything you might have missed. This chapter is not about how to use all of the out of the box web parts, rather it's a somewhat random collection of things a customizer needs to know about web parts.

What's in this chapter?

- Does this page have web parts?
- My page won't load… how do I delete a "bad" web part?
- Exporting, Importing and Reusing Web Parts
- Using "Static" web parts
- SharePoint 2010, the Content Editor Web Part, and Broken Views…

Does this page have web parts?

Easy one… If there is an **Edit Page** option in the **Site Actions** menu, then the page is a web part page. Some web part pages that do not have an **Edit Page** option still may have web parts, so read on…

Getting to web parts when there is no "Edit Page" in Site Actions

Some pages support web parts, but do not have **Edit Page** in the **Site Actions** menu. These include the Display, New and Edit pages for lists. For these you can add **&ToolPaneView=2** to the end of the URL. The following example will let you see the web parts on a list's NewForm.aspx page.

```
http://……/NewForm.aspx?……&ToolPaneView=2
```

```
http://demoserver/sites/demosite/Lists/Announcements/NewForm.aspx?RootFolder= … &ToolPaneView=2
```

This works in both SharePoint 2007 and 2010.

 SharePoint 2010 often opens New, Edit and Display pages in a dialog box where you cannot see the URL. To explore the web parts on these pages you can right-click in any empty area of the dialog box, select **Properties** and copy the full URL. Paste this URL into the browser's address box to display the page without the dialog box. You can then work with the page by itself, including the &ToolPaneView option.

My page won't load... how do I delete a "bad" web part?

It is possible to delete a web part that prevents a web part page from loading or causes SharePoint to display the error message page. Simply add "?Contents=1" or "&Contents=1" to the page's URL.

If the URL does not include a question mark then add "**?Contents=1**" to the end of the URL:

```
http://……/default.aspx?Contents=1
```

If the URL already includes a question mark then add "**&Contents=1**" to the end of the URL:

```
http://……/default.aspx?someotherparamerter=value&Contents=1
```

You can now delete the offending web part. Prior to deleting the bad web part you may want to open the site and the page in SharePoint Designer to see if you can find the cause of the error, or maybe to make a copy of the page before deleting the web part.

This works in both SharePoint 2007 and 2010.

SharePoint 2007 after adding **?Contents=1**:

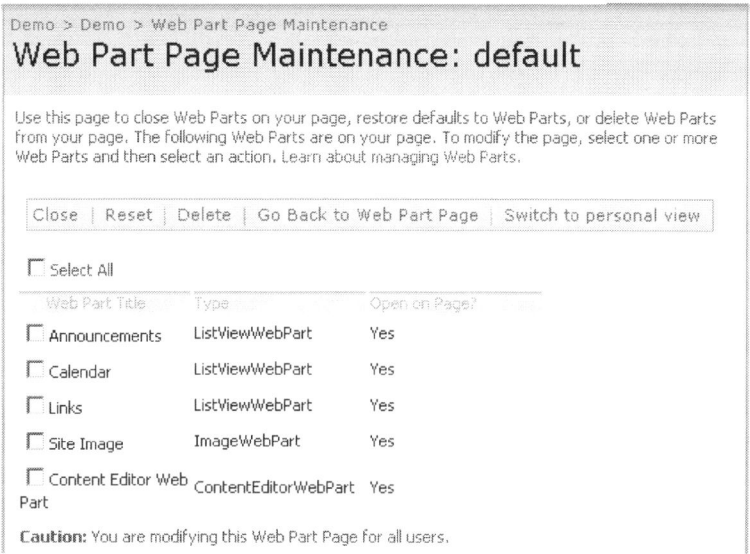

SharePoint 2010 after adding **?Contents=1**:

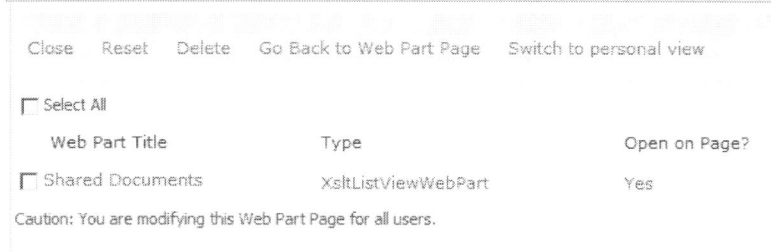

Exporting, Importing and Reusing Web Parts

Most web parts can be exported and loaded into other pages or other sites. There are a few details though:

- List and Library web parts do not have an Export option (See the "One Library, Multiple Sites" article in chapter 11 for an example of how you can add "Export" to a list or library web part)
- When you "export a web part" you are only exporting the settings for the web part - for example: you cannot add a MOSS web part to a WSS server by using Export
- For SharePoint 2007, the file extension for an exported web part is .DWP and for SharePoint 2010 it is .WEBPART
- SharePoint 2007 and 2010 export files are not compatible

Web Part Must Knows

- A web part file is an XML file that can be opened in Notepad for study or editing

Using "Static" web parts

A "static" web part is a web part added outside of a web part zone. A typical use would be when you want to add a web part to a master page so it can be seen on all site pages.

Notes:

- You cannot make changes from the browser to static Web Parts in either shared or personal views
- The static web part's properties can only be changed by editing the HTML/XML of the web part
- A good "trick" is to add the web part to a normal web part page and edit the properties there, then open the page in SharePoint Designer, copy the code for the web part and then paste into the master page
- Another good "trick" is to right-click the web part in SharePoint Designer and convert it to an XSLT Data View and add customizations not available in a normal View

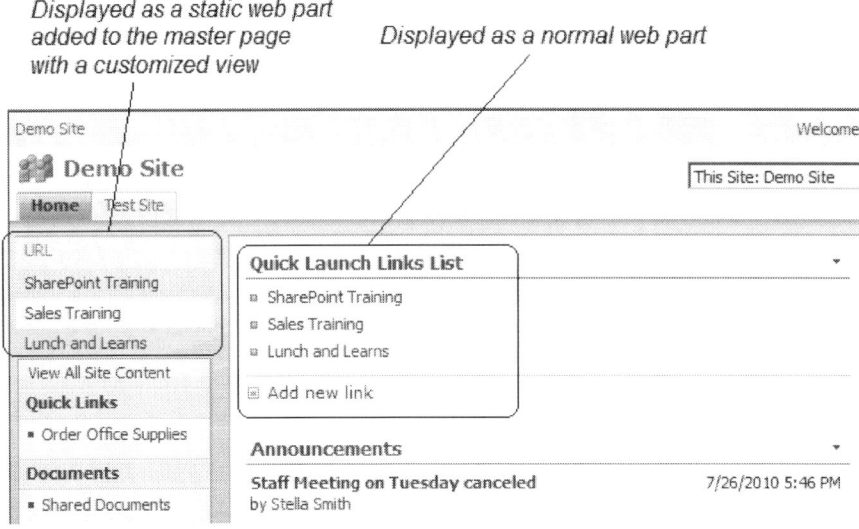

SharePoint 2010, the Content Editor Web Part, and Broken Views...

Adding a Content Editor Web Part to a view page like "Allitems.aspx" is a great way of customizing views in SharePoint 2007. This generally had no negative impact, was easy to do and produced some major improvements with little work.

The Problem in 2010?

SharePoint 2010 treats view pages with added web parts as non-views and removes many view related features.

Here's a typical Task list All Tasks ("Allitems.aspx") view:

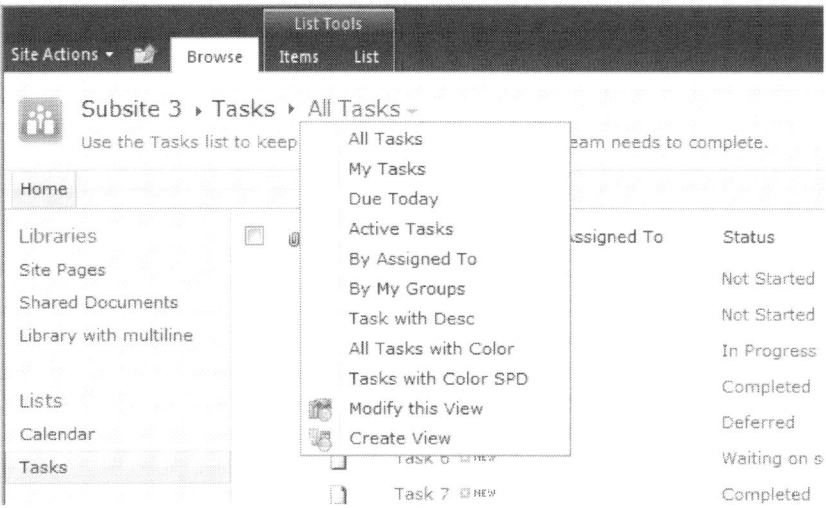

Note these features:

- The name of the view is displayed: Subsite 3 > Tasks > **All Tasks**
- There are ribbon tabs for Items and List (or for a library, Documents and Library)
- There is a dropdown arrow after "**All Tasks**" in the crumb trail

Here is the same view after the addition of a Content Editor Web Part (and the JavaScript to color code the task list):

Web Part Must Knows

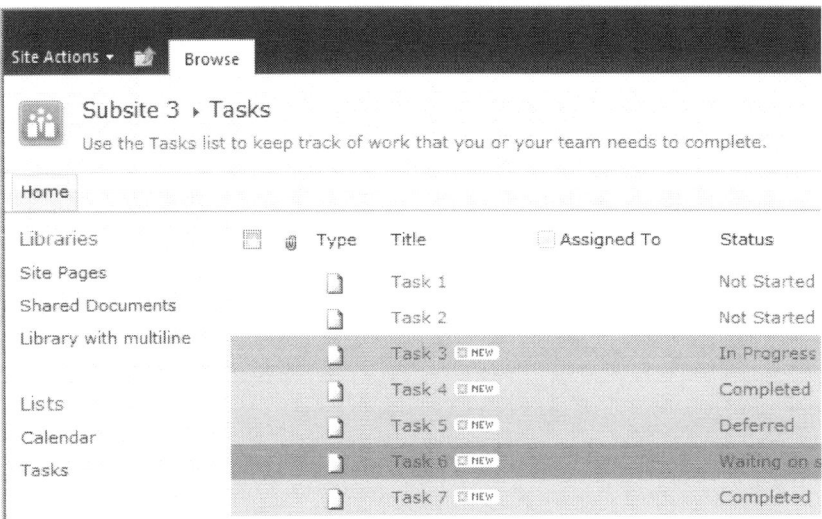

Note what's missing:

- The name of the view in the crumb trail is missing
- The ribbon tabs for Items and List are missing
- The dropdown arrow after "All Tasks" in the crumb trail is missing

You can still get to the ribbon tabs, but you have to first click a row in the list:

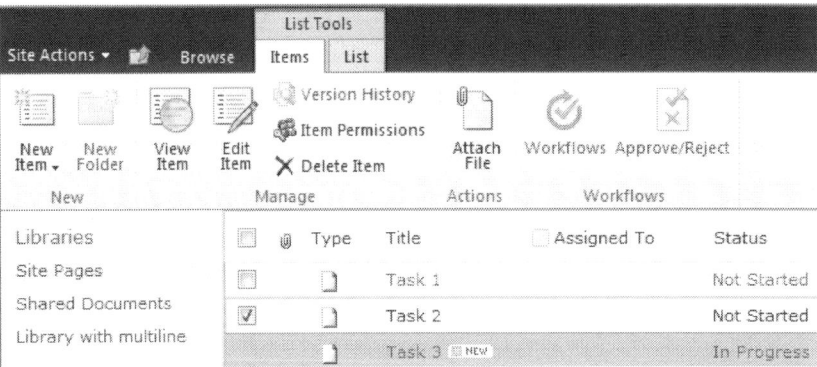

The Fix?

Don't add web parts to a 2010 view! (Duh) Instead, edit the page using SharePoint Designer 2010 and add your JavaScript code between the end tag for the Web Part Zone and the end tag for the **PlaceHolderMain** content tag.

Web Part Must Knows

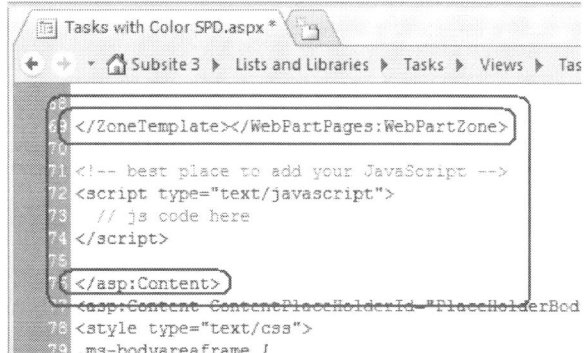

You can either embed the JavaScript:

```
<script type="text/javascript">
  // js code here
</script>
```

Or you can link to a text file with the JavaScript that you've uploaded to a library:

```
<script src="../../SitePages/ColorCodedTaskList.txt" type="text/javascript"></script>
```

✎ See chapter 6 for more on editing site pages in SharePoint Designer.

Prevent the Closing of web parts

If you have worked with SharePoint for a while you probably have found that in most cases Closing a web part is "bad" and Deleting a web part is "good". (If you didn't know this, do a web search on "SharePoint web part close vs delete".)

So how can you prevent the closing of a web part?

How about five ways...

1) Every time you add a web part go to the **Advanced** section of the properties panel and un-checkmark **Allow Close** (too much work!)

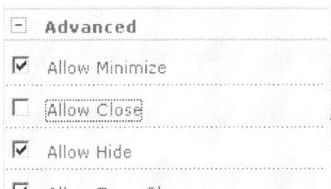

125

Web Part Must Knows

2) Add a little JavaScript code to prevent the Close:

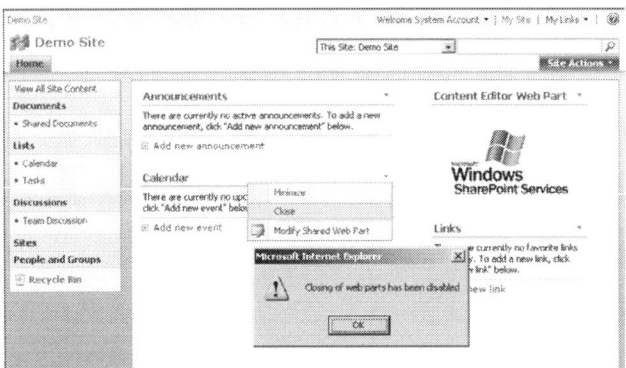

3) Add a little JavaScript code to disable the Close option

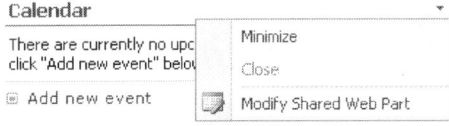

4) Add a little JavaScript code to hide the Close option (probably the best choice)

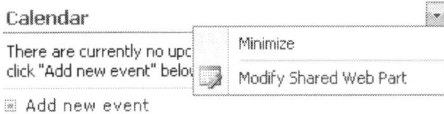

5) Add a CSS style to hide the Close option (easy to do, but it leaves a blank line)

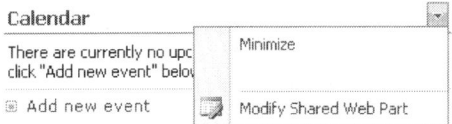

I prefer #4! Below are details on all five ways.

The JavaScript to prevent the close and display a popup:

Add the following to your site's master page just before the </BODY> tag (A SharePoint Designer task!) or in a Content Editor Web Part (last one on the page) if you just want this for a single page. This code replaces the SharePoint close function with our own that just displays a message.

```
<script type="text/javascript">
  MSOLayout_RemoveWebPart = function (x)
  {
```

```
    alert("Closing of web parts has been disabled");
  }
</script>
```

The JavaScript to Disable or Hide the Close option:

Add the following to your site's master page just before the </BODY> tag (A SharePoint Designer task!) or in a Content Editor Web Part (last one on the page) if you just want this for a single page. This code has two options; you will need to uncomment either **x.disabled=true** or **x.hidden=true**.

```
<script type="text/javascript">
// hide or disable the web part Close option
_spBodyOnLoadFunctionNames.push('hideWebPartClose');  // delay the load of this code

function hideWebPartClose()
{
  var x = document.getElementById("MSOMenu_Close")

  // uncomment the next line to just disable (gray out)
  // x.disabled=true

  // uncomment the next line to hide the close option
  x.hidden=true

}
</script>
```

The CSS to hide the Close option:

Add this to your master page, your linked style sheet file or to a Content Editor Web Part:

```
<style type="text/css">
 #MSOMenu_Close
 {
   display:none;
 }
</style>
```

9. The Content Editor Web Part

Do you need this chapter?

As the Content Editor Web Part is used in a large number of the customizations in this book, and the chapter is quite short, yes you should read it.

What's in this chapter?

- What about the Form Web Part and the Page Viewer Web Part?
- What about direct page edits using SharePoint Designer?
- The CEWP in SharePoint 2007
- The CEWP in SharePoint 2010
- Reusing a Content Editor Web Part Customization
- Best Practices

A Gift to Customizers!

The Content Editor Web Part (CEWP) is SharePoint's gift to site customizers! It's most common use is to create ad-hoc rich text content for a page that can include text, images, hyperlinks, bulleted lists, and just about anything else you associate with a rich text HTML editor. The bonus for customizers is the ability to inject our own JavaScript code, Cascading Style Sheets and custom HTML into a SharePoint page. Most of the tricks and tips in the rest of this book that impact a single page will be using the CEWP.

You can use the CEWP for:

- Custom HTML - tables, images, videos, Silverlight, Flash, etc
- Custom CSS
- Custom JavaScript, including jQuery

You cannot use the CEWP for:

- any HTML that needs a <FORM> tag
- Connect to other web parts using "Edit, Connections"
- any code that needs a server side control such as the ASP controls (<asp:*controlname*>) or SharePoint controls (<sharepoint:*controlname*>)

 Most of the customizations that use the CEWP can also be directly added to a site page by using SharePoint Designer. See chapter 6.

What about the Form Web Part and the Page Viewer Web Part?

SharePoint has two other web parts that might lend themselves to the customization tricks we do in this book; the Form Web Part and the Page Viewer Web Part.

Form Web Part / HTML Form Web Part

The Form Web Part in 2007 and the HTML Form Web Part in 2010, have a Source Editor button just like the Content Editor Web Part. Unlike the Content Editor Web Part, the Form Web Part can be connected to other web parts. A common use of this web part is to create a "form" that a user can complete to filter another web part. The Form Web Part is missing the Rich Edit button and the Content Link box that lets you link to HTML, CSS and JavaScript stored in a separate text file. While this web part can be used for some of our customizations, the CEWP is usually a better choice.

For more information on the Form Web Part see Links 901 and 902.

Page Viewer Web Part

The Page Viewer Web Part can display HTML from a linked file or web site. It uses an <IFRAME> tag to enclose and isolate the displayed content. *For security reasons the HTML, CSS and JavaScript in the linked page cannot impact the HTML in the SharePoint page using the Page Viewer Web Part.* While this web part is excellent to display reports and web pages from other systems and sites, it is not too useful for our customization purposes.

   For more information on the Page Viewer Web Part see Link 903

   For an example of a customization use see "Add a Web part for a Document Library Folder" in chapter 11

What about direct page edits using SharePoint Designer?

Almost everything you can do with the CEWP can also be done by adding your customizations directly to the page using SharePoint Designer.

Advantages of direct page edits:

- Edits are completely hidden from site users, especially site members as there are no web parts they can edit or delete
- Code added directly to a SharePoint 2010 view page will not break crumb trail and view menu features (See "The CEWP in SharePoint 2010" later in this chapter)
- SharePoint Designer's editors make writing JavaScript, HTML and CSS easier with color coding and auto completion features

Disadvantages:

- You must use SharePoint Designer - and your company may have a policy against this
- The page will changed from un-customized (ghosted) to customized (un-ghosted), which has a small impact on performance (See chapter 6 for more details)
- Customizations are harder to find by the next site owner who inherits your site
- More steps are needed for each edit

To add code directly to a page:

Add your JavaScript code between the end tag for the Web Part Zone and the end tag for the PlaceHolderMain content tag. (See chapter 6 - "Editing a SharePoint Page")

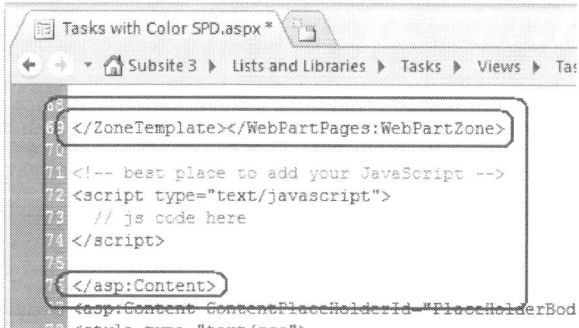

The CEWP in SharePoint 2007

The CEWP in SharePoint 2007 is a simple web part that includes four options to add content:

- a Rich Text Editor with all of the HTML editing options you might expect
- the Edit HTML Source button ( ) inside of the Rich Text Editor toolbar
- a Source Editor that is very simple text editor, so simple you many want to use another tool to write your code, and then just copy it to the Source Editor
- a Content Link box to link to an external file containing your code - this file would typically be stored in a library

To add a Content Editor Web Part

1. Display any web part page, click **Site Actions**, **Edit Page** then **Add a web part**:

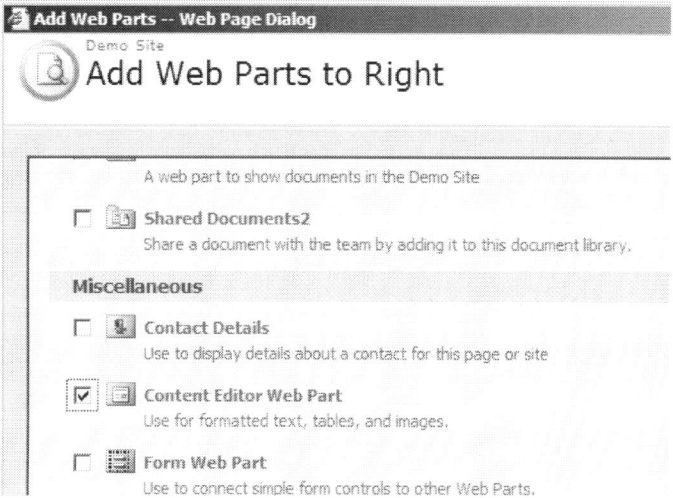

The Content Editor Web Part

To edit a Content Editor Web Part

1. Click the web part's edit button then select **Modify Shared Web Part**
2. Or, if you have linked to a text file, then just open that text file directly from a library, make your edits and then save. No need to open the CEWP.

 You can open linked code files from within SharePoint Designer by just expanding the library's folder and double-clicking the file. You will then be able to use SharePoint Designer's JavaScript, HTML and CSS editors with their color coding and auto completion features.

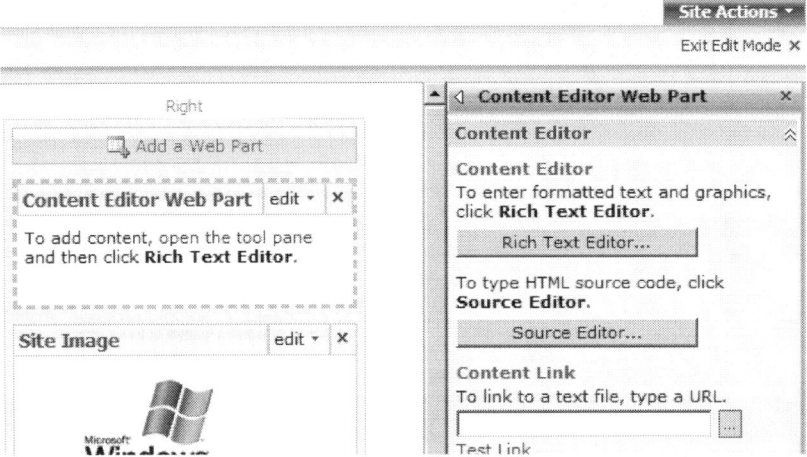

Hiding the CEWP title bar

The CEWP will often be used to store code and will not need a title or title bar displayed on the page.

- In the properties editor, expand **Appearance**, click the **Chrome Type** dropdown and select **None**

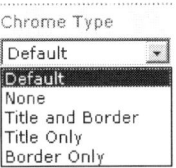

The CEWP in SharePoint 2010

In 2010 it's now just called "Content Editor" and is in the **Media and Content** section of **Add a Web Part**:

132

The Content Editor Web Part

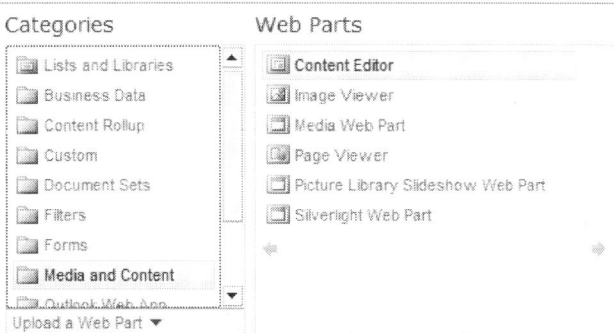

The page with the new web part:

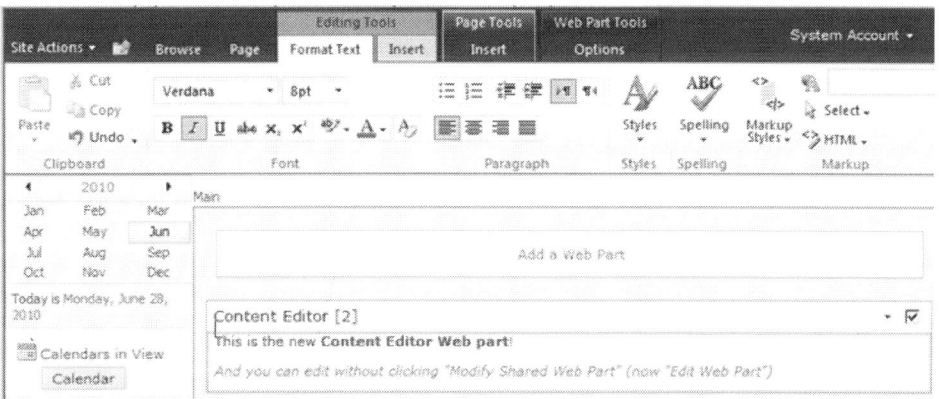

How do you add HTML?

When you add this web part you get a "wiki style" editor for normal rich text editing. When you use the web part's edit dropdown and click **Edit Web Part** you will find that the **Source Editor** button is gone! So how do you add your JavaScript and CSS? You could just click the HTML button in the Ribbon ( ), but read on for some fun issues with this option…

The Content Editor Web Part

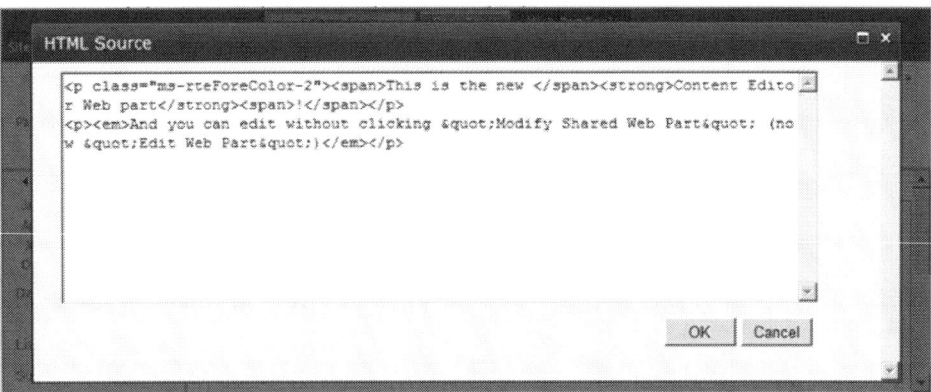

When you add CSS or JavaScript you may get this nice little message:

Warning: The HTML source you entered might have been modified.

Consider this trivial example:

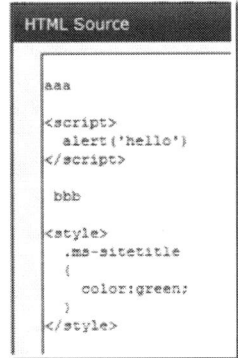

Each time you go back into the HTML editor and click **OK** it adds another blank line after the script tag and removes line breaks elsewhere!

The Content Editor Web Part

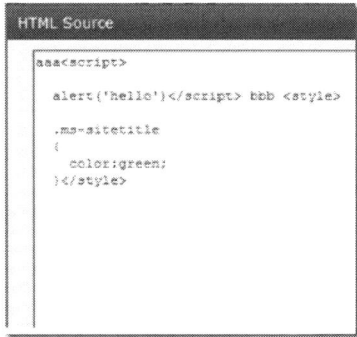

It has even sometimes changes the capitalization. In one of my edits it changed color:red to COLOR:red.

Who knows why...

The fix? Just link to your code!

Both 2007 and 2010 offer the option to link from the CEWP to a text file with your content. To avoid the problem with the random edits made by 2010 just upload a text file containing the code to a library. Then in the CEWP just click the Edit Web Part option in the dropdown and add the link to the code file. This has added benefit of using any HTML, CSS and JavaScript editor such as Visual Studio or SharePoint Designer to edit your code.

To edit a Content Editor Web Part

1. If the CEWP includes displayable text, the just click anywhere in the web part to open up the editor ribbon and start typing.
2. If you have linked to a text file, then just open that text file from the library, make your edits and then save. No need to open the CEWP during each edit, just refresh the page to see the changes.

 You can open linked code files from within SharePoint Designer. Click All Files, click the "push pin" to expand the list of files, expand the library, and double-click your file. You will then be able to use SharePoint Designer's JavaScript, HTML and CSS editors with their color coding and auto completion features.

Reusing a Content Editor Web Part Customization

You can easily reuse many CEWP customizations by exporting the web part to a file and then uploading it into another site. As the CEWP is just a container for text (HTML, JavaScript, CSS, etc) it will have few external dependencies and should be reusable in other pages and sites.

A few watch outs:

The Content Editor Web Part

- If the CEWP code has an absolute URL to an image, JavaScript file or other resource, then the links will still work, as long as the users of the new site have permissions to the linked files in the original site
- If the CEWP has relative URLs, then the new site will need the same files stored in libraries with the same library name and file names
- Some of the customizations in this book may not work when a site has a heavily modified master page, so a CEWP customization that works in one site might not work in another

Best Practices

- Document everything! Add comments to all of your HTML, JavaScript and CSS!
- Document everything! Create a document for each site that lists all of the customization. Some day you will need to rebuild your site from scratch, figure how you did what, or help the poor sole who will someday inherit your site!

Tip! Store a copy of these documents outside of SharePoint. Otherwise, if you lose the SharePoint site, or the entire farm, you will lose all of your documentation with it.

- Store all of your customizations in text files in a library and use the Content Link feature to link from the Content Editor Web Part to this file. Advantages:
    - You can write the code and upload it to a library once, then use it in multiple Content Editor Web Parts (…edit in one place… update in many…)
    - You can use your HTML, CSS or JavaScript editor's Intellisense, copy and paste, and other editing features to help write the code
    - When it comes time to upgrade from SharePoint 20xx to SharePoint 20yy you will have everything that needs to be reviewed and updated in one place.

10. User Interface Customization

Do you need this chapter?

Only if you want to do cool things with your site! The real content of the book starts here. This is a very busy chapter! Here you will see how to make customizations that impact entire pages, and even an entire site. Prior to starting here you should have read, or at least skimmed, the chapters on the Content Editor Web Part (9), SharePoint Designer (6), JavaScript (4) and Cascading Style Sheets (3).

User interface customization can cover just about anything in SharePoint that is displayed in the browser. In this chapter we are looking at basic page and navigation features such as the Top Link Bar, Quick Launch, copyright and warning messages and the Tree View. List and Library customizations are covered in chapters 11 through 15.

What's in this chapter?

- Is this branding?
- Adding messages to sites
- Changing the site title and icon
- Redesign the 2010 title area
- Hiding menu options
- Quick Launch and Top Link bar tricks
- Quick Launch pop outs and accordions
- "Fixing" basic pages and web part pages
- Adding, removing and hiding web part zones
- Customizing the Tree View
- Adding dropdowns to the Top Link bar
- Creating custom menus
- Replacing your home page with another page
- Add Colors, Borders and Fonts to Web Parts

User Interface Customization

Is this Branding?

This book will not cover the complete rebranding of a site or the complete rearrangement of the master page. That is a big project, and well beyond the scope of this book. There are numerous books and web sites with articles on SharePoint branding, so do a web search or check out the links here: (Link 1001)

Some of the customizations in this chapter:

- Add a message at the top of the page
- Site Title - Size, Font or Hide It
- Add / hide menus
- Change the site title
- Quick Launch - hide/show, add back to basic pages and web part pages
- Add a top message bar to every page
- Add a footer to every page
- Modify / Add / remove web part zones
- Customizing the Basic Page
- How to hide the right web part column
- Hide the TreeView Icons

Also see: Chapter 7: How to Hide View All Site Content

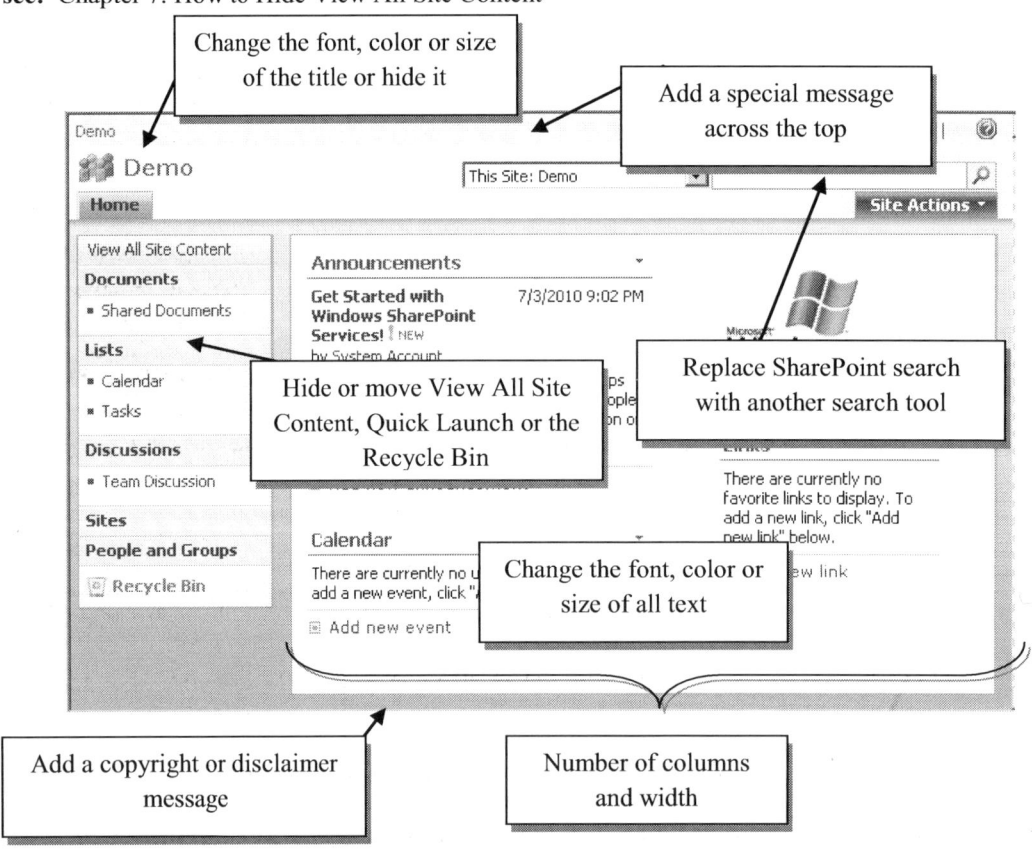

Add a message at the top or bottom of a page

You may want to add a message bar at the top of a page for a "Site update in progress" message or a policy statement. You can use a Content Editor Web Part to update a single page or use SharePoint Designer to add it to every page in the site.

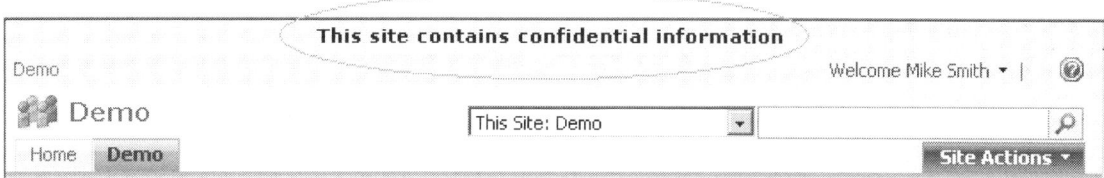

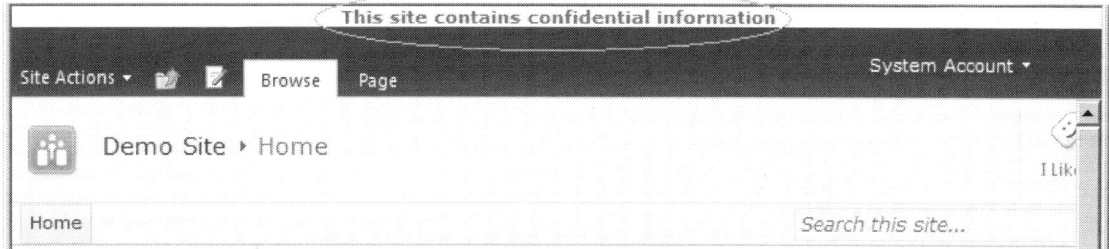

SharePoint 2007 Steps

How it works: SharePoint 2007 uses HTML tables to layout a page. The basic table structure is not defined in your page, but rather in a master page, so we will use JavaScript to make the update after our page loads. A three line JavaScript routine will be used to add a new row to the main table used to layout the page.

How would you have discovered this? If you use the "View Source" option of your browser you can see that SharePoint 2007 uses HTML tables for page layout. In order to add text at the top of the page you would want to find the main layout table on the page (it happens to be the first one), add a new row to the table and then in that row add your HTML for the message.

Steps:

1. Add a Content Editor Web Part (see the basic steps in Chapter 9)
2. Decide whether to add the JavaScript code using the **Source Editor** button or store it in a linked file (again see the basic steps in Chapter 9)
3. Add the following JavaScript code to the linked file or by using the **Source Editor** button:

```
<script type="text/javascript">
 var newrow = document.getElementsByTagName('table')[0].insertRow(0);
 nvar newcell = newrow.insertCell(0);
 newcell.innerHTML = "<span style='width:100%;'>This site contains confidential information</style>";
```

User Interface Customization

```
</script>
```

4. Edit the SPAN's style to format the text as desired - Formatting examples:

   Centered text:
   `<span style='width:100%;text-align:center'>`

   Text formatted the same as the normal first line of the page:
   `<span class='ms-globalbreadcrumb' style='text-align:center;width:100%'>`

   Text formatted the same as the normal first line plus bold and red text:
   `<span class='ms-globalbreadcrumb' style=' width:100%;color:red;text-align:center; font-weight: bold;'>`

A jQuery version:

If you are using jQuery you can accomplish the above with one (long) line of jQuery. (See "jQuery" in chapter 4)

```
$("table:first tr:first").before("<tr><td><span class='ms-globalbreadcrumb' style='width:100%;color:red;text-align:center; font-weight: bold;'>Site Message</span></td></tr>");
```

Hoes does it work? The jQuery selector "table:first tr:first" picks the first table found in the page and then picks the first table row (<TR>) in the table. Then ".before" is added to insert a string of HTML in front of this table row. In this example the HTML is a complete table row plus the content.

The full jQuery version would look like this:

```
<script type="text/javascript">
$("table:first tr:first").before("<tr><td><span class='ms-globalbreadcrumb' style='width:100%;color:red;text-align:center; font-weight: bold;'>Site Message</span></td></tr>");
</script>
```

or if the jQuery library is not already loaded in the page or the master page we will need to load the library and then run our script:

```
<script src="/sites/demo /CustomizationFiles/jquery-1.4.2.min.js" type="text/javascript"></script>

<script type="text/javascript">
```

```
$("table:first tr:first").before("<tr><td><span class='ms-globalbreadcrumb'
style='width:100%;color:red;text-align:center; font-weight: bold;'>Site
Message</span></td></tr>");
</script>
```

See "jQuery" in Chapter 4 for more on jQuery and how to use the library.

SharePoint 2010 Steps

How it works: SharePoint 2010 uses DIVs instead of tables to layout a page. Here we will also use JavaScript, but this time to insert a new DIV, center its contents and then add a SPAN with our text.

How would you have discovered this? If you use the "View Source" option of your browser you can see that SharePoint 2010 uses DIVs for page layout. To add text at the top of the page you would want to find the first DIV used to display content. This appears to be the one with the ID of "s4-ribbonrow". So all we need to do is create a new DIV with our content and insert it in front of that DIV.

Steps for a single page:

1. Open Notepad (or your favorite HTML or JavaScript editor), add the following script and save to, or upload to, your "Customization Files" library

```
<script type="text/javascript">
  var NewDiv = document.createElement('div');
  NewDiv.align='center';
  NewDiv.innerHTML="<span style='font-weight:bold;'>This site contains confidential information</span>";

  var RibbonDiv = document.getElementById('s4-ribbonrow');
  RibbonDiv.parentNode.insertBefore(NewDiv, RibbonDiv);
</script>
```

2. Add a Content Editor Web Part and link to the file (see the basic steps in Chapter 9)
3. Edit the SPAN's style to format the text as desired - Formatting examples:
    Text and background formatted the same as the normal first line of the page:
       `<span class='ms-cui-topBar1' style=' color:white;'>`
    Text and background formatted the same as the normal first line plus bold text:
       `<span class='ms-cui-topBar1' style='color:white;font-weight: bold;'>`

User Interface Customization

jQuery version:

As the first displayed DIV very conveniently has an ID, we can grab (query) it by searching for the ID prefixed with the "#" selector and then use the "before" method to add a string of HTML with our message before that DIV:

```
$("#s4-ribbonrow").before("<div align='center'><span style='font-weight:bold;'>This site contains confidential information</span></div>");
```

The full jQuery version would look like this:

```
<script type="text/javascript">
$("#s4-ribbonrow").before("<div align='center'><span style='font-weight:bold;'>This site contains confidential information</span></div>");
</script>
```

or if the jQuery library is not already loaded in the page or the master page:

```
<script src="/sites/demo /CustomizationFiles/jquery-1.4.2.min.js" type="text/javascript"></script>

<script type="text/javascript">
$("#s4-ribbonrow").before("<div align='center'><span style='font-weight:bold;'>This site contains confidential information</span></div>");
</script>
```

See "jQuery" in Chapter 4 for more on jQuery and how to use the library.

Add a message at the top of every page using SharePoint Designer

If you want to add a message to every page in the site you could either add a CEWP to every page, or make a quick edit to the site's master page. The master page contains the core set of HTML that all of the site pages are built from. Any edits there are seen on every page in the site. For SharePoint 2007, "every page" means every site page except for pages with "_layouts" in their URL. LAYOUTS pages can only be updated on the SharePoint 2007 web servers.

To add this top line we will use SharePoint Designer to edit the site's master page. This edit uses simple HTML and does not require any JavaScript code.

SharePoint 2007 Steps

As described in the CEWP version earlier, SharePoint 2007 uses tables to layout a page. All we need to do is find the main table and insert a new row.

Steps:

1. Open your site in SharePoint Designer 2007 (see chapter 93)
2. Expand the _catalogs folder and expand the masterpage folder
3. Double click the master page (typically default.master)
4. If not already selected, click the Code button at the bottom of the window

   ![Design Split Code]
5. Find the first <TABLE> tag in the page
6. Insert a new line under the TABLE tag and add the following HTML:

   <tr><td><span style='width:100%;text-align:center'>CONFIDENTIAL</span> </td></tr>

   This is how it should look in SharePoint Designer:

   ```
   </HEAD>
   <BODY scroll="yes" onload="javascript:if (typeof(_spBodyOnLoadWrapper) != 'undefined') _sp
     <form runat="server" onsubmit="return _spFormOnSubmitWrapper();">
       <WebPartPages:SPWebPartManager id="m" runat="Server"/>
   <TABLE class="ms-main" CELLPADDING=0 CELLSPACING=0 BORDER=0 WIDTH="100%" HEIGHT="100%">

       <tr><td><span style='width:100%;text-align:center'>CONFIDENTIAL</span></td></tr>

       <tr><td><asp:ContentPlaceHolder id="PlaceHolderGlobalNavigation" runat="server">
   ```

7. Save the page, and if prompted, click OK for the "Saving changes will customize" prompt
8. Open a browser and test your change

Add a footer

Adding a message at the bottom of the page is almost identical to adding one to the top of the page. All you need to do is locate the end tag for the main TABLE and add a new row.

Steps:

1. With SharePoint Designer and the master page opened using the steps seen earlier, right-click on the main TABLE tag (class=ms-main) and select "Find matching tag" (or just scroll to the bottom of the page and find the last </TABLE> tag)
2. Insert a new row just above the </TABLE> tag and add the following HTML

   <tr><td><span class="ms-pagebottommargin" style='width:100%; text-align:center'>Copyright © 2010</span></td></tr>

User Interface Customization

```
415        </TABLE></TD></TR>
416
417        <tr><td><span class="ms-pagebottommargin" style='width:100%;text-align:left'>Copyright &cop
418
419        </TABLE>
420        <asp:ContentPlaceHolder id="PlaceHolderFormDigest" runat="server">
421            <SharePoint:FormDigest runat=server/>
422        </asp:ContentPlaceHolder>
423        <input type="text" name="__spDummyText1" style="display:none;" size=1/>
424        <input type="text" name="__spDummyText2" style="display:none;" size=1/>
425        </form>
426        <asp:ContentPlaceHolder id="PlaceHolderUtilityContent" runat="server"/>
427          <asp:ContentPlaceHolder id="PlaceHolderBodyAreaClass" runat="server"/>
428          <asp:ContentPlaceHolder id="PlaceHolderTitleAreaClass" runat="server"/>
429   </BODY>
430   </HTML>
```

3. Save the changes and test

📓 The "@copy;" is an HTML "entity" for the copyright symbol. (See Link 1002 for more on HTML entities)

📓 The style reference, **class='ms-pagebottommargin'**, sets the colors used on the bottom of the page to the current SharePoint theme.

SharePoint 2010 Steps

Steps:

1. Open your site in SharePoint Designer 2010 (see Chapter 6)
2. In the **Navigation - Site Objects** pane click **Master Pages**
3. Right-click your site's master page (typically **v4.master**) and select "Edit in Advanced Mode"
4. Search for "s4-ribbonrow"
5. Insert a line in front of this DIV and add the following HTML:

   This site contains confidential information

```
58   <SharePoint:DelegateControl runat="server" ControlId="GlobalNavigation"/>
59
60   <div style='font-weight:bold; text-align:center'>This site contains confidential informatio
61
62   <div id="s4-ribbonrow" class="s4-pr s4-ribbonrowhidetitle">
```

6. Save the page, and if prompted, click YES for the "Saving your changes will customize" prompt
7. Open a browser and test your change

Add a footer

When adding the footer DIV you may be tempted to put it after the last DIV in the page. The way the v4.master master page was designed, the last DIV is "forced" to the bottom of the screen and anything that follows it is off of the screen (hidden). A footer DIV works best if placed just above the last DIV.

```
<div style=" clear:both; text-align:center; ">Copyright &copy; 2010</div>
```

To style the footer text to match the rest of the page consider using " class='s4-notdlg' ". You may also want to add a border style and some padding:

```
<div style="clear:both;text-align:center;border: 1px solid gray; padding:10px">Copyright &copy; 2010</div>
```

Site Title and Icon (2007) - Change the Font Size, Face or Hide It

One of the most common requests I have had in my SharePoint classes is how to change the display of the site title. The requests have included changing colors, larger fonts, replacing the title with a graphic and hiding it altogether.

First of all, make sure you can't already do what you want with the **Site Actions, Site Settings** options.

Remove the image using Site Actions, Site Settings

You can't just leave the URL box blank, otherwise it just displays the default image. You must include some type of image and the most common solution is a 1 pixel by 1 pixel transparent image. SharePoint actually has one of these available in the LAYOUTS folder: /_layouts/images/blank.gif. Add that image to the **Title, Description and Icon** page and… no more icon!

User Interface Customization

Here's the result in 2007 and 2010:

Hide the Site Title (2007)

To hide the site title you may be tempted to go back to **Site Actions, Site Settings, Title Description and Icon** and just delete the title. SharePoint won't let you do this, besides the site title is used in many places in SharePoint to identify your site. These include search, the Tree View, crumb trails, reports and user bookmarks.

So, if you should keep it, how can you hide it? In SharePoint 2007 it's easy, just add a little piece of CSS (Cascading Style Sheet) code into a Content Editor Web Part or into the site's master page. SharePoint 2010's title is part of the crumb trail navigation and will take a little bit more work and will be covered separately.

SharePoint 2007 Steps for a Single Page

1. Add a Content Editor Web Part (See the basic steps in chapter 9)
2. Decide whether to add the CSS to the Source Editor button or in a linked file (again see the basic steps in chapter 9)
3. Add the following CSS to the linked file or by using the Source Editor button:

```
<style type="text/css">
 .ms-sitetitle h1
 { display:none; }
</style>
```

Note: The "h1" is needed in the CSS selector so you also don't hide the table cell containing the title. Doing so would change the position of the search box.

4. Save your changes and... no more title!

Site with hidden title:

Replace the site title with a big image

Now you can create a nice big image to fill the space and add it as usual from **Site Actions, Site Settings, Title Description and Icon.**

1. Create and pre-size your logo in your favorite drawing or paint program, save it as a web compatible format (.jpeg, .gif, etc) and upload it to a SharePoint library (maybe named CustomizationFiles) - Make sure all of your users have at least View permissions to this library!
2. Right-click the new image in the library, click **Properties** and copy the URL of the image
3. Go to **Site Actions, Site Settings, Title Description and Icon,** and paste in the copied URL

    Important! Whenever possible you should use a relative URL. If your site has both an internal URL (http://intranet) and an external URL (http://sharepoint.xyz.com) then an absolute URL will fail for one set of users while a relative URL will work for both.
    An absolute URL: http://myserver/sites/Demo/CustomizationFiles/WideLogo.jpg
    A relative URL: /sites/Demo/CustomizationFiles/WideLogo.jpg

4. Add a description for the image as a mouse over tip and so users with screen reading programs will know what the image is all about
5. Click **OK** and test!

Change the Site Title font

The steps to change the site title font are the same as hiding it, but with different CSS. Here is an example:

```
<style type="text/css">
  .ms-sitetitle a
  {
    font-size:48pt;
    color:blue;
    font-family:"Comic Sans MS"
  }
</style>
```

Note: the "a" is needed as the title is enclosed in an anchor "<A>" tag.

Again, you can put the CSS in either the master page to impact all pages in the site or in a Content Editor Web Part to impact a single page.

For samples of CSS for styling text see Link 1003

Site Title and Icon (2010) - Change the Font Size, Face or Hide It

Customizing the site title is a bit harder in 2010 as the site title is part of a larger navigation area that includes the title, a "crumb trail" and the View menu. In this section we will look at using CSS to change the font, color or size of the text. In the next section we will change how the navigation works.

Here's the home page of a sample site. The text "Demo Site" is the name of the site as set in **Site Actions, Site Settings, Title Description and Icon**.

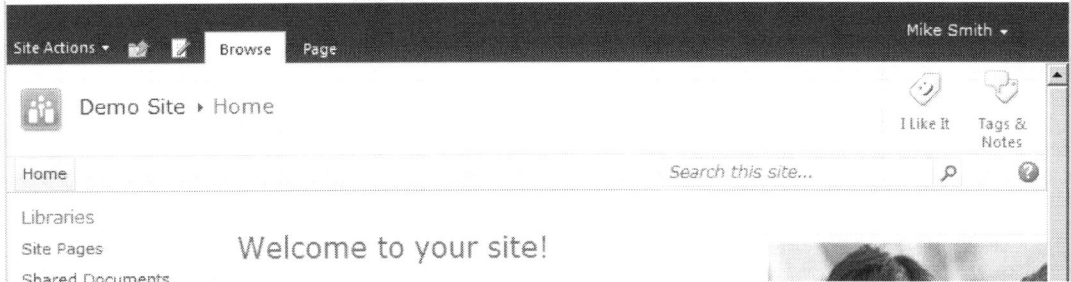

User Interface Customization

The following shows the title, crumb trail and view menu for a library page. "Demo Site" is the site title, "Shared Documents" is a library and "All Documents" is both the current view and the view dropdown menu button.

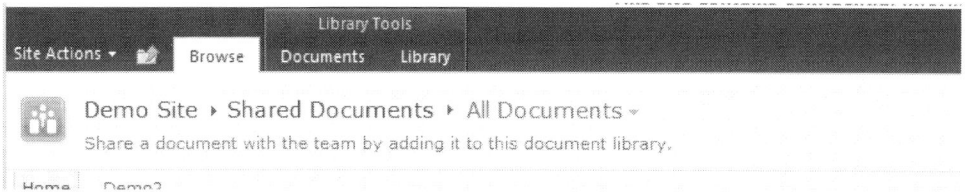

Here's a similar page with the view menu clicked:

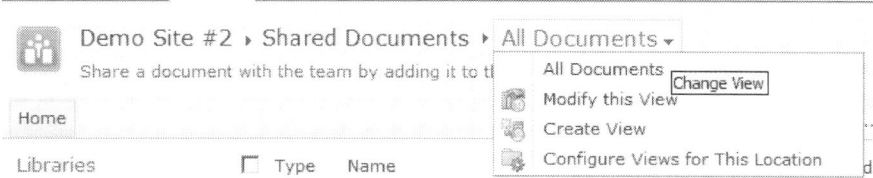

Changing fonts and colors using CSS

Each part of the page can be hidden or changed by using a CSS style. Here are the style names and the part of the title impacted by the style:

Style	Description
.s4-titlelogo	
#s4-titlerow	The entire title row including "I Like It" and "Tags & Notes"
.s4-titletext h1 a	The site title text Demo Site
.ms-WikiPageNameEditor-Display	Title of any wiki-style page (home page of a Team Site or a page added with "Site Actions, New page") Home
.s4-titletext h2 a	List/Library name Shared Documents

User Interface Customization

.s4-titletext h2	Folder name
#zz17_ListTitleViewSelectorMenu_t	Current view and view selector All Documents ▾
#onetidPageTitleSeparator	The triangles between the items " ▸ "

Note: "." indicates a class while "#" indicates an ID

To hide everything after the title:

```
<style type="text/css">
.s4-titletext h2     <!-- everything after the site title  -->
{
        display:none;
}
#onetidPageTitleSeparator  <!-- The triangles between the items -->
{
        display:none
}
</style>
```

Here's a set of sample styles to change the Site Title, the List Name and the View Selector:

```
<style type="text/css">
.s4-titletext h1 a   <!-- The site title text  -->
{
  color:Blue;
  font-size:24pt;
}

.s4-titletext h2 a    <!-- list / library name  -->
{
  color:red;
  font-size:18pt;
}

#zz17_ListTitleViewSelectorMenu_t    <!-- current view and menu  -->
{
  color:green;
  font-size:12pt;
}
```

```
</style>
```

And here's the page after adding the above styles:

SharePoint 2010 Steps for a Single Page

You would most likely want to do this kind of customization for an entire site rather than a single page by using a master page edit. To make these changes for a single page just add a CEWP (See chapter 9) and add your CSS styles.

SharePoint 2010 Steps for a Master Page

To make your changes available for all pages in your site, add them to the site's master page.

1. Open your site in SharePoint Designer 2010 (see chapter 6)
2. In the **Navigation - Site Objects** pane click **Master Pages**
3. Right-click your site's master page (typically **v4.master**) and select **Edit in Advanced Mode**
4. Search for "</head>" and insert your style block before the </head> tag

```
<SharePoint:SPHelpPageComponent Visible=...
  <style type="text/css">
    <!-- add your styles here -->
  </style>
</head>
```

A Redesign of the SharePoint 2010 Site Title and Crumb Trail

The SharePoint 2010 approach to merging three features, the Site Title, the crumb trail and the View menu is less than ideal for site customization. Here are a few of the issues:

- The Site Title is small and not resizable (We had that issue in 2007 also, but we could fix it with a simple CSS addition)
- Can you even tell if a site is a subsite of another site? (You have to click the **Navigate Up** button to find out.)
- The "Home" text is almost ok, but we can't edit this. (easily anyway)
- In a document library section there is no room for a long site title plus a long a library name
- The View dropdown menu is now in the crumb trail! Any redesign/branding we do may lose the view menu!
- When you get down to a sub-site the crumb trail fails, it is no longer a complete trail. There is no one-click way up to the parent folder. Your only option is to use Navigate Up (two clicks), or go to the top of the library and drill back down.

In this section we will convert the standard Team Site from this out of the box design:

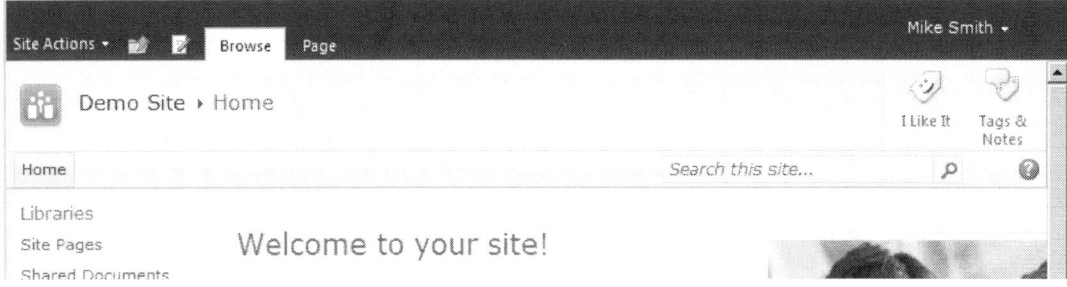

to a design with a large title and a true and complete crumb trail where our users expect it:

User Interface Customization

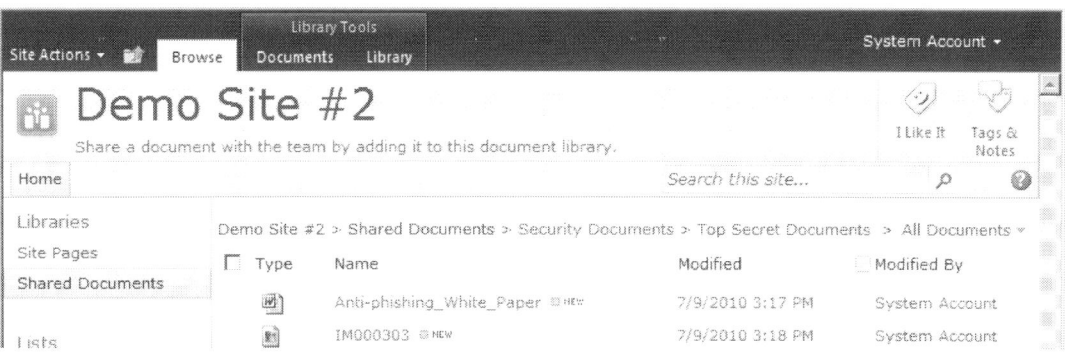

How to get there?

1. Hide the existing crumb trail, but leave the Site Title
2. Restyle the Site Title (color, font, size, etc)
3. Add the SharePoint 2007 crumb trail control
4. Copy the part of the hidden crumb trail's HTML that displays the View dropdown and add it just after the 2007 crumb trail
5. Restyle the View dropdown to match the 2007 crumb trail

Steps:

1. Open your site in SharePoint Designer 2010 (See chapter 6)
2. In the **Navigation - Site Objects** pane click **Master Pages**
3. Right-click your site's master page (typically **v4.master**) and select **Edit in Advanced Mode**
4. Hide the existing crumb trail:
    a. Search for "**PlaceHolderPageTitleInTitleArea**", add a DIV block around the two lines before, and one line after this text, and set the display style to "**none**" (new HTML in **bold**):

```
<td class="s4-titletext">
 <h1 name="onetidProjectPropertyTitle">
  <asp:ContentPlaceHolder id="PlaceHolderSiteName" runat="server">
   <SharePoint:SPLinkButton runat="server" NavigateUrl="~site/" ...
  </asp:ContentPlaceHolder>
 </h1>
 <div style="display:none">
  <span id="onetidPageTitleSeparator" class="s4-nothome s4-bcsep s4-titlesep">
  <SharePoint:ClusteredDirectionalSeparatorArrow runat="server"/> </span>
  <h2>
   <asp:ContentPlaceHolder id="PlaceHolderPageTitleInTitleArea" runat="server" />
  </h2>
 </div>
```

User Interface Customization

```
<div class="s4-pagedescription" tabindex="0" >
 <asp:ContentPlaceHolder id="PlaceHolderPageDescription" runat="server"/>
</div>
</td>
```

5. Restyle the Site Title (color, font, size, etc)
    a. At the end of the page, just before the </BODY> tag add a <STYLE> block something like this: (new code in bold)
    b. Note: These style tags can also be placed at the end of the <head> section of the page

```
<style type="text/css">
 .s4-titletext h1 a
 {
   color:Blue;
   font-size:24pt;
 }
</style>

<style type="text/css">
 .s4-titletext h1 a
 {
   color:Blue;
   font-size:24pt;
 }
</style>
</body>
```

6. Add the SharePoint 2007 crumb trail control and a DIV for the View dropdown – I put it just before "PlaceHolderMain" to be near where it was in 2007: (new code in bold)

```
<a name="mainContent"></a>

<div>
  <br/>

  <!-- the following is all one line -->
   <asp:SiteMapPath SiteMapProvider="SPContentMapProvider" id="ContentMap2" SkipLinkText="" NodeStyle-CssClass="ms-sitemapdirectional" runat="server"/> 

  <span id="myViewDiv"></span>
```

154

```
    <br/>
</div>

<asp:ContentPlaceHolder id="PlaceHolderMain" runat="server">
</asp:ContentPlaceHolder>
```

7. We hid the old crumb trail earlier, but we need the HTML that displays the View dropdown menu. The code here moves that HTML to our crumb trail and should be placed at the end of the master page, just before the </body> tag:

```
<script type="text/javascript">
  var OldCrumbTrail = document.getElementById("ctl00_PlaceHolderPageTitleInTitleArea_ctl01_ctl00");
  var NewCrumbTrail = document.getElementById("myViewDiv");
  OldCrumbTrail.childNodes[0].innerHTML=">";
  NewCrumbTrail.outerHTML = OldCrumbTrail.outerHTML;
  OldCrumbTrail.innerHTML = "";
  OldCrumbTrail.id = "NOT_ctl00_PlaceHolderPageTitleInTitleArea_ctl01_ctl00";
</script>
```

8. Restyle the View dropdown to match the 2007 crumb trail – just add the following to the style block we created above:

```
# <style type="text/css">
  .s4-titletext h1 a
  {
    color:Blue;
    font-size:24pt;
  }

  #zz17_ListTitleViewSelectorMenu
  {
     font-size:8pt;
  }
</style>
```

Note: If you don't see the font size change, display the page in a browser and use the View Source option. Search for "ListTitleViewSelectorMenu" and use the ID you find in place of "#zz17_ListTitleViewSelectorMenu".

Hide the SharePoint 2010 Ribbon from Visitors and Anonymous Users

The ribbon adds little or no value to site visitors. This is especially true for internet facing sites with anonymous users who generally have no rights to edit anything in the site. Here we will look at hiding the ribbon based on a user's permissions by using a SharePoint SPSecurityTrimmedControl control. For more on this control see chapter 7, Security Tricks.

There are three possible steps to this customization:

- Hide the ribbon
- Optionally hide the View All Site Content (Visitors don't need to see this either)
- Optionally move the "Welcome" menu out of the ribbon area so anonymous users can still logon

Before:

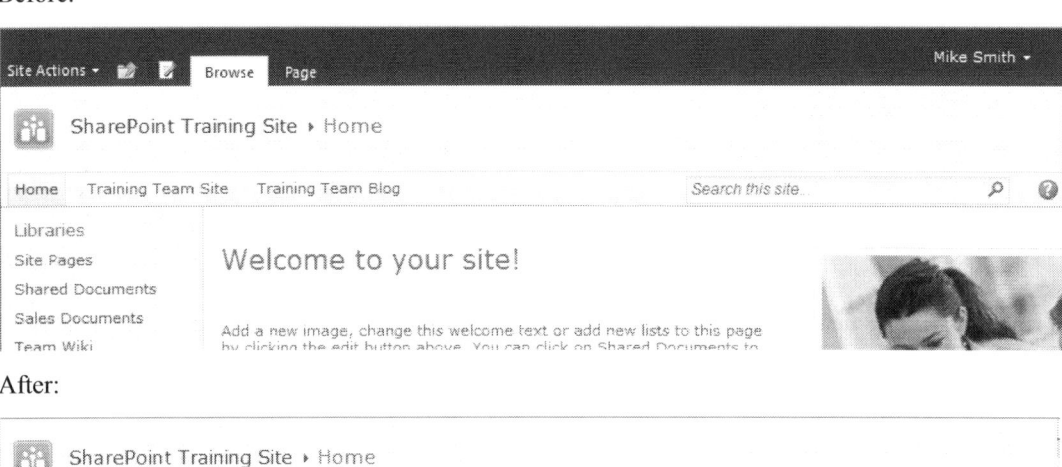

After:

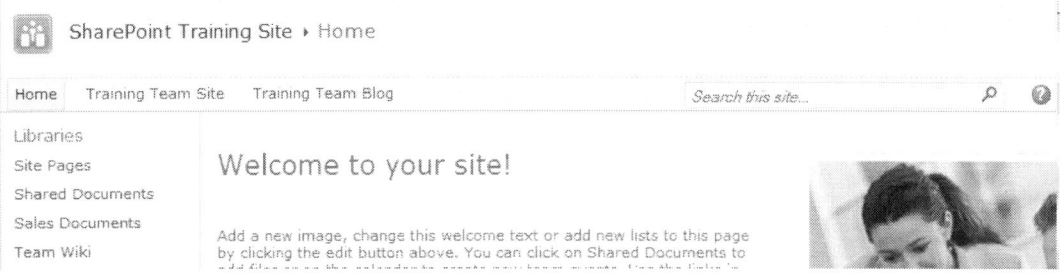

Hide the Ribbon

Steps:

1. Open SharePoint Designer and open your site

User Interface Customization

2. Open your master page
   a. In the Site Objects panel click Master Pages
   b. Click your master page (most likely v4.master)
   c. Click Edit File
3. If the code view is not displayed, click the Code tab or the Split tab
4. Search for " s4-ribbonrow"
   You should find this DIV:
   <div id="s4-ribbonrow" class="s4-pr s4-ribbonrowhidetitle">
5. Just before the DIV add a SPSecurityTrimmedControl control:

```
<SharePoint:SPSecurityTrimmedControl runat="server"
PermissionsString="EditListItems">
<div id="s4-ribbonrow" class="s4-pr s4-ribbonrowhidetitle">
```

6. Set the PermissionsString to a permission common to users who need to see the ribbon. A good choice would be EditListItems
7. Right-click the DIV you found above and click Select Tag - this will highlight the entire ribbon area DIV and let you locate the ending </DIV> for the block
8. Add the ending tag for the SPSecurityTrimmedControl:

```
</div>
</SharePoint:SPSecurityTrimmedControl>
```

9. Save your changes and test - you will either need to visit the site using an account with visitor permissions or as an anonymous user

Move the Welcome menu

If you are hiding the ribbon from members of the Visitors group then the steps above may be all that you need. If your users need access to the "Sign In" link or to the "Welcome" menu, then you need one more edit as the Welcome menu was in the ribbon area we just hid.

In the steps below we will move the Welcome menu control to the top of the Quick Launch area.

157

User Interface Customization

Steps:

1. Starting with the master page still open, search for "**wssuc:Welcome**"
2. Select and cut the following code:

```
<wssuc:Welcome id="IdWelcome" runat="server" EnableViewState="false">
</wssuc:Welcome>
```

3. Search for "**SharePoint:SPNavigationManager**" and insert a few blank lines in front of this tag
4. Add a <DIV> similar to the following (your choice of background color - the color listed here is the default theme's ribbon background color)

```
<div style="background:#3b4f65;clear:both">
</div>
```

5. Paste the Welcome control you cut in step 2 inside of the DIV

```
<div style="background:#3b4f65;clear:both">
  <wssuc:Welcome id="IdWelcome" runat="server" EnableViewState="false">
  </wssuc:Welcome>
</div>
```

6. Save your changes and test - the result should look like the example on the left for your non-visitor and like the example on the right for your visitor:

Hide Menu Options (2007)

Often there are features you don't want your users to have, either in a certain list or library, or in the entire site. All it takes is a little JavaScript and they're gone!

Here's a before and after sample of a menu with "Open with Windows Explorer" removed:

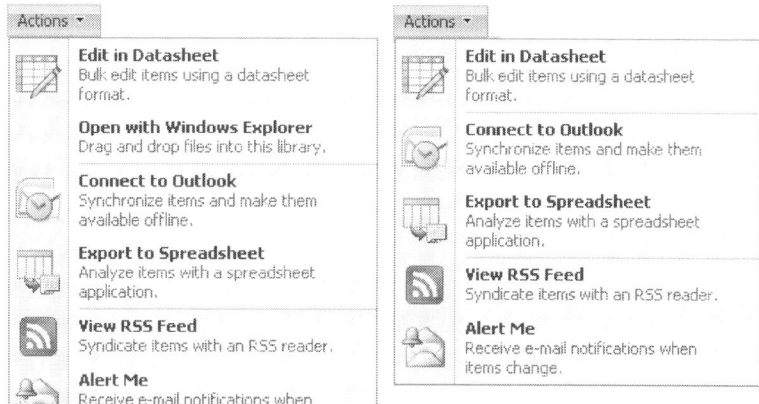

How it works: SharePoint menus are generated either with "in the page" HTML or with JavaScript "on demand" HTML. The first is easy to deal with; the second will take a little more work.

How would you have discovered this? The "in the page" HTML can be studied by displaying the page and using the browser's View Source feature to find the menu options. For example, let's look at hiding "Open in Windows Explorer" in the Actions menu. Go to a library page, view the page source code and search for "Explorer". You will find "<ie:menuitem id='zz22_OpenInExplorer' ". Now all you have to do is write some JavaScript to find tags with an ID equal to zz22_OpenInExplorer, except... the first part of the ID, the "zz22", is not consistent or predictable. To play it safe you must assume that the "zz22" might change from page to page (it's "zz25" in a picture library). You should look for an ID that contains some reasonably unique part of the ID such as "OpenInExplorer". To do this we can just loop through all of the tags of type "<ie:menuitem>" and check the IDs.

So the script will look something like this:

```
<script type="text/javascript">
 var doc = document.getElementsByTagName('ie:menuitem');
 for (var i = 0; i < doc.length; i++)
  {
    itm = doc[i];
    if (itm.id.match('OpenInExplorer') != null)
     {
       itm.hidden=true;
       break;
     }
  }
</script>
```

User Interface Customization

jQuery version:

The jQuery solution is only one line, but may need some explaining…

```
$('ie\\:menuitem[id*=OpenInExplorer]').attr("hidden","true")
```

The selector is first looking for a tag named "ie:menuitem", but the colon in the name must be escaped so the tag selector looks like this: "ie\\:menuitem". There are lots of menus in the page so we to refine the selection by selecting those tags with an ID attribute that contains "OpenInExplorer". The asterisk after the ID is a wildcard. Now that we have found the menu item, set its "hidden" attribute to "true".

Like all jQuery solutions, you have either loaded the jQuery library in the master page, or added it to the Content Editor Web Part. The following is how it would look in a CEWP:

```html
<!-- needed if not loaded in the master page -->
<script src="/sites/demo /CustomizationFiles/jquery-1.4.2.min.js" type="text/javascript"></script>

<script type="text/javascript">
  $('ie\\:menuitem[id*=OpenInExplorer]').attr("hidden","true")
</script>
```

Where should I put this JavaScript code?

If you want to impact just one list or library, then you will need to edit each page used to display the list that includes a menu bar. Typically this would be all of the views.

If you want to impact all lists and libraries in a site, then add this code to the site's master page somewhere just before the </body> tag.

ID Names for Menu Items

If you are writing client JavaScript code to interact with the SharePoint menus you will need to know the IDs of the <ie:menuitem> tags. Below are some of the IDs used by menu items. Remember that in the SharePoint page these will include a prefix that looks like "zz22_" or "ct100_".

If the ID you need is not listed here then view the source of your SharePoint page and search for the name of the menu item ("Edit Page" or the text "ie:menuitem" until you find the one you need.

```
menuGroupId="100"></ie:menuitem><ie:menuitem
id="ct100_PlaceHolderTopNavBar_SiteActionsMenuMain_ct100_MenuItem_EditPage"
type="option" IconSrc="/_layouts/images/ActionsEditPage.gif"
onMenuClick="window.location = 'javascript:MSOLayout_ChangeLayoutMode(false);';"
text="Edit Page" description="Add, remove, or update Web Parts on this page."
menuGroupId="100"></ie:menuitem><ie:menuitem id="zz11_MenuItem_Settings" type="
```

160

✎ For a current, and possibly more complete, list of the menu codes see Link 1004

This is a list of menu items created by a typical WSS Master Page:

Menu ID name	Menu	Menu text
PersonalInformation	The Welcome menu	My Settings
LoginAsDifferentUser	The Welcome menu	Sign in as Different User
RequestAccess	The Welcome menu	Request Access
Logout	The Welcome menu	Sign Out
MenuItem_Create	Site Actions	Create
MenuItem_Settings	Site Actions	Site Settings
MenuItem_EditPage	Site Actions	Edit Page

This is a list of items created by a typical document library "allitems.aspx" page:

(all of the above plus the following)

Menu ID name	Menu	Menu text
New0 (zero, not O)	New	New Document (default click)
NewFolder	New	New Folder
_Upload [1]	Upload	Upload Document
MultipleUpload	Upload	Upload Multiple Documents
EditInGridButton	Actions	Edit in Datasheet
OpenInExplorer	Actions	Open with Windows Explorer
OfflineButton	Actions	Connect to Outlook
ExportToSpreadsheet	Actions	Export to Spreadsheet
ViewRSS	Actions	View RSS Feed
SubscribeButton	Actions	Alert Me
AddColumn	Settings	Create Column
AddView	Settings	Create View
ListSettings	Settings	Document Library Settings
DefaultView	View	All Documents (in typical library)
View1	View	Explorer View
ModifyView	View	Modify this view
CreateView	View	Create view

(1) Prefix the keyword "Upload" with the underline to not confuse with "MultipleUpload"

Unique to a Picture Library

Menu ID name	Menu	Menu text
EditPictures	Actions	Edit
DeletePictures	Actions	Delete
DownloadPictures	Actions	Download
SendPictures	Actions	Send To
ViewSlideShow	Actions	View Slide Show

Lists

Menu ID name	Menu	Menu text
EditInGridButton	Actions	Edit in Datasheet
ExportToDatabase	Actions	Open with Access

Hide Menu Options (2010)

Menus in 2010? Isn't there a ribbon now?

SharePoint 2010 has ribbons everywhere... except for Picture libraries and Surveys. Those two lists seem to have been overlooked in the upgrade process. The code to hide items in the list and library menus in 2007 appears to work just fine in 2010 for Picture libraries and Surveys. Also the Site Actions link and the Welcome link still display menus and these require the same code as for 2007.

Finding the Menu ID names for these menus uses the same process as described above for 2007. Display a page that has the menu option you want to hide and use the browser's "view source" option to display the HTML. Search for the text of the menu, "New Page" for example, and note the ID.

```
this site on your computer." menuGroupId=":
<ie:menuitem id="zz3_MenuItem_CreatePage" t:
 (LaunchCreateHandler("Page")) t OpenCreateI
 text="New Page" description="Create a page
<ie:menuitem id="zz4 MenuItem CreateDocLib"
```

Pick a part of the ID that is likely to be the same in every page in every site such as "MenuItem_CreatePage" and use that in the JavaScript in the 2007 example or in the example in the next section. (The "zz3" might vary between pages and versions, but the rest of the name should be consistent.)

Where should I put this JavaScript code?

If you want to impact just one list or library, then you will need to edit each page used to display the list that includes a menu bar. Typically this would be all of the list's views.

User Interface Customization

If you want to impact all lists and libraries in a site, then add this code to the site's master page somewhere just before the </body> tag.

This is a list of menu items created in a typical Team Site home page (v4.master) for the Site Actions and Welcome menus:

Menu ID name	Menu	Menu text
ID_PersonalInformation	The Welcome menu	My Settings
ID_LoginAsDifferentUser	The Welcome menu	Sign in as Different User
ID_RequestAccess	The Welcome menu	Request Access
ID_Logout	The Welcome menu	Sign Out
MenuItem_EditPage	Site Actions	Edit Page
MenuItem_TakeOffline	Site Actions	Sync to SharePoint Workspace
MenuItem_CreatePage	Site Actions	New Page
MenuItem_CreateDocLib	Site Actions	New Document Library
MenuItem_CreateSite	Site Actions	New Site
MenuItem_Create	Site Actions	More Options…
MenuItem_ViewAllSiteContents	Site Actions	View All Site Content
MenuItem_EditSite	Site Actions	Edit in SharePoint Designer
MenuItem_SitePermissions	Site Actions	Site Permissions
MenuItem_Settings	Site Actions	Site Settings

This is a list of menu items created by a picture library view page:

(all of the above table plus the following)

Menu ID name	Menu	Menu text
NewFolder	New	New Folder
_Upload [1]	Upload	Upload Document
MultipleUpload	Upload	Upload Multiple Pictures
EditPictures	Actions	Edit
DeletePictures	Actions	Delete
DownloadPictures	Actions	Download
SendPictures	Actions	Send To
ViewSlideShow	Actions	View Slide Show
OpenInExplorer	Actions	Open with Windows Explorer
OfflineButton	Actions	Connect to Outlook

163

TakeOfflineToClient	Actions	Sync To Computer
ViewRSS	Actions	View RSS Feed
SubscribeButton	Actions	Alert Me
AddColumn	Settings	Create Column
AddView	Settings	Create View
ListSettingsMenu_t	Settings	Settings
ModifyView	View	Modify this view
CreateView	View	Create view

(1) Prefix the keyword "Upload" with the underline to not confuse with "MultipleUpload"

Hide Menu Options for Selected Users (2007 and 2010)

As you saw in chapter 7 you can hide content from users based on their permissions by using the SPSecurityTrimmedControl. Revisit the "Identify the user by their permissions" section in chapter 7 for details on how this works. Here's how we might limit one of the above examples, "Hide Windows Explorer", to just users with the **ManagePermissions** permission (typically only Site Owners and Site Collection Administrators) by using the SPSecurityTrimmedControl:

```
<script type="text/javascript">
  <!-- assume no is allowed to see the menu option -->
  var userCanSeeWindowsExplorer = false;
</script>

<SharePoint:SPSecurityTrimmedControl runat="server"
  PermissionsString="ManageWeb">
<script type="text/javascript">
  <!-- users with ViewFormPages can see the menu option -->
  userCanSeeWindowsExplorer = true;
</script>
</SharePoint:SPSecurityTrimmedControl>

<script type="text/javascript">
  <!-- Hide the menu option for some users -->
  if ( userCanSeeWindowsExplorer == false)
  {
   var doc = document.getElementsByTagName('ie:menuitem');
   for (var i = 0; i < doc.length; i++)
```

User Interface Customization

```
{
  itm = doc[i];
  if (itm.id.match('OpenInExplorer') != null)
   {
     itm.hidden = true;
     break;
   }
  }
 }
}
</script>
```

 Big reminder! The SPSecurityTrimmedControl cannot be used inside of Content Editor Web Part as it must be processed on the web servers. You must add this control directly to an ASPX page or the master page using SharePoint Designer.

Where should I put this JavaScript code?

If you want to impact just one list or library, then you will need to edit each page used to display the list that includes a menu bar. Typically this would be all of the list's views.

If you want to impact all lists and libraries in a site, then add this code to the site's master page somewhere just before the </body> tag.

Hide Disabled Ribbon Options (2010)

In SharePoint 2007 users do not see menu options for features that they do not have rights to. In 2010 the ribbon just grays out ribbon options when the option does not apply or the user does not have rights to the option. While the following customization will hide disabled ribbon buttons, it does not hide any now empty sections. So while this works, it's not ideal, but may reduce the number of calls to support about "why can't I click the XYZ button?"

```
<style type="text/css">
.ms-cui-disabled
 {
   display:none !important;
 }
</style>
```

Before hiding disabled buttons:

165

User Interface Customization

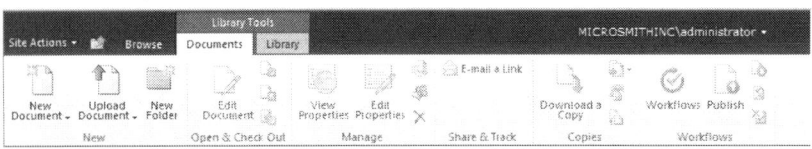

After hiding disabled buttons:

Quick Launch and Top Link Bar Tricks - Add Message Pop-ups (2007 and 2010)

Need to add a message to a Quick Launch or Top Link bar? How about adding a custom "Help" link? Or maybe change the almost useless Quick Launch headings ("Document, Lists, Discussions…) into help links? You can add JavaScript routines to Quick Launch and the Top Link Bar without using page edits or web parts. This trick depends on the fact that you can use JavaScript code in most places where you can use a URL. As example consider the HTML <A> tag:

```
<A HREF="http://www.maxtrain.com">  Click here </A>
```

The HREF attribute usually has a simple URL, but can also use "JavaScript:" followed by some JavaScript code:

```
<A HREF="JavaScript:alert('hi there!')">  Click here </A>
```

When you enter the URLs into Quick Launch and the Top Link bar you are just entering the URL for an <A> tag generated by SharePoint… so just replace it with some JavaScript do display a message:

User Interface Customization

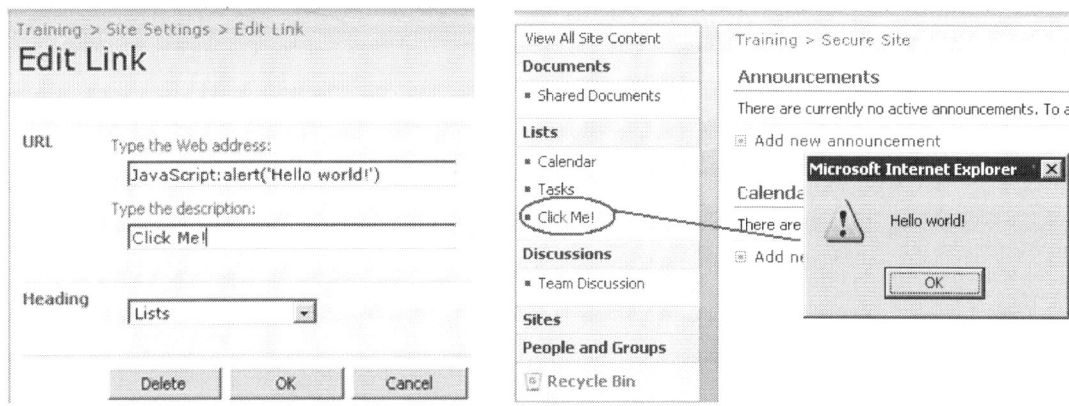

The above example will just display an annoying message, but you could add a more useful message like this one:

JavaScript:alert('For site help call Sam at 123-1234 or email Sam at sam@someserver.com')

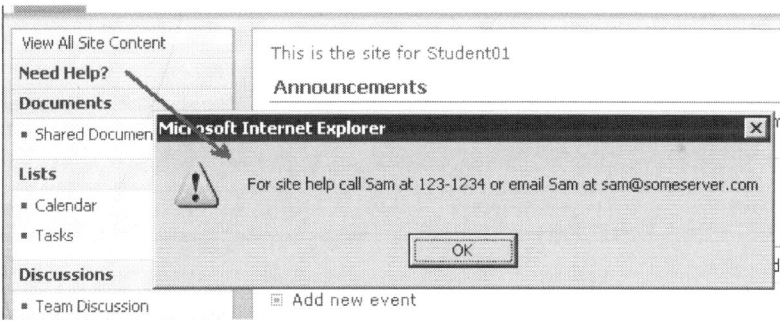

Quick Launch and Top Link Bar Tricks - Confirm Site Exit (2007 and 2010)

You may want to warn a user that they are about to leave your site and also to make sure that they know that you are not responsible for the linked external content. Out of the box SharePoint cannot do this, but this turns out to be a simple change, if you know just a little JavaScript and the previous trick!

Here's the normal link found in Quick Launch for the Calendar:

/sites/training/secure/Lists/Calendar/calendar.aspx

User Interface Customization

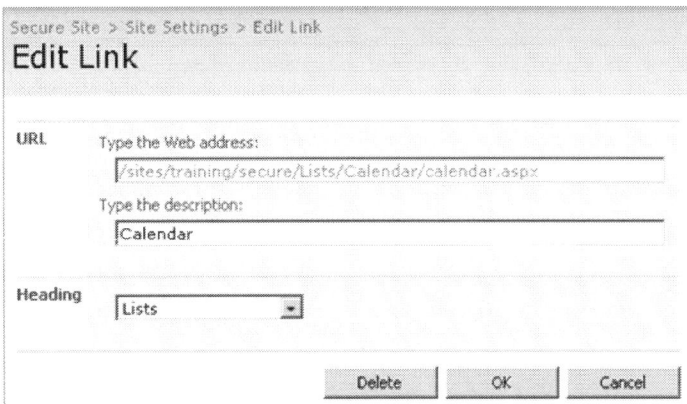

Here's a link that will prompt to see if you really want to go to the calendar: (all one line!)

```
JavaScript: if ( confirm('do you really want to see the calendar?') )
document.location='/sites/training/secure/Lists/Calendar/calendar.aspx';
```

The JavaScript confirm function creates a pop-up that displays a message along with OK and Cancel buttons. Here's a Quick Launch (or Top Link Bar) entry to confirm that the user really wants to see the link destination:

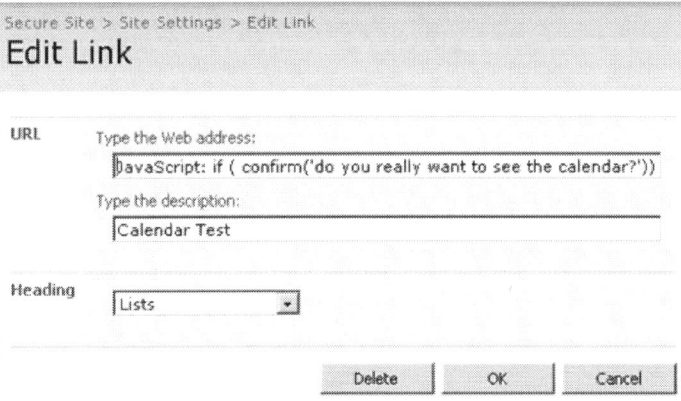

And here is what the user sees when they click that link:

User Interface Customization

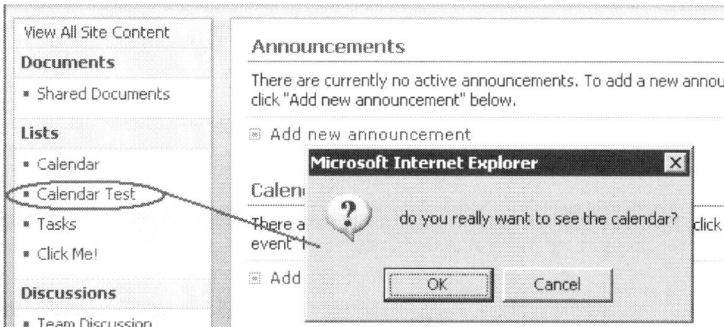

Here's a more practical link that will prompt to see if they really want to go to an external site: (all one line!)

```
JavaScript: if ( confirm('This web site is external to the company and may not be safe!') )
document.location='http://somesiteontheweb.com';
```

And this is what the user sees when they click that link:

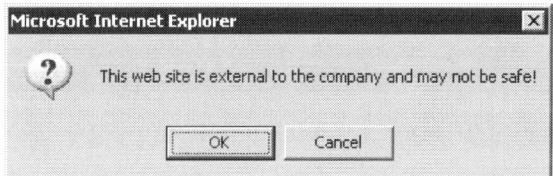

Quick Launch Pop outs (2007 and 2010)

A Quick Launch menu with a large number of items can be a nuisance for users if they have to keep scrolling up and down to find items. There are two common ways of making the Quick Launch a little more compact: convert them into pop out sub-menus or into accordion (expand/collapse) menus. Both hide the details of each section of Quick Launch until the user mouses over a menu heading (or clicks it). Let's first take a look at pop outs as they are a bit easier to implement.

Quick Launch is generated from a SharePoint control (<SharePoint:AspMenu>) which is an enhanced version of the ASP menu control (<asp:Menu>). Many of the features and tricks documented on the web for the ASP control will work with the SharePoint version, so you may want to a little web searching for ideas. In SharePoint 2007 this control has an ID of "**QuickLaunchMenu**". SharePoint 2010 has two versions of the control, one named "**QuickLaunchMenu**" and the other named "**V4QuickLaunchMenu**". The first version will be used for sites that have been upgraded from 2007, but still use the 2007 user interface. The second is used for all sites using the 2010 interface (i.e. with the ribbon).

169

User Interface Customization

✎ Quick Launch master page customizations in SharePoint 2007 will not impact the "_LAYOUTS" pages such as View All Site Content. Similar customizations in SharePoint 2010 will impact all site pages.

	Before	After:
2007		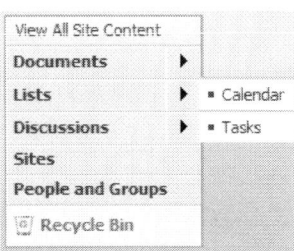
2010	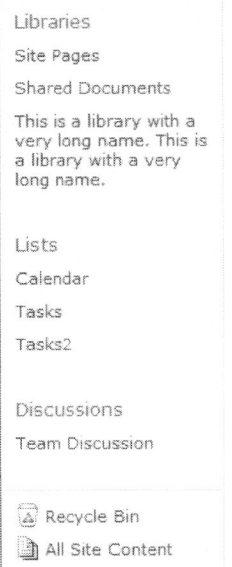	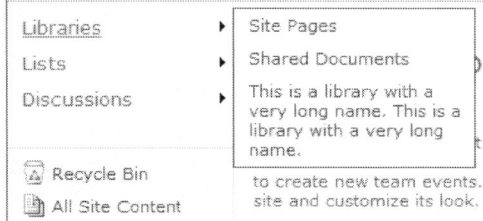

To add pop outs:

1. Open the site's master page in SharePoint Designer (See chapter 6)
2. In SharePoint 2010 click **Edit Page**
3. Display the **Code** view of the page (Design Split Code)
4. Search for **QuickLaunchMenu** or for 2010 search for **V4QuickLaunchMenu**

User Interface Customization

5. In that line find and change **StaticDisplayLevels** from 2 to 1 (only headings will now be displayed)
6. Find and change **MaximumDynamicDisplayLevels** from 0 to 1
7. Save and test

Your code should now look similar to this (may all be on one line):

```
<SharePoint:AspMenu id="QuickLaunchMenu"
  DataSourceId="QuickLaunchSiteMap"
  runat="server"
  Orientation="Vertical"
  StaticDisplayLevels="1"
  ItemWrap="true"
  MaximumDynamicDisplayLevels="1"
  StaticSubMenuIndent="0"    SkipLinkText=""
>
  ...
</SharePoint:AspMenu>
```

While the above works, the pop outs are not very pretty. In 2007 they are not clearly defined. In 2010 they have transparent backgrounds. The pop outs need some CSS styling.

Before styling: 2007   2010

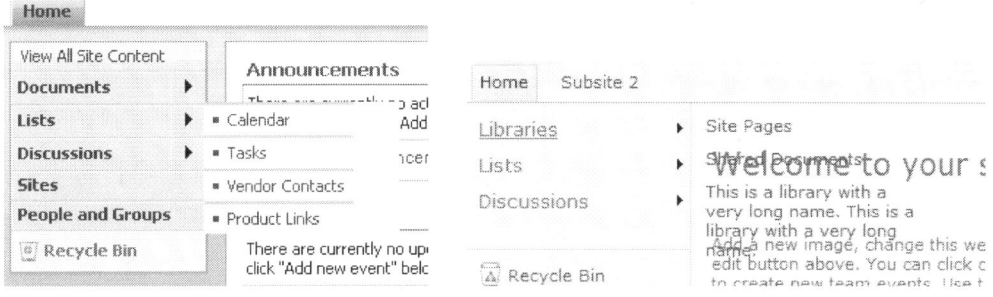

To style the pop outs:

1. In the master page search for the Quick Launch control and then explore down to find the end tag: </SharePoint:AspMenu>
2. Any where after this tag and before the **</body>** tag add a **<style>** block

```
</SharePoint:AspMenu>
<style type="text/css">
  ... CSS goes here ...
</style>
```

171

Styles for 2007:

You need to override two style classes to recolor or resize Quick Launch pop outs in SharePoint 2007: **ms-navSubMenu1** for the headings and **ms-navSubMenu2** for the items. If you want to override the font styles, such as size, then you also need to use the "**!important**" declaration. The following demonstrates an extreme change in styles just to test the CSS.

```
<!-- Style the menu headings -->
.ms-navSubMenu1 td a
{
        font-size:24pt !important;
        width:200px;
        color:red;
        background-color:yellow;
}

<!-- Style the menu items / pop outs-->
.ms-navSubMenu2 td a
{
        font-size:24pt !important;
        width:200px;
        color:yellow;
        background-color:green;
}
```

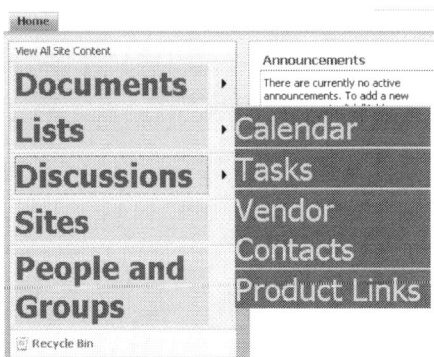

A more practical version might only change the pop outs and look like this:

```
<!-- Style the menu items / pop outs -->
.ms-navSubMenu2 td a
{
        font-weight:bold;
```

```
        width:150px !important;
        background-color:#D6E8FF;
        border:thin !important;
        border-width:1px !important;
        border-color:darkblue;
        border-style:solid !important;
        padding:5px;
}
```

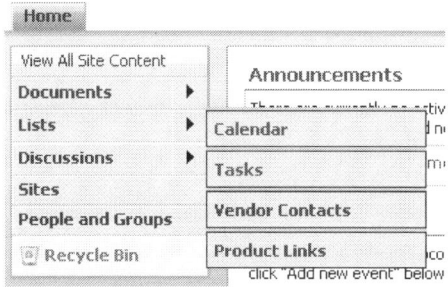

Styles for 2010:

To style the pop out in SharePoint 2010 you will need to override a series of classes. The following demonstrates an extreme change in styles to test the CSS. You will probably only override the pop outs (.s4-ql .dynamic .menu-item).

```
<!-- Style the menu headings -->
.s4-ql .static .menu-item
{
        font-size:14pt !important;
        color:green;
        background-color:yellow;
        border:solid !important;
        border-color:black;
        border-width:thin;
}

<!-- Style the menu items / pop outs-->
.s4-ql .dynamic .menu-item
{
        font-size:14pt;
        color:red;
```

```
    background-color:#D6E8FF;
    border:solid;
    border-color:black;
    border-width:thin;
}
```

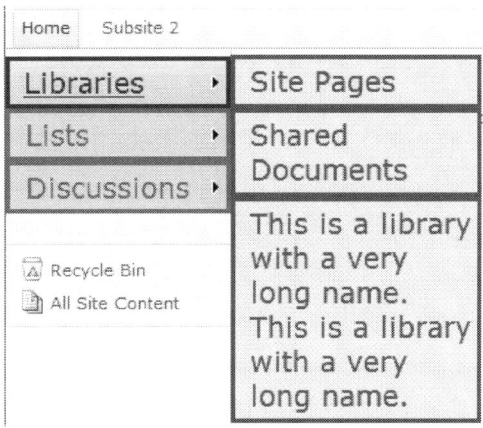

A more practical version might only change the pop outs and look like this:

```
<!-- Style the menu items / pop outs-->
.s4-ql .dynamic .menu-item
{
    background-color:#E1F3FF;
    border:solid;
    border-width:1px;
}
```

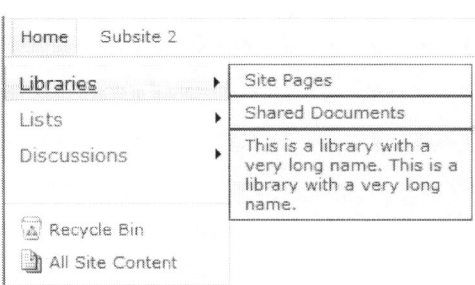

User Interface Customization

Quick Launch Accordions

While a pop-out menu, well, pops out and then back, an accordion expands one section of a menu at a time. The expansion can be triggered using a mouse click or a simple mouse move over the menu heading. As Quick Launch headings are clickable out of the box, this accordion will be designed to use a "mouse over" to trigger the expansion.

2007:   **Unmodified**   **Collapsed**   **After mouse moved over Lists**

2010:   **Unmodified**   **Collapsed**   **After mouse moved over Lists**

As you saw in the previous customization, the Quick Launch area is generated from a SharePoint control that supports pop-outs. As this control does not support an accordion option we will need to create our own accordion effect using JavaScript. SharePoint 2007 and 2010 use different styles of HTML to create and display Quick Launch, so each will have its own JavaScript routine. 2007 uses tables (<TABLE>) while 2010 uses unordered lists (<UL> and <LI>).

175

User Interface Customization

Quick Launch Accordions (2007)

Quick Launch in SharePoint 2007 has a mouse over event already in place on the header rows. All we need to do is to intercept this event and add our own code to hide and show the menu items in each section. We will also need a routine to hide all of the sections when the page first loads and every time the mouse is moved up and down across the menu.

Steps:

1. Open SharePoint Designer 2007, open your site and open your master page (see chapter 6)
2. Scroll to the end of the master page and add the JavaScript code just before **</body>** tag

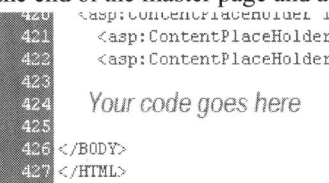

Note: If you just wanted this feature on a single page you could add a Content Editor Web Part or edit the page in SharePoint Designer and add the code just before the **</asp:Content>** for PlaceHolderMain.

3. Save your changes and test!

The JavaScript:

```
<script type="text/javascript">

// intercept the existing mouseover event function
var oldMenu_HoverRoot= Menu_HoverRoot;
// and replace it with our own
Menu_HoverRoot= function (x)
{

if (x.childNodes[0].childNodes[0].className.indexOf("ms-navheader") > -1)
{
  if (x.nextSibling)
  {
    // first hide all sections
    AccordionQLHideRows();
    // then expand the current section
    var items = x.nextSibling.childNodes[0].childNodes[0];
    items.style.display="";
  }
}
```

User Interface Customization

```
// then call the intercepted function
return oldMenu_HoverRoot.apply(this, arguments);

}

// hide all of the sections when the page first loads
AccordionQLHideRows();


function AccordionQLHideRows()
{
  // close any open sections
  var nav = document.getElementById("LeftNavigationAreaCell");
  var tables = nav.getElementsByTagName("table")

  for (var i=0;i<tables.length;i++)
  {
    if (tables[i].className.indexOf("ms-navSubMenu2")>-1)
    {
      tables[i].style.display="none";
    }
  }
}
</script>
```

Quick Launch Accordions (2010)

Quick Launch in SharePoint 2010 does not have the built-in mouse over event that was available in 2007. We will need to add our own mouse over event to the Quick Launch header HTML. The steps for this customization are identical to those for 2007, except for the JavaScript used.

Steps:

1. Open SharePoint Designer 2010, open your site and open your master page (see chapter 6)

User Interface Customization

2. Scroll to the end of the master page and add the JavaScript code just before </body> tag

```
631  </form>
632  <asp:ContentPlaceHolder id="Plac
633    <SharePoint:WarnOnUnsupportedE
634
635      Your code goes here
636
637 </body>
638 </html>
```

Note: If you just wanted this feature on a single page you could add a Content Editor Web Part or edit the page in SharePoint Designer and add the code just before the </asp:Content> for PlaceHolderMain.

3. Save your changes and test!

The JavaScript:

```
<script type="text/javascript">

// this functions hides the menu sections and adds a mouse over event handler
function AccordianQL()
{
 // find all divs on the page
 var AccordianQLdivs = document.getElementsByTagName("div");
 for (var i=0; i<AccordianQLdivs.length;i++)
 {
  // find the Quick Launch div
  if (AccordianQLdivs[i].className=="ms-quickLaunch")
  {
   // find all UL tags
   var AccordianQLuls = AccordianQLdivs[i].getElementsByTagName("ul");
   for (var j=0; j<AccordianQLuls.length;j++)
   {
    // find the "master" UL for Quick Launch
    if (AccordianQLuls[j].className == "root static")
    {
     // for each child (LI) of the UL:
     //   add the event handler
     //   change the style for LI's contents
     for (var k=0; k<AccordianQLuls[j].children.length; k++)
     {
      AccordianQLuls[j].children[k].onmouseover =
            function () { AccordianQLExpandSection(this) }
      AccordianQLuls[j].children[k].childNodes[1].style.display="none";
     }
```

```
        // all done - no more divs to check
        break;
      }
    }
   }
  }
}

// Call once here to collapse the Quick Launch on page load
AccordianQL();

// respond to the mouse over event
function AccordianQLExpandSection(t)
{
  // collapase all open sections
  AccordianQL();
  // expand the current section
  t.childNodes[1].style.display = "";
}
</script>
```

Add Quick Launch Back Into Basic Pages and Web Part Pages (2007)

2007 Basic Pages and Web Part Pages include all of the top navigation of a SharePoint page, but excludes the Quick Launch area, breaking the navigation interface your users expect. You also get a big empty blue band, and a site title that looks like it might be part of the article. You won't need to do this in SharePoint 2010 as the same pages in 2010 do include Quick Launch.

A web part page and a basic page:

User Interface Customization

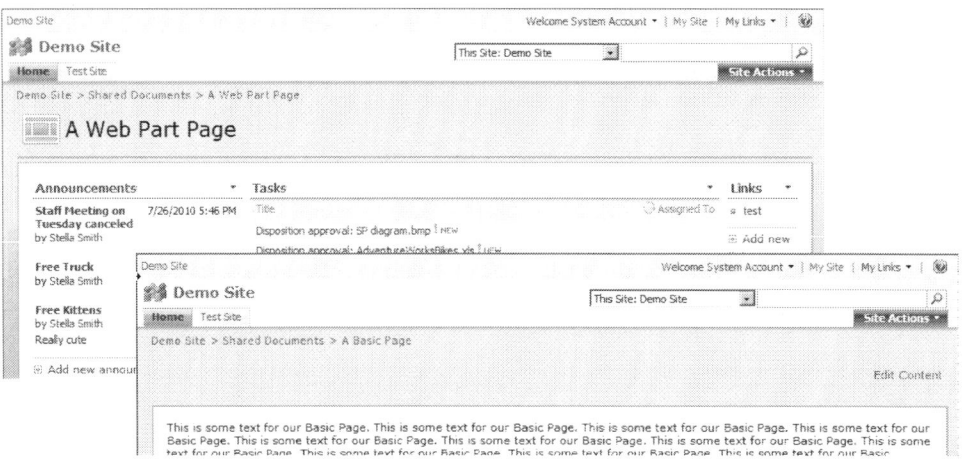

Restore Quick Launch

Getting Quick Launch back is rather easy. This time we will delete something from a page instead of adding something to the page.

1. Open your site in SharePoint Designer and open this page (remember you created the page a library)
2. Display the code view of the page and search for **PlaceHolderLeftNavBar**
3. Select the following two lines and delete them:

```
<asp:Content ContentPlaceHolderId="PlaceHolderLeftNavBar" runat="server"></asp:Content>
<asp:Content ContentPlaceHolderId="PlaceHolderNavSpacer" runat="server"></asp:Content>
```

User Interface Customization

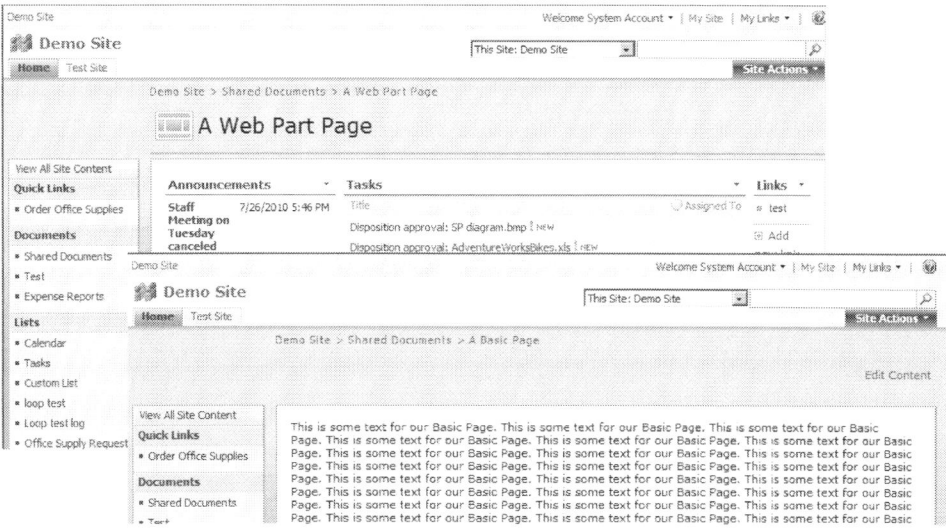

Now we have Quick Launch back... but what about all of that blue space in the Basic Page?

Cleaning up the Basic Page (2007)

Now you need to get rid of that big blue band and the oddly placed Site Title. I'm not sure why they designed this page this way, but it's easy to fix.

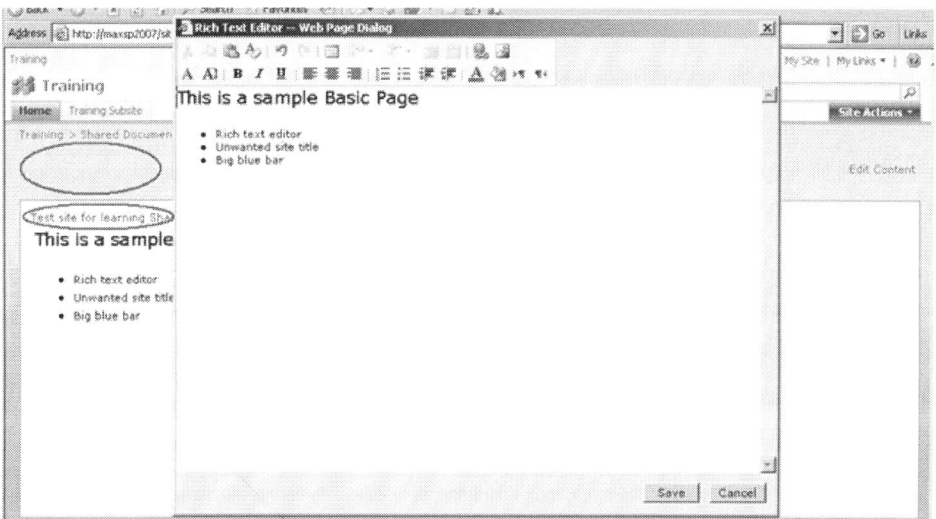

181

Hide the oddly placed site title

The site title looks like it is part of the basic page's text, which most likely not what you want:

To hide the title:

1. Open your site in SharePoint Designer and open this page (remember you created it a library)
2. Find the **PlaceHolderPageDescription** placeholder
3. Either delete the entire placeholder or delete the **SharePoint:ProjectProperty** control inside of the placeholder

```
<asp:Content ContentPlaceHolderId="PlaceHolderPageDescription" runat="server">
<SharePoint:ProjectProperty Property="Description" runat="server"/>
</asp:Content>
```

After removing the title:

Hide the Blue Bar

It turns out there are several ways of hiding the blue area, depending on what you would like to hide along with it.

Method #1: Hide the blue area, but keep the crumb trail.

1. Return to the page you opened in SharePoint Designer and find the following area:

```
<style type="text/css">
Div.ms-titleareaframe {
   height: 100%;
}
.ms-pagetitleareaframe table {
   background: none;
}
</style>
```

2. And change it to:

```
<style type="text/css">
Div.ms-titleareaframe
{
   height: 100%;
}
.ms-pagetitleareaframe table {
   background: none;
   height:25px;
}
#onetidPageTitle
{
   display:none
}
</style>
```

The blue bar is now gone!

Training > Shared Documents > Sample Basic P

Test site for learning SharePoint

This is a sample Basic Page

- Rich text editor
- Unwanted site description
- Big blue bar

But the Edit Content link is also now gone... how are you going to edit this page?

One way is to just modify the URL and add "?PageView=Shared&ContentEditorPopUp=True" to the end of the page's URL.

The URL will look something like this:

```
http://yourserver/sites/yoursite/Shared%20Documents/Sample%20Basic%20Page.aspx?PageView=Shared&ContentEditorPopUp=True
```

That's not an easy way to edit a page, so let's hide the blue bar for everyone except for Site Owners (who have the "**ManageWeb**" permission). To do this we will repeat the <STYLE> section, once customized for non-Site Owners and once again for Site Owners. But the second time we will wrap the style code in a "SPSecurityTrimmedControl". (For more on this control and other permission options see chapter7.) This edit depends on how multiple blocks of CSS "cascade", i.e. how the second occurrence of the CSS will override the first.

```
<style type="text/css">
Div.ms-titleareaframe {
   height: 100%;
}
.ms-pagetitleareaframe table {
   background: none;
   height:25px;
}
#onetidPageTitle
{
   display:none
}
</style>
<SharePoint:SPSecurityTrimmedControl runat="server" PermissionsString="ManageWeb">
   <style type="text/css">
   .ms-pagetitleareaframe table
   {
      height:53px;
   }
   #onetidPageTitle
   {
      display:inline
```

```
    }
    </style>
</SharePoint:SPSecurityTrimmedControl>
```

Method #2: Hide the blue bar AND the crumb trail

If you have already tried Method #1, then either reset that page back to the site definition or create another Basic Page to test with.

1. Open your site in SharePoint Designer and open this page (remember you created it a library)
2. Find the **PlaceHolderAdditionalPageHead** placeholder
3. Add **display:none** to the **.ms-pagetitleareaframe** style section (see the line in bold below)

```
<asp:Content ContentPlaceHolderId="PlaceHolderAdditionalPageHead" runat="server">
    <META Name="GENERATOR" Content="Microsoft SharePoint">
...
    <style type="text/css">
    Div.ms-titleareaframe {
       height: 100%;
    }
    .ms-pagetitleareaframe table {
    background: none;
    display:none;
    }
    </style>
</asp:Content>
```

After this edit we no longer have the big blue bar, or the crumb trail:

This is a sample Basic Page

- Rich text editor
- Unwanted site description
- Big blue bar

185

Method #3: Hide the blue bar and the crumb trail from "some" users, based on user permissions.

This is similar to what we did in #1 to hide the blue bars from everyone except for Site Owners.

1. Make the change as above to hide the blue bar
2. Add an SPSecurityTrimmedControl to contain custom CSS for selected users (by permission)
3. Set PermissionsString="ManageWeb" to target Site Owners, or maybe set it to EditListItems to target contributors.

```
<asp:Content ContentPlaceHolderId="PlaceHolderAdditionalPageHead" runat="server">
    <META Name="GENERATOR" Content="Microsoft SharePoint">
...
    <style type="text/css">
    Div.ms-titleareaframe
    {
       height: 100%;
    }
    .ms-pagetitleareaframe table
    {
       background: none;
       display:none;
    }
    </style>

    <SharePoint:SPSecurityTrimmedControl runat="server"
        PermissionsString="ManageWeb">
     <style type="text/css">
     .ms-pagetitleareaframe table
     {
       display:inline;
     }

     </style>
    </SharePoint:SPSecurityTrimmedControl>

</asp:Content>
```

Cleaning up the Basic Page (2010)

Unlike the SharePoint 2007 basic page, the 2010 version already includes Quick Launch and does not have the "blue bar" problem. Instead it has an additional, and probably unwanted, "Recently Modified" box above the Quick Launch area.

Steps:

1. Open your site in SharePoint Designer and open this page (remember you created it a library)
2. Click the **Advanced Mode** button in the ribbon to permit the editing of the entire page
3. Find the placeholder named **PlaceHolderLeftActions** and either delete the entire placeholder or delete the **SharePoint:RecentChangesMenu** control inside of that placeholder

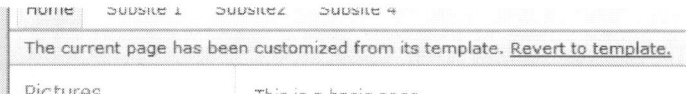

4. Save your changes and click **OK** to the **"will customize"** dialog box and click **OK** to the next warning
5. Test the page

You will probably now see this message in the page

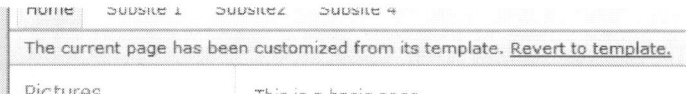

While this message should only display for site owners, you can hide it if you like:

4. Go back to SharePoint Designer and scroll to the end of the page
5. Just before the end tag for **PlaceHolderMain** add this style block

```
<style type="text/css">
  #s4-statusbarcontainer
  {
        display:none;
  }
</style>
```

187

User Interface Customization

```
79      </Triggers>
80    </asp:UpdatePanel>
81    <style type="text/css">
82      #s4-statusbarcontainer
83      {
84        display:none;
85      }
86    </style>
87  </asp:Content>
88
```

6. Save and test the page

Remove Quick Launch from a Basic Page (2010)

If you want to have the full width of a Basic Page available for text then you will need to hide the Quick Launch area. This requires three pieces of CSS: one to hide Quick Launch, one to make the main area full width and one to hide the annoying "Revert to template" message.

Before:

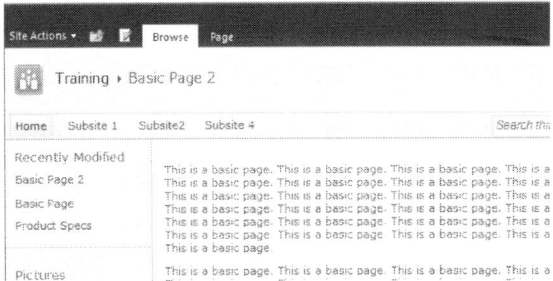

After:

Steps:

1. Open your site in SharePoint Designer and open this page (remember you created it a library)
2. Click the **Advanced Mode** button in the ribbon to permit the editing of the entire page
3. Just before the end tag for **PlaceHolderMain** add this style block:

<style type="text/css">

188

```
.s4-ca
{
  margin-left:0px;
}

#s4-leftpanel
{
      display:none;
}

#s4-statusbarcontainer
{
  display:none;
}
</style>
```

4. Save your changes and test

How to hide the right web part column (2007)

In a later section, "Modify / Add / remove web part zones", we will take a look at formally adding and removing web part zones by using SharePoint Designer. Here we will take a look at a quick trick using a Content Editor Web Part to hide a web part zone.

The Team Site template creates a home page with two columns, one 70% wide and one 30% wide. Actually there are two more columns, one between the two web part columns and one to the right. We want to hide the right web part column and change the width of the left web part column.

How is it done?

- The trick is to identify the columns to hide. It turns out only two columns in the page have widths of 30% and 70% defined.
- Add a Content Editor Web Part to the zone not being hidden. Modify the web part and click the **Source Editor** button.
- Add the JavaScript code listed below to change column widths and hide the other columns.

User Interface Customization

Steps:

1. Click **Site Actions** and **Edit Page**
2. Click **Add a Web Part** and add a Content Editor Web Part - Make sure you add it to the left column, i.e. the one you aren't going to hide!
3. Click the web part's dropdown menu and click **Modify Shared Web Part**
4. Click the **Source Editor** button
5. Add the following code

The Code:

```javascript
<script type="text/javascript">

function HideWebPartZone()
{
  var x = document.getElementsByTagName("TD");
  for (var i=0; i<x.length; i++)
  {
   if (x[i].width == "70%")
   {
     // we found the left column, now change the width
     x[i].style.width="100%";

     // the next column is the center (otherwise empty) column
     var x2=x[i].nextSibling;
     x2.style.width="0";
     x2.style.display="none";
     x2.innerHTML="";

     // and then there's the right column
     x2=x[i].nextSibling.nextSibling;
     x2.style.width="0";
     x2.style.display="none";
     x2.innerHTML="";

     // and an otherwise empty right margin column
     x2=x[i].nextSibling.nextSibling.nextSibling;
     x2.style.width="0";
     x2.style.display="none";
     x2.innerHTML="";

     //all done
     return;
```

```
      }
     }
  }

  _spBodyOnLoadFunctionNames.push("HideWebPartZone")

</script>
```

Setting the Web Part Zones to 50% and 50%

The steps here are basically the same as in the previous example, just add a Content Editor Web Part and add some JavaScript code.

Steps:

1. Click **Site Actions** and **Edit Page**
2. Click **Add a Web Part** and add a Content Editor Web Part (either column)
3. Click the web part's dropdown menu and click **Modify Shared Web Part**
4. Click the **Source Editor** button
5. Add the following code, save your changes and test

The Code:

```
<script type="text/javascript">

function ReformatWebPartZone()
{
  var x = document.getElementsByTagName("TD");
  for (var i=0;i<x.length;i++)
   {
    if (x[i].width=="30%")
      {
        x[i].style.width="50%";
      }
    if (x[i].width=="70%")
      {
        x[i].style.width="50%";
      }
   }
}
```

User Interface Customization

```
}
_spBodyOnLoadFunctionNames.push("ReformatWebPartZone")
</script>
```

Modify / Add / remove web part zones (2007 and 2010)

The SharePoint 2007 home page, and 2010 home pages named default.aspx, have only two web part zones. If you need only one zone, or you need five zones, you will need to edit the page in SharePoint Designer. You will generally need to update the HTML <table> or <div> structures and add ASP.Net web part zone controls.

> Also see "Change or Replace Your Home Page" later in this chapter.

To add a new web part zone:

1. Open SharePoint Designer, open your site and open the page for editing
2. In SharePoint Designer 2010 you will also need to click the **Advanced** button in the ribbon to enable full page editing
3. Decide where to put the web part zone (it does not have to go in the same table as the existing web part zones)
4. You will need to alter the <table> or <div> structures of the page to manage the page layout (this has nothing to do with the web part zones themselves, just basic page design work)
5. You will need to create a web part zone either by typing code or using the **Insert** menu. The new zone code will look something like this:

```
<WebPartPages:WebPartZone runat="server" FrameType="TitleBarOnly" ID="center" Title="Center">
    <ZoneTemplate></ZoneTemplate>
</WebPartPages:WebPartZone>
```

6. You will need to pick a display name and a unique ID
   (Example: Title="Center" ID="centerwebpartzone")

Adding Center and Top Web Part Zones

As an example of adding a new web part zone let's take a look at adding a new zone across the top of the existing web part zones and a new zone between the two existing zones. The result will look like the following page where the Shared Documents web part has been added to the new "Top" zone and a Tasks web part has been added to the new "Center" zone. (This sample is for SP 2007, but is the same for 2010.)

User Interface Customization

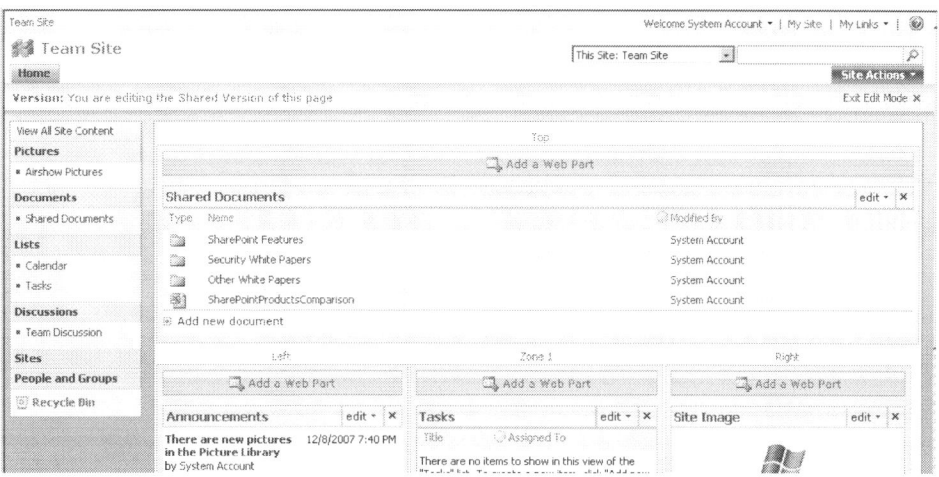

To add a new center zone:

1. There's already a handy center column in the existing <table>, so in the design view click in the empty cell between the two existing web part zones. If this were not the case you would need to add a new column to the table (<td> ... </td>)
2. Edit the <TD> tag to set the width to 33% and add " valign='top' "
3. Edit the other two columns (td's) to set their widths to 33%
4. Either type the WebPartZone sample from above, or insert the web zone from the menus: **Insert, SharePoint Controls, Web Part Zone** in SharePoint 2007
5. Use either the properties panel or the code window to change the Title to **"Center"** and optionally supply a unique ID
6. You could add a web part from within SharePoint Designer, but for this example we will wait and add it from a browser
7. Save the changes and accept the customization warnings
8. In a browser navigate to your site's home page
9. Click **Site Actions, Edit Page** and add new web parts to the new zones

To add a new top zone:

We will need to add a new row to the table with one cell that spans all three columns:

1. In the SharePoint Designer **Design** view of the page click the "tab" for the left zone
2. In the code view find the <table> tag for the web part zones

```
<table width="100%" cellpadding=0 cellspacing=0 style="padding: 5px 0px 0px 0px;">
 <tr>
  <td valign="top" width="33%">
```

193

User Interface Customization

3. Add the tags for the new row:

```
<table width="100%" cellpadding=0 cellspacing=0 style="padding: 5px 0px 0px 0px;">
 <tr><td colspan="4"> </td></tr>
 <tr>
  <td valign="top" width="33%"
```

Note: The value for "colspan" should be the number of columns in the table.

4. Return to the Design view and insert a new web part zone like you did before
5. Save the changes
6. In a browser navigate to your site's home page
7. Click Site Actions, Edit Page and add a new web part to the new zone

Change or Hide the Bullet Image in Quick Launch (2007)

> This is only for SharePoint 2007, as the default design in SharePoint 2010 does not add bullets to Quick Launch.

Sometimes it's the little things... I had a request where a site owner wanted to change just the bullet used in Quick Launch. They did not want to create a custom theme or do a complete rebranding of the entire site, just change the bullet.

So...

1. Create your new bullet image in your favorite paint program (JPG or GIF format) and upload it to a library in your site, or if you have server access upload it to the Images folder in Layouts
   Here's my fantastic example "bullet": → (Hopefully you are a better artist than I am!)
2. Use SharePoint Designer to edit the master page and add the CSS just after these two lines:

```
<SharePoint:CssLink runat="server"/>
<SharePoint:Theme runat="server"/>
     <!-- your custom styles go here -->
```

Or, if you want to do a quick test, instead of editing the master page add a Content Editor Web Part (CEWP), edit the CEWP, click the Source Editor button and paste the following style code.

The CSS to change the bullet image:

```
<style type="text/css">
table.ms-navitem td,span.ms-navitem
{
```

194

```
  background-image:url("/sites/training/Shared%20Documents/myBullet.gif");
}
</style>
```

The result (with my horrible bullet image!):

If you just want to hide the bullet then just set **background-image** to "none":

```
<style type="text/css">
table.ms-navitem td,span.ms-navitem
{
  background-image:none;
}
</style>
```

Customizing the Tree View (2007 and 2010)

The Tree View is an optional navigation tool that is useful for content oriented sites, i.e. sites that largely consist of lists and libraries with nested folders. The Tree View can be displayed with or without Quick Launch, and out of the box it is always displayed below Quick Launch.

Show the Tree View

Displaying the Tree View in your site is as easy as **Site Actions, Site Settings, Tree View**, and checking **Enable Tree View**.

How the Tree View works

The Tree View is built from two SharePoint controls, SharePoint:SPHierarchyDataSourceControl and SharePoint:SPTreeView. The data displayed in the Tree View is retrieved by the SPHierarchyDataSourceControl and it is this control that we will configure to choose what content is to be displayed in the Tree View. The SPTreeView control displays the Tree View using the data retrieved by the SPHierarchyDataSourceControl. Changes to the SPTreeView control will only impact the formatting of the Tree View data.

Customize Tree View Contents

The SPHierarchyDataSourceControl in the master page initially looks like this:

```
<SharePoint:SPHierarchyDataSourceControl
 runat="server"
 id="TreeViewDataSource"
 RootContextObject="Web"
 IncludeDiscussionFolders="true"
/>
```

The IncludeDiscussionFolders is a hint that this control can be configured. Here's the complete list of options we are interested in: ("true" is the default value if these options are not included in the HTML)

- **IncludeDiscussionFolders** - set to true to show individual discussions as folders in the tree view (Note: **ShowFolderChildren="false"** overrides this option)
- **ShowDocLibChildren** - set to false to hide document libraries
- **ShowFolderChildren** - set to false to hide all folders within all lists and libraries
- **ShowListChildren** - set to false to hide all lists, including calendars, tasks and discussions

- ShowWebChildren - set to false to hide sub sites

If you add these properties to the control then you can start experimenting with the content options:

```
<SharePoint:SPHierarchyDataSourceControl
 runat="server"
 id="TreeViewDataSource"
 RootContextObject="Web"
 IncludeDiscussionFolders="true"
 ShowDocLibChildren="true"
 ShowFolderChildren="true"
 ShowListChildren="true"
 ShowWebChildren="true"
/>
```

Example: Sites-only Tree View

To create a Tree View that only displays subsites of the current site you will need to make these changes:

- Set all of the "include" and "show" options in the SPHierarchyDataSourceControl to false except for ShowWebChildren
- Optional: Pre-expand the tree by changing the SPTreeView control by setting ExpandDepth to number larger than 0 - this example has it set to 5
- Optional: Add lines to improve the appearance of the tree by setting ShowLines to true

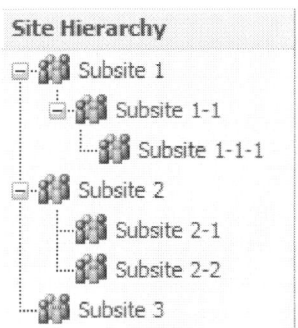

```
<SharePoint:SPHierarchyDataSourceControl
 runat="server" id="TreeViewDataSource" RootContextObject="Web"
 IncludeDiscussionFolders="false"
 ShowDocLibChildren="false "
```

User Interface Customization

```
  ShowFolderChildren="false "
  ShowListChildren="false "
  ShowWebChildren="true"
/>
<SharePoint:SPRememberScroll ...... >
  <SharePoint:SPTreeView id="WebTreeView" runat="server"
   ShowLines="true"
   ExpandDepth="5"
     ...
  </SharePoint:SPTreeView>
</SharePoint:SPRememberScroll>
```

Styling the Tree View

SharePoint uses two style definitions to control the appearance of the Tree View fonts and colors: .ms-navitem and .ms-tvselected. When you create a style for the "selected" item you will need to define ".ms-tvselected a". You can also define your own styles and assign them to the Tree View's SelectedNodeStyle-CssClass and NodeStyle-CssClass properties.

```
.ms-tvselected a
{
        color:maroon;
        background-color:blue;
}
.ms-navitem
{
        color:yellow;
        background-color:red;
}
```

Pre-Expanding the Tree View

The default Tree View only displays the top level of any hierarchy. For example, it will display the library's name, but not its folders. You can set the level of expansion by editing **ExpandDepth** in the SharePoint:SPTreeView control.

```
<SharePoint:SPTreeView id="WebTreeView" runat="server"
  ShowLines="true"
  ExpandDepth="10"
     ...
</SharePoint:SPTreeView>
```

User Interface Customization

ExpandDepth="0"   ExpandDepth="1"   ExpandDepth="2"

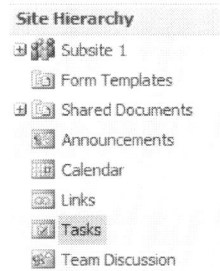 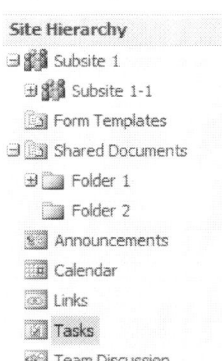 

Adding Lines and Indent to the Tree View Control

Adding lines to a Tree View can improve readability of more complex hierarchies. Lines are enabled by changing **ShowLines** to "true" in the SPTreeView control. You can increase or decrease the indention of each level by setting **NodeIndent** to a value in pixels. The default indent is 12 pixels.

```
<SharePoint:SPTreeView id="WebTreeView" runat="server"
    ...
  ShowLines="true"
  NodeIndent="12"
    ...
</SharePoint:SPTreeView>
```

ShowLines="false"   ShowLines="true"

 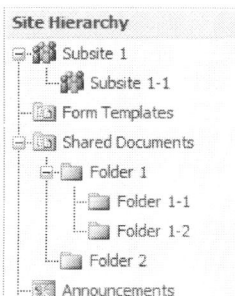

199

Change the Site Hierarchy (2007) / Site Content (2010) link and text

2007

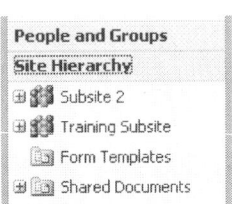

2010

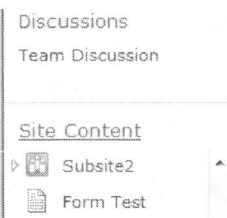

The link just above the Tree View goes to the View All Site Content page. You can change this link to point anywhere by editing the SharePoint:SPLinkButton control and changing the **NavigateUrl** attribute. As an example, if you have modified the Tree View to only display subsites then you might want to change the link to go to a View All Site Content page that lists only subsites:

NavigateUrl="~site/_layouts/viewlsts.aspx?ShowSites=1"

The unmodified version:

```
<SharePoint:SPLinkButton runat="server"
NavigateUrl="~site/_layouts/viewlsts.aspx"
id="idNavLinkSiteHierarchy"
Text="<%$Resources:wss,treeview_header%>"
accesskey="<%$Resources:wss,quiklnch_allcontent_AK%>" />
```

 What's that "<%$Resources" stuff all about? SharePoint stores almost all of its displayed text, such as the words "Site Hierarchy", in external files called resource files. This is how SharePoint can support multiple languages without having to have a different version of SharePoint for each language. These files are XML files with an extension of .resx that are stored in the SharePoint installation folders on the web servers. (C:\Program Files\Common Files\Microsoft Shared\web server extensions\12\Resources or \14\ for SharePoint 2010)

In most cases you can replace these resource references with your own text. For example, to change "Site Hierarchy" to "All lists and libraries" just change:
  Text="<%$Resources:wss,treeview_header%>"
to
  Text="All lists and libraries"

Hide the Tree View Icons

The Tree View displays icons to represent the document or folder type. While these do add value to the display, they also add clutter in an otherwise clean page design.

User Interface Customization

The before:	and the after:	and with lines:
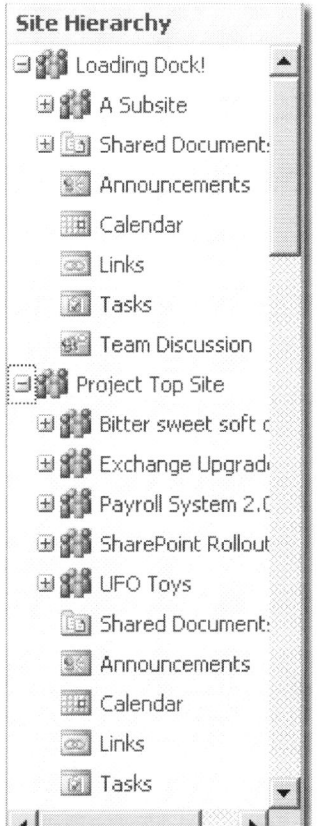	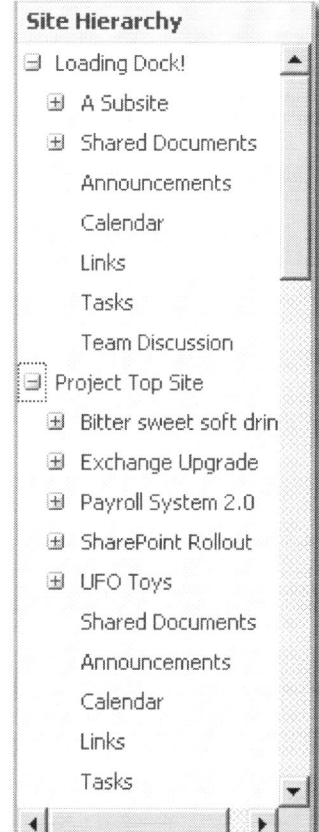	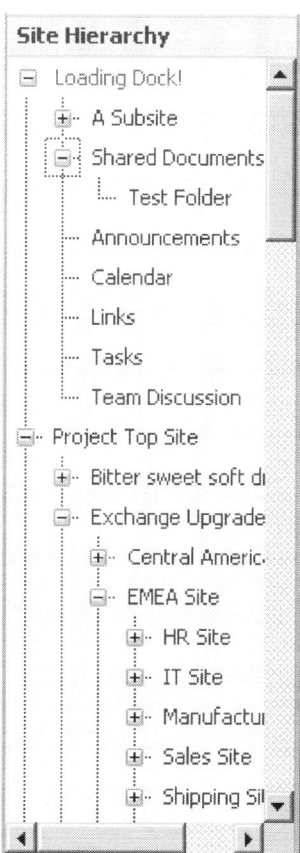

How it works

Hiding the icons requires two JavaScript tricks. The first one removes the images on the initial page load. The second intercepts the web service calls to retrieve data for further expansions of the tree. I may have missed one or more of the icon types in the sample code, but that is easy for you to fix.

- For testing: Add a Content Editor Web Part to the page. In 2007 click the **Source Editor** button and paste the code from below. For 2010, save the code below to a text file, upload the file to a library and in the CEWP add a link to the uploaded text file.
- For actual use: Add this code to the master page anywhere after where the tree is loaded

You will need to use SharePoint Designer to add the tree view lines.

1. Open the site in SharePoint Designer
2. Open the master page and search for **ShowLines**
3. Change **ShowLines** = "false" to **ShowLines** = "true"

201

User Interface Customization

```
<Sharepoint:SPTreeView
    id="WebTreeView"
    runat="server"
    ShowLines="true"
    DataSourceId="TreeViewDataSource"
    ExpandDepth="0"
```

The JavaScript:

```
<script>

// Step 1: hide icons on the initial page load...

//get the tree DIV by ID (different ID for 2007 and 2010)
if ( typeof _fV4UI == "undefined" )   // check version
  {
   // THIS LINE FOR 2007
   var tree = document.getElementById("ctl00_PlaceHolderLeftNavBar_WebTreeView");
  }
  else
  {
   // THIS LINE FOR 2010
   var tree = document.getElementById("ctl00_PlaceHolderLeftNavBar_ctl01_WebTreeViewV4");
  }

//get the tree view rows
var trs = tree.getElementsByTagName("TR");

//loop through the rows and hide the images
for (i=0;i<trs.length;i++)
{
  var tds = trs[i].getElementsByTagName("TD");
  if (tds.length>0)
  {
    tds[1].style.display="none";
  }
}

// Step 2: intercept the web service call and fix up the returned data

// make a copy of the SharePoint return handler
var backup=TreeView_ProcessNodeData;
```

User Interface Customization

```
// create our replacement function
TreeView_ProcessNodeData = function(result, context)
{
  //replace the images with blank.gif  (it*.gif, stsicon.gif and folder.gif)
  result = result.replace(/\/_layouts\/images\/it/g,'/_layouts/images/blank.gif" x="');
  result = result.replace(/\/_layouts\/images\/stsicon/g,'/_layouts/images/blank.gif" x="');
  result = result.replace(/\/_layouts\/images\/folder/g,'/_layouts/images/blank.gif" x="');

  //call the SharePoint return handler
  backup(result, context);
}

</script>
```

Add Dropdown Menus to the Top Link Bar (2007)

SharePoint 2007 Publishing templates include a feature to add dropdowns to the Top Link Bar. As it appears that they forgot to give us a similar option in WSS we will need to create our own. And we will do one better and add a way to populate the dropdown list from a SharePoint list or library. To be fair to all, this new menu feature will work in both WSS and MOSS and in Publishing and non-Publishing sites.

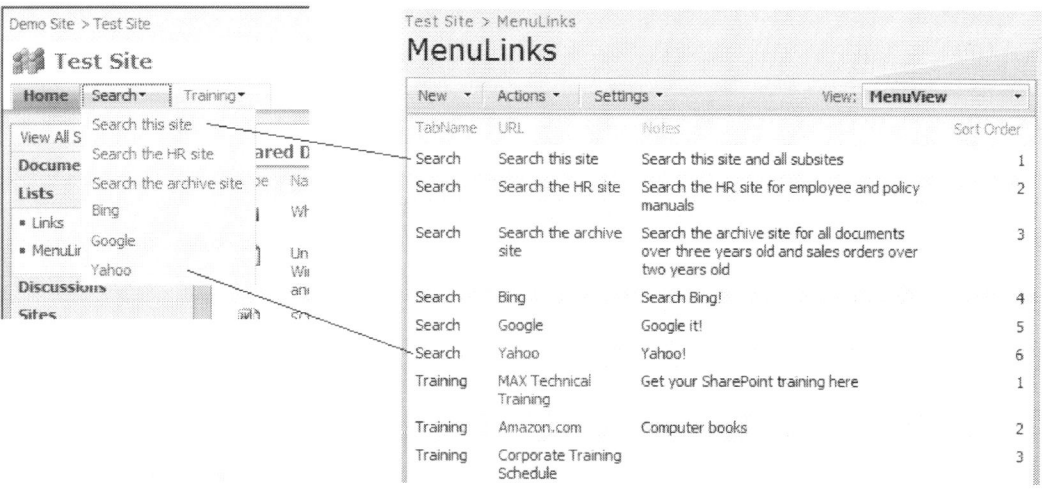

How it works: SharePoint Top Link Bar tabs are represented in HTML as a <TABLE>. All we need to do is to write some JavaScript to create our own table with the new menu choices and to move this table to display just under the tab. The second part of the solution is getting a list of items for the menu. The sample code below lets you manually enter a list of links or find them in a hidden list web part. In order for this to

203

work, the hidden web part must be placed directly in the master page. This is an uncommon use of web parts, especially as we are not adding it to a web part zone. These types of web parts are called Static Web Parts as they cannot be edited from within the browser. If you need to update the web part you will need to either edit the HTML directly or delete the web part, update the default view and then add it back.

How would you have discovered this? This is not an easy one as it depends on a collection of tricks. Pulling the data from the web part is similar to how the "Convert a Links list to a Dropdown list" works. Figuring out how the table structure for the Top Link Bar was done using the browser's View Source feature. The adding and positioning of the dropdown itself requires basic HTML, CSS and JavaScript skills, along with some trial and error and a pinch of magic. Finding the exact location of the Top Link Bar tab requires a block of JavaScript downloaded from www.codeplex.com.

What's needed to build these dropdown menus:

- A Links list with an extra column or two and a new default view
- SharePoint Designer to edit the master page
- Knowing how to add a web part directly to a master page
- A JavaScript routine from www.codeplex.com

Setup Work

You will need to create a Links list, add new columns and then add some new tabs in the Top Link Bar.

1. Create a new Links List and name it "MenuLinks"
2. Add a new column named "TabName"
3. Create a new view on this list named "MenuView" based on "Standard View", make it the default view and then list the columns in this order: **TabName**, **URL** (not URL with edit menu), **Notes**
4. Optionally add a column to use for sorting the list and then when you create the view for the list sort it by this column

5. Add an entry for each item for the menu - the example below has data for dropdowns for a Search tab and a Training tab.

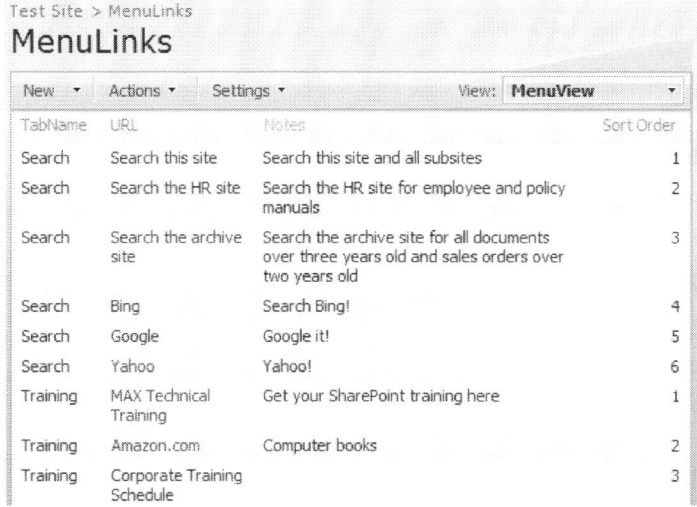

6. Create a new view
   a. add the columns in this order: **TabName, URL, Notes** and optionally add **Sort Order**
      Note: use the URL column, not the "URL with edit menu" column
   b. (optional) sort the view by TabName and then by Sort Order
   c. set this view to be the Default view (important!)
7. Add a tab in the Top Link Bar for each of your new menus. For WSS, just go to **Site Actions, Site Settings** and **Top Link Bar** and add the links. For a MOSS publishing template, go to **Site Actions, Site Settings** and **Navigation** and add "global" links. (Do not add these as headings!)
   a. For each link enter the text to display on the tab - this will need to match the text you added to the **TabName** column of the **MenuView** list
   b. For the URL, just enter the site's home page URL for now as this will get changed when the JavaScript runs to update the tab

Changes to the Master Page

Most of the work will be done in the site's master page. Here you will add a Links List web part as a static web part, add a DIV to hold the new menus and a large block of JavaScript to read data from the web part and display it in the dropdown menus.

1. Go to **www.codeproject.com/KB/scripting/dom-element-abs-pos.aspx** (Link 1006) and copy the big block of code in the tan box and paste it into a Notepad
2. Open SharePoint Designer and open your site
3. Open the master page (most likely **default.master** for 2007 and **v4.master** for 2010)
4. Scroll to the bottom of the page and insert the code below just before the **</body>** tag

User Interface Customization

5. Copy the code you downloaded from www.codeplex.com to where you see "download the code from codeplex.com and paste it here!"
6. Add the web part to the page:
   a. In SharePoint Designer, switch to the Design view of the editor
   b. Scroll to the bottom of the page and click as close to the end of the page as possible
   c. Click the Insert menu and select SharePoint Controls, Web Part - this will display the Web Parts pane
   d. In the Web Parts pane find MenuLinks and drag it to the very bottom of the page

The result should look something like this:

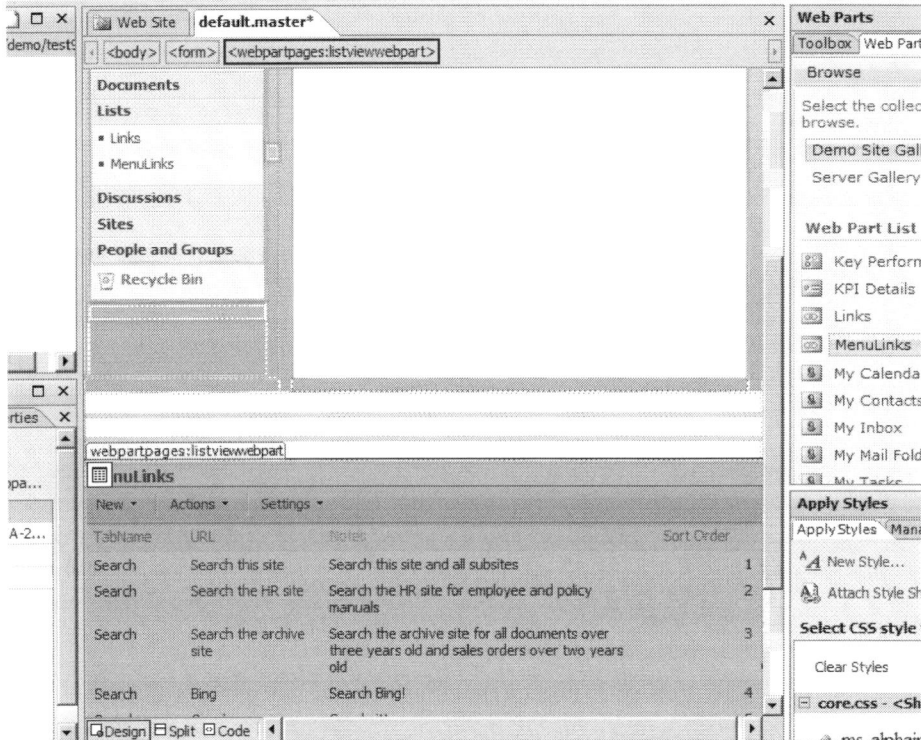

When you save the master page and return to the browser you should now see little arrows in the tabs, and when you mouse over the tabs the dropdowns should appear.

The Code

Now I know you are not going to type everything needed for this little project, so go to the book's website and download the code (See chapter 1 for details). If you do try to type this by hand, watch out for line wraps in odd places.

```html
<!-- the DIV that will hold the dropdown menu -->
<div id='customdropdowns' style="position:absolute;display:none;"
 onblur="javascript:  document.getElementById('customdropdowns').style.display='none'">
</div>
```

```javascript
<script type="text/javascript">
//////
// Start of code borrowed from
// http://www.codeproject.com/KB/scripting/dom-element-abs-pos.aspx
//////

    // download the code from codeplex.com and paste it here!

//////
// End of code borrowed from
// http://www.codeproject.com/KB/scripting/dom-element-abs-pos.aspx
//////


// Code to add dropdown menus to the Top Link Bar
var CustomMenuArray = Array();
function CustomMenuSetup()
{

  // build a manual list of menus and items (examples)
  // CustomMenuArray[0] = ["Search","Bing",  "http://www.bing.com",   "Search Bing"];
  // CustomMenuArray[1] = ["Search","Google","http://www.google.com", "Google It!"];
  // CustomMenuArray[2] = ["Search","Yahoo", "http://www.yahoo.com",  "Yahoo!"];


  // or read a list from a Links web part

  //Find the link list and hide it
  var x = document.getElementsByTagName("TABLE"); // find all of the Tables
  var LinkList;
  for (var i=0; i<x.length; i++)
  {
    if (x[i].summary == "MenuLinks")
    {
      // OK, we found it
```

```
      LinkList = x[i];
      // now hide it, unless we are in the maintenance pages for the list
      if (document.location.href.indexOf("MenuLinks")<0)
      {
        //hide the links list web part (tables in tables in tables!)
  x[i].parentNode.parentNode.parentNode.parentNode.parentNode.parentNode.parentNode.pare
  ntNode.parentNode.style.display="none";
      }
    }
  }

  // Copy all of the links from the link list to the select list
  if (LinkList)
  {
    var links = LinkList.getElementsByTagName("A");  // find all of the links
    for (i=2; i<links.length; i++)
    {
    var a = Array(3);
      if (document.all) // is IE
       { a[0] = links[i].parentNode.previousSibling.innerText; }
      else            // is Firefox or other
       { a[0] = links[i].parentNode.previousSibling.textContent;}

      a[1] = links[i].innerHTML;
      a[2] = links[i].href;
      if (document.all) // is IE
       { a[3] = links[i].parentNode.nextSibling.innerText; }
      else            // is Firefox or other
       { a[3] = links[i].parentNode.nextSibling.textContent;}

      CustomMenuArray.push(a);
    }
  }

  // Find the Top Link Bar area and update the links that match the MenuLinks table
  var navArea = document.getElementById('onetIdTopNavBarContainer');
  var tds = navArea.getElementsByTagName('a');

  // find tabs that match the first column of the array
  for (var i=0; i<tds.length; i++)
  {
```

```
   for (var itm=0; itm<CustomMenuArray.length; itm++)
   {
     var innerText;
     if (document.all) // is IE
      { innerText = tds[i].innerText; }
     else           // is Firefox or other
      { innerText = tds[i].textContent;}

     if (innerText == CustomMenuArray[itm][0])
     {
       // change the hyperlink to display the custom menu
       var t = tds[i];
       t.href="#";
       t.onclick= function() {CustomMenuToggle(this)};
       t.onmouseover= function() {CustomMenuToggle(this)};

       // add a dropdown arrow
       tds[i].innerHTML += ' <img src="_layouts/images/menudark.gif" border="0" style="border-style:none;vertical-align:middle;"/>'
       break;
     }
   }

  }
}
// Code to handle the mouse over or click on the Top Link Bar tab
function CustomMenuToggle(mnu)
{
  var tab = mnu.parentNode.parentNode.parentNode.parentNode;
  var mydiv = document.getElementById('customdropdowns');

  // if menu is displayed, then hide it and exit
  if (mydiv.style.display != 'none')
  {
    mydiv.style.display='none';
    return false;
  }

  // position the dropdown DIV
  var x= getElementAbsolutePos(tab).x
```

```
  var y= getElementAbsolutePos(tab).y
  mydiv.style.left = x;
  mydiv.style.top = y + 18;



  // build the menu
  var s = "";
  s += '<table class="ms-banner ms-topnav"  cellpadding=0 cellspacing=0 >';

  for (var j=0; j<CustomMenuArray.length; j++)
  {
    var innerText;
      if (document.all) // is IE
      { innerText = mnu.innerText; }
      else          // is Firefox or other
      { innerText = mnu.textContent;}

    if (CustomMenuArray[j][0] + " " == innerText) // then add to the menu
    {
      s += '<tr xonmouseout="CustomMenu_Unhover(this)" xonkeyup="Menu_Key(this)" xonmouseover="CustomMenu_HoverDynamic(this)" onmouseover="Menu_HoverDynamic(this)" onmouseout="Menu_Unhover(this)" >';
      s += '<td >';
      s += '<table class="ms-topNavFlyOuts" cellpadding="0" cellspacing="0" border="0" width="100%">';
      s += '<tr>';
      s += '<td style="white-space:nowrap;width:100%;">';
      s += '<a class="ms-topNavFlyOuts" href="';
      s += CustomMenuArray[j][2] + '" ';
      if (CustomMenuArray[j].length>2)
        s += ' title="' + CustomMenuArray[j][3] + '" ';
      else
        s += ' title="' + CustomMenuArray[j][2] + '" ';

      s +='" style="border-style:none;font-size:1em;">';

      s +=CustomMenuArray[j][1];

      s += '</a>';
      s += '</td>';
      s += '</tr>';
```

```
    s += '</table></td>';
    s += '</tr>';
  }

 }
 s += '</table>';
 mydiv.innerHTML = s;
 mydiv.style.display='inline';

 return false;
}


// change the Top Link Bar highlights
function CustomMenu_Unhover(item)
{
  item.childNodes[0].childNodes[0].className="ms-topNavFlyOuts";

item.childNodes[0].childNodes[0].childNodes[0].childNodes[0].childNodes[0].childNodes[0].className="ms-topNavFlyOuts";
}
function CustomMenu_HoverDynamic(item)
{
  item.childNodes[0].childNodes[0].className="ms-topNavFlyOuts ms-topNavFlyOutsHover";

item.childNodes[0].childNodes[0].childNodes[0].childNodes[0].childNodes[0].childNodes[0].className="ms-topNavFlyOuts ms-topNavFlyOutsHover";
}

// make sure SharePoint has completely loaded the page
_spBodyOnLoadFunctionNames.push("CustomMenuSetup");

</script>
```

Add Dropdown Menus to the Top Link Bar (2010)

With a number of edits, I have gotten the 2007 example above to work with SharePoint 2010, but I'm not satisfied with the appearance of the result. Check Link 1000 every once in a while for updates.

User Interface Customization

Create Your Own Custom Menus

SharePoint creates Quick Launch using a slightly customized version of the ASP.NET menu control (<asp:Menu>). You can use the asp:Menu control to create your own custom menus. The example given here is for a static menu. While in this example all of the menu items will be hard coded in the page, if you have AJAX or 2010 client side API skills then you could populate the menu with data from a SharePoint list. (Check Link 1000 to see if I have finally put together an example of this.)

The asp:Menu control has two parts, a header that controls the display of the menu and an Items section with the individual menu items. Notice that the items section is hierarchical and can support many levels of sub-menus. Do a web search for "asp:menu" for more information on the customization options.

- **Menu controls are "server controls" and cannot be used in a Content Editor Web Part.** These controls must be added to pages using SharePoint Designer.

- **When added to a master page, the menu controls must be between the page's <form> and </form> tags.**

- **When added to a site pages the controls must be placed inside of an <asp:content> area.** The most common location would be inside the PlaceHolderMain content area.

Sample asp:Menu:

```
<asp:Menu ID="Menu1" runat="server"
      StaticDisplayLevels="1"
      MaximumDynamicDisplayLevels="2"
      Orientation="Vertical"
>
 <Items>
  <asp:MenuItem Text="Forms" >
   <asp:MenuItem Text="Expense Reimbursement" ToolTip="Travel and non-entertainment" navigateurl="/forms/expenses.xls"/>
   <asp:MenuItem Text="Purchase Order" ToolTip="Purchase Orders under $500" navigateurl="/forms/po.xls"/>
  </asp:MenuItem>
  <asp:MenuItem Text="Mangement Reports">
   <asp:MenuItem Text="Sales Year To Date" ToolTip="for sales team only" navigateurl="/reports/salesYTD.xls"/>
   <asp:MenuItem Text="Plant Floor KPIs" ToolTip="Key Performance Indicators" navigateurl="/forms/plantfloorkpis.xls"/>
   <asp:MenuItem Text="Product Inventory" ToolTip="Product Inventory Report" navigateurl="/forms/inventory.xls"/>
```

```
      </asp:MenuItem>
    </Items>
</asp:Menu>
```

Here is what the above would look like when added to the bottom of a 2010 Basic Page. With **StaticDisplayLevels** set to "1" this is a pop-out menu

With **StaticDisplayLevels** set to "2" there are no pop-outs and the menu is a more fixed design. You can also see the ToolTip here.

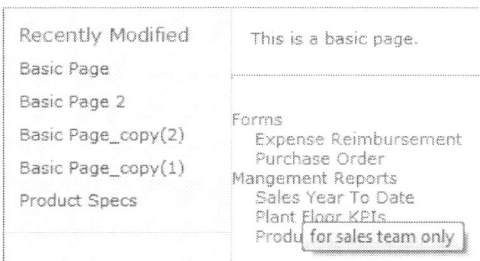

Asp:Menu or SharePoint:AspMenu

The **SharePoint:AspMenu** control can do everything the **Asp:Menu** can do, plus it can format itself to look like QuickLanch! When working with SharePoint 2010 you can simply add two more attributes, **CssClass="s4-ql"** and **UseSimpleRendering="true"** and get a SharePoint Quick Launch style menu.

2010 version:

```
<SharePoint:AspMenu ID="Menu1" runat="server"
      StaticDisplayLevels="2"
      MaximumDynamicDisplayLevels="2"
      Orientation="Vertical"
      UseSimpleRendering="true"
      CssClass="s4-ql"
      >
<Items>
    ...
</Items>
```

User Interface Customization

```
</SharePoint:AspMenu>
```

And now it looks like Quick Launch (this is the SP 2010 example):

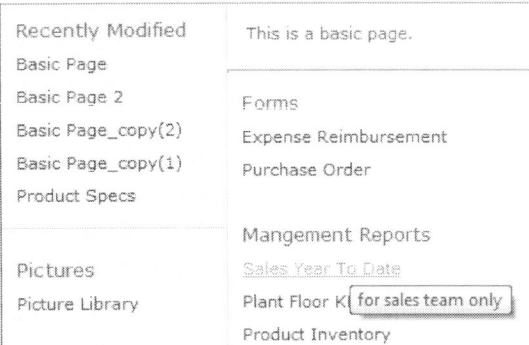

If you want the SharePoint 2007 version to be an exact match to Quick Launch formatting then you will need to wrap the entire menu inside of a <div> or <span> and set the class to **"ms-quickLaunch"**. You will also need to add the CSS classes by adding **LevelMenuItemStyles, LevelSubMenuStyles** and **LevelSelectedStyles** sections to the menu control.

2007 version:

```
<div class="ms-quickLaunch">
 <SharePoint:AspMenu ID="Menu1" runat="server"
      StaticDisplayLevels="2"
      MaximumDynamicDisplayLevels="2"
      Orientation="Vertical"
      >
      <LevelMenuItemStyles>
            <asp:MenuItemStyle CssClass="ms-navheader"/>
            <asp:MenuItemStyle CssClass="ms-navitem"/>
      </LevelMenuItemStyles>
      <LevelSubMenuStyles>
            <asp:SubMenuStyle CssClass="ms-navSubMenu1"/>
            <asp:SubMenuStyle CssClass="ms-navSubMenu2"/>
      </LevelSubMenuStyles>
      <LevelSelectedStyles>
            <asp:MenuItemStyle CssClass="ms-selectednavheader"/>
            <asp:MenuItemStyle CssClass="ms-selectednav"/>
      </LevelSelectedStyles>
   <Items>
      ...
```

```
    </Items>
  </SharePoint:AspMenu>
</div>
```

2007 version:

> **Forms**
> * Expense Reimbursement
> * Purchase Order
>
> **Mangement Reports**
> * Sales Year To Date
> * Plant Fl[for sales team only]
> * Product Inventory

More menu options!

You have a number of options to further customize the menu. First start by looking at the QuickLaunch use of <SharePoint:AspMenu> in the master page. Then do a web search for "asp:menu" to find the MSDN documentation and to see what others are doing with this control.

As a teaser, here are some of the attributes for the asp:Menu control that will work with both SharePoint menus (Quick Launch) and your own custom ASP menus.

Images:

- PopOutImageUrl - An optional image displayed in a menu item to indicate that the menu item has a dynamic submenu.
- SeparatorImageUrl - An optional image displayed at the bottom of a menu item to separate it from other menu items.

Menu item CSS style properties:

- DynamicHoverStyle - The style settings for a dynamic menu item when the mouse pointer is positioned over it.
- DynamicMenuItemStyle - The style settings for an individual dynamic menu item.
- DynamicMenuStyle - The style settings for a dynamic menu.
- DynamicSelectedStyle - The style settings for the currently selected dynamic menu item.
- StaticHoverStyle - The style settings for a static menu item when the mouse pointer is positioned over it.

- StaticMenuItemStyle - The style settings for an individual static menu item.
- StaticMenuStyle - The style settings for a static menu.
- StaticSelectedStyle - The style settings for the currently selected static menu item.

Image properties:

- DynamicBottomSeparatorImageUrl - An optional image displayed at the bottom of a dynamic menu item to separate it from other menu items.
- DynamicPopOutImageUrl - An optional image displayed in a dynamic menu item to indicate that it has a submenu.
- DynamicTopSeparatorImageUrl - An optional image displayed at the top of a dynamic menu item to separate it from other menu items.
- ScrollDownImageUrl - The image displayed at the bottom of a menu item to indicate that the user can scroll down to view additional menu items.
- ScrollUpImageUrl - The image displayed at the top of a menu item to indicate that the user can scroll up to view additional menu items.
- StaticBottomSeparatorImageUrl - An optional image displayed at the bottom of a static menu item to separate it from other menu items.
- StaticPopOutImageUrl - An optional image displayed in a static menu item to indicate that it has a submenu.
- StaticTopSeparatorImageUrl - An optional image displayed at the top of a static menu item to separate it from other menu items.

Template properties:

- DynamicItemTemplate - The template that contains the custom content to render for a dynamic menu item.
- StaticItemTemplate - The template that contains the custom content to render for a static menu item.

Change or Replace Your Home Page

I frequently get questions on changing the home page or using another page as the home page:

- Can I have three (or four or five or…) columns in the default home page?
- Do I have to use the new wiki home page in my Team Site?

- I want to test a new home page design, but I don't want to lose the existing home page... (just in case you know...)
- How can I use a page from my wiki library as my home page?

If you don't want to directly edit the home page you can create a new Basic Page, Web Part page, or in 2010 a wiki page

Below are two ways to set another page as your home page: (both work for both 2007 and 2010)

- From Site Settings (If the publishing features are enabled)
- From SharePoint Designer

If you are a developer or a SharePoint server administrator then you can also change the default home page by using SharePoint API or PowerShell. See Link 1007

Important note for all all methods: Make sure all of your users have at least read access to the new home page, and if in a library that you have it checked in and published.

If the publishing features are enabled for a site then:

1. Click Site Actions, Site Settings, Welcome Page
   2007:

   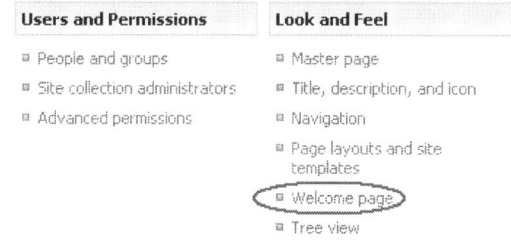

   2010:

2. Enter the URL to the page (that was easy!)

From SharePoint Designer:

1. Open your site in SharePoint Designer
2. In SharePoint 2010 click the push pin in All Files to expand the file list
3. Find your new web page, either in the root of the site or in a library

User Interface Customization

4. Right-click the new page and click "Set as Home Page".

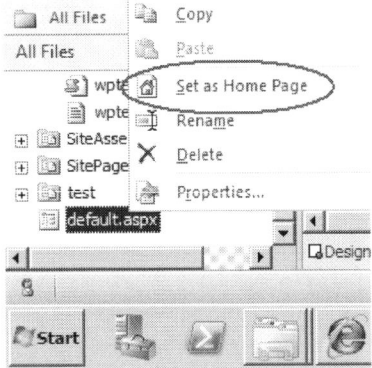

> For SharePoint 2007 this only appears to work from SharePoint Designer if the file is in the root of the site. I.e. the same place as **default.aspx**.

Add Colors, Borders and Fonts to Web Parts

You will often want to make one web part stand out from all of the others on a page. Or you may even want to change the way all web parts are displayed. You can easily do this with Cascading Style Sheets (CSS).

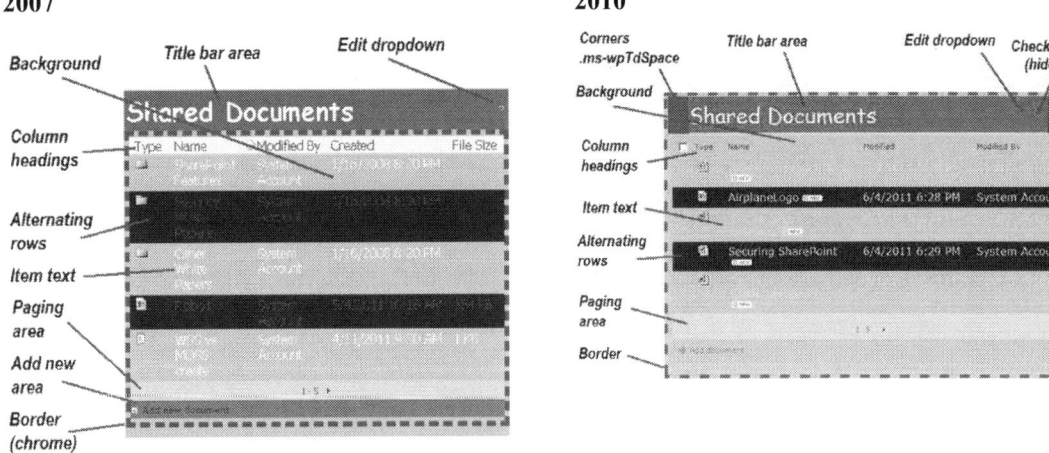

> Full size and full color versions of these pictures are available at Link 1009 and Link 1010.

> You can make similar changes dynamically using JavaScript or jQuery, See Link 1008.

Do you want to change all the web parts in all of the site's pages, all web parts in a single page or just one web part? Each of these will require a slightly different approach.

- **All web parts in all pages?**
  Add the CSS to the master page, either inline or linked to a file
- **All web parts in a single page?**
  Add the CSS directly to the page using SharePoint Designer or in a Content Editor Web Part
  (If using a CEWP, add the web part below the web parts to change, i.e. last zone, last web part)
- **Just one web part?**
  Add the CSS the same way as for a single page, but prefix all of the CSS entries with the ID of the web part to change

CSS Examples

Below you will find samples of CSS to customize web parts. These are offered as examples to get you started. You probably will never use all of them, and will certainly use different values for the fonts, colors and sizes.

Single web part?

In the sample CSS you will find a selector named #MSOZoneCell_WebPartWPQ*somenumber*. This selector is used to select a single web part. To find the selector for your web part, visit the web part page, use the browser's "View Source" option and search for your web part's name ("Shared Documents") and browse up to find the ID. You could also search for "#MSOZoneCell_WebPartWPQ" and browse down to find your web part's name. Be aware that this ID may change if you rearrange the web parts on the page! It will also likely change if you delete a web part and later put it back.

All web parts?

SharePoint 2010 has a CSS class defined for all web parts, **s4-wpcell**, that is useful for setting properties for the entire web part. SharePoint 2007 does not have a class defined for the entire web part table. This is why in the sample CSS below you will see #MSOZoneCell_WebPartWPQ1 to #MSOZoneCell_WebPartWPQ*somenumber*. In theory you could have up to fifty web parts on a page, so I guess "somenumber" could go as high as fifty. Check the source of your web part page to confirm your ID numbers.

2007 or 2010?

The CSS used for SharePoint 2010 is quite different from the CSS used in SharePoint 2007. Make sure you are using the right set of CSS in the sample that follow.

SharePoint 2007 Web Parts

Here is a terribly abused web part :-) that has an exaggerated set of colors and fonts to make each area stand out. The CSS for web parts is quite complicated and there are many parts of the web part that can be

User Interface Customization

changed. The CSS below will create the example shown here. In your work you would add CSS for only the parts you want to change.

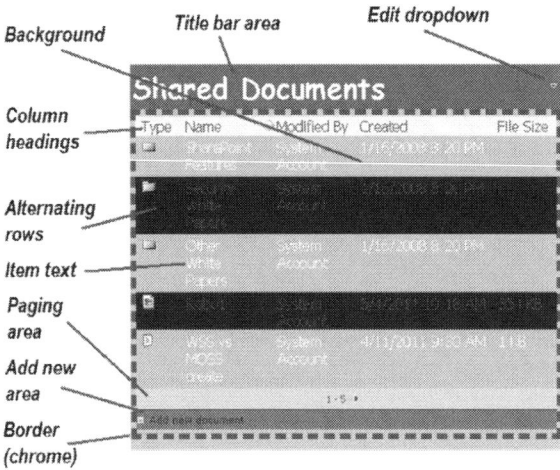

The 2007 CSS

As you play with the web part CSS, try one edit at a time.

Notes:

- The order you define the CSS can impact the final result.
- The use of "!important" after the CSS can override existing inline styles.
- You don't need to use all of the CSS in these examples. Pick and choose as needed.
- Any area can be hidden by using: display:none
- This is not a complete list of what you can change in a web part. Search the HTML source of your web part page for ideas, or do a web search to see what other people are doing.
- "#MSOZoneCell_WebPartWPQ5" is the ID of a single web part to change. This is only needed when changing a single web part on a single page. Your web part will have a similar ID, but with a different number.
- The number in the web part ID may change if the web part is moved on the page.
- Anywhere that there is a CSS background property you can usually set a background image by using:
  background-image:url(' someimagepath ');
- Colors can be set using color names ("green") and color numbers ("#00FF00")

2007 CSS to change all of the web parts on a page

To change all pages, add this CSS to your master page. To change a single page, add this CSS to a Content Editor Web Part or edit the page with SharePoint Designer and add the CSS just before the end tag for the PlaceHolderMain <asp:Content> tag. If using a Content Editor Web Part, it should be placed as the last web part on the page. This would usually be the last web part in the last column of the bottom most web part zone.

Note that the following is only a collection of samples. This is not a copy and paste for your web part.

```css
<style type="text/css">

/* CSS for web parts */


/* === Title bar CSS === */

/* TR - title bar for web part */
.ms-WPHeader
{
  background-color:green;
}

/*  H3 - Text in title bar of web part */
.ms-WPTitle, .ms-WPTitle a
{
  color:white !important;
  font-family:"Comic Sans MS";
  font-size:24pt;
}



/* === Web part background CSS === */

/* TD - paging area (i.e. 1 - 5) */
.ms-bottompaging td
{
  background-color:yellow !important;
}
```

```css
/* hide or change the gray line above "add new" link */
.ms-partline
{
  /* display:none; */
  background-color:red;
}

/* "add new" area */
.ms-addnew
{
  background-color:gray !important;
}

/* There could be up to 50 web parts on a page (only 20 in this example) */
/* Use your browser's View Source feature to check your zone names */
#MSOZoneCell_WebPartWPQ1,
#MSOZoneCell_WebPartWPQ2,
#MSOZoneCell_WebPartWPQ3,
#MSOZoneCell_WebPartWPQ4,
#MSOZoneCell_WebPartWPQ5,
#MSOZoneCell_WebPartWPQ6,
#MSOZoneCell_WebPartWPQ7,
#MSOZoneCell_WebPartWPQ8,
#MSOZoneCell_WebPartWPQ9,
#MSOZoneCell_WebPartWPQ10,
#MSOZoneCell_WebPartWPQ11,
#MSOZoneCell_WebPartWPQ12,
#MSOZoneCell_WebPartWPQ13,
#MSOZoneCell_WebPartWPQ14,
#MSOZoneCell_WebPartWPQ15,
#MSOZoneCell_WebPartWPQ16,
#MSOZoneCell_WebPartWPQ17,
#MSOZoneCell_WebPartWPQ18,
#MSOZoneCell_WebPartWPQ19,
#MSOZoneCell_WebPartWPQ20
{
  background-color:lightgreen;
}
```

```css
/* === Column headings === */

/* color for sortable column headings */
/* there are many "diid" IDs, and this list is not complete */
.ms-vh2 .ms-vb, .ms-vh2 .ms-vb a,
#diidSortEditor, #diidSortAuthor,
#diidSortCheckoutUser, #diidSortAssignedTo,
#diidSortTaskGroup, #diidSortLinkFilenameNoMenu, #diidSortCustomUrl,
th.ms-vh2-nograd
{
  color:red !important;
  font-size:12pt;
}


/* === List text CSS === */

/* TD - item description text (for odd numbered rows) */
.ms-vb,
.ms-vb2,
.ms-vb a,
.ms-vb2 a
{
  color:white !important;
  font-size:12pt;
}

/*  TR - background alternating (for even numbered rows) */
 .ms-alternating
{
  background-color:navy;
}

/*  TD - text for alternating (for even numbered rows) */
.ms-alternating .ms-vb,
.ms-alternating .ms-vb2,
.ms-alternating .ms-vb a,
.ms-alternating .ms-vb2 a
{
  color:red !important;
}
```

User Interface Customization

```css
/* border (if enabled in the web part's properties */
.ms-WPBorder
{
  border-color:red;
  border-width:thick;
  border-style:dashed;
}



/* background and text for list web parts without column headings */
/* links list, calendar list... */
/* web parts with no items "There are currently no..." */
.ms-summarycustombody td,
.ms-summarycustombody td a
{
  background-color:yellow !important;
  color:red !important;
}


</style>
```

2007 CSS to change a single web part

To select a single web part you will use the same CSS as above, but prefix each item with the ID of the web part. To find this ID use your browser's View Source feature and search for the name of your web part. Somewhere above this you will find a #MSOZoneCell_WebPartWPQ*somenumber* that represents your web part.

Here's what you might find if looking for the "Airshow Pictures" web part:

```html
<table width="100%" cellpadding="0" cellspacing="0" border="0">
    <tr>
        <td id="MSOZoneCell_WebPartWPQ16" valign="top">
        <table toplevel="" border="0" cellpadding="0" cellspacing="0" wi
            <tr>
                <td>
                <table border="0" cellpadding="0" cellspacing="0" width=
                    <tr class="ms-WPHeader">
                        <td title="Airshow Pictures"> - Pictures from the
                        <h3 class="ms-standardheader ms-WPTitle">
                        <a accesskey="W" tabindex="0" href="/sites/train
```

2007 CSS for web part #MSOZoneCell_WebPartWPQ17

Note that the following is only a collection of samples. This is not a copy and paste for your web part.

```css
<style type="text/css">

/* CSS for web parts */


/* === Title bar CSS === */

/* TR - title bar for web part */
#MSOZoneCell_WebPartWPQ17 .ms-WPHeader
{
  background-color:green;
}

/*  H3 - Text in title bar of web part */
#MSOZoneCell_WebPartWPQ17 .ms-WPTitle, #MSOZoneCell_WebPartWPQ17 .ms-WPTitle a
{
  color:white !important;
  font-family:"Comic Sans MS";
  font-size:24pt;
}



/* === Web part background CSS === */

/* TD - paging area (i.e. 1 - 5) */
#MSOZoneCell_WebPartWPQ17 .ms-bottompaging td
{
  background-color:yellow !important;
}

/* hide or change the gray line above "add new" link */
#MSOZoneCell_WebPartWPQ17 .ms-partline
{
  /* display:none; */
  background-color:red;
}
```

```css
/* "add new" area */
#MSOZoneCell_WebPartWPQ17 .ms-addnew
{
  background-color:gray !important;
}

/* There could be up to 50 web parts on a page */
/* Use your browser's View Source feature to check your zone names */
#MSOZoneCell_WebPartWPQ17
{
  background-color:lightgreen;
}



/* === Column headings === */

/* color for sortable column headings */
/* there are many "diid" IDs, and this list is not complete */
#MSOZoneCell_WebPartWPQ17 .ms-vh2 .ms-vb, #MSOZoneCell_WebPartWPQ17 .ms-vh2 .ms-vb a,
#MSOZoneCell_WebPartWPQ17 #diidSortEditor, #MSOZoneCell_WebPartWPQ17 #diidSortAuthor,
#MSOZoneCell_WebPartWPQ17 #diidSortCheckoutUser, #MSOZoneCell_WebPartWPQ17 #diidSortAssignedTo,
#MSOZoneCell_WebPartWPQ17 #diidSortTaskGroup, #MSOZoneCell_WebPartWPQ17 #diidSortLinkFilenameNoMenu,
#MSOZoneCell_WebPartWPQ17 #diidSortCustomUrl,
#MSOZoneCell_WebPartWPQ17 th.ms-vh2-nograd
{
  color:red !important;
  font-size:12pt;
}



/* === List text CSS === */

/* TD - item description text (for odd numbered rows) */
#MSOZoneCell_WebPartWPQ17 .ms-vb,
```

```css
#MSOZoneCell_WebPartWPQ17 .ms-vb2,
#MSOZoneCell_WebPartWPQ17 .ms-vb a,
#MSOZoneCell_WebPartWPQ17 .ms-vb2 a
{
  color:white !important;
  font-size:12pt;
}

/* TR - background alternating (for even numbered rows) */
#MSOZoneCell_WebPartWPQ17 .ms-alternating
{
  background-color:navy;
}

/* TD - text for alternating (for even numbered rows) */
#MSOZoneCell_WebPartWPQ17 .ms-alternating .ms-vb,
#MSOZoneCell_WebPartWPQ17 .ms-alternating .ms-vb2,
#MSOZoneCell_WebPartWPQ17 .ms-alternating .ms-vb a,
#MSOZoneCell_WebPartWPQ17 .ms-alternating .ms-vb2 a
{
  color:red !important;
}

/* border (if enabled in the web part's properties */
#MSOZoneCell_WebPartWPQ17 .ms-WPBorder
{
  border-color:red;
  border-width:thick;
  border-style:dashed;
}


/* background and text for list web parts without column headings */
/* links list, calendar list... */
/* web parts with no items "There are currently no..." */
#MSOZoneCell_WebPartWPQ17 .ms-summarycustombody td,
#MSOZoneCell_WebPartWPQ17 .ms-summarycustombody td a
{
  background-color:yellow !important;
  color:red !important;
```

User Interface Customization

```
}
</style>
```

More?

There's always more you can change! Use your browser's "View Source" feature to explorer the HTML and CSS delivered by SharePoint to see what else you can do. You can also use the add-in developer tool bars for Internet Explorer and Firefox to explore the CSS. Some of the cool CSS things you may want to do will probably not work in all browsers, especially Internet Explorer 6, so test, test, test.

Also take a look at the CSS reference and branding blogs on the web like these: Link 1011 and Link 1012.

SharePoint 2010 Web Parts

Here is another terribly abused web part :-) that has an exaggerated set of colors and fonts to make each area stand out. The CSS for web parts is quite complicated and there are many parts of the web part that can be changed. The CSS below will create the example shown here. In your work you would add CSS for only the area you want to change.

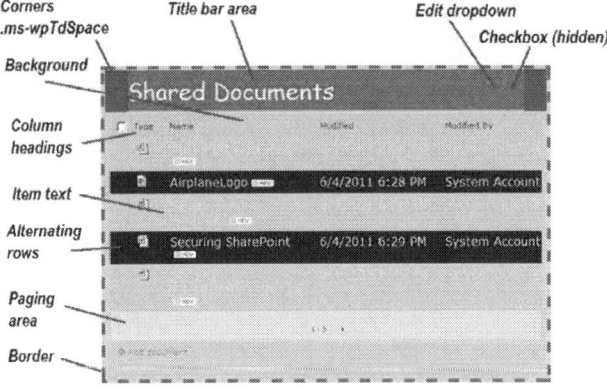

The 2010 CSS

Notes:

- The order you define the CSS can impact the final result.
- The use of "!important" after the CSS can override existing inline styles.
- You don't need to use all of the CSS. Pick and choose as needed.

User Interface Customization

- This is not a complete list of what you can change in a web part. Search the HTML source of your web part page for ideas, or do a web search to see what other people are doing.
- "#MSOZoneCell_WebPartWPQ5" is the ID of a single web part to change. This is only need when changing a single web part on a single page. Your web part will have a similar ID, but with a different number.
- The number in the web part ID may change if the web part is moved on the page.
- "#MSOZoneCell_WebPartWPQ5.ms…" vs. "#MSOZoneCell_WebPartWPQ5<space>.ms…"
  The space is used to indicate a CSS parent-child relationship. With the space, CSS looks for an element with an ID of "#MSOZoneCell_WebPartWPQ5" and then looks for a child element with a class name of "ms…". Without the space, CSS looks for single element that has both the ID and the class name.
- Anywhere there is a CSS background property you can also set a background image by using:
  background-image:url(' someimagepath ');
- Colors can be set using color names ("green") and color numbers ("#00FF00")
- The .ms-wpTdSpace class name is used to identify the corners or ends of the web part's title area. If you don't define anything for these they stay hidden. See the links at the end of this article for ideas for taking advantage of these corner areas. (How about rounded tab-like corners!)

2010 CSS for a single web part (#MSOZoneCell_WebPartWPQ5 in this example)

Note that the following is only a collection of samples. This is not a copy and paste for your web part.

```
<style type="text/css">

/* === Title bar CSS === */

/* TR - title bar for web part */
#MSOZoneCell_WebPartWPQ5 .ms-WPHeader
{
  background-color:green;
}

/*  H3 - Text in title bar of web part */
#MSOZoneCell_WebPartWPQ5 .ms-WPTitle a
{
  color:white;
  font-family:"Comic Sans MS";
  font-size:24pt;
}
```

```css
/* TD - far left and far right (corner) cells of title bar - useful for round corner tricks */
#MSOZoneCell_WebPartWPQ5 .ms-wpTdSpace
{
  /* background-image:url(' someimagepath '); */
  width:30px !important;
  background-color:red;
}

/* web part check box */
#MSOZoneCell_WebPartWPQ5 .ms-WPHeaderCbxHidden
{
  display:none;
}


/* === Web part background CSS === */

/*  TD - background for all but title bar of web part */
#MSOZoneCell_WebPartWPQ5.s4-wpcell
{
  background-color:lightgreen;
  /* border-style:dashed; */
  border-style:dashed;
  border-width:5px;
}

/* TD - paging area (i.e. 1 - 5) */
#MSOZoneCell_WebPartWPQ5 .ms-bottompaging td
{
    background-color:yellow !important;
}

/* hide the gray line above "add new" link */
#MSOZoneCell_WebPartWPQ5 .ms-partline
{
  display:none;
}

/* selected (clicked) web part background */
#MSOZoneCell_WebPartWPQ5.s4-wpActive
```

```css
{
  background-color:fuchsia;
  border-color:red;
    /* border-style:dotted; */
}


/* === Column headings === */

/* color for sortable column headings */
#MSOZoneCell_WebPartWPQ5 .ms-vh-div a
{
  color:red !important;
}
/* color for non-sortable column headings */
#MSOZoneCell_WebPartWPQ5 .ms-vh-div
{
  color:red !important;
}


/* === List text CSS === */

/* item description text */
#MSOZoneCell_WebPartWPQ5 .ms-vb2,
#MSOZoneCell_WebPartWPQ5 .ms-vb-user a,
#MSOZoneCell_WebPartWPQ5 .ms-vb-title a
{
  color:yellow !important;
  font-size:12pt;
}

/*  TR - alternating (#2,#4,#6...) row of web part */
#MSOZoneCell_WebPartWPQ5 .ms-alternating
{
  background-color:navy;
}

</style>
```

2010 CSS for all web parts in a page or site (masterpage)

Note that the following is only a collection of samples. This is not a copy and paste for your web part.

```css
<style type="text/css">

/* === Title bar CSS === */

/* TR - title bar for web part */
.ms-WPHeader
{
  background-color:green;
}

/*  H3 - Text in title bar of web part */
.ms-WPTitle a
{
  color:white;
  font-family:"Comic Sans MS";
  font-size:24pt;
}

/* TD - far left and far right (corner) cells of title bar - useful for round corner tricks */
.ms-wpTdSpace
{
  /* background-image:url(' someimagepath '); */
  width:30px !important;
  background-color:red;
}

/* web part check box */
.ms-WPHeaderCbxHidden
{
  display:none;
}


/* === Web part background CSS === */

/*  TD - background for all but title bar of web part */
```

```css
.s4-wpcell
{
  background-color:lightgreen;
  /* border-style:dashed; */
  border-style:dashed;
  border-width:5px;
}

/* TD - paging area (i.e. 1 - 5) */
.ms-bottompaging td
{
    background-color:yellow !important;
}

/* hide the gray line above "add new" link */
.ms-partline
{
  display:none;
}

/* selected (clicked) web part background */
.s4-wpActive
{
  background-color:fuchsia;
  border-color:red;
    /* border-style:dotted; */
}


/* === Column headings === */

/* color for sortable column headings */
.ms-vh-div a
{
  color:red !important;
}
/* color for non-sortable column headings */
.ms-vh-div
{
  color:red !important;
}
```

```
/* === List text CSS === */

/* item description text */
.ms-vb2,
.ms-vb-user a,
.ms-vb-title a
{
  color:yellow !important;
  font-size:12pt;
}

/*  TR - alternating (#2,#4,#6...) row of web part */
.ms-alternating
{
  background-color:navy;
}
</style>
```

More?

There's always more you can change! Use your browser's "View Source" feature to explorer the HTML and CSS delivered by SharePoint to see what else you can do. You can also use the add-in developer tool bars for Internet Explorer and Firefox to explore the CSS. Some of the cool CSS things you may want to do will probably not work in all browsers, especially Internet Explorer 6, so test, test, test.

Want rounded corners on your web parts? See these web articles: Link 1013 and Link 1014

Don't forget Links lists!

Navigation is more than just the Top Link Bar, Quick Launch and the Tree View. Anything the user can click on is part of site navigation. This includes announcement web parts and especially Links lists. Links lists are so much fun they have their own chapter. Chapter 14 includes:

- Adding Pop-ups to Links lists (open the link in a in new window)
- Add a "You are leaving this site" message
- Convert a Links list to a Dropdown list
- and more…

11. List and Library Customization

Do you need this chapter?

Yes... nuff said.

Lists and libraries are the heart of SharePoint. The old over used phrase "everything is a list in SharePoint" is almost true, and because so many things are lists, many of the customizations in this chapter can be used on multiple list types.

What's in this chapter?

- The list is so long that you will need to take a look at the next page: "What's in this chapter?"

A few of the list types invite special customization and have received their own chapters:

- Surveys - chapter 12
- Links Lists - chapter 13
- Task Lists - chapter 14
- Calendars - chapter 15

✏ Also see " Add Colors, Borders and Fonts to Web Parts" in chapter 10.

List and Library Customization

Before you get started

In this chapter we will be looking at a number of customizations that can be applied to several list types. If you would really like to know how these kinds of customizations work then you should take the time to go through the first one, "Color coded lists", in step by step detail.

The Content Editor Web Part

Most of the customizations in this chapter impact a single list or web part and will most likely be added using a Content Editor Web Part (CEWP). Before attempting these, go and read chapter 9 as in this chapter I am assuming you know how to add JavaScript and CSS to a Content Editor Web Part or a linked file. Because of changes to the CEWP in 2010 there are often separate instructions and code for SharePoint 2007 and 2010.

SharePoint Designer

Many of the customizations can be added directly to a page using a CEWP or SharePoint Designer. To impact all pages in all sites they can be added to the master page using SharePoint Designer. For details on editing with SharePoint Designer see chapter 6.

Has your site been "branded" or your lists customized?

If you have a customized master page, or you have customized or changed the order of columns in the lists, then you may have to adjust the code in the examples to match your customizations.

What's in this chapter?

In this chapter the customizations are grouped by the primary list or library type. While reviewing these, keep in mind that many of these customizations can be used on other list and library types.

- General
    - Color coded lists
    - Redirecting to a page after adding a New item to a list
    - Group By on more than two columns in a view
    - Removing Group Headings from a View's Group By
    - Adding a bar chart to a list

- Web Part Customizations
    - Create a "What's New" web part for a library or list
    - Add a Web part for a document library folder
    - Hide a web part with zero rows
    - Change the "No Items" message in a discussion web part
    - Change the "Add New" message for a web part

List and Library Customization

- Libraries
    - Adding hyperlinks to document libraries
    - How do to add a column (meta data) to SharePoint folders
    - Hiding Upload Multiple and Explorer View
    - Hiding the Checked Out Icon from Anonymous Users
    - One library, multiple sites!
    - Synchronize Document Library Web Part Column Widths
    - Prevent Accidental Overwrites when Uploading to a Library
    - The List, the Whole List, Nothing but the List

- Picture Libraries
    - Rotating Pictures, Random Pictures

Color coded lists

SharePoint lists can be boring with nothing but row after row of text. We often need to make selected list items stand out from the rest, in progress tasks for example, and color is one way we might do this. SharePoint does not have an out of the box way to set colors based on the data in a list or a library. There are both third party web parts and open source projects, such as those at codeplex.com, that can color code lists, but these usually require installing code on the SharePoint web servers. In this customization we will look at color coding lists just using the built-in Content Editor Web Part along with a little JavaScript.

Each list will need a slightly different fragment of JavaScript to set the colors. This customization will show a generic approach, but there are a few other customizations in the book that focus on specific lists:

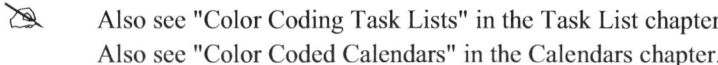
Also see "Color Coding Task Lists" in the Task List chapter.
Also see "Color Coded Calendars" in the Calendars chapter.

Here are three examples:
- Set color backgrounds for rows in a task list to show the status of the task:

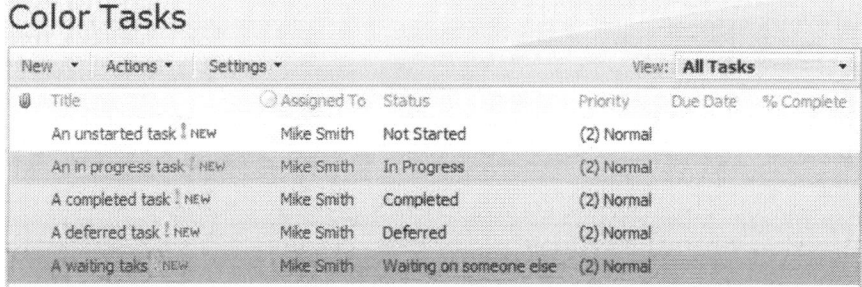

237

List and Library Customization

- Set colors in libraries to show approval status:

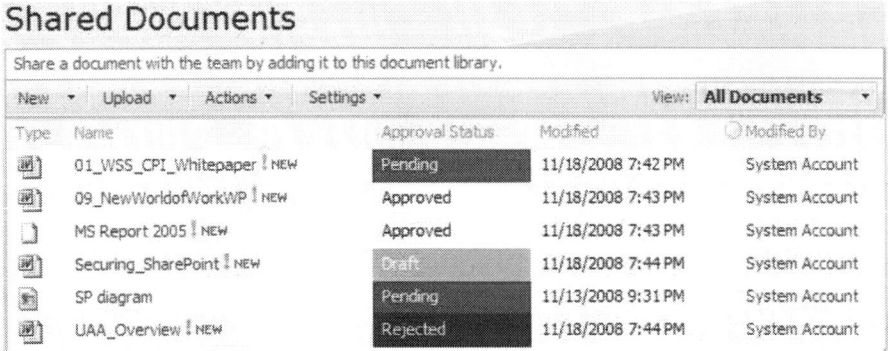

- Set the color of a single column based on its value:

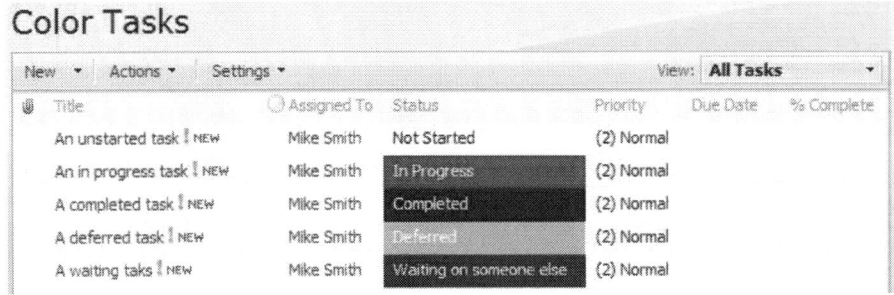

How can you do this?

Microsoft used HTML tables to layout SharePoint lists. HTML table tags have nice parent/child relations that let us easily determine the cell (<TD>), row (<TR>) or table (<TABLE>) that contains a piece of data, and once found, an easy way to find the parent or child of a tag. For example, the parent of a <TD> is a <TR>. If we have found a <TD> using JavaScript and stored it in a variable named **MyTD** we can modify the <TR> with **MyTD.parentNode.***propertyToChange*. As an example, once we have found a <TD> we can make the entire row green with **MyTD.parentNode.style.backgroundColor='green'**.

Finding the <TD>

We can just create a JavaScript loop using a FOR statement to check every <TD> in a page, but there are a lot of <TD> tags in a SharePoint page, especially SharePoint 2007. A better way is to find a pattern for <TD> tags in web parts. With a little detective work with your browser's View Page Source feature you will find that <TD> tags in web parts have a CSS class of "ms-vb2". Here's a loop to find a <TD> that contains a certain piece of text and then change the row's background to green:

```
// get all of the TDs
var x = document.getElementsByTagName("TD");   // find all of the TDs
```

List and Library Customization

```
// loop through all of the TDs
for (var i=0;i<x.length;i++)
{
  // find those that are in web parts
  if (x[i].className == "ms-vb2") //find the TDs styled for lists
  {
    // find a TD that has the text "Not Started"
    if (x[i].innerHTML == "Not Started")   //find the data to use to determine the color
    {
      // do some work (like set a color)
      x[i].parentNode.style.backgroundColor = 'lightgreen';
    }
  }
}
```

To make the above work you will need to know exactly what is inside of the <TD>. For a task list Status column there is just the text, "Not Started" for example. (<TD>Not Started</TD>) In some lists there may be additional HTML tags such as a <NOBR>, <SPAN> or <IMG>. This additional text/html will need to be considered in your code. Let's look at a few of the list TD's and their content.

A typical cell in a task list Status column:

```
<TD Class="ms-vb2">Not Started</TD>
```

A typical cell in a date valued column:

```
<TD Class="ms-vb2"><NOBR>4/13/2009 10:17 AM</NOBR></TD>
```

A typical cell with a numeric column:

```
<TD Class="ms-vb2"><DIV align=right>123</DIV></TD>
```

A typical cell with is the item's title (has the item options dropdown list):

```
<td width="100%" Class="ms-vb">
  <a onfocus="OnLink(this)" href="/sites/training/Lists/Tasks/ ….
    This is a task title
    <img src="/_layouts/images/blank.gif" class="ms-hidden" ….
  </a>
  <IMG SRC="/_layouts/1033/images/new.gif" alt="New">
```

List and Library Customization

```
</td>
```

To deal with these more complex examples you can just change your IF test from an exact match test:

```
if (x[i].innerHTML == "your search text")
```

To a partial match test:

```
if (x[i].innerHTML.toString().indexOf("your search text ") > -1)
```

☞ indexOf returns the position of the first matching character. It returns -1 if there is no match.

Let's color code a library

The example below uses a custom column to decide which color to use, but you could use Approval Status or any other column with predictable text.

Add a custom column (optional):

This example adds a "Review Status" choice column to a document library.

1. In 2007, click **Settings** and **Create Column**
   In 2010 click the **Library** ribbon tab and then the **Create Column** button
2. Add a title such as "**Review Status**", select the column type of **Choice**, add a few choices (my example uses "Pending", "In progress" and "Completed") and click **OK** to save the column (Leave "Add to default view" checked!)

Create a new view (optional)

This customization will work with both a view page and with a web part in any other page. If you are working with a view page you may want to leave the default views alone when first experimenting with these customizations. Also, if you add a Content Editor Web Part to a SharePoint 2010 view page you will "break" a few view features (more on this later - also see "SharePoint 2010, the Content Editor Web Part, and Broken Views" in chapter 8).

1. SharePoint 2007: In the library click **Settings** and **Create View** (or click **Create View** from the **View** dropdown menu)
   SharePoint 2010: In the library, click the **Library** tab of the ribbon and click the **Create View** button
2. Create a **Standard View** (or start from a copy of the **All Documents** view)
   Note: The sample steps below only work on Standard views - there is a example for Calendar views in chapter 15.
3. Select your columns for the view and be sure to include the column used to determine the color ("Review Status" in this example)

4. If you enable grouping, set the groups to be expanded
5. Save the view

A view with a custom "Review Status" column:

Type	Name	Modified	Modified By	Review Status
	01_WSS_CPI_Whitepaper	3/1/2011 9:18 PM	MICROSMITHINC\admin	Pending
	05_IDCReportcomparing_WS03	3/1/2011 9:18 PM	MICROSMITHINC\admin	In progress
	07_FY05_Vision_Paper_Connected Productivity_IW_Ent.MM_Final.06_16_04	3/1/2011 9:18 PM	MICROSMITHINC\admin	Pending
	08_Navigant2005_Connecting_people_to_info	3/1/2011 9:18 PM	MICROSMITHINC\admin	Completed
	09_NewWorldofWorkWP	3/1/2011 9:18 PM	MICROSMITHINC\admin	Pending
	10_Windows_XP_Upgrade_Business_Benefits	3/1/2011 9:18 PM	MICROSMITHINC\admin	Pending
	11_WinXP_and_Office_with_abstract	3/1/2011 9:18 PM	MICROSMITHINC\admin	In progress
	Anti-phishing_White_Paper	3/1/2011 9:18 PM	MICROSMITHINC\admin	Completed
	MicrosoftCRMSQL2005Upgrade	3/1/2011 9:32 PM	MICROSMITHINC\admin	Completed

Determine how the <TD> tag is formed in the page

Display the new view and use the browser's View Source option. Search the source HTML for one of the key words ("In progress") and note what's inside of the <TD>...</TD> tag pair. In a choice column you will just find the <TD> tags and the text:

```
<td class="ms-vb2">In progress</td>
```

Add the JavaScript

We have several options for adding JavaScript to a page:

- Add a Content Editor Web Part and add the JavaScript using the **Source Editor** button (2007) or the **HTML** button in the ribbon (2010) (see chapter 9)
- Add the JavaScript to a text file, upload the file to a library, add a Content Editor Web Part and add the URL to the text file to the **Content Link** box (see chapter 9)
- Edit the page in SharePoint Designer and add the JavaScript somewhere below the list web part (see chapter 6)

The first option works well for SharePoint 2007 because the page is never customized or "un-ghosted". In SharePoint 2010 the first option can fail as 2010 "edits" the JavaScript and may damage the code.

The second option works in both versions, but SharePoint 2010 will not consider a page with a web part to be a view. When 2010 displays this page, the view dropdown in the crumb trail is not displayed and the page is not listed in the ribbon's view menu. (See "SharePoint 2010, the Content Editor Web Part, and Broken Views" in chapter8) If you are not customizing a view page, then either the second or third option will work for 2010.

List and Library Customization

The third approach works for both versions with no side issues for 2010. The page will be customized (un-ghosted) and will have a minor impact on performance.

I recommend the first and second for SharePoint 2007 and the third for 2010, especially when working with a view page.

SharePoint 2007: Add the Content Editor Web Part and JavaScript:

1. Display the view page to color code (if you want to color code multiple views of a list then each view will need its own web part and JavaScript)
2. Add a Content Editor web part:
    a. Site Actions, Site Settings, Edit Page
    b. Add a Content Editor web part and move it below the calendar web part
    c. Move this web part so it is below the list you are color coding
    d. Click in the web part, click **Edit, Modify Shared Web Part**, and in the **Appearance** section change **Chrome** to **None**.
3. Add the JavaScript
    a. Click the **Source Editor** button
    b. Type or paste the JavaScript (examples below)

SharePoint 2010: Use SharePoint Designer to add the code to a view page:

1. From the view page click **Site Actions** and then **Edit in SharePoint Designer**
2. Click **Lists and Libraries** in the **Site Object** pane and click on your list or library name
3. In the **Views** section of the screen click your view
4. After the view has loaded, click the **Code** tab at the bottom of the page and then click the **Advanced Mode** button in the ribbon
5. Find the two lines below in the page code and insert the JavaScript between these two lines

```
</ZoneTemplate></WebPartPages:WebPartZone>
    your code goes here
</asp:Content>
```

6. Save your changes and click **OK** for the customization message
7. Go to a browser and test your page

The result, color! (as if most of you holding a black and white book could tell)

Type	Name	Modified	Modified By	Review Status
	01_WSS_CPI_Whitepaper	3/1/2011 9:18 PM	MICROSMITHINC\admin	Pending
	05_IDCReportcomparing_WS03_to_previous	3/1/2011 9:18 PM	MICROSMITHINC\admin	In progress
	07_FY05_Vision_Paper_Connected Productivity_IW_Ent.MM_Final.06_16_04	3/1/2011 9:18 PM	MICROSMITHINC\admin	Pending
	08_Navigant2005_Connecting_people_to_info	3/1/2011 9:18 PM	MICROSMITHINC\admin	Completed
	09_NewWorldofWorkWP	3/1/2011 9:18 PM	MICROSMITHINC\admin	Pending
	10_Windows_XP_Upgrade_Business_Benefits	3/1/2011 9:18 PM	MICROSMITHINC\admin	Pending
	11_WinXP_and_Office_with_abstract	3/1/2011 9:18 PM	MICROSMITHINC\admin	In progress
	Anti-phishing_White_Paper	3/1/2011 9:18 PM	MICROSMITHINC\admin	Completed
	MicrosoftCRMSQL2005Upgrade	3/1/2011 9:32 PM	MICROSMITHINC\admin	Completed

The JavaScript

```javascript
<script type="text/javascript">

var x = document.getElementsByTagName("TD") // find all of the TDs
for (var i=0; i<x.length; i++)
{

  if (x[i].className == "ms-vb2") //find the TDs styled for lists
  {

   if (x[i].innerHTML == "Pending") //find the data to use to determine the color
   {
     x[i].parentNode.style.backgroundColor='white';   // set the color
   }

  // repeat the above for each additional data value

   if (x[i].innerHTML == "In progress")
   {
     x[i].parentNode.style.backgroundColor = 'lightgreen'; // set the color
   }

   if (x[i].innerHTML=="Completed")
   {
     x[i].parentNode.style.backgroundColor = 'lightblue'; // set the color
   }

  // add additional IF blocks for each key word
```

List and Library Customization

```
    }

}
</script>
```

Customizing the "New" button

Let's say you wanted to put a link on the home page of your site that your users could click to add a site comment, meeting request or any other list entry. When they complete the list's "new" form you might want the user to be directed to a "Thank You" page, or even back to the home page. This is actually pretty easy to do using a little copy and paste and some more detective work.

In the examples that follow we will use an office supplies request list. It's a simple list, but not one where most users need to browse through all of the list items. They only need to add new items.

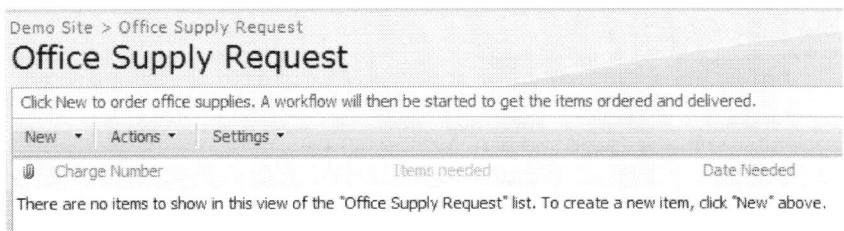

While we can do this customization in both SharePoint 2007 and 2010, there are a few differences in details, so we will show each separately.

Add Quick Launch Link to Create a New Item - 2007

To get the user to the newpage.aspx form of a list without the user first going to the list is easy. Go to the list, click the **New** button and note the URL. Copy the URL and paste it as a link in Quick Launch, a link in an Announcement, a entry in a Links list or a link in a Content Editor Web Part. Here is the link added to Quick Launch:

When the user clicks your link they will go directly to the New item page of the Office Supplies list.

List and Library Customization

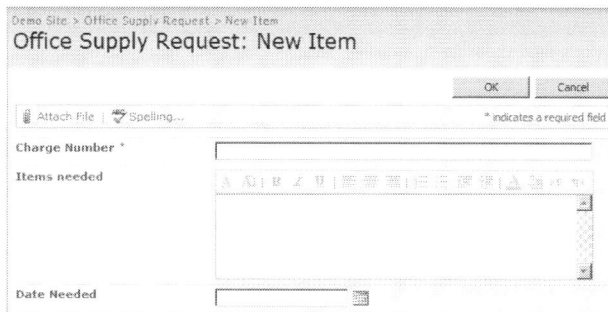

Absolute or Relative URLs?

Best practice for links from one page in a site to another page in the same site is to use a relative URL (no HTTP or server name) so your link will work when you have both internet and intranet access to the same site, or even after IT renames your SharePoint server. If you are sending the URL in an Email or adding it to another SharePoint site collection then you will need to use the absolute URL.

Look at the "new item" URL again; it will be something like this:

```
http://www.yourserver.com/sites/demo/Lists/OfficeSupplyRequest/NewForm.aspx?RootFolder=%2Fsites%2Fdemo%2FLists%2FOfficeSupplyRequest&Source=http%3A%2F%2Fwww%2Eyourserver%2Ecom%2Fsites%2Fdemo%2FLists%2FOfficeSupplyRequest%2FAllItems%2Easpx
```

The name of the server is in the URL twice. To convert it into a relative URL remove the "http://" and the server name both places.

```
/sites/demo/Lists/OfficeSupplyRequest/NewForm.aspx?RootFolder=%2Fsites%2Fdemo%2FLists%2FOfficeSupplyRequest&Source=%2Fsites%2Fdemo%2FLists%2FOfficeSupplyRequest%2FAllItems%2Easpx
```

Now use this edited URL as your Quick Launch link.

Redirect to another Page after Clicking OK - 2007

By default, after a new item is added, the user is redirected to the default view of the list. If the user linked from a home page to the New Item page you will probably want to return them to the home page when finished. Or, you may want to send them to a "thank you" page or a confirmation page. The solution is pretty simple, just edit the URL again and replace the URL text after "&Source=" with the URL of your destination page.

/sites/demo/Lists/OfficeSupplyRequest/NewForm.aspx?RootFolder=%2Fsites%2Fdemo%2FLists%2FOfficeSupplyRequest**&Source=%2Fsites%2Fdemo**

"%2Fsites%2Fdemo" is the escaped version of the relative URL that would otherwise look like "/sites/demo" if it was not escaped. If you wanted to send them to a "thank you" page that you created from a Basic Page you might have a URL that looks like this:

/sites/demo/Lists/OfficeSupplyRequest/NewForm.aspx?RootFolder=%2Fsites%2Fdemo%2FLists%2FOfficeSupplyRequest**&Source=%2Fsites%2Fdemo/Shared%20Documents/ThankYou.aspx**

 Is the escaping of special characters required? The safe answer is yes. In many cases you can get away without escaping the special characters, but if you have two question marks or an unescaped ampersand in the wrong spot the URL may not work.

Common character encoding:

%2F	/
%2E	. (period)
%27	& (ampersand)
%20	a space
%25	% (percent)

See Link 1105 for a complete list.

Add Quick Launch Link to Create a New Item - 2010

The steps in 2010 are similar to the steps for the 2007 version above, once we adjust for the new pop-up dialog box way of display the New and Edit forms. Go to the list, click the **New** button in the ribbon and you will see the New form display in a dialog box. Now right-click in any blank area outside of the text boxes of the pop-up form, click **Properties** and then copy the URL.

List and Library Customization

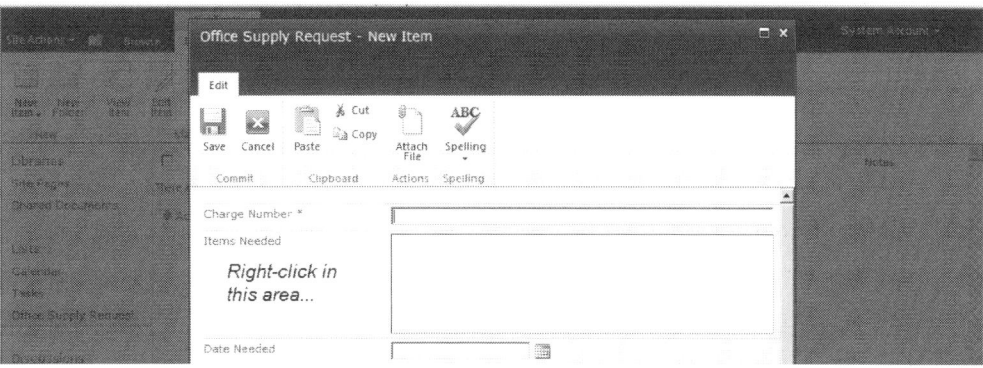

The 2010 URL will look like this:

http://www.yourserver.com/sites/training/Lists/OfficeSupplyRequest/NewForm.aspx?RootFolder=%2Fsites%2Ftraining%2FLists%2FOfficeSupplyRequest**&IsDlg=1**

To directly link to this page remove the "&IsDlg=1" from the end of the URL. Best practice is to also convert the URL to a relative URL by removing the server name.

/sites/training/Lists/OfficeSupplyRequest/NewForm.aspx?RootFolder=%2Fsites%2Ftraining%2FLists%2FOfficeSupplyRequest

 Adding "&IsDlg=1" to a URL will not cause the page to open in a dialog box, rather it will cause the page to open with formatting appropriate for a dialog box and will not display most of the master page, including the navigation tabs and Quick Launch.

Now add the URL to Quick Launch, an Announcement or a Content Editor Web Part hyperlink.

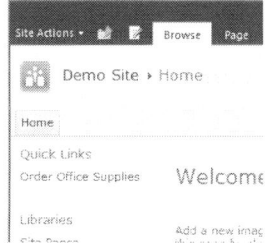

List and Library Customization

Redirect to another Page after Clicking OK - 2010

The steps here are the same as the 2007 steps except you are adding, instead of replacing, "&Source=" to the URL to specify where to go after the user clicks OK.

> http://www.yourserver.com/sites/training/Lists/OfficeSupplyRequest/NewForm.aspx?RootFolder=/sites/training/Lists/OfficeSupplyRequest**&Source=/sites/training/SitePages/ThankYou.aspx**

Note: the "RootFolder=" part of the URL should only be needed when you are using folders in the list. So when not using folders, a shorter version of the above might look like this:

> http://www.yourserver.com/sites/training/Lists/OfficeSupplyRequest/NewForm.aspx**?Source=/sites/training/SitePages/ThankYou.aspx**

Note that the first parameter in the URL uses a "?" while all that follow use "&". You should also convert this to a relative URL.

Redirect the Cancel Button (2007)

The redirect steps above redirect both the OK and the Cancel button to the "Source" URL. Here's how to add a "CancelDestination" parameter to the query string to set the destination for the cancel button.

Steps:

1. Go the "New Item" page in your browser
2. Edit the URL and add "&ToolPaneView=2" to the end of the URL to put the page in edit mode

> http://yourserver/sites/sales/Lists/Announcements/NewForm.aspx?RootFolder=%2fsites%2fsales%2fLists%2fAnnouncements&Source=http%3a%2f%2fyourserver%2fsales%2fyoursite**&ToolPaneView=2**

3. Click "**Add a Web Part**" and add a Content Editor Web Part (CEWP)
4. Move the CEWP below the existing list web part
5. Edit the CEWP and click the **Source Editor** button
6. Add the JavaScript from below
7. Save your changes and exit the edit mode of the page
8. Create a URL similar to the one earlier in the article, but add a new parameter named "&CancelDestination=http://yourcanceldestination"

248

List and Library Customization

```
http://www.yourserver.com/sites/sales/Lists/Tasks/NewForm.aspx?RootFolder=%2FLists%2FT
asks&Source=http%3A%2F%2Fwww.yourserver.com%2Fsites%2Fsales&CancelDestination
=http%3A%2F%2Fwww.yourserver.com%2Fsites%2Fsales%2FCancelPage.aspx
```

9. Test!

The JavaScript:

```
<script type="text/javascript">

var querystring = window.location.search.substring(1);
var parameters = querystring.split("&");
var QueryString = Array();
for (var i=0;i<parameters.length;i++)
{
  QueryString[parameters[i].split("=")[0]] = parameters[i].split("=")[1];
}
if (QueryString["CancelDestination"] != undefined)
{
  var inputs = document.getElementsByTagName("INPUT");
  for (var i=0; i<inputs.length; i++)
  {
   if (inputs[i].value == "Cancel")
   {
     inputs[i].onclick =
      function () {document.location.href = unescape(QueryString["CancelDestination"])};
   }
  }
}
</script>
```

Redirect the Cancel Button (2010)

The steps for 2010 are identical to the steps for 2007, except for some changes due to the ribbon. These steps use a Content Editor Web Part. You could also add the code directly to the page. See chapter 6.

Steps:

1. Go to the list and click the new item button in the ribbon

2. Right-click any blank area in the dialog box (except for the text boxes) and select **Properties**

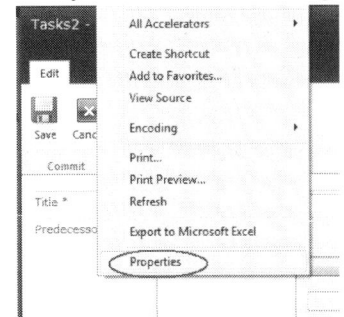

3. Copy the URL from the Properties box excluding "&IsDlg=1" and paste it into a Notepad file so you can get to it later
4. Paste this URL into the browser's address bar and press Enter
5. Click **Site Actions** and **Edit Page**
6. In the page click **Add a Web Part** and add a Content Editor Web Part
7. Move the new web part below the existing list web part
8. In the new web part click "**Click here to add new content**" and then click **HTML** and **Edit HTML Source** in the ribbon
9. Add the JavaScript from the 2007 version listed earlier and click **OK**
10. Click the **Page** ribbon tab and then click **Stop Editing**
11. Copy the URL you pasted to Notepad and paste it into the browser's address bar and append "&CancelDestination=" plus the URL to your cancellation page:

    &CancelDestination=http%3A%2F%2Fwww.yourserver.com%2Fsites%2Fsales%2FCancelPage.aspx

    or: (encoded version above is preferred)

    &CancelDestination=http://www.yourserver.com/sites/sales/CancelPage.aspx

12. Press Enter, click one of the Cancel buttons and see if it works!

Group By on more than 2 columns in a view

In my SharePoint classes I have often been asked how to group on more than two levels in a view. I have always given the quick answer of "use SharePoint Designer"! That was not fair as there are a number of steps needed to get there, a large number.

The problem

SharePoint views in both 2007 and 2010 are limited to only two levels of grouping. So while you can group State and then City, you cannot group on State, then City, then Customer. SharePoint views also have a few quirks you might also want to fix while you are at it.

Here's an example with three levels of grouping and sub totals at the bottom of each group:

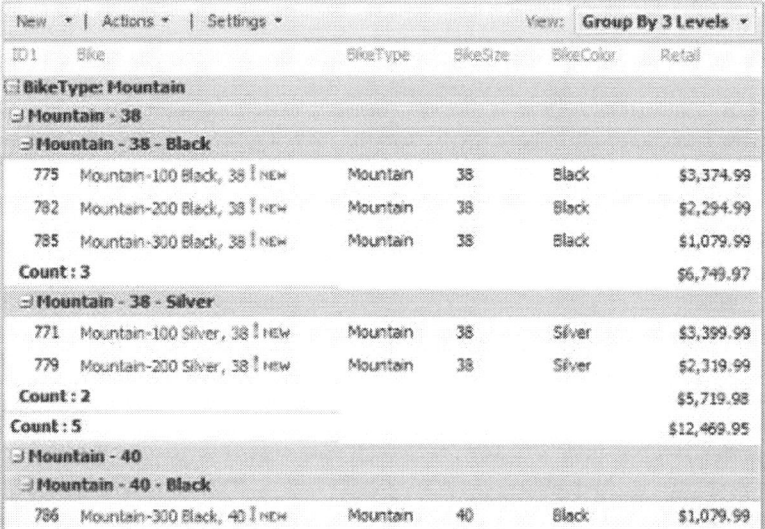

So in this section we will:

- See how to create views with grouping on more than two levels
- Optionally put counts and totals at the bottom of each section instead of at the top
- Optionally remove unwanted group heading text
- Optionally add some color to the view
- Over all, create a nice looking report!

Secrets and Tricks needed:

- It can't be done "out of the box" in the browser - SharePoint Designer is needed
- You need to convert the view web part to a SharePoint Designer Data Form Web Part
- You need a Sort and Group secret
- You need to fix the footer rows
- You need to manually add your totals, averages, counts etc.

SharePoint 2007 vs. 2010

SharePoint 2010 uses a new web part to display lists in views. That along with a much changed SharePoint Designer means that we will have two sets of steps in this customization, one for 2007 and one for 2010.

List and Library Customization

Just for some background here are some of the details on how 2007 and 2010 are different. (You can skip this and go right to the steps.)

SharePoint 2007:

- A list in a view is displayed with a ListViewWebPart. This web part is what has all of the limitations that we are trying to fix in this article.
- Using SharePoint Designer we can convert this web part into a DataViewWebPart that does not have these limitations, but also is not nearly as easy to setup as a normal view.

SharePoint 2010:

- A list's view is now being displayed in 2010 using a XsltListViewWebPart and can only be customized with the same options as found when using a browser ("Modify View"). It has the same limitations as found in 2007 (2 levels of grouping etc.).
- For more info on what has changed from the 2007 ListViewWebPart and the XsltListViewWebPart see Link 1102 and Link 1103
- SharePoint Designer 2010 has two web parts for lists:
    - XsltListViewWebPart - this is the web part used when you create a new view
    - DataFormWebPart - created within SharePoint Designer using **Insert, Empty Data View**
- SPD 2010 adds a bit of confusion when trying to add a "Data View":
    - When you click **Insert** and pick an existing list, SPD inserts an XsltListViewWebPart
    - When you click **Insert, Empty Data View**, SPD inserts a DataFormWebPart
- SharePoint 2010 does not consider a page with a DataFormWebPart to be a "view". It only believes that a page is a "view" when it has an XsltListViewWebPart. In 2007 we could create a new view, edit it in SharePoint Designer as much as we wanted, and it was still a view. In 2010, SharePoint will not recognize a page without an XsltListViewWebPart as a view.

My Example:

- I have a simple list with these columns: ID1, Bike, BikeType, BikeSize, BikeColor and Retail (price).
- I want to group this on BikeType, BikeSize, BikeColor, count the items and sum or average the price in each group.

Group By on more than 2 columns in a view (2007)

Steps: (and yes, a lot of them!)

Tip: There are many, many options available in the Data View Web Part used here. For the first time through this process don't change any of the options not listed below. You can always come back and experiment with the rest of the options later!

1. Create a new **Standard View** from the list's **View** menu.
   - Generally don't bother with any options other than selecting the desired columns.
     - Don't set any grouping options, they will mess up the expand / collapse functionality
     - Don't set up any Totals options, they will be ignored
     - Do select the columns needed in your view, both display and grouping
     - Optionally set the filter options (this can also be done in SharePoint Designer)

The "before" – just a standard view with selected columns:

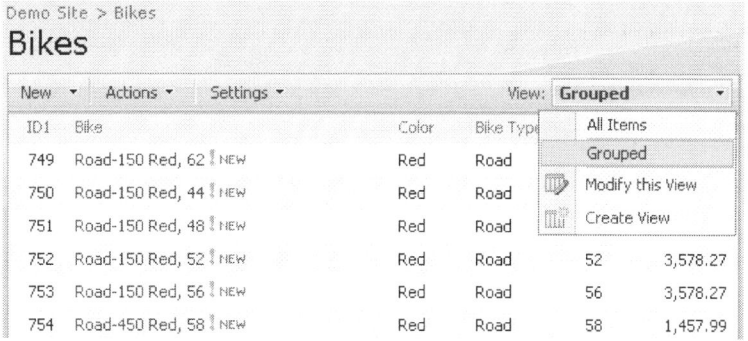

2. Open your site with SharePoint Designer and expand the **Lists** node in the **Folder List** pane.
3. Expand your list's node and double-click on your new view.

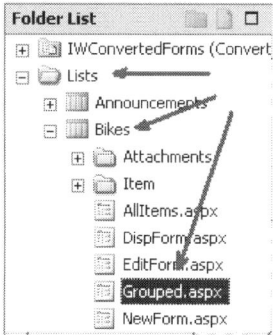

253

List and Library Customization

4. If your view page is not being displayed in the Design view, click the **Design** tab at the bottom of the page.

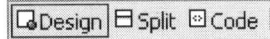

Note: The view is now being displayed using a ListViewWebPart and can only be customized from the browser ("**Modify View**")

5. Right-click in the middle of the view and select **Convert to XSLT Data View**

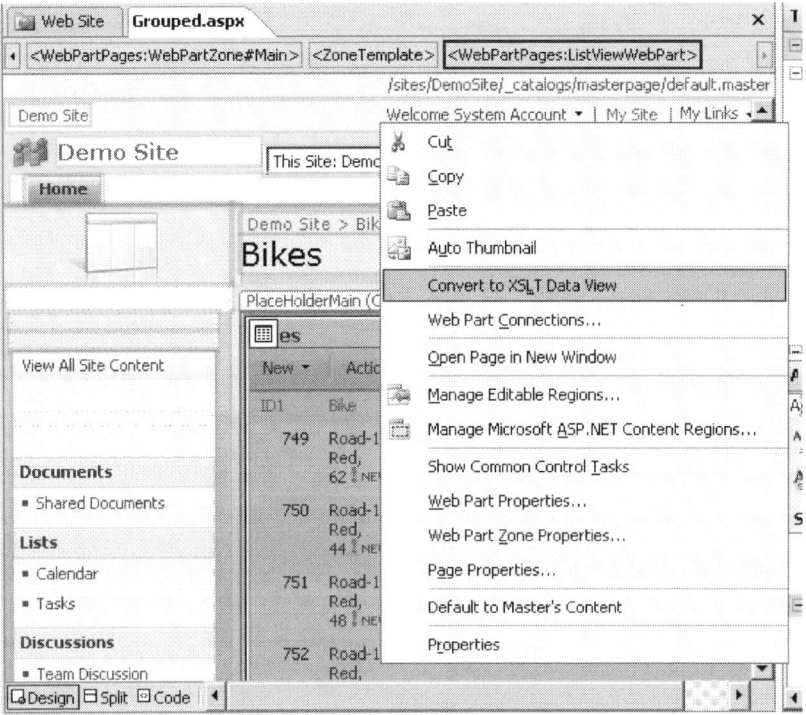

Note: The view is now being displayed using a DataFormWebPart and:

- is no longer a "View" and can no longer be modified from the "Modify this view" - you can now only delete it or rename it from "Modify this view"

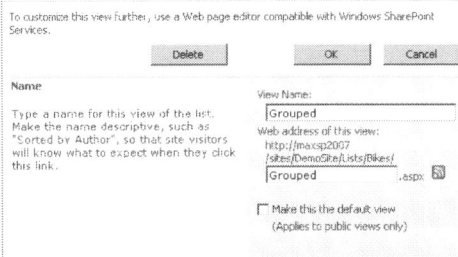

254

- can be customized from SharePoint Designer
- from the browser you can only rename the view
- from the browser you can also use **Site Actions, Edit Page, Modify Shared Web Part** to hand edit the XSLT (but you are very unlikely to want to do this)
- going forward, columns added to the list will not be automatically added to the DataFormWebPart (you can add them from SharePoint Designer)

Your data should now be displayed using the DataFormWebPart. Before moving on, you could also fix up the display of the data (right align some columns, rename column headings, select color, bold, etc). Just click, select and use the SharePoint Designer toolbar for normal HTML style editing.

6. **Save your work!** At this point you may want to click **Save** and review the results so far in a browser. Review the formatting and note the things you need to change. This page is now an unghosted, or customized, page.

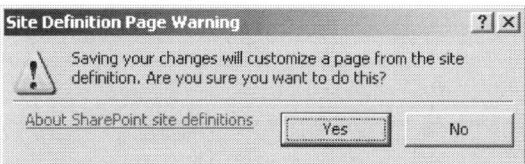

Now add the Sorting and Grouping options...

- For my example I am first grouping on Bike Type, then by Size and Color

7. Right-click the web part and select **Show Common Control Tasks** (or click the pop-out arrow at the top right corner of the control The pop-out is named **Common Data View Tasks**)

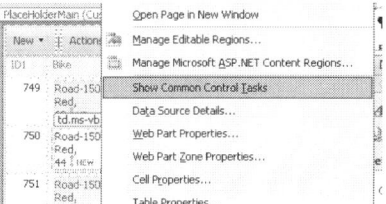

8. Click **Sort and Group**

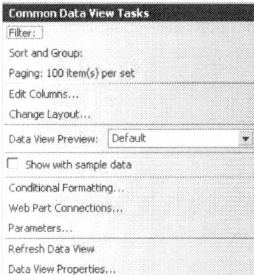

List and Library Customization

9. Remove any sort fields listed in the **Sort order** box

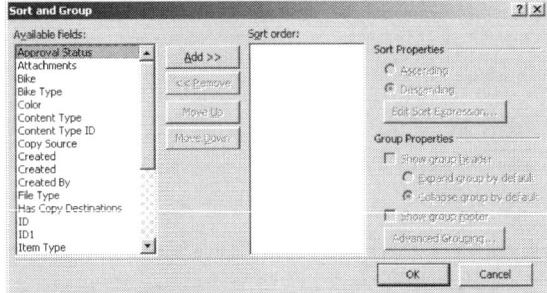

10. Add your top most group:
    - Click the field (BikeType) and
    - Click **Add**
    - Click **Show group header**
    - Click **Collapse group** (optional)
    - Click **Show group footer** (if you want counts and totals)

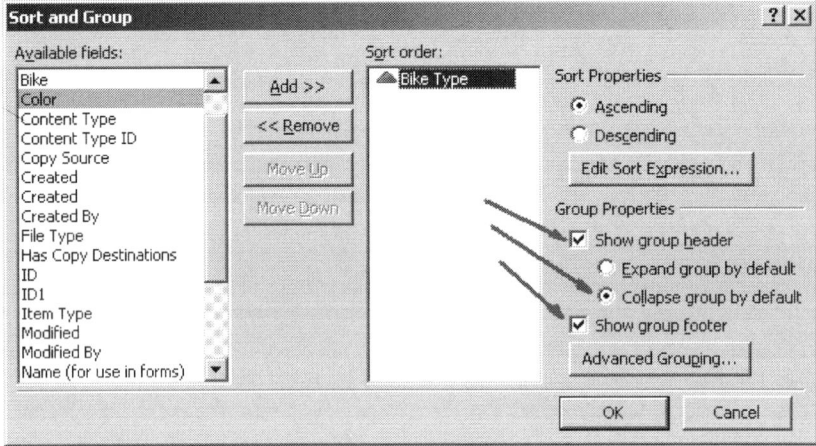

11. Add your second group by clicking the field (Example: Size) and clicking **Add**

    - If you stop here you will have groups, but all of your counts and totals will be wrong! We need to create both the text to display for the group and the hierarchy for the grouping. At the second level of our grouping we need to group on the combination of both columns, "Bike Type" plus "Size"

12. For each grouping field added after the first field, click **Edit Sort Expression** (my example here will add the Size column as the second column)

List and Library Customization

- At a minimum you will need to concatenate the current grouping column with the previous grouping columns, and while you are at it you can add some formatting like adding a "-" as a separator
- Enter:

    concat(@Bike_x0020_Type, " - ", @Size)

    Watch the capitalization! Use the exact name the Intelisense offers – spaces are "encoded" so "Bike Type" in the list is "Bike**_x0020_**Type" in the web part
- Note the preview at the bottom of the dialog box…

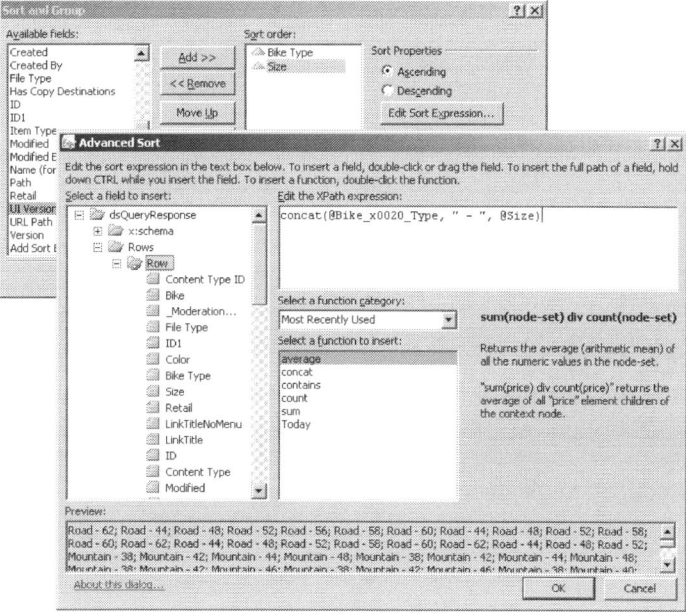

13. For the third and following groups repeat the step above with a Sort Expression similar to:

    concat(@Bike_x0020_Type, " - ", @Size, " - ", @Color)

In each new group include all of the fields from the previous groups along with any separators (dashes, etc.):

concat(@group1field, @group2field, @group3field, @group4field, @group5field, etc)

or

concat(@group1field, " - ", @group2field, " - ", @group3field, " - ", @group4field, " - ", @group5field, etc)

14. Before clicking OK to leave this dialog box, check the order of the groups. They may have changed. The result should look something like this

257

List and Library Customization

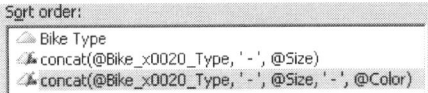

Recheck each of the sort levels to see if these options are still checked:

    Click **Show group header**

    Click **Collapse group** (optional)

    Click **Show group footer** (if you want counts and totals)

15. Optionally add one more column just to sort the data within the last group - do not turn on the group header or group footer options for this sort-only field
16. Click **OK** to close the **Sort and Group** dialog box
    - You will probably want to change the **Paging** options as they default to 100 items per page
    - Right-click the new data and select **Show Common Control Tasks** (or click the pop-out arrow at the top right corner of the control, or select **Paging** from the **Data View** menu)
    - Click **Paging** and pick your options

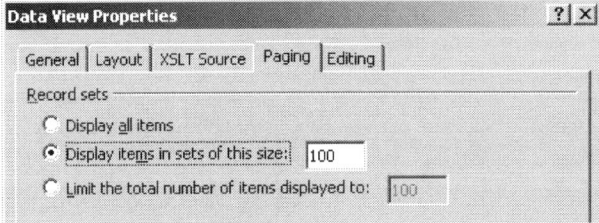

Tip: If you have a lot of data in the list, SharePoint Designer can get really slow. There are two things you could do here, set paging to a small number (not so good for testing multi-level grouping) or from the **Common Control Tasks** popup select **Show With Sample Data**.

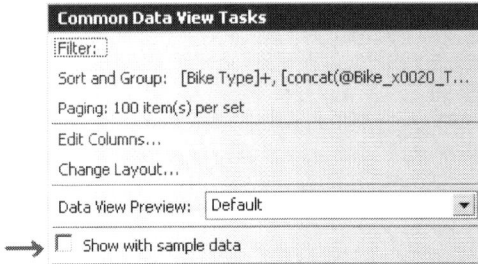

258

List and Library Customization

Tip: If you have a problem finding the **Common Control Tasks** popup, click anywhere in the Data View Web Part and then right-click the little "tab":

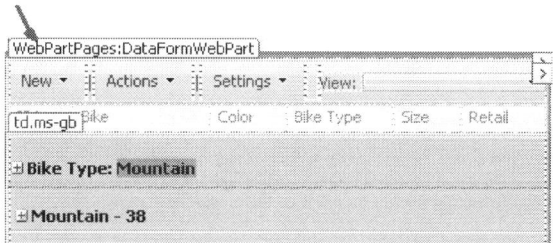

Add Totals to the view

A SharePoint view adds totals and counts at the top of each group. Most reporting tools will have these at the bottom of each group. When you are working with the DataFormWebPart you can choose where to put your summary data, at the top, the bottom or both.

- These steps describe adding totals to the footer rows, but also apply to modifying the header (top of each group) rows.
- The Data View sets up the header and footer rows as a single cell with a column span of 99! To display totals in the same columns as the data you will need to fix these rows.
- You will need to fix each of the group footer rows plus the view footer (last) row.

Explore the HTML to see what's there and what needs to be done:

- In the **Code** view of the page do a search for **colspan="99"**. In my example there will be many of these, one for each grouping footer, one for each grouping header and one for the view footer.
- Now you need to do a little planning. In my example I'd like to put the "**Count=**" in a two column spanned cell under the ID and Bike columns. Then I would like to have one cell under each additional column. So something like:

<td colspan='2'>count stuff</td><td></td><td></td><td></td><td>total goes here</td>

Here's what this footer should look like with the cells (TD's), the count and the total:

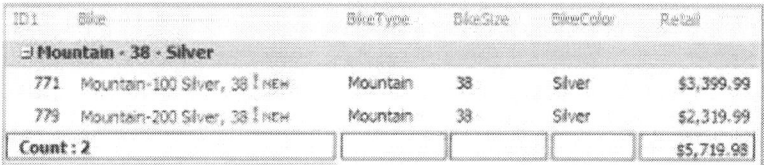

259

List and Library Customization

Steps:
1. Find **colspan="99"** for the first group footer row.
   Tip: Did you find a header or footer row? Look up two lines and you should see either "**<xsl:if test="$showheader"**" or "**<xsl:if test="$showfooter"**"
2. Change the **99** to **2** (The 2 is for my example where I want the count spread out under the ID and Bike columns.)
3. Find the end tag for the cell (**</td>**)   (down about 16 lines of html)
4. After the end tag add the other cells (TD tag pairs), one for each additional column (I need four more for my sample data)
   <td></td> <td></td><td></td><td></td>

Now to add the total...

5. Switch to the **Design** view and you should see the new cells in one of the footer rows
6. Click in the cell where you want to add the total
7. Right-click and select **Insert Formula**
8. Build your formula. For a total, double click "**sum**" in the function list then select your field from the dropdown list. My example needed: **sum(@Retail)**
9. The formula editor does not know one extra piece of information needed here. The **@Retail** field needs to come from the current group only. To get this, update the formula like this:
   sum($nodeset/@Retail)   ("nodeset" is all lower case)

   Tip: How would you have discovered this? Go look at how they calculated the Count: **count($nodeset)**.

10. Notice that the formatting is wrong. The total is left aligned and the wrong size. To match the font and size find the style used for the data in the row above. In my example it looked like this:
    <TD Class="{$IDADW3HE}">
11. Copy the class info (**Class="{$IDADW3HE}"**) into your total cell (the TD tag). The result will look something like this:
    <td Class="{$IDADW3HE}"><xsl:value-of select="sum(@Retail)" /></td>
12. The last step is to right align the cell (you can use the SharePoint Designer toolbar button) and to format the total. To format the number, click in the cell with the total, right-click and select **Format Item As...** and pick your formatting options.

    Note: SharePoint Designer may get creative and merge your formatting into new styles with great names like style1, style2, style3 etc.. If you are curious, do a search for **.style1** (dot style1) and you will find they have placed the style class definition in the **PlaceHolderBodyAreaClass** content placeholder.

13. Fix up each footer row, including the **View Footer**, the same way. Add the extra TDs, add the totals, counts, etc, and format the results

Now about the View Footer... and some things to make your head hurt...

New ▼	Actions ▼	Settings ▼			View:	Group By 3 Levels ▼
ID1	Bike	BikeType	BikeSize	BikeColor		Retail
⊟ BikeType: Mountain						
Count : 18						$45,264.82
⊟ BikeType: Road						
Count : 27						$57,134.51
⊟ BikeType: Touring						
Count : 12						$23,931.96
Totals Count : 57						$126,331.29

The View Footer is built with its own HTML table, so the column widths are not going to line up with the rest of the list. You will need to do some work to create the correct number of TD's and get the width's right. My example above was fairly easy as the count was the first column and the total was the last column, both easy to get lined up.

The grand totals need a special calculation to sum all of the rows. The @Retail field (or @yourfield) needs to come from the entire set of rows. To get this, update the formula like this:

  sum(**/dsQueryResponse/Rows/Row/**@yourfield)   (make sure the capitalization is correct!)

Tip: How would you have discovered this? Go look at how they calculated the Count for the View Footer:
  count(/dsQueryResponse/Rows/Row)

A Bug?

There's a bug with how SharePoint handles the clicks on the Expand and Collapse buttons in the web part. When you click Expand at the top level it also expands all the detail levels. For one possible solution to the problem see Link 1106.

What else can you do with the Data View Web Part?

- Display pictures or thumbnails - See Link 1104

Group By on more than 2 columns in a view (2010)

Warning! SharePoint 2010 does not consider a page with a DataFormWebPart to be a "view". It only believes that a page is a "view" when it has an XsltListViewWebPart". In 2007 we could create a new view, edit it in SharePoint Designer as much as we wanted, and it was still a view. In 2010, SharePoint will not recognize a page without an XsltListViewWebPart as a view.

So before you start...

- If you just need a page with your list nicely grouped, it may be best just to create a web part page and store it in a library, then add the Data Form Web Part using the steps below.
- If you want the page to be treated as a view, leave the XsltListViewWebPart on the page, but make it hidden. Then add the Data Form Web Part below the existing web using the steps below.
- In SharePoint 2010, a view page with an added web part introduces a bug or two. The ribbon will not be displayed. The view name in the page title area will be missing the dropdown to select another view.

Steps: (and yes, a lot of them!)

Tip: There are many, many options available in the Data View Web Part used here. For the first time through this process don't change any of the options not listed below. You can always come back and experiment with the rest of the options later!

1. Create a new **Standard View** from the list's view menu.
   - Don't bother with any view options as we are just going to delete the default list web part.
   - Or just create an empty web part page. (see "Warning" above)

The "before" – just a standard view with selected columns:

	ID1	Bike		Color	Bike Type	Size	Retail
	749	Road-150 Red, 62	NEW	Red	Road	62	3,578.27
	750	Road-150 Red, 44	NEW	Red	Road	44	3,578.27
	751	Road-150 Red, 48	NEW	Red	Road	48	3,578.27
	752	Road-150 Red, 52	NEW	Red	Road	52	3,578.27
	753	Road-150 Red, 56	NEW	Red	Road	56	3,578.27
	754	Road-450 Red, 58	NEW	Red	Road	58	1,457.99
	755	Road-450 Red, 60	NEW	Red	Road	60	1,457.99
	756	Road-450 Red, 44	NEW	Red	Road	44	1,457.99
	757	Road-450 Red, 48	NEW	Red	Road	48	1,457.99
	758	Road-450 Red, 52	NEW	Red	Road	52	1,457.99
	759	Road-650 Red, 58	NEW	Red	Road	58	782.99
	760	Road-650 Red, 60	NEW	Red	Road	60	782.99

2. If starting with an existing view page:
   a. Open your site with SharePoint Designer and click the **Lists and Libraries** node in the **Site Objects** pane
   b. Click your list ("Bikes" in my example)
   c. Click the view you created earlier ("Grouped" in my example)
3. Otherwise create a new web part page in a library
4. If starting with an existing view, delete or hide the existing web part:

List and Library Customization

      a. Delete: In the **Design** window click in the web part, click the **WebPartPages:XsltListViewWebPart** tab, press the Delete key
         or
         in the **Code** window select the entire <WebPartPages:XsltListViewWebPart tag (including the start and end tags) and delete the code
      b. Hide: In the **Design** window click in the web part. In the ribbon in the **List View Tools** section click the **Web Part** tab and then click **Properties**. In the **Layouts** section of properties click **Hidden**

5. Insert an **Empty Data View Web** part
      a. Click the **Insert** ribbon tab and click the **Data View** button
      b. Click **Empty Data View**
6. In the new web part click "**Click here to select a data source**"
7. Click your list and click **OK** (this will open the **Data Source Details Pane**)
8. Select the columns you want in your list (click a field, then Shift-click each additional field)
9. Click the **Insert Selected Fields as** button and click **Multiple Item View**

Note: the view is now being displayed using a DataFormWebPart and:
- it is no longer a "View" and can no longer be modified from the browser
- it can be customized from SharePoint Designer,
- from the browser you can only rename the view,
- from the browser you can also use **Site Actions, Edit Page, Modify Shared Web Part** to hand edit the XSLT,
- new columns added to the list will not be automatically added to the DataFormWebPart. You will need to use SharePoint Designer to manually add the columns to the "view".

Save! At this point you may want to click **Save** and review the results so far in a browser. Review the formatting and note the things you need to change.

Edit the Data View Web Part...

10. Click the web part and note that you now have a **Data View Tools** section in the SharePoint Designer ribbon

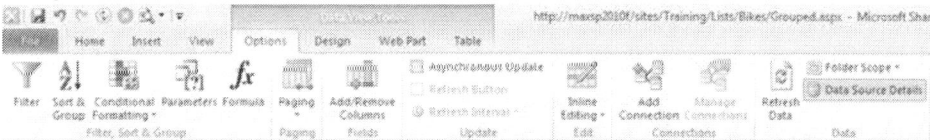

List and Library Customization

11. Click **Sort and Group**

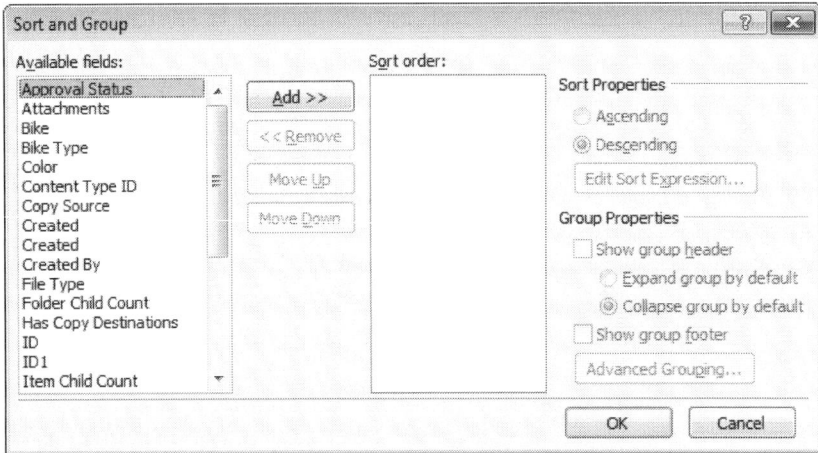

12. Remove any sort fields that may already be in the **Sort Order** box
13. Add your top most group:
    a. Click the field (**BikeType**) and
    b. Click **Add**
    c. Click **Show group header**
    d. Click **Collapse group by default** (optional)
    e. Click **Show group footer** (if you want counts and totals)

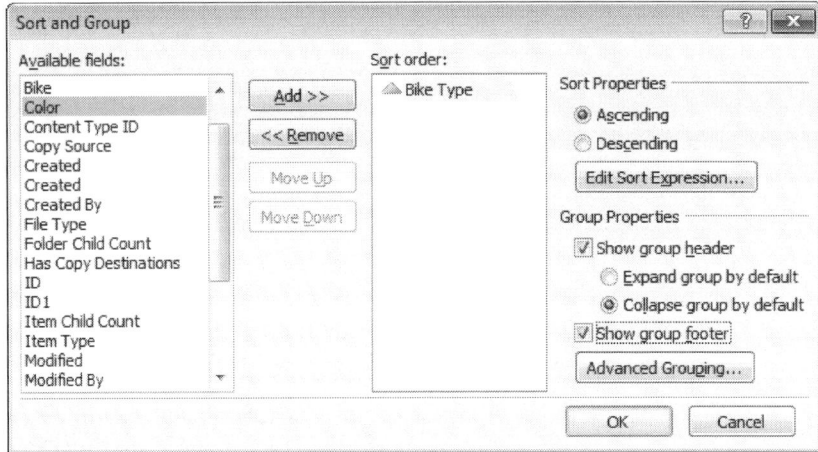

14. Add your second group by clicking the field (Example: Size) and clicking **Add**

    If you stop here you will have groups, but all of your counts and totals will be wrong! You need to create both the text to display for the group and a hierarchy for the grouping. At the second level of grouping you need to group on the combination of both columns, "Bike Type" plus "Size"

15. Click **Edit Sort Expression**

264

a. At a minimum you will need to concatenate the current grouping column with the previous grouping columns, and while you are at it you can add some "pretty" formatting (maybe a "-" or a comma)
b. Enter: concat(@Bike_x0020_Type, " - ", @Size)
Watch the capitalization! Use the exact name the Intelisense offers – spaces are "encoded" so "Bike Type" in the list is "Bike**_x0020_**Type" in the web part.)
c. Note the preview at the bottom of the dialog box…

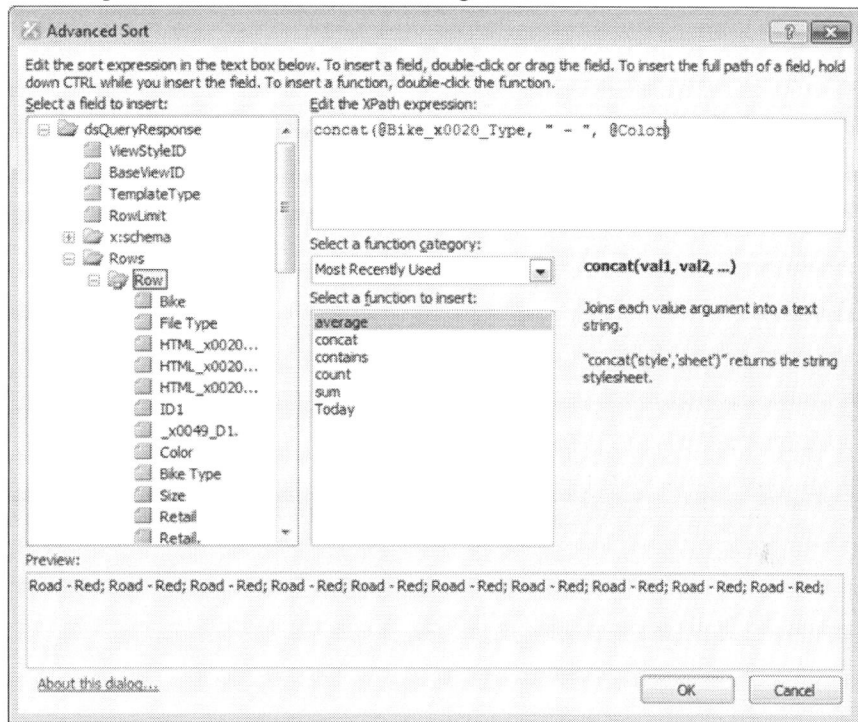

d. Click **OK**
e. Click **Show group header**
f. Click **Collapse group** (optional)
g. Click **Show group footer** (if you want counts and totals)

16. For the third and following groups - repeat the step above with sort expressions similar to:
    a. Formula: concat(@Bike_x0020_Type, " - ", @Size, " - ", @Bike_x0020_Color)
    b. More columns? In each new group include all of the fields from the previous groups along with any separators you like:
       concat(@group1field, @group2field, @group3field, @group4field, @group5field)
          or maybe:
       concat(@group1field, " - ", @group2field, " - ", @group3field, " - ", @group4field, " - ", @group5field, etc)

List and Library Customization

c. If you could see the full width of these you would see:

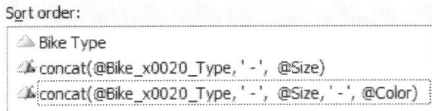

17. Before clicking **OK** to leave this dialog box, check the order of the groups to see if they have changed (bug?)
    a. Make sure they are in order something like:
       @BikeType
       concat(@Bike_x0020_Type, " - ", @Size)
       concat(@Bike_x0020_Type, " - ", @Size, " - ", @Bike_x0020_Color)
    b. Recheck each of the sort levels to see if these are still checked:
       i. Click **Show group** header
       ii. Click **Collapse group** (optional)
       iii. Click **Show group footer** (if you want counts and totals)
18. Optionally add one more column just to sort the data within the last group. Do not turn on the group header or group footer options for this sort-only field.
19. Click **OK** to close the **Sort and Group** dialog box.
20. You will probably want to change the Paging options as they default to 10 items. Click the **Paging** button in the Ribbon (**Data View Tools** group, **Options** tab)

Tip: If you have a lot of data in the list SharePoint Designer can get really slow. There are two things you could do here, set paging to a small number (not so good for testing multi-level grouping) or from the **Common Control Tasks** pop-out select **Show With Sample Data** (or click **Sample Data** in the ribbon).

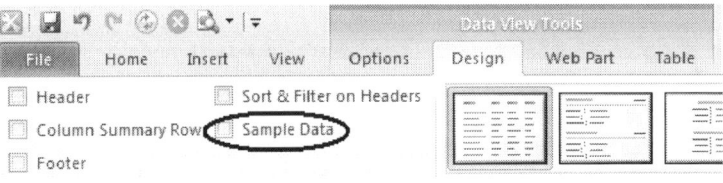

21. If you want grand totals you will also need to click **Data View Properties** and check **Show View Footer**

22. **Save!** At this point you may want to click **Save** and review the results so far in a browser. You should now have all of your groups. (Click the + to expand a section.)

23. Now is a good time to clean up the formatting, such as the gray background and odd row height in the group header and footer rows. (Right-click in the row in **Design** view and select **Cell Properties**.)

ID1	Bike	Color	Bike Type	Size	Retail
⊞ Bike Type: Mountain					
⊞ Bike Type: Road					
⊟ Bike Type: Touring					
⊞ Touring - 44					
⊞ Touring - 46					
⊞ Touring - 50					
⊟ Touring - 54					
⊟ Touring - 54 - Blue					
958	Touring-3000 Blue, 54	Blue	Touring	54	742.35
968	Touring-1000 Blue, 54	Blue	Touring	54	2,384.07
972	Touring-2000 Blue, 54	Blue	Touring	54	1,214.85
⊞ Touring - 54 - Yellow					

Your grouping work is now done. The following steps are only needed if you want to add totals, counts, averages, etc.

Add Totals to the view

A SharePoint view adds totals and counts at the top of each group. Most reporting tools will have these at the bottom of each group. When you are working with the DataFormWebPart you can choose where to put your summary data, at the top, the bottom or both.

- These steps describe adding totals to the footer rows, but also apply to modifying the header (top of each group) rows.
- The Data View sets up the header and footer rows as a single cell with a column span of 99! To display totals in the same columns as the data you will need to fix these rows.
- You will need to fix each of the group footer rows plus the view footer row.

Explore the HTML to see what's there and what needs to be done:

- In the Code View do a search for **colspan="99"**. In my example there will be many of these, one for each grouping footer, one for each grouping header and one for the view footer.
- Now you need to do a little planning. In my example I'd like to put the "**Count=**" in a two column spanned cell under the ID and Bike columns. Then I would like to have one cell under each additional column. So something like:

  <td colspan='2'>count stuff</td><td></td><td></td><td></td><td>total goes here</td>

Here's what this footer should look like with the cells (TD's), the count and the total:

List and Library Customization

Steps:

Fix the footer row...

24. Find "colspan="99"" for the first group footer row.
    Tip: Did you find a header or footer row? Look up two lines and you should see either "<xsl:if test="$showheader"" or "<xsl:if test="$showfooter""
25. Change the 99 to 2 (The 2 is for my example where I want the count spread under the ID and Bike columns)
26. Find the end tag for the cell (</td>)   (down about 16 lines of html)
27. After the end tag add the other cells (TD tag pairs), one for each additional column (I need four more for my sample data)
    <td></td> <td></td><td></td><td></td>

Now to add the total...

28. Switch to **Design** view and you should see the new cells in one of the footer rows.
29. Click in the cell where you want the total
30. Right-click and select **Insert Formula**
31. Build your formula. For a total double click "sum" in the function list then select your field from the dropdown list. My example needed this: **sum(@Retail)**
32. The formula editor does not know one extra piece of information needed here. The **@Retail** field needs to come from the current group only. To get this, update the formula like this:
    sum($nodeset/@Retail)   ("nodeset" is all lower case)

    Tip: How would you have discovered this? Go look at how they calculated the Count: **count($nodeset)**.

33. Notice that the formatting is wrong. The total is left aligned and the wrong size. To match the font and size find the style used for the data in the row above. In my example it looked like this:
    <TD Class="{$IDADW3HE}">
34. Copy the class info (**Class="{$IDADW3HE}"**) into your total cell (the TD tag). The result will look something like this:
    <td Class="{$IDADW3HE}"><xsl:value-of select="sum(@Retail)" /></td>
35. The last step is to right align the cell (you can use the ribbon button) and to format the total. To format the number, click in the cell with the total, right-click and select **Format Item As...** and pick your formatting options.

List and Library Customization

Note: SharePoint Designer may get creative and merge your formatting into new styles with great names like style1, style2, style3 etc.. If you are curious, do a search for .style1 (dot style1) and you will find they have placed the style class definition in the **PlaceHolderBodyAreaClass** content placeholder.

36. Fix up each footer row, including the **View Footer**, the same way. Add the extra TDs, add the totals, counts, etc, and format the results

Now about the View Footer... and some things to make your head hurt...

ID	Bike	BikeType	BikeSize	BikeColor	Retail
BikeType: Mountain					
Count : 18					$45,264.82
BikeType: Road					
Count : 27					$57,134.51
BikeType: Touring					
Count : 12					$23,931.96
Totals Count : 57					$126,331.29

The View Footer is built with its own HTML table, so the column widths are not going to line up with the rest of the list. You will need to some work to create the correct number of TD's and to get the widths right. My example above was fairly easy as the count was the first column and the total was the last column, both are easy to get lined up.

The grand totals need a special calculation to sum all of the rows. The @Retail field (or @yourfield) needs to come from the entire set of rows. To get this, update the formula like this:

sum(/dsQueryResponse/Rows/Row/@yourfield)   (make sure the capitalization is correct!)

Tip: How would you have discovered this? Go look at how they calculated the count for the View Footer:
count(/dsQueryResponse/Rows/Row)

A Bug?

The steps above show how to convert a View into a DataView web part and how to add as many levels of grouping as you want. There's a bug with how SharePoint handles the clicks on the Expand and Collapse buttons in the web part. When you click Expand at the top level it also expands all the detail levels. For one possible solution to the problem see Link 1106.

What else can you do with the Data View Web Part?

- Display pictures or thumbnails - See Link 1104

Quote of the Day / Tip of the Day

Want to display some "wise words" for your coworkers, or maybe a "product of the day" for your customers? You need a Quote of the Day web part!

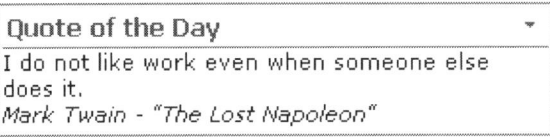

To build this you will need:

- A list with the quotes / tips
- A web part with a customized view of the list
- A Content Editor web part with a little HTML and some JavaScript

This web part is another simple Content Editor Web Part solution. It:

- Works from a normal SharePoint list
- Displays a random quote from the list
- Can display a new quote on each page view, or just one new quote a day
- Can be used to display quotes, product announcements or any kind of text
- Uses a Rich Text field so you can include formatting

Create the Quotes list

While you could use a Custom List, I used an Announcements list as it already had what I needed, a Title field and a Rich Text field.

1. Go to **Site Actions, Create** (or for 2010, **Site Actions, More Options**)
2. Click **Announcements**
3. Add a name for the list such as "Quotes"
4. The description is optional, but is best left blank as it adds a little complication later on
5. Click **OK**
6. If you are not using the Announcements list type then add a **Multiple Lines of Text** column. Name the column "Quote" (although any name will work) and click **Rich text (Bold, italics, text alignment)**

List and Library Customization

7. Add a few quotes by clicking **New**:

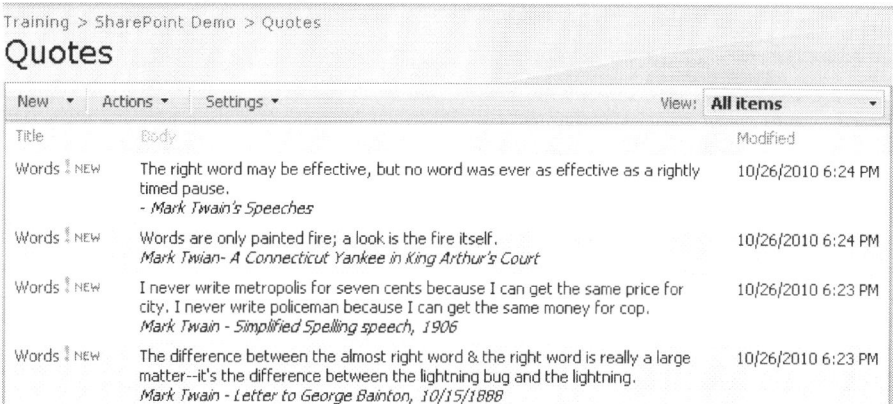

8. Create a new view (2007: click the "View:" dropdown and click **Create View**) (2010: click **Create View** in the ribbon)
9. Create the view as a **Standard** view and name it something like "Web Part View". Un-checkmark all of the columns except for the "Quote" column (the "Body" column if using an announcements list)
10. In 2010, expand the **Tabular View** section and un-checkmark Allow individual item checkboxes
11. Click **OK** to save the view

Add the Quotes list web part to the page

1. Go to the page where you want to add the "Quote of the Day"
2. Click **Site Actions, Edit Page**
3. Click **Add a web part** and add the web part for the quotes list
4. In the web part click **Edit** and **Modify Shared Web Part**
5. Select the view you created above ("Web Part View")
6. Click **OK**

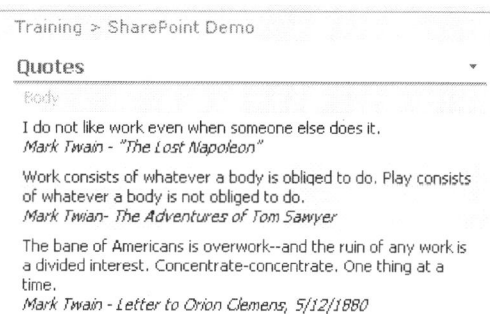

271

The Content Editor Web Part

1. Add a Content Editor Web Part (CEWP) and move it so it is below the quotes web part
2. Click the CEWP's dropdown menu and select **Modify Shared Web Part** (**Edit Web Part** in 2010)
3. In the **Appearance** section add a title for the web part (perhaps "Quote of the Day")
4. Now you have two choices:
   - For 2007, click the **Source Editor** button and add the JavaScript that you will find later in this article

   or (good idea for 2007 and the best practice for 2010)

   - Create the JavaScript in your favorite HTML editor (Visual Studio, SharePoint Designer, Notepad, etc), upload it to a library and enter the path to the file in the Content Editor Web Part's **Content Link** box.

This second choice is preferred for a few reasons:

- You can use your editor's auto-completion, copy and paste, and other features to help write the code
- You can write the code and upload to a library once, then use it in multiple Content Editor Web Parts (…edit in one place… update in many…)
- Easier to backup, share with other site owners and document

ID'ing your Web Part

In order to write JavaScript code to interact with the HTML of a web part you need to indentify the web part's HTML. SharePoint's web parts have a custom attribute named "title". This title consists of two parts: the title entered in the **Appearance** section of the web part's properties and the description entered in the list's **Title, Description and Navigation** settings. Note that when you have a description, the title attribute includes a "-" or space as separator.

Examples:

Web Part Title	List Description	HTML "title"
Quotes	none entered	Quotes
Quotes	Cool words of wisdom	Quotes - Cool words of wisdom

List and Library Customization

So how do you find the title? Display the SharePoint page with the list's web part (probably your site's home page), use the browser's "View Source" feature (In IE 6 click the **View** menu, then click **Source**) and search for the name of the web part. What you are looking for should be something like this:

```
<td id="MSOZoneCell_WebPartWPQ7" vAlign="top"><table TOPLEVEL border="0" cellpadding=
    <tr>
        <td><table border="0" cellpadding="0" cellspacing="0" width="100%">
            <tr class="ms-WPHeader">
                <td title="Vendor Links - Preferred vendors" id="webP
            </tr>
        </table></td>
    </tr><tr>
```

Or like this if there is no list description:

```
<td id="MSOZoneCell_WebPartWPQ7" vAlign="top"><table TOPLEVEL border="0" cellpadding=
    <tr>
        <td><table border="0" cellpadding="0" cellspacing="0" width="100%">
            <tr class="ms-WPHeader">
                <td title="Vendor Links" id="webPartTitlewPQ7" style=
            </tr>
        </table></td>
    </tr><tr>
```

The JavaScript

Add the following JavaScript into your Content Editor Web Part or a linked text file. (see the two options described above) Remember to edit the **quotesWebPartName** variable.

```
<!-- add your own formatting here... -->
<span name="QuoteText" id="QuoteText"></span>

<script type="text/javascript">
// another CEWP trick from http://TechTrainingNotes.blogspot.com

// name of the quotes library web part
var quotesWebPartName="QuoteOfTheDay";

// set this to "true" so the user will see the same quote
// for 12 hours or until they close and reopen the browser
var OneQuotePerVisit = false;

// don't change these
var QuoteList;
var QuoteArray = [];
var quoteCount = 0;

//Find the quotes web part and hide it
var x = document.getElementsByTagName("TD"); // find all of the table cells

var i=0;
```

List and Library Customization

```javascript
for (i=0; i<x.length; i++)
{
  if (x[i].title == quotesWebPartName)
  {
    // tables in tables in tables... ah SharePoint!
    QuoteList = x[i].parentNode.parentNode.parentNode.parentNode.parentNode.parentNode.parentNode;

    // hide the links list web part
    QuoteList.style.display="none";
    break;
  }
}

if ( ! QuoteList )
{
  document.getElementById("QuoteText").innerHTML="Web Part '" +
        quotesWebPartName + "' not found!";
}

//Count the quotes

var links = QuoteList.getElementsByTagName("TR") // find all of the rows
var url;
var quoteCount = 0;
for (var i=0; i<links.length; i++)
{

  if (links[i].childNodes[0].className=="ms-vb2")
  {
    QuoteArray[quoteCount] = i;
    quoteCount++;
  }
}

if (quoteCount == 0)
{
  document.getElementById("QuoteText").innerHTML =
        "No quotes found in web part'" + quotesWebPartName + "'!";
}

var id=-1;
```

```
// check for a cookie and use last ID if found

if (OneQuotePerVisit)
{
  // check for a cookie with the last quote ID
  if (document.cookie.length > 0)
  {
    c_start = document.cookie.indexOf("LastQuoteDisplayedID=");
    if (c_start! = -1)
    {
      c_start = c_start + "LastQuoteDisplayedID".length + 1;
      c_end = document.cookie.indexOf(";",c_start);
      if (c_end == -1) c_end = document.cookie.length;
      id = unescape(document.cookie.substring(c_start,c_end));
    }
  }
}

if (id == -1)
{
  // generate a random quote ID
  id = Math.floor(Math.random() * QuoteArray.length);
}

// display the quote
document.getElementById("QuoteText").innerHTML=
QuoteList.getElementsByTagName("TR")[QuoteArray[id]].childNodes[0].innerHTML;

if (OneQuotePerVisit)
{
  // set a cookie so they see the same quote for xx hours (.5 = 1/2 day = 12 hours)
  var exdate = new Date();
  exdate.setDate(exdate.getDate() + 1);
  document.cookie="LastQuoteDisplayedID=" + id //+ ";expires=" + exdate.toUTCString();
}

</script>
```

Removing View Group Headings and Group Counts

If your groups have obvious names, such as North America, Europe and Asia, you may find the Group By heading to be redundant. Here we will show how to remove both this heading and the group counts.

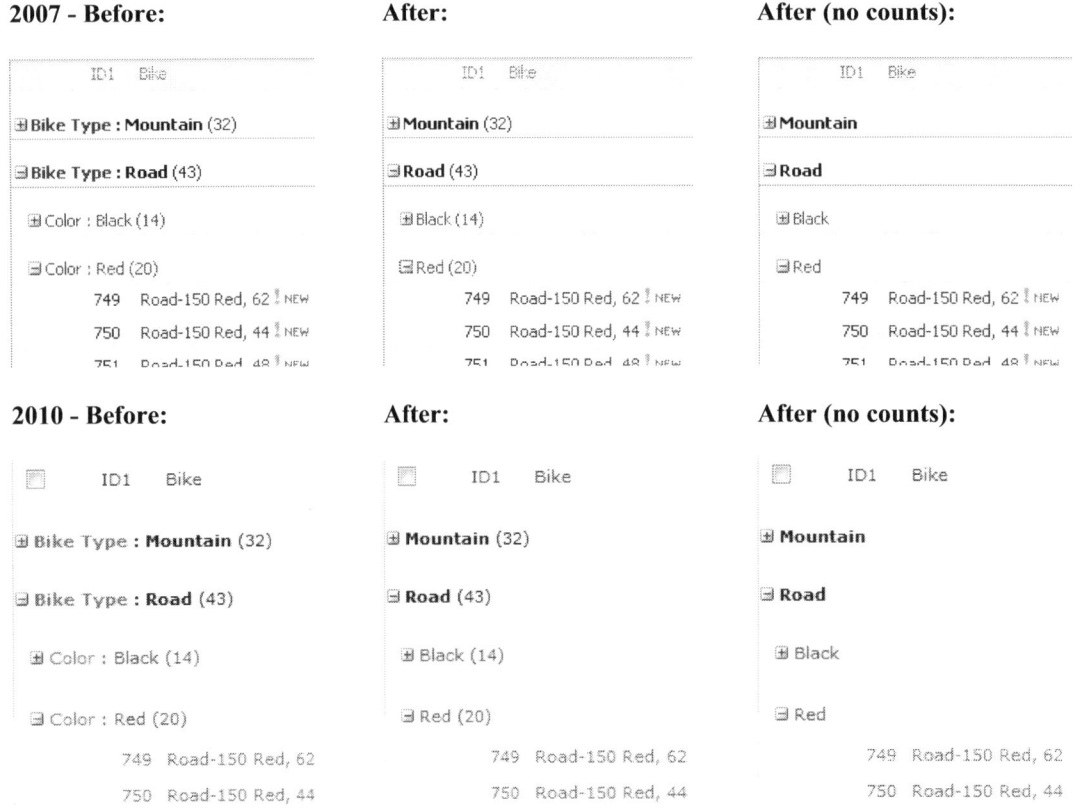

How it works:

As all of the data for a grouped list is not downloaded on the first load of a page we need to first find the HTML for the group heading and make our updates. We then need to intercept the SharePoint function that handles the expansion of groups so we can clean up the expanded sub-headings each time a heading is clicked. Though similar, 2007 and 2010 use different HTML for the grouping.

Steps for 2007:

For SP 2007 you can add the code to a Content Editor Web Part added to the view page, in a text file stored in a library and linked from a Content Editor Web Part, or directly to the page using SharePoint Designer. For the SPD approach add the code just before the **</asp:Content** tag for **PlaceHolderMain**. The steps below add a web part to the view page.

List and Library Customization

1. Display the view page with the grouped list and click **Site Actions, Edit Page**
2. Add a Content Editor Web Part and move the new web part just after the list's web part
3. Click the web part's **Edit** menu and click **Modify Shared Web Part**
4. Click the **Source Editor** button and add the JavaScript code from below
5. Click **OK** and test

The code - 2007 version

```
<script>

// do the initial cleanup
CleanUpGroups()

_spBodyOnLoadFunctionNames.push("CustomGrouping");

function CustomGrouping()
{
  // intercept the old function
  var oldExpCollGroup = ExpCollGroup;

  // and replace it with our version
  ExpCollGroup= function (a,b,c)
  {
    // call the old version
    oldExpCollGroup(a,b,c)
    // then do our cleanup
    CleanUpGroups()
  }
}


function CleanUpGroups()
{
  // get all of the TDs in the page
  var tds = document.getElementsByTagName("TD");
  for (var i=0; i<tds.length; i++)
  {
    if (tds[i].className=="ms-gb" || tds[i].className=="ms-gb2")
    {
      if (tds[i].childNodes[4].data.substring(2,1) == ":")
      {
```

List and Library Customization

```
      // hide the group column name
      tds[i].childNodes[3].style.display="none";
      // hide the colon ":"
      tds[i].childNodes[4].data=tds[i].childNodes[4].data.substring(3,99)
      // hide the group count
      tds[i].childNodes[5].style.display="none";
    }
   }
  }
 }
</script>
```

Steps for 2010:

When you add a web part to a view page in 2010 you also break a few view related features. (See chapter 8.) The best solution therefore is to add the code directly to the page using SharePoint Designer.

1. Open SharePoint Designer 2010 and open your site
2. In the **Site Objects** pane expand **Lists and Libraries**, click your list and click your view page
3. Click the **Advanced Mode** button in the **Edit** ribbon
4. Find the end tag for the **PlaceHolderMain** content area (</asp:content>):

```
65 </WebPartPages:XsltListViewWebPart>
66
67 </ZoneTemplate></WebPartPages:WebPartZone>
68
69     Your code goes here...
70
71 </asp:Content>
72 <asp:Content ContentPlaceHolderId="PlaceHolderBodyAreaClass"
```

5. Add the JavaScript from below, save your work and test

The JavaScript - 2010 version:

```
<script>

// do the initial cleanup
CleanUpGroups()

_spBodyOnLoadFunctionNames.push("CustomGrouping");

function CustomGrouping()
{
  // intercept the expand function
```

```
  var oldExpCollGroup = ExpCollGroup;

  // and replace it with our version
  ExpCollGroup= function (a,b,c)
  {
    // call the old function
    oldExpCollGroup(a,b,c);
    // then do our cleanup
    CleanUpGroups();
  }
}

function CleanUpGroups()
{
  // get all of the TDs in the page
  var tds = document.getElementsByTagName("TD");
  for (var i=0; i<tds.length; i++)
  {
    if (tds[i].className=="ms-gb")
    {
      if (tds[i].childNodes[1].data.substring(2,1) == ":")
      {
        // hide the group column name
        tds[i].childNodes[0].childNodes[0].nextSibling.data=" ";
        // hide the colon ":"
        tds[i].childNodes[1].data=tds[i].childNodes[1].data.substring(3,99);
        // hide the group count
        tds[i].childNodes[2].style.display="none";
      }
    }

    // repeat for the second level
    if (tds[i].className=="ms-gb2")
    {
      if (tds[i].childNodes[2].data.substring(2,1) == ":")
      {
        // hide the group column name
        tds[i].childNodes[1].childNodes[0].nextSibling.data=" ";
        // hide the colon ":"
        tds[i].childNodes[2].data=tds[i].childNodes[2].data.substring(3,99);
        // hide the group count
```

List and Library Customization

```
      // hide the group count
      tds[i].childNodes[3].style.display="none";
    }
   }
  }
 }
}
</script>
```

Web Part Customizations

The next set of customizations do not modify lists themselves, but rather modify the web parts that display lists.

Create a "What's New" web part for a library or list (2007 and 2010)

If your library has folders in folders in folders... the only quick way to find the library's new documents is to display the RSS feed for the library. Or, you could create a custom view so your users can find the new items right on the home page. There's no JavaScript code or SharePoint Designer needed for this one as you can quickly create a view with the Sort, Limit and Expand Folders features to create a "what's new" web part.

Steps:
1. Add a web part to the page for the list or library (Example: add the Shared Documents web part)
2. From the web part's dropdown menu select **Modify Shared Web Part** (or **Edit Web Part** in 2010)
3. From the properties panel on the right, click the **Edit the current view** (just below the **Selected View** dropdown)
4. In the **Sort** section select the **Modified** column and then click **Show items in descending order**
5. Expand the **Folders** section and select **Show all items without folders** to show all of the documents in the library as a single list
6. Expand **Item Limit** and enter the number of items to display
7. Optionally select what to do if there are more than that number of items:
   a. select **Display items in batches** so the users can click next / previous links to page through the data, or
   b. select **Limit** to display just xx number of items and then display a **More** link to take the user to the library's page
8. Click **OK** to save the view and click **OK** to update the web part.

Add a web part to display a document library folder

When a library web part is added to a page it will default to display the root folder of the library. If you want to just display a single folder from the library you will need to find a way to specify the URL of the library that includes the folder name. To do this we can use SharePoint Designer to create a new page with a single web part to display the folder. The challenge is not the web part, but displaying just a single folder out of the list. To do this we will create a new page that only displays the web part, and then we will display that page in a Page Viewer Web Part. It of course would be ideal if the library's web part properties or the view options included a way to filter by URL or folder. The goal of the following approach is to create this folder display with no code, no custom web parts, no access to the servers and no custom XML or HTML.

Before - the normal library web part:

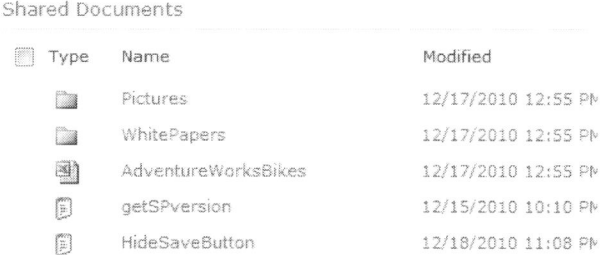

After - the custom web part that just displays the "WhitePapers" folder:

Overview Steps:

- Create a web part to display the view
- Edit the view as needed
- Create a page that displays only the web part and no other SharePoint page content
- In your final page add a Page Viewer Web Part and link to our new page

Steps:

1. Create a web part page or navigate to an existing web part page
2. Edit the page and insert the web part for your library

List and Library Customization

3. If you would like to customize the view then click the web part's edit button and edit the web part and then click Edit the current view
4. You may also want to change the title or "chrome" of the web part to rename it or just hide the title area
    a. Rename the web part: Appearance, Title
    b. Hide the web part's title and border: Appearance, Chrome Type, None
5. In 2007 click Exit Edit Mode or in 2010 if the Page tab is displayed in the ribbon click Page and Save
6. Click the library's folder you want to display in the final web part and copy this URL (you may want to paste it into a Notepad file)
   This will look something like:
   http://*yourserver*/sites/*yoursite*/SitePages/*yournewpage*.aspx?RootFolder=%2Fsites%2F*yoursite*%2F*yourlibrary*%2F*yourfolder*&FolderCTID=0x012000799ECACE4DFBE947B4036269AAA6B428&View={130CD9E4-1E01-4A42-BD9F-94F0FA3896C0}
7. Open your site in SharePoint Designer (See chapter 6)
8. In SharePoint Designer 2007:
   click File, New, ASPX
   click File Save as, select a library and click Save
   In SharePoint Designer 2010:
   click File, More Pages, ASPX and Create
   select a library (most likely Site Pages), enter a filename and click Save
   click Yes to open the page in Advanced Mode
9. Click the Design button at the bottom of the editor window to display the page in Design view
10. In SharePoint Designer open the web part page you worked with in step 1
    a. In SPD 2010 you may need to click All Files in the Site Objects panel and then click your library name to see all of the files
11. Display/edit the page in Design view, click and copy the web part
12. Return to the new page you just created and paste the web part
13. Save the page and exit from SharePoint Designer
14. In your browser go to the page where you want to display the folder web part
15. Edit the page and insert a Page Viewer Web Part
16. Edit the web part and enter the URL (the one you copied in step 5) to the page you just created into the Link box
17. Optional:
    a. Rename the web part: Appearance, Title
    b. Hide the web part's title and border: Appearance, Chrome Type, None
    c. Adjust the height and width of the web part: Appearance, Height/Width
18. Save your changes and test

Hide a web part with zero rows

Often you will have a web part such as Announcements or Relevant Documents that is empty for some users. For a clean looking page you will probably want to hide these empty web parts.

Two web parts that both have content: **Two web parts, one without content:**

Two web parts, one without content and hidden:

How it works...

While 2007 and 2010 use different messages, most empty web parts display a message that can be used as a test to see if the web part is empty. The code needs to first find the web part you want to hide and then check for one of the "empty" messages. Once the web part has been found, the code just needs to change the display style to "none".

As we probably don't want any of these web parts hidden while we are in page edit mode we will also check to see if we are in edit mode. In 2007 the code to do this is:

```
if (document.getElementById("edmc2") == null)  // then not in edit mode
{
  // stuff to do only when not in edit mode
}
```

283

SharePoint 2007

There are three versions of the JavaScript here: hide one selected empty web part, hide several empty web parts and hide all empty web parts.

Steps:

1. Go to the page with the web part to hide
2. Add a Content Editor Web Part
3. Edit the web part, click the **Source Editor** and paste one of the three JavaScript samples
4. If you are not using the "all web parts" code then edit the code and add your web part names:
   a. Use the browser's View Source feature to display the page's HTML, search for "Title=" and your first part of your web part's name (example: Title="Announcements ...)
   b. Copy the entire name (this is usually composed of two parts, the web part's name and the list's description)
   c. Paste the name into your JavaScript's code
      (See "How to Find a Web Part in Code" in chapter 5 for more details)
5. Save your changes and test

2007 JavaScript to hide a single empty web part:

Replace yourTitleGoesHere with your web part title!

```
<script>
var a = document.getElementsByTagName("TD");
for (var i=0;i<a.length;i++)
{
  if ( a[i].title=="yourTitleForWebPartGoesHere" )
  {

    // the following is all one line
    var x =
a[i].parentNode.parentNode.parentNode.parentNode.parentNode.parentNode.parentNode.parentNode;

    if (x.innerHTML.indexOf("There are no items to show in this view") > -1
      || x.innerHTML.indexOf("There are currently no ") > -1
    )
    {
      x.style.display="none";
    }
  }
}
```

```
}
</script>
```

2007 JavaScript to hide several empty web parts:

```
<script>
var a = document.getElementsByTagName("TD");
for (var i=0;i<a.length;i++)
{
  if (
      a[i].title=="yourTitleForWebPart1GoesHere" ||
      a[i].title=="yourTitleForWebPart2GoesHere" ||
      a[i].title=="yourTitleForWebPart3GoesHere" ||
      a[i].title=="yourTitleForWebPart4GoesHere"
  )
  {

    // the following is all one line
    var x =
a[i].parentNode.parentNode.parentNode.parentNode.parentNode.parentNode.parentNode.parentNode;

    if (x.innerHTML.indexOf("There are no items to show in this view") > -1
      || x.innerHTML.indexOf("There are currently no ") > -1
    )
    {
      x.style.display="none";
    }
  }
}
</script>
```

2007 JavaScript to hide all empty web parts:

Note: the following makes the assumption that all TD tags that have a TITLE attribute and an "empty" message are web parts. This may not always be the case, so do some testing with your web page.

```
<script>
var a = document.getElementsByTagName("TD");
```

```
for (var i=0;i<a.length;i++)
{
  if (a[i].title)    // if the TD has a TITLE attribute
  {

    // the following is all one line
    var x =
a[i].parentNode.parentNode.parentNode.parentNode.parentNode.parentNode.parentNode.parentNode;

    if (x.innerHTML.indexOf("There are no items to show in this view") > -1
      || x.innerHTML.indexOf("There are currently no ") > -1
    )
    {
      x.style.display="none";
    }
  }
}
</script>
```

SharePoint 2010

This is fairly easy to do in 2010 as every web part displays a consistent message, or rather all do except for the Picture Library. Most libraries display a message that starts with "There are no items to show in this view" while the Picture Library displays "There are no pictures to show in this view".

Overview Steps:

1. Display the page with the web part to hide
2. Display the source of the page to search and find the "Title" of the TD that contains the web part
3. Hide the table that contains the web part

Note: There are three versions of the JavaScript, one to hide a single empty web part, one to hide any number of empty web parts and one to hide all empty web parts.

Steps:

1. Go to the page with the web part
2. Use the browser's View Source feature to display the page's HTML
3. Search for the web part's name - example: "Announcements"
4. Repeat the search until you find: Title="*yourwebpartname*
5. Copy the entire name (note that the name includes the web part's title and the list's description)

List and Library Customization

6. Create a text file using Notepad that contains the JavaScript from below
7. Edit the line that contains " if (a[i].title==" and replace the sample title with the one you just copied:

    if (a[i].title=="*yourTitleGoesHere*")

    Something like this: (this is all one line)

    if (a[i].title=="**Announcements - Use this list to track upcoming events, status updates or other team news.**")

8. If you are want to hide multiple web parts then in the multiple web part version of the JavaScript copy and paste a line for each web part:

    || a[i].title=="*yourTitleGoesHere*"

9. Upload this file to a library such as Site Assets or Site Pages
10. Add a Content Editor Web Part to the page, edit the web part, and set the link to the location of the file you just uploaded

2010 JavaScript for a single web part

Replace yourTitleGoesHere with your web part title!

```
<script>
function HideWebPartWithZeroRows()
{

  var a = document.getElementsByTagName("TD")
  for (var i=0;i<a.length;i++)
  {
   if (a[i].title=="yourTitleGoesHere")
   {
     // the following is all one line
     var x =
a[i].parentNode.parentNode.parentNode.parentNode.parentNode.parentNode.parentNode.parentNode;

     if (x.innerHTML.indexOf("There are no items to show in this view") > -1
      || x.innerHTML.indexOf("There are no pictures to show in this view") > -1
     )
      {
         x.style.display="none";
      }
   }
  }
}
```

287

```
_spBodyOnLoadFunctionNames.push("HideWebPartWithZeroRows");

</script>
```

2010 JavaScript for multiple web parts

The follow code is the same as above except the IF statement has multiple OR tests ("||").

```
<script>
function HideWebPartWithZeroRows()
{
  var a = document.getElementsByTagName("TD")
  for (var i=0;i<a.length;i++)
  {
    if (
        a[i].title=="yourTitleForWebPart1GoesHere" ||
        a[i].title=="yourTitleForWebPart2GoesHere" ||
        a[i].title=="yourTitleForWebPart3GoesHere" ||
        a[i].title=="yourTitleForWebPart4GoesHere"
    )
    {
      // the following is all one line
      var x = a[i].parentNode.parentNode.parentNode.parentNode.parentNode.parentNode.parentNode.parentNode;

      if (x.innerHTML.indexOf("There are no items to show in this view") > -1
       || x.innerHTML.indexOf("There are no pictures to show in this view") > -1
      )
      {
         x.style.display="none";
      }
    }
  }
}

_spBodyOnLoadFunctionNames.push("HideWebPartWithZeroRows");

</script>
```

List and Library Customization

2010 JavaScript for all web parts

Note: The following makes the assumption that all TD tags that have a TITLE attribute and an "empty message" are web parts. This may not always be the case, so do some testing with your web page.

```
<script>
function HideWebPartWithZeroRows()
{

  var a = document.getElementsByTagName("TD")
  for (var i=0; i<a.length; i++)
  {
    if ( a[i].title  )
    {
      // the following is all one line
      var x =
a[i].parentNode.parentNode.parentNode.parentNode.parentNode.parentNode.parentNode.parentNode;

      if (x.innerHTML.indexOf("There are no items to show in this view") > -1
       || x.innerHTML.indexOf("There are no pictures to show in this view") > -1
      )
        {
           x.style.display = "none";
        }
    }
  }
}

_spBodyOnLoadFunctionNames.push("HideWebPartWithZeroRows");

</script>
```

Change the "No Items" message in a discussion web part (2007 & 2010)

When you create a new team site or add a new discussion list to a site the discussion web part initially displays a "no items" message. If you would like to change this message all you need is a little JavaScript added to the web part page or to the master page. If you would rather hide this web part anytime there are no discussions then see the previous customization: "Hide a web part with zero rows".

List and Library Customization

The JavaScript

The code to change this message could be as easy as the following sample; as long as we can insure that the code is run after the page has been loaded. This code searches all of the TD tags for any that are styled as "ms-vb" and has the text found in the discussion web part. It then replaces that text with the text of our choice.

```
<script type="text/javascript">
  var a = document.getElementsByTagName("TD");
  for (var i=0; i<a.length; i++)
  {
    if (a[i].className == "ms-vb")
    {
      if (a[i].innerHTML.indexOf("There are no items to show in this view")>-1 &&
          a[i].innerHTML.indexOf("discussion board")>-1)
      {
        a[i].innerHTML = "There are no active discussions";
      }
    }
  }
</script>
```

One way to ensure that the code runs after the web part has been loaded is to add this code to the bottom of the master page somewhere before the </BODY> tag or in a Content Editor Web Part that has been added below the discussion board's web part. If you want to add the code somewhere before the web part then we need a delayed load using _spBodyOnLoadFunctionNames. (See chapter 5 "Controlling when JavaScript Runs" for more information on the use of _spBodyOnLoadFunctionNames.)

```
<script type="text/javascript">
function ChangeDiscussionMessage()
{
  var a = document.getElementsByTagName("TD");
  for (var i=0;i<a.length;i++)
```

List and Library Customization

```
{
  if (a[i].className=="ms-vb")
  {
    if (a[i].innerHTML.indexOf("There are no items to show in this view")>-1 &&
       a[i].innerHTML.indexOf("discussion board")>-1)
    {
      a[i].innerHTML = "There are no active discussions";
    }
  }
}
}

_spBodyOnLoadFunctionNames.push("ChangeDiscussionMessage");

</script>
```

jQuery

Here's a jQuery version of the above: (For more on jQuery see Chapter 4)

```
<script type="text/javascript">
function ChangeDiscussionMessage()
{
  // the following is all one line:
  $("TD .ms-vb:contains('discussion board'):contains('There are no items')").text("There are no active discussions ")}
}

_spBodyOnLoadFunctionNames.push("ChangeDiscussionMessage");

</script>
```

If you are not loading the jQuery library in the master page then you will need to load it for this example:

```
<script src="http://maxsp2010f/sites/Training/Shared%20Documents/jquery-1.3.2.min.js"></script>

<script type="text/javascript">
function ChangeDiscussionMessage()
{
  // the following is all one line:
```

List and Library Customization

```
    $("TD .ms-vb:contains('discussion board'):contains('There are no items')").text("There are no active discussions ")}
}

_spBodyOnLoadFunctionNames.push("ChangeDiscussionMessage");

</script>
```

Change the "Add New" message for a web part

Most list and library web parts have a "summary toolbar" enabled with a generic message similar to "Add new item". You can change this "add new" text to anything you like using JavaScript and a little detective work.

Here's the before and after for this customization:

Project Tasks					Project Tasks				
☐ 📎	Title	Start Date	Due Date	% C	☐ 📎	Title	Start Date	Due Date	% Co
	Task 1	7/1/2010	7/15/2010			Task 1	7/1/2010	7/15/2010	
	Task 2	7/8/2010	7/20/2010			Task 2	7/8/2010	7/20/2010	
✣ Add new item					✣ Click here to add team tasks				

How does this work?

Each web part's "add new" link has an ID. A few even share a common ID. The JavaScript code just needs to find the <A> tag with this ID and update the text. You will need to modify the following code examples to use the ID used by your list. Note that some lists share the same ID; these include Tasks and KPIs.

Here's the <A> tag in SharePoint 2010 for a document library, with some text removed for clarity, that you might find while looking at the source of the page:

```
<a class="ms-addnew" id="idHomePageNewDocument" href="..." onclick="..." target="_self">Add document</a>
```

IDs for SharePoint 2007

Web Part	Default message	ID for ".getElementById"
Announcements	Add new announcement	"Add new announcement"
Links	Add new link	"idHomePageNewLink"
Calendar	Add new event	"idHomePageNewEvent"

List and Library Customization

Picture Library	Add new picture	"idAddPicture"
KPI List	Add new item	"idAddNewItem"
Tasks	Add new item	"idAddNewTask" *
Project Tasks	Add new item	"idAddNewTask" *
Document Library	Add new document	"idAddNewDoc" *
Wiki	Add new Wiki page	"idAddNewDoc" *
Survey	Respond to this survey	"idNewSurveyResponse"
Discussion	Add new discussion	"idAddNewDiscuss"

* = Shared with another list

IDs for SharePoint 2010

Web Part	Default message	ID for ".getElementById"
Announcements	Add new announcement	"idHomePageNewAnnouncement" (changed in 2010)
Links	Add new link	"idHomePageNewLink"
Calendar	Add new event	"idHomePageNewEvent"
Picture Library	Add new picture	"idHomePageNewItem" * (changed in 2010)
KPI List	Add new item	"idHomePageNewItem" * (changed in 2010)
Tasks	Add new item	"idHomePageNewItem" * (changed in 2010)
Project Tasks	Add new item	"idHomePageNewItem" * (changed in 2010)
Document Library	Add new document	"idHomePageNewDocument" (changed in 2010)
Wiki	Add new Wiki page	"idHomePageNewWikiPage" (changed in 2010)
Discussion	Add new discussion	"idHomePageNewDiscussion" (changed in 2010)
Custom List	Add new item	"idHomePageNewItem" * (changed in 2010)

* = *Shared with another list*

Changing the message for a single web part

Once you know the ID, the update should be as easy as:

```
document.getElementById("idHomePageNewDocument").innerHTML='your new text goes here'
```

List and Library Customization

Changing the message for multiple web parts

But… if you have two library web parts on the same page you will have two identical IDs. While in good HTML there should never be two identical IDs, this does happen in SharePoint. **getElementById** will only return the first one found and not give us a way to update both web parts.

The following JavaScript will find all of the web parts with the ID you are searching for, but only update the web part if it has the title you are looking for. To find this title you will need to view the source of the page and search for the name of the web part.

```
<script type="text/javascript">

var As = document.getElementsByTagName('A');
for (var j=0; j<As.length; j++)
{
  if (As[j].id == 'idHomePageNewDocument')
  {

    // the following is all one line
    if (
As[j].parentNode.parentNode.parentNode.parentNode.parentNode.parentNode.parentNode.parentNode.innerHTML.indexOf("Shared Documents [2] - Share a document with the team by adding it to this document library.") > -1
)

    {
      As[j].innerHTML='your new text goes here';
    }

  }
}
</script>
```

Where to add the code

This customization is similar to many of the others in that you need to add this JavaScript to the page somewhere after the web part you want to change. You can do this by adding a Content Editor Web Part or by editing the page in SharePoint Designer.

Steps using a Content Editor Web Part:

1. Go to the page with the web part
2. Use the browser's View Source feature to display the page's HTML
3. Search for the "add new item" text - example: "Add new announcement"
4. Read backwards in the code to find the <A> tag and note its ID - example: idHomePageNewDocument
5. If you are wanting to change only one web part of several that share the same ID then search for the title of the web part and copy the entire "title=" value - example: Shared Documents [2] - Share a document with the team by adding it to this document library.
6. For SharePoint 2007
    a. Add a Content Editor Web Part to the page, edit the web part, and click the Source Editor button
    b. Add the JavaScript from above
    c. Edit the code to use the ID you found in step 4
    d. If you are wanting to change only one web part of several that share the same ID then update the code with the text copied in step 5
    e. Save your changes
7. For SharePoint 2010 (or 2007)
    a. Create a text file using Notepad that contains the JavaScript from above
    b. Edit the code to use the ID you found in step 4
    c. If you are wanting to change only one web part of several that share the same ID then update the code with the text copied in step 5
    d. Upload this file to a library such as Site Assets or Site Pages
    e. Add a Content Editor Web Part to the page, edit the web part, and set the link to the location of the file you just uploaded
    f. Save your changes and test

Adding hyperlinks to document libraries

Sometimes you have external content that you would like to make available from your document library without uploading a file. Or you may want to provide easy access to a single document from multiple libraries without having to create multiple copies of the file. Examples include documents in other SharePoint sites or libraries, and even links to other web pages including SharePoint pages and external web sites. Adding hyperlinks to a document library is not a customization, but just the discovery of a well hidden SharePoint feature!

SharePoint has a built-in Content Type called "Link to a Document". Add this to your library and then just click the "New" dropdown and select "Link to a Document"! SharePoint will simply ask you for a document name and URL. You can supply a URL to anything that starts with "http://", including both SharePoint documents and external web pages. It does not support a link to a network share such as "\\myfileserver\folder1\somedoc.doc".

List and Library Customization

2007 Steps:

1. Display your library (Example: Shared Documents)
2. Click Settings and Library Settings
3. Click Advanced Settings
4. Check "Allow management of content types" and then OK
5. In the Settings page scroll down to Content Types and click "Add from existing site content types"
6. Select Link to a Document, click Add and then click OK
7. Go back to your library and click the New dropdown and select Link to a Document
8. Enter a display name (document name) and the URL (must start with http://) and click OK

2010 Steps:

1. Display your library (Example: Shared Documents)
2. Click the Library tab in the ribbon then click Library Settings and Library Settings
3. Click Advanced Settings
4. Check Allow management of content types and then OK
5. In the Settings page scroll down to Content Types and click Add from existing site content types
6. Select Link to a Document, click Add and then click OK
7. Go back to your library and click the Documents tab of the ribbon, click the New dropdown and select Link to a Document
8. Enter a display name (document name) and the URL (must start with http://) and click OK

So how does it work? The Content Type has a template that is an ASPX page that contains a server side control named SharePoint:UrlRedirector. When this page is rendered it simply redirects to the address listed in the items URL property. Also experiment with adding these built-in content types to your library:

- Basic Page
- Web Part Page
- Dublin Core Columns (Do a web or wikipedia.com search for "Dublin Core")
- Picture

Need to add custom columns / meta data to any of the above? Just create a new Content Type based on one of the above and add it to your library.

Add hyperlinks for special URLs

The Link to Document content type described only works with URLs that start with HTTP://. If you have a need to link to a special URL, such as mms:// (Microsoft Multimedia) or FTP://, you can create your own custom web page that includes a JavaScript redirect command.

Steps:

1. Use Notepad to create a text file named **redirect.aspx** (or any name you choose that ends with .aspx)
2. In this file add this little JavaScript routine: (no other HTML or text needed!)

```
<script>
  window.location.href = window.location.search.substring(1);
</script>
```

3. Upload this file to a library in SharePoint and note the URL (something like http://yourserver/sites/yoursite/shared documents/redirect.aspx)
4. Setup the **Link to Document** content type per the previous article
5. When you add a new **Link to Document** enter the URL this way:
   http://yourserver/sites/yoursite/shared documents/redirect.aspx?**mms://pathtoyourdocument**

You can take this one step further and warn the user that they are about to leave your SharePoint site:

```
<script>
  if ( confirm("Are you sure you want to go there?") )
  {
    window.location.href = window.location.search.substring(1);
  }
  else
  {
    history.go(-1)  // same as clicking the back button
  }
</script>
Click your back button to return to the library.
```

When they click the link the user will see:

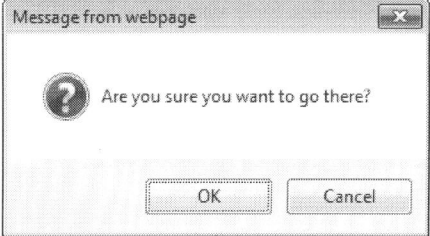

How to truncate a Multiline column and add a "More" link (2007 & 2010)

Lists with a lot of text are difficult to display as a web part as SharePoint does not include any options to truncate text. In this customization we will display a part of a field and append a "more…" link so we can display the list as a compact web part while letting the user click a link to see all of the text.

A picture is worth a thousand words, so here's two thousand worth…

The list before any customizations:

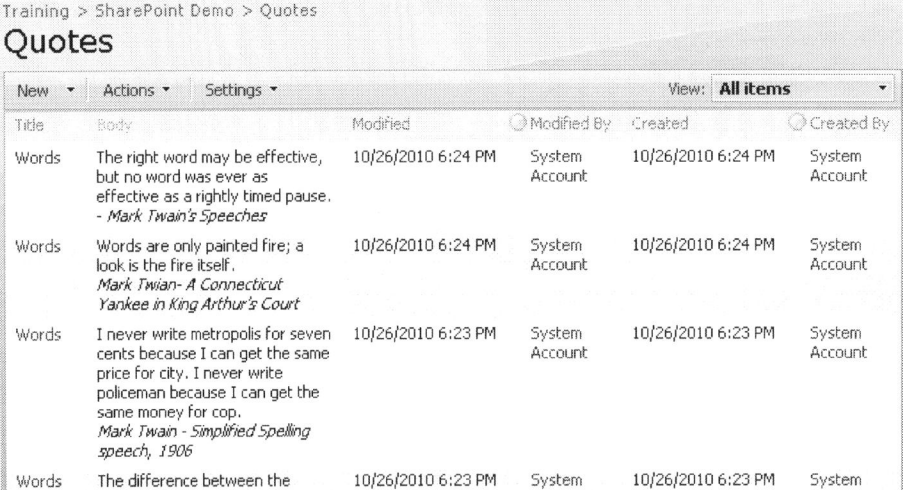

This is the list with the truncated text:

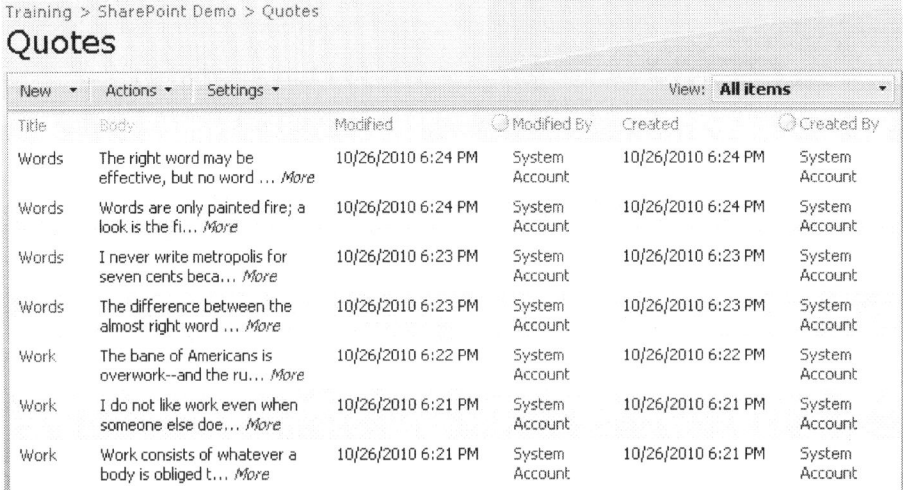

We want to take the text from a long multiline text column and truncate it to say 50 characters and then add a "More" link to take the user to the DispForm.aspx page so they can read all of the text. The JavaScript below is similar to many of the JavaScript customizations in this book. It first searches for an HTML table with an attribute named "summary" that contains the name of the list. It then looks inside of this table for <TR> tags to find the rows. It then filters these to only rows containing more than 2 <TD> tags. We then extract the HREF (URL) to the DispForm.aspx page that's in the default link for the list item. Next we extract the long text from the text column (<TD>), shorten it to "xx" characters, append the "More" link using the HREF found earlier and then write this back into the <DIV> in the <TD>.

Steps:

These steps show adding a Content Editor Web Part to hold the link to the JavaScript. You can also edit the page in SharePoint Designer and add the code from below to just before then end tag of the **PlaceHolderMain** block. See chapter 9 for more details on these options.

1. Go to the page with the list displayed as a web part
2. Edit the web part and customize the view - at least two columns must be displayed: one with the long text and one which is the column called "**Name (linked to document with edit menu)**".
3. Save the changes to the web part
4. Click **Site Actions, Edit Page**
5. Add a Content Editor Web Part and move it below the list's web part
6. For SharePoint 2007:
    a. Edit the web part, click the **Source Editor** button and paste the JavaScript code from below
    b. Edit the five variables in the code (see notes below)
7. For SharePoint 2007 or 2010:
    a. Copy the JavaScript code from below and paste into Windows Notepad
    b. Edit the five variables in the code (see notes below)
    c. Save or upload the file to a SharePoint library
    d. Copy the URL for the file in the library (right-click the file and click **Properties**)
    e. Return to your web part page, edit the Content Editor Web Part and paste the URL into the **Content Link** box
8. Test

The JavaScript:

When adding the JavaScript code you must change the following variables:

- **var SummaryName** – Make sure this is correct! The best way to get the correct text is to right-click on the page with the list web part and select View Source. Do a search for "summary=" and copy the name. SharePoint 2010 may add a space at the end of the summary name. Don't delete

List and Library Customization

this! Both versions will include the web part name and the list description as part of the "summary="

- **var ColumnWithDropDown** - When creating a view this column is called "Name (linked to document with edit menu)" - Remember, the first column is #0 and the second is #1…
- **var ColumnWithLongText** – The column with the text that needs to be trimmed - Remember, the first column is #0 and the second is #1…
- **var CharactersToShow** – Just what its name implies… If the column as fewer than this many characters, then there is no change, but if more, then the column is truncated and a "More" link is added.
- **var isEnhancedRichText** – If the column is Enhanced Rich Text then the HTML is a bit different.

```
<script>

// Update the next five variables to match your list
var SummaryName = "Tasks Use the Tasks list to keep track of work that you or your team needs to complete." ;
var ColumnWithDropDown = 2;  //first column is 0
var ColumnWithLongText = 8;
var CharactersToShow   = 100;
var isEnhancedRichText = false;

var tables = document.getElementsByTagName("TABLE");
for (var i=0;i<tables.length;i++)
{
  if ( tables[i].summary == SummaryName )
  {
    var rows = tables[i].getElementsByTagName("TR");
    for (var j=1;j<rows.length;j++)
    {
      if (rows[j].childNodes.length > 2)
      {
        if ( rows[j].childNodes[ColumnWithDropDown ] == "[object Text]")
          continue; // fix for Firefox

        var href = rows[j].childNodes[ColumnWithDropDown ].getElementsByTagName("A")[0].href

        // the following is all one line
        if (href.toLowerCase().indexOf("dispform.aspx") == -1 &&
href.toLowerCase().indexOf("listid=") == -1  )
        {
```

```
        var docID = rows[j].childNodes[ColumnWithDropDown].childNodes[0].id

      // if not "dispform.aspx" then must be a library or links list
      // if "listid=" then must be a task list in 2010
      var parts = href.split("/");
      parts[parts.length-1] = "forms/DispForm.aspx?ID=" + docID;
      href = parts.join("/");
    }


    var theNode;
    if (isEnhancedRichText)
    {
      theNode = rows[j].childNodes[ColumnWithLongText].childNodes[0].childNodes[0];
    }
    else
    {
      theNode = rows[j].childNodes[ColumnWithLongText].childNodes[0];
    }
    if (theNode.innerHTML.length>CharactersToShow)
    {
      if (document.all)  // IE
        theNode.innerHTML = theNode.innerText.substring(0,CharactersToShow)
        + "... <a href='" + href + "'><i>More</i></a>"
      else // Firefox
        try {
        theNode.innerHTML = theNode.textContent.substring(0,CharactersToShow)
        + "... <a href='" + href + "'><i>More</i></a>"
        } catch (e) {}
    }
   }
  }
  break; // no need to check the other tables
 }
}
</script>
```

Code Notes:

- **theNode.innerHTML = theNode.innerText**… – This strips out all of the HTML formatting from the text and loads back the clear text and the MORE link
- **if (rows[j].childNodes[ColumnWithDropDown] == "[object Text]")**
  Firefox and IE handle white space differently.
- **theNode.innerText vs. theNode.textContent** – IE and Firefox don't work the same (so what's new…)

How do to add columns (metadata) to SharePoint folders (2007 & 2010)

The question was: "How do I add a column (meta data) to SharePoint folders?" My first thought is to modify the Content Type named Folder, but it is "sealed". (Microsoft locked the door!) So I created a new Content Type based on Folder, added the custom columns, added the content type to the library and magically I found my custom folder type in the New dropdown.

Note that this process will add metadata to folders, but this metadata will not carry down to items in the folder. I.e. A search for a meta data keyword will find the folder, not the documents in the folder. SharePoint 2010 has a special content type called a Document Set that cause its metadata to be inherited by items within the Document Set. Do a web search on "Document Set" to find out what else it can do.

Steps:

1. Go to **Site Actions, Site Settings**
2. Click **Site Content Types**
3. Click **Create**
4. Give the new content type a name such as **Enhanced Folder** or **Product Spec Folder**
5. Set the parent content type group as **Folder Content Types**
6. Set the parent content type to **Folder**
7. Add the new Content Type to a content type group. I put it in the exiting **Folder Content Types** group
8. Click **OK**
9. Scroll down to the columns section and click **Add from new site column**
10. Name the column and set all the usual column options.
11. Repeat for any additional columns (**Release Date**, etc)
12. Click **OK**
13. Go to your document library
14. 2007: Click **Settings** and **Library Settings**
    2010: Click the **Library** tab of the ribbon and click **Library Settings**
15. Click **Advanced** and set **Allow management of content types** to **Yes** and click **OK**

List and Library Customization

16. Scroll down to **Content Types** and click **Add from existing site content types** and add your new folder content type
17. Go to your document library and click the **New** dropdown and add your new folder!
18. Go to the View dropdown and click **Modify this view** and add your new folder meta data columns (you will probably want to move them to just after the **Name** column)

Hiding the Checked Out icon from anonymous users (2007 & 2010)

When a document has been checked out, SharePoint will overlay a little icon to show the checked out status. When a user moves their mouse over the icon it will display a popup with the name of the user who has it checked out.

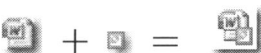

And when they mouse-over this icon they see this popup:

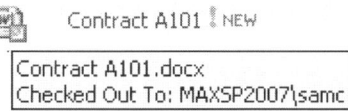

Anonymous users can see it too!

You may want to display this icon to most users, but very likely not to read only and anonymous users.

Hiding it:

There is no out of the box way to turn off this icon, so we need a trick to hide it. You could use JavaScript or jQuery, but best bet is to use a tiny piece of Cascading Style Sheet (CSS) code.

The code to display the icon looks like this:

<img src="/_layouts/images/checkoutoverlay.gif" class="ms-vb-icon-overlay" ...

The CSS to hide it looks like this:

```
<style type="text/css">
  .ms-vb-icon-overlay
  {
    display:none
  }
</style>
```

List and Library Customization

The only problem with this is that it hides the icon from everyone. A better solution would be to hide it from selected users. So what we do is:

- Add a style to hide it from all users (display:none)
- Add a SPSecurityTrimmedControl to then show it for any user with appropriate permissions (the example below uses the "AddListItems" permission)

The "code": (CSS + a SharePoint Control)

```
<style type="text/css">
  .ms-vb-icon-overlay
  {
    display:none;
  }
</style>

<SharePoint:SPSecurityTrimmedControl runat="server" PermissionsString="AddListItems">
  <style type="text/css">
    .ms-vb-icon-overlay
    {
      display:inline;
    }
  </style>
</SharePoint:SPSecurityTrimmedControl>
```

Where should you put this code?

- If you want this for just a single page, put this CSS in a Content Editor Web Part on that page (see chapter 9)
- If you want this for an entire site then add this to your master page somewhere after where SharePoint add its CSS links (**SharePoint:CssLink** and **SharePoint:Theme** tags). Anywhere just before </BODY> should work. (see chapter 6)

```
<SharePoint:CssLink runat="server"/>
<SharePoint:Theme runat="server"/>

  <style type="text/css">
    <!-- your CSS goes here -->
  </style>
```

List and Library Customization

What might go wrong?

SharePoint might be using the **ms-vb-icon-overlay** style for something other than checkout status. I've not run across it yet, but you never know...

One library, multiple sites!

We often have data in one place that we need in another. SharePoint libraries have the "Link to Document" content type (see "Adding hyperlinks to document libraries" earlier in this chapter), but you have to create a link for each document and there is no automatic feature to create new links. In this customization we are going to create a library web part in one site and, with a few customizations, move it to another web site while still displaying data from the original site.

This customization has an interesting history. The question that started this was "why don't list and library web parts have an 'Export' option?" Most other web parts do.

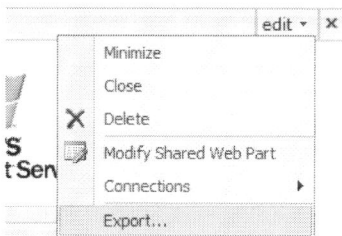

A little background:

- While editing a web part page, click a web part's menu and you will usually see an **Export** option, except when working with list and library web parts
- List and library view pages are web part pages (they have "**Edit Page**" in the **Site Actions** menu") and the displayed list is a web part

So, why are these web parts different? And, if we could export a list or library web part, could we import it into another site and have it still work? Turns out, with a little work, they can be exported, and imported back into any site in the same site collection.

Tools Needed:

- SharePoint Designer
- A little utility you will need to download to get the GUID (Globally Unique Identifier) for the site
- Access rights to the top level site of the site collection, or at least rights to the Web Part Gallery (or ask your Site Administrator to upload the web part for you)

305

List and Library Customization

So how can you export a list web part?

It turns out to be pretty easy. Edit the page in SharePoint Designer and change one word.

Steps:

1. Open the site in SharePoint Designer then locate and double click on a page with the web part (default.aspx, Shared Documents/Forms/Allitems.aspx, etc)
2. In the code view find the web part and find
   <ExportControlledProperties>false</ExportControlledProperties>
   and change from "false" to "true"
   Tip: to find the web part code: display the page in Split view, click the web part - the web part's code will be highlighted
3. Save the page
   (This will "unghost" the page, but you can undo the changes after the export is complete by right-clicking the file in the Folder List and selecting Reset to Site Definition)
4. Go to a browser, visit this page and go to Site Actions, Edit Page
5. Click the Edit dropdown menu in the web part you just modified and click Export
6. Give the file a name and save it somewhere where you can find it in the next step

Import the exported settings as a new web part <u>back into the same site</u>:

7. Visit your top level site in the site collection and go to Site Actions, Site Settings, and in the Galleries column click Web Parts
8. Upload the web part (.DWP or .WEBPART) you just exported in step 6 - while you don't need to change any of the options, you may want to rename it for clarity

Add the web part <u>to the same site</u>

9. Nothing special here. Add this web part just to a page just like any other web part.

Some differences to note...

- Oddly, the displayed columns are different. The All Items view displayed four columns: Type, Name, Modified and Modified By. The new web part displays three columns: Type, Name and Modified By. This is easy to fix. Edit the web part and change the Selected View property to All Documents. You will then have the same list of columns in both displays.
- The new web part does not display a toolbar by default, but this can be enabled from the web part's properties panel. If the toolbar is enabled you will see all of the buttons found in the All Items page: New, Upload, Actions and Settings (depending on the current user's security rights).

Now test the web part in a sub site....

If you add the web part to a subsite you will get an error!

List and Library Customization

> **Unable to add selected web part(s).**
> **List does not exist.**
> **The page you selected contains a list that does not exist.**

On the first attempt it appears that the new exported web part will not work on another site. Time for more research…

Open the web part file created by the Export by using Notepad or other text editor. Find these two lines:

<ListName …..>{ *guid_here* } </ListName>

<WebId ….> *guid_here* </WebId>

SharePoint uses Globally Unique IDs (GUIDS) to identify just about everything stored in the databases. Notice that the **ListName** element has a GUID, but the **WebId** element's GUID is all zeros. Replace the zeros with the GUID for the site that owns the list and all will then work.

Finding the site's GUID

I have not found any place in the pages where SharePoint exposes web site's GUID. (Although a list's GUID can be found in some of the URLs - for example after clicking **Settings, List Settings** or **Library Settings**) I wrote a little utility to display a site's GUIDs that you can download from Link 1102.

1. Download the file (it's a ZIP file)
2. Extract the program from the ZIP file and run it
3. Enter the URL to your site along with your username and password and click **Go**
4. Click the "**Web:**" URL and the copy it from the "**Selected ID**" box

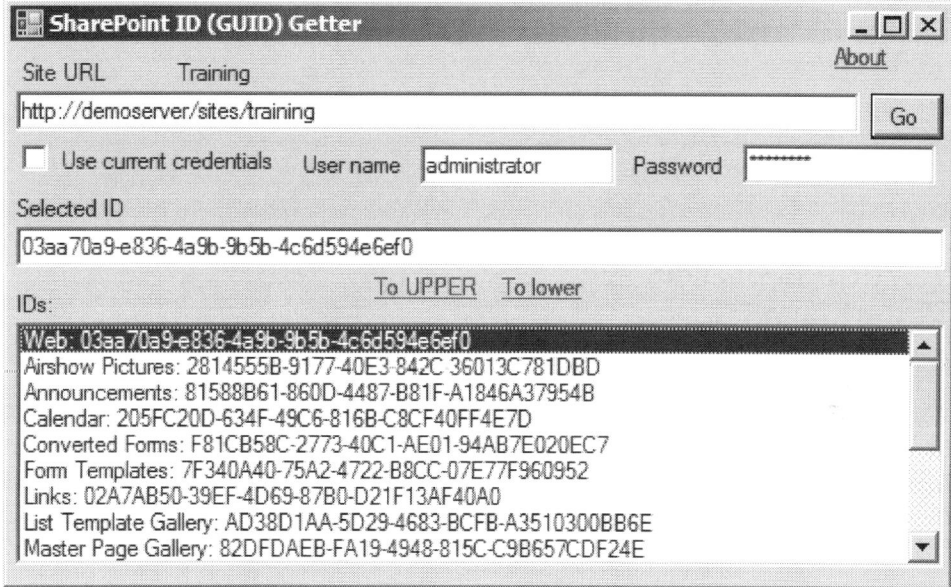

307

List and Library Customization

Update the web part file

Edit the **WebId** element and replace the all zeros GUID with the site's GUID:

SP 2007:   <WebId ....> all_zeros_guid_here </WebId>

SP 2010 :   <property name="WebId" ...>all_zeros_guid_here </property>

After updating the .DWP or .WEBPART file with the site's (web's) GUID, re-upload it to the web part gallery and test the web part in a subsite.

And something for the "Strange Things" list... the GUID for the web site does not include brackets ({ }) and is in lower case. The GUID for the list must have brackets and MUST be in UPPER CASE or it will not work.

Notes:

- Users will need rights to the original list or library. This web part is only a view of the real list.
- This will only work within the same site, or within the same site collection. It will not work between site collections, between applications or between servers.
- So far I have only tested this on a MOSS 2007 Enterprise installation and in SharePoint Server 2010.
- I have tested this so far with document libraries and several lists such as Announcements, but not with every list and library.
- The view displayed in the web part is a copy of the view in the original list or library. Use Edit, Modify Shared Web Part to pick another view or to refresh the view.
- Alerts will be stored in the site with the original list so alert management will need to be done from that site's Site Actions, Site Settings menu.
- Most menu options will display pages from the site with the original list, but when the user clicks OK, Cancel, Close, etc, they will return to the site with the web part. One exception is if an operation generates as error, the "Go back to site" link will take them to the list's site, not the web part's site.

List and Library Customization

Rotating Pictures, Random Pictures

Many web sites have a picture that either changes on each visit to the site or randomly changes while the user is viewing the page. This is often done to highlight a product or to display pictures from a team event. SharePoint provides two options to do something similar, but are probably not quite what you are looking for. In SharePoint 2007 you can add a "This week in pictures" web part. All this does is display the last picture uploaded to a picture library. While it also has a "View slide show" button, this opens a new window where the user has to click the Play button to see the "show". SharePoint 2010 has removed "This week in pictures" web part and replaced it with the "Picture Library Slideshow" web part. This web part is closer to what you want, but it does a number of weird things! It seems to scan all of the images in the library to find the largest one and then sizes the web part for that picture. This web part is also downloading the full size picture and then resizing it to fit the web part, which can slow down page loads.

The 2010 Picture Library Slideshow Web Part with the largest picture setting the web part size:

A JavaScript Solution

This customization will give you a lot more control over how your images are presented. One possible result of this custom solution might look like this:

309

List and Library Customization

How it works

This customization takes advantage of the out of the box Picture Library to hold the pictures and to automatically create a "thumbnail" version of the picture. It also uses a regular library web part to list the pictures and their URLs. This library web part will be hidden, but is on the page to bring the list of pictures to the home page so our JavaScript code can access them. A Content Editor Web Part is used to both display the pictures and to hold the JavaScript. The JavaScript finds the library web part, hides it and extracts the list of pictures. The code then displays the pictures with the options you have selected.

The basic steps:

- Add a picture library and upload some pictures
- Add a the web part for this new library on your home page
- Customize the view used by the web part
- Add a Content Editor Web Part to the same page and add the HTML and JavaScript code from below to display the pictures

Options:

When you paste the JavaScript you can set a few options to control the appearance of the images:

- One is required:
    - The name of the web part
- The rest are optional:
    - Show the pictures in thumbnail size (160 pixels wide) or full size
    - Show in the order found in the web part or random
    - Set how long each picture is displayed
    - Set how long to take to transition between images (Note: the feature used here works in IE 6, but is not supported in Firefox and is buggy in IE 8)
    - Set if you would like to make the images clickable to navigate to a custom URL
    - Set if you would like to display the First, Previous, Play, Next and Last buttons
    - Set a column that contains a "caption" or custom text

Steps

Upload pictures and add the library's web part:

1. Create a picture library
2. If you would like to have the pictures clickable, add a Hyperlink column

3. If you would like to supply descriptive text or captions for the pictures, add a "**Multiple lines of text**" column

Column (click to edit)	Type
Title	Single line of text
Date Picture Taken	Date and Time
Description	Multiple lines of text
Keywords	Multiple lines of text
CustomUrl	Hyperlink or Picture
CustomText	Multiple lines of text
Created By	Person or Group

4. If you would like to filter the list of pictures to be displayed then add additional columns to the filter data (Event name, department, product, etc)
5. Ideally, clean up your pictures in a picture editor program to crop them and resize them to no larger than needed on your site (but you can also use the consistently sized thumbnails created during the upload)
6. Upload your pictures and add the custom URL and text if desired
7. Go to your web part page and add the web part for the new library - not the SharePoint "View slide show" or "Picture Library Slideshow" web parts, just the regular library web part
8. Click **Edit, Modify Shared Web Part**
9. Optional: In the appearance section give the web part a meaningful name
10. Click **Edit the Current View**
11. Un-checkmark all of the columns except for **Name (linked to document)**
12. Checkmark a column to use for the custom URL
    - if you don't have a custom URL then select any column
    - this must be the second column in the view
13. Checkmark a column to use as a custom text/caption
    - this must be the third column in the view
    - this must be a "Multiple lines of text" column
14. Optional: Set the sort order (if not using the "random picture" option)
15. Optional: Set filter options to select only the pictures you want displayed
16. Make sure the list web part view is not using an "Item Limit" less than the number of pictures in the list (You could just set this to be BIG number)
17. Click **OK** to save the view changes
18. Click **OK** to save the web part changes

    Your library web part might look something like this:
    2010:

List and Library Customization

2007:

Add the Content Editor Web Part

19. For 2010:
    a. Open Notepad and add the JavaScript from below
    b. Edit the **"vars"** in the code per step 23 C
    c. Save the file and upload to a library in the same site as the picture library

20. Add a Content Editor Web Part (CEWP) **below** the picture library web part
21. Click **Edit, Modify Shared Web Part**
22. Change the web part's title or set the **Chrome** to **None**

23. For 2007:
    a. Click the **Source Editor** button
    b. Copy and paste the code from below
    c. Edit the **"vars"** at the beginning of the JavaScript:
    pictureWebPartName – enter the web part, and if your library has a description, then include it:
    If the library name is "Airshow Pictures" and has no Description
    var pictureWebPartName="Airshow Pictures"
    If the library name is "Airshow Pictures" and has a description of "Pictures from the Dayton Airshow"
    var pictureWebPartName="Airshow Pictures - Pictures from the Airshow"

```
var pictureWebPartName="Airshow Pictures"; // name of the picture
var showThumbnails = true;       //otherwise show full sized images
var randomImg = true;            //set to true to show in random or
var useCustomLinks = true;       //true to use second column as URL
var RotatingPicturesLoopTime = 5000;  //2000 = 2 seconds
var manualClick = true;          //true to use the play pause butto
var customTextColumn = true;     //true to display text / caption
```

Also edit **showThumbnails, randomImg, useCustomLinks, RotatingPicturesLoopTime, imgToImgTransition, manualClick** and **customTextColumn** as needed
  d. Click **OK** for the Source Editor
  e. Click **OK** to save the web part changes
  f. Click Exit Edit Mode and see if it works! (The library web part should disappear)

24. For 2010:
  a. Enter the URL for the Notepad file uploaded earlier in step 19 in the **Content Link** box
  b. Click **OK** to save the web part changes
  c. Save the page and see if it works!

Most common errors

- The list web part does not have the "Name (linked to document)" as the first column
- If you are using the Custom Hyperlink option, the second column must be a Hyperlink column
- If you are using the Custom Text option, the third column must be a "Multiple lines of text"
- The name used for pictureWebPartName is the name of the web part, plus the description from the picture library. View the source of the page with the library web part and search for the name of your picture library looking for: title="*name of your web part - library description*"   or title="*name of your web part*".

The Code

This code sample has two major sections; the JavaScript (lots of it!) and the HTML (at the beginning) that is used to format the picture, caption and navigation controls. You may want to revise the HTML section to change the appearance of the final web part.

There is no way you want to type this one! Go to the web site and copy it from there.

```
<!--
  add your own formatting in the HTML below...
  - add borders
  - change fonts and colors
  - set a background
  - use images for the navigation links
-->
<table border="0" cellpadding="0" cellspacing="0" width="100%">
  <tr>
    <td id="VU" height="125" width="160" align="center" valign="middle">
      <a name="RotatingImageLnk" id="RotatingImageLnk" alt="click for larger picture">
```

```
      <img src="/_layouts/images/dot.gif" name="RotatingImage" id="RotatingImage" border=0>
    </a>
    <span name="RotatingImageMsg" id="RotatingImageMsg"></span>
  </td>
  <td ID="customTextTD" name="customTextTD" width="100%" style="padding: 4px 1ex 4px 4px;">
     <span name="RotatingImageText" id="RotatingImageText"></span>
  </td>
 </tr>
 <tr id="buttonRow" style="display:none">
  <td colspan="2" align="left">
    <a href="" onclick="moveFirst();return false;">First</a>
    <a href="" onclick="movePrev();return false;">Previous</a>
    <a href="" onclick="movePlay();return false;" name="PlayButton" ID="PlayButton">Play</a>
    <a href="" onclick="moveNext();return false;">Next</a>
    <a href="" onclick="moveLast();return false;">Last</a>
  </td>
 </tr>
</table>


<script>

// another CEWP trick from http://techtrainingnotes.blogspot.com

var pictureWebPartName="Airshow Pictures"; // name of the picture library web part
var showThumbnails = true;       //otherwise show full sized images
var randomImg = true;          //set to true to show in random order
var useCustomLinks = true;     //true to use second column as URL for picture clicks
var RotatingPicturesLoopTime = 5000;  //2000 = 2 seconds
var manualClick = true;        //true to use the play pause buttons
var customTextColumn = true;    //true to display text / caption

// this is not supported in Firefox and is buggie in IE 8, so it has been removed
//var imgToImgTransition = 0;        //2 = 2 seconds


// don't change these
var selectedImg = 0;
var imgCache = [];
```

```
var imgTag;
var listFound = false;


function RotatingPictures()
{
  if (manualClick) {document.getElementById("buttonRow").style.display="inline"};
  if (!customTextColumn) {document.getElementById("customTextTD").style.display="none"}

  imgTag = document.getElementById("RotatingImage");

  //Find the picture web part and hide it
  var Imgs = [];
  var LinkList;

  var TDs = document.getElementsByTagName("TD"); // find all of the table cells
  for (var i=0; i<TDs.length; i++)
  {
    if (TDs[i].title == pictureWebPartName)
    {
      // tables in tables in tables... ah SharePoint!
      LinkList = 
TDs[i].parentNode.parentNode.parentNode.parentNode.parentNode.parentNode.parentNode;
      // hide the links list web part
      LinkList.style.display="none";

      listFound = true;
      break;
    }
  }
  if (!LinkList)
  {
    document.getElementById("RotatingImageMsg").innerHTML="Web Part '" + 
pictureWebPartName + "' not found!";
    return;
  }


  // SharePoint 2010 code
  if ( typeof _fV4UI != "undefined" )
  {
```

```
var tbl = document.getElementsByTagName("TABLE") // find all of the tables
var len=0

for (i=0; i<tbl.length; i++)
{
  if (tbl[i].className=="ms-unselectedtitle")
  {
    var Url="";
    if (document.all) // is IE
     { Url = tbl[i].Url; }
    else            // is Firefox or other
     { Url = tbl[i].getAttribute("url"); }

    if (Url != null)
    {
      Imgs[len]=[];
      Imgs[len][0] = Url;

      Imgs[len][1] = "";
      if (document.all) // is IE
       { Imgs[len][1] = tbl[i].parentNode.nextSibling.innerText; }
      else            // is Firefox or other
       { Imgs[len][1] = tbl[i].parentNode.nextSibling.textContent; }

      Imgs[len][2] = "";
      if (document.all) // is IE
       { Imgs[len][2] = tbl[i].parentNode.nextSibling.nextSibling.innerText; }
      else            // is Firefox or other
       { Imgs[len][2] = tbl[i].parentNode.nextSibling.nextSibling.textContent; }

      len++;
    }
  }
}
// end of 2010 code


// SharePoint 2007 code
if ( typeof _fV4UI == "undefined" )
```

List and Library Customization

```
{

  var links = LinkList.getElementsByTagName("TR") // find all of the rows
  var url;
  var len;
  for (i=0;i<links.length;i++)
  {

   if (links[i].childNodes[0].className=="ms-vb2")
   {
     len=Imgs.length
     Imgs[len]=[]
     Imgs[len][0] = links[i].childNodes[0].childNodes[0].href;
     if (useCustomLinks)
     {
       if (links[i].childNodes[1].childNodes.length>0)
        { Imgs[len][1] = links[i].childNodes[1].childNodes[0].href; }
       else
        { Imgs[len][1] = "" }
     }
     if (customTextColumn)
     {
       if (links[i].childNodes[1].childNodes.length>0)
        {Imgs[len][2] = links[i].childNodes[1].nextSibling.childNodes[0].innerHTML;}
       else
        {Imgs[len][2] = "" }
     }
   }
  }
}
// end of 2007 code


 if (Imgs.length==0)
 {
   document.getElementById("RotatingImageMsg").innerHTML="No images found in web part '"
+ pictureWebPartName + "'!";
   return;
 }
 for (i = 0; i < Imgs.length; i++)
```

```
   {
     imgCache[i] = new Image();
     imgCache[i].src = Imgs[i][0];
     if (useCustomLinks)
     {
//     imgCache[i].customlink=Imgs[i][1];
       imgCache[i].setAttribute("customlink",Imgs[i][1]);
     }
     if (customTextColumn)
     {
//     imgCache[i].customtext=Imgs[i][2];
       imgCache[i].setAttribute("customtext",Imgs[i][2]);
     }

   }

   RotatingPicturesLoop();
 }


 // now show the pictures...
 function RotatingPicturesLoop()
 {
   if (imgCache.length == 0)
   {
     document.getElementById("RotatingImageMsg").innerHTML="No image cache found in web part '" + pictureWebPartName + "'!";
     LinkList.style.display="";
     return;
   }

   if (!manualClick)
     if (randomImg)
     {
       selectedImg=Math.floor( Math.random() * imgCache.length );
     }

   // this is not supported in Firefox and is buggie in IE 8, so it has been removed
   //if (document.all && imgToImgTransition>0 ){
   //   imgTag.style.filter="blendTrans(duration=" + imgToImgTransition + ")";
   //   imgTag.filters.blendTrans.Apply();
```

```
  //}

  url=imgCache[selectedImg].src
  if (useCustomLinks)
  {
document.getElementById("RotatingImageLnk").href=imgCache[selectedImg].getAttribute("customlink"); }
  else
  { RotatingImageLnk.href = url; }

  if (customTextColumn)
  {
    var ctext = imgCache[selectedImg].getAttribute("customtext") + ""
    document.getElementById("customTextTD").innerHTML = ctext.replace(/&lt;/g,'<').replace(/&gt;/g,'>');
  }
  else
    document.getElementById("customTextTD").innerHTML = "";

  if (showThumbnails)
  {
    // convert URLs to point to the thumbnails...
    //   from  airshow%20pictures/helicopter.jpg
    //   to    airshow%20pictures/_t/helicopter_jpg.jpg

    url = revString(url);
    var c = url.indexOf(".");
    url = url.substring(0,c) + "_" + url.substring(c+1,url.length);
    c = url.indexOf("/");
    url = url.substring(0,c) + "/t_" + url.substring(c,url.length);
    url = revString(url) + ".jpg";
  }

  imgTag.src = url;

  // this is not supported in Firefox and is buggie in IE 8, so it has been removed
  //if (document.all){
  //   imgTag.filters.blendTrans.Play();
  //}

  if (!manualClick)
```

```
  {
    selectedImg += 1;
    if (selectedImg > (imgCache.length-1)) selectedImg=0;

    setTimeout(RotatingPicturesLoop, RotatingPicturesLoopTime);
  }
}


// utility function revString found here:
// http://www.java2s.com/Code/JavaScript/Language-Basics/PlayingwithStrings.htm
function revString(str) {
  var retStr = "";
  for (i=str.length - 1 ; i > - 1 ; i--){
    retStr += str.substr(i,1);
  }
  return retStr;
}

function moveFirst() {setManual(); selectedImg = 0; RotatingPicturesLoop()}
function moveNext()  {setManual(); selectedImg += 1; if (selectedImg > (imgCache.length-1)) selectedImg=0; RotatingPicturesLoop()}
function movePrev()  {setManual(); selectedImg -= 1; if (selectedImg < 0 ) selectedImg=imgCache.length-1; RotatingPicturesLoop()}
function moveLast()  {setManual(); selectedImg = imgCache.length-1;  RotatingPicturesLoop()}

function setManual()
{
  manualClick = true;
  document.getElementById("PlayButton").innerHTML="Play";
}

function movePlay() {
  if (document.getElementById("PlayButton").innerHTML=="Play")
  {
    manualClick = false;
    document.getElementById("PlayButton").innerHTML="Pause";
  }
  else
  {
    manualClick = true;
```

```
    document.getElementById("PlayButton").innerHTML="Play";
  }
if (listFound)
{
  RotatingPicturesLoop()}
}



RotatingPictures()

</script>
```

The List, the Whole List, Nothing but the List

SharePoint does not provide a clean way to display or print just a list or library. It only displays the list inside of the master page and that includes all of the navigation, search and graphics.

Here are a few workarounds:

- Display the list in the mobile view (http://yoursitename/m)
  (ok, that's not pretty, but it does hide the master page!)

- Install the PrintList sample feature from Ishai Sagi:
  http://www.sharepoint-tips.com/2007/01/how-to-add-print-list-option-to-list.html
  (very cool, works, but requires a Feature deployment to the web front end servers)

- Create a new page using SharePoint Designer that has the web part for the list or library, but does not use the master page, which is what we do in this customization…

Here is the goal:

The list, the whole list, nothing but the list (and maybe a crumb trail…). No site icons, site title, search box, Quick Launch or other clutter.

List and Library Customization

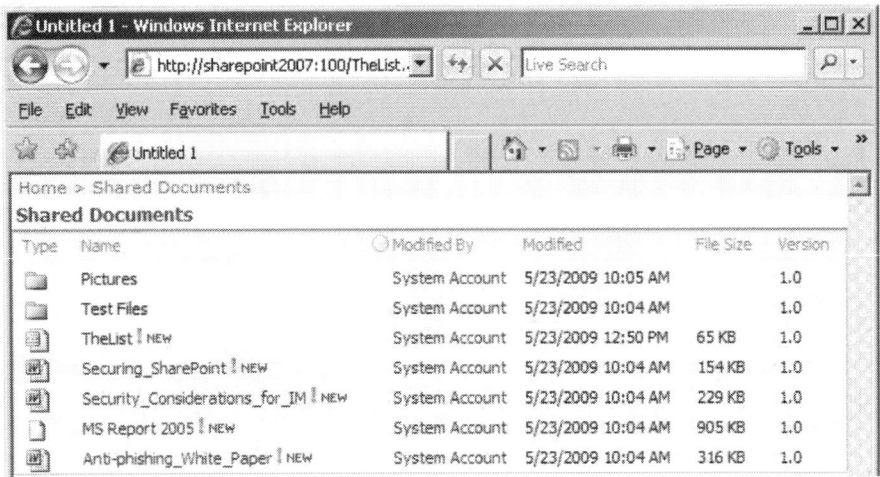

Steps for SP 2007:

1. Open SharePoint Designer 2007
2. Open your site
3. Right-click in a library (in the Folder List in 2007 and in the Navigation panel in 2010)
4. Select **New** and **ASPX** to create a new .ASPX web page

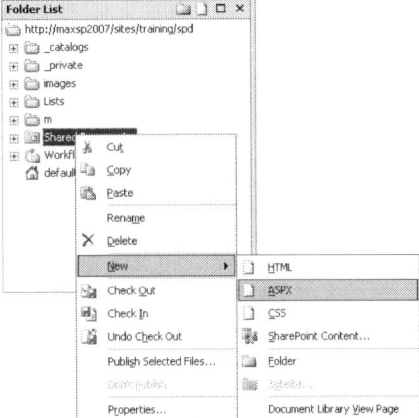

5. Rename the file (**JustTheList.aspx**, or whatever you like)
6. Double click the new file to open it
7. Select the code view by clicking the **Code** tab at the bottom of the editor
8. Add two blank lines between </title> and </head>

322

List and Library Customization

9. Select **Insert, SharePoint Controls, More SharePoint Controls**

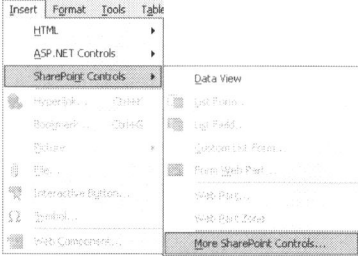

10. Scroll down through the Toolbox pane to find the "**Server Controls (SharePoint)**" section

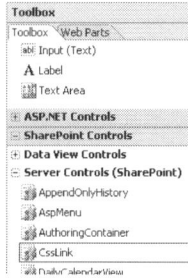

11. Drag a **CssLink** control to the new blank line
12. Drag a **Theme** control to just after the **CssLink** control
13. Select the design view by clicking the **Design** tab at the bottom of the editor
14. Select **Insert, SharePoint Controls, Web Part Zone**
15. Click "**Click to insert a Web Part**"
16. From the Web Parts pane select your list or library and drag it into the web part zone of your new page
17. Save the page and test in a browser (Pressing F12 is the shortcut to open the current page)
18. Click the web part's edit menu dropdown and click **Modify Shared Web Part**

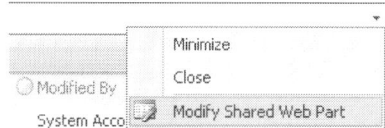

19. Most likely changes you will want to make:
    a. Select another view, or edit the current view
    b. Set the **Toolbar Type** to "No Toolbar"
20. Add a link to this new page in Quick Launch, a links list or as a link from some other page

Steps for SP 2010:

1. Open SharePoint Designer 2010
2. Open your site
3. Click **File, Add Item, More Pages, ASPX, Create** and name the file

List and Library Customization

4. Click **Yes** for the **Advanced Edit** mode
5. Select the code view by clicking the **Code** tab at the bottom of the editor
6. Add two blank lines between </title> and </head>
7. Click in the first blank line, click the **Insert** tab in the ribbon, then click **SharePoint Controls**
8. In the **Service Controls** section click **More SharePoint Controls**
9. Double click the **CssLink** control to add it to the head section
10. Repeat steps 7 and 8 and add the **Theme** control to the head section
11. In the **Insert** tab in the ribbon click **Web Part Zone** to add a new zone
12. In the **Insert** tab in the ribbon click **DataView** and select your list or library
13. Save the page and test in a browser (Pressing F12 is the shortcut to open the current page)
14. Click the web part's edit menu dropdown and click **Edit Web Part**
15. Most likely changes you will want to make:
    a. Select another view, or edit the current view
    b. Set the **Toolbar Type** to "No Toolbar"
16. Add a link to this new page in Quick Launch, a links list or as a link from some other page

Final cleanup?

- Add some HTML comments about how you did all of this so you can fix this up in the future.
- Find the <title> tags at the top of the page and add a proper title to display at the top of the browser and as the title for Favorites.

And I suppose you want a crumb trail too...

Libraries can have folders, and once a user drills down into the folders they need a way back out. I tried most of the things I found on the web to create SharePoint crumb trails and none have worked to create a correct path to use with a web part. As a temporary workaround I created some JavaScript to emulate the crumb trail feature. (Check Link 1101 to see if I have found a better way.)

JavaScript crumb trail for SP 2007:

This JavaScript takes the URL for the page apart to build a crumb trail.

```
<div id="navtrick" class='ms-globalbreadcrumb' style="text-align:left;" ></div>
<script type="text/javascript">
  var fullURL = parent.document.URL;
  var splitURL = fullURL.substring(fullURL.indexOf('?')+1, fullURL.length).split("&");
  var siteURL = fullURL.substring(0,fullURL.indexOf('?'), fullURL.length);
  siteURL = siteURL.substring(0,siteURL.lastIndexOf('/') );
  var rootURL = fullURL.substring(0,fullURL.indexOf('?')) + "?RootFolder=";
  var path = unescape(splitURL[0].split("=")[1]);
  var folders=path.split("/");
```

List and Library Customization

```
  document.getElementById("navtrick").innerHTML = " <a href='" + siteURL + "'>Home</a>";
  for (i=1;i<folders.length;i++)
  {
    rootURL += "/" + folders[i];
    document.getElementById("navtrick").innerHTML += " &gt; <a href='" + rootURL + "'>"
       + folders[i] + "</a>";
  }
</script>
```

To add the crumb trail:

1. Switch back to SharePoint Designer
2. Click **View** and **Refresh** to reload the page (make sure you see the same view and options you just selected above)
3. Add the JavaScript above just after the **<form>** tag
4. Save and test

With the crumb trail (**Chrome** is set to **Title Only**):

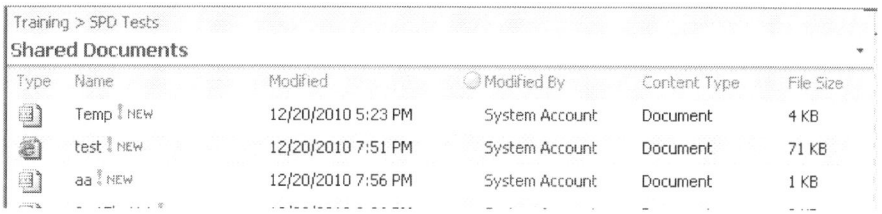

JavaScript crumb trail for SP 2010:

Add just before the **<WebPartPages:XsltListViewWebPart ...>** tag:

```
<div id="navtrick" class='ms-globalbreadcrumb' style="text-align:left;" ></div>
```

Add just after the **</WebPartPages:XsltListViewWebPart>** tag:

```
<script type="text/javascript">
  var fullURL = parent.document.URL;
  var splitURL = fullURL.substring(fullURL.indexOf('?')+1, fullURL.length).split("&");
  var siteURL = fullURL.substring(0,fullURL.indexOf('?'), fullURL.length);
     siteURL = siteURL.substring(0,siteURL.lastIndexOf('/') );
  var rootURL = fullURL.substring(0,fullURL.indexOf('?')) + "?RootFolder=";
  var path = unescape(splitURL[0].split("=")[1]);
```

List and Library Customization

```
   path = path.substring(ctx.HttpRoot.length);

 var folders=path.split("/");

 document.getElementById("navtrick").innerHTML = " <a href='" + ctx.HttpRoot+ "'>"
   + ctx.SiteTitle + "</a>"
   + " &gt; "
   + " <a href='" + rootURL + "'>" + ctx.ListTitle + "</a>";

 rootURL += ctx.listUrlDir;

 for (i=1;i<folders.length;i++)
 {
   rootURL += "/" + folders[i];
   document.getElementById("navtrick").innerHTML += " &gt; <a href='" + rootURL + "'>"
     + folders[i] + "</a>";
 }
 </script>
```

To add the crumb trail:

1. Switch back to SharePoint Designer
2. Click **View** and **Refresh** to reload the page (make sure you see the same view and options you just selected above)
3. Add the JavaScript above just after the **<form>** tag
4. Save and test

With the crumb trail (**Chrome** is set to **None**):

326

12. Surveys

Do you need this chapter?

If you want to do anything beyond basic surveys, then take a look here for a few ways to fancy up your surveys.

What's in this chapter?

- A list of survey tips, including how to create custom views
- A better Yes/No field for surveys and lists
- Adding a Welcome or Instructions message to the Overview page
- Adding a Welcome, Instructions or Thank You message to the survey
- Adding Color, Fonts and HTML to Surveys

Surveys

Surveys are one of those list types like Discussions and Wikis that don't look like a list. Behind the scenes a survey is just another SharePoint list that has a special user interface. You create a survey just like any other list, except you can choose from two additional column types: Rating and Page Break. A survey also has two special pages named overview.aspx and summary.aspx that serve as a "home page" and a report page.

2007 vs. 2010

Surveys are largely unchanged between 2007 and 2010. SharePoint 2010 Surveys don't even have a ribbon! They still have the "old" 2007 toolbar and view dropdowns.

2010 Issues:

- The lack of a ribbon prevents the use of a Rich Text Editor with the Content Editor Web Part. You will need to create any text, JavaScript or HTML in a separate text file, upload it to a library and then link it using the Content Editor Web Part's "Content Link" property.
- Adding a web part to a list page causes 2010 to hide the title area view dropdown. This is not currently a problem with the Survey page as the ribbon and other 2010 enhancements are not supported. If a future update brings the Survey list up to 2010 standards (ribbon, view menu only in the title area, etc), then the customizations in this chapter would break the view menu.
- 2010 lists include a Column Validation feature so you can write a formula to test user input --- for example, you could require that a number must be greater than a certain value "[Age] > 17". As of the current release, an invalid entry in a validated question will generate an error. This is a known bug and hopefully will be fixed in a future update.

Survey Pages

Surveys use the following pages:

overview.aspx	This is the "home" page for the survey. It lists the name, description, time created, number of responses and includes links to the summary.aspx and allitems.aspx pages.
NewForm.aspx	This is the page used to start a new survey and is the destination for the "Respond to this survey" link.
	Tip: Email the URL to NewForm.aspx to your users so they can start a survey in one click.
EditForm.aspx	This page has two uses:

	- to edit an existing survey
	- to display the second through the last pages of a multipage survey (a survey with page separators)
AllItems.aspx	This page has a list of all responses to the survey. You can display it by clicking "Show all responses" on the overview page or by selecting "All Responses" from the view dropdown.
Summary.aspx	This page shows a graphical summary of all responses. You can display it by clicking "Show a graphical summary of responses" on the overview page or by selecting "Graphical Summary" from the view dropdown.

SharePoint 2010 uses the same pages listed above, but displays the NewForm.aspx and EditForm.aspx pages in a pop-up dialog box.

Survey Tips

Before we get into customization, here are a few tips for working with surveys.

Use a Direct URL to a Survey

You can send your users directly to a new survey by giving them the URL to the NewForm.aspx page. Send this URL in an email, add it to Quick Launch or add it to an announcement to provide a "one-click" link to the survey.

To discover the URL:

- Go to the survey and click "Respond to this survey"
- For 2007, copy the URL from the browser's address bar up to, and including, "NewForm.aspx", but exclude "?Source=…"
- For 2010, right-click in the dialog box and click **Properties** then copy the URL up to, and including, "NewForm.aspx", but exclude "?IsDlg=1"
- Paste this URL into an email, Quick Launch or an announcement
- Optional: At the end of the URL add "?Source=" and the URL of a page you would like to send the user to after they complete the survey. Two important notes:
    - This URL must be to a page in a SharePoint site
    - "Source" is ignored on multipage surveys (surveys with Page Separators)

  The following example would be typed as all one line:

Surveys

> http://*yourserver*/sites/*yoursite*/Lists/*yoursurveyname*/**NewForm.aspx?Source=**
> http://*yourserver*/sites/*yoursite*/Shared Document/*thankyou.aspx*

SharePoint 2010 users...

SharePoint 2010 hides many of the options when you create new lists. When you create a new list using **Site Actions, More Options,** always click the **More Options** button instead of **Create** so you can see and set the options.

Survey

Type: List
Categories: Data

A list of questions which you would like to have people answer. Surveys allow you to quickly create questions and view graphical summaries of the responses.

Survey Options:

This is the screen displayed when you create a new survey: (SP 2010 users need to click the **More Options** button to get here.)

Name and Description

Type a new name as you want it to appear in headings and links throughout the site. Type descriptive text that will help site visitors use this survey.

Name:
Description:

Navigation

Specify whether a link to this survey appears in the Quick Launch.

Display this survey on the Quick Launch?
● Yes   ○ No

Survey Options

Specify whether users' names will appear in survey results and whether users can respond to the same survey multiple times.

Show user names in survey results?
● Yes   ○ No
Allow multiple responses?
○ Yes   ● No

Don't add to Quick Launch

Surveys are often used for only a few days and then rarely need to be seen by your users again. When you create the survey select the option to not add the survey to Quick Launch.

Surveys

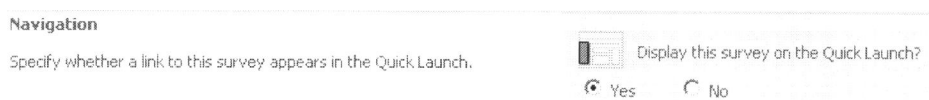

Instead of using Quick Launch, notify your users by adding a link to an Announcement or an email. To get the link, click the **Respond to this Survey** button and then copy the URL. (In 2010, right-click the form and select **Properties** to see the URL.)

Allow testing by allowing multiple responses

If you would like to test your new survey, you will need to fill it out more than once. The default settings only let you fill out a survey once. After you are finished testing, go back to the survey, click **Show All Responses**, delete the test responses, then go and change the option back to **No**.

You can create custom views! (2007 only)

Or at least in SharePoint 2007 you can. In SharePoint 2010 you can create the custom view, but 2010 ignores the view's "Style" setting and always displays the default view. The workaround so far is to create the custom view in SharePoint Designer 2010, delete the default web part and add back a Data View Web Part. While this is not identical to a common view, you can get pretty close. So, the "Custom Views" discussion that follows is for SharePoint 2007 for now. Check Link 1200 to see if I have found a better way or detailed the SharePoint Designer approach.

SharePoint surveys only have three views out of the box:

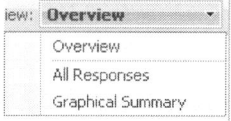

You often hear that if you want to see your survey data any other way, then export it to Excel and tweak it there. But SharePoint lets you create views everywhere else, why not in surveys? As an example, I created a survey about our department's existing computer hardware. While there are a number of questions in the survey, I just wanted a quick view of the final comments, a "Hardware Survey Comments" view, and I wanted it in the menus like this:

331

Surveys

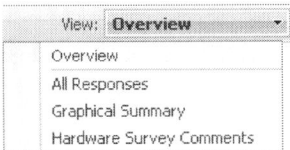

The built-in views supplied with a survey cannot be edited and the "Create View" option is missing. But, you can create new views, if you know a trick. The page that's missing in the survey's view menu is **Create View** (ViewType.aspx). This page usually has a URL similar to:

http://*yourserver/sites/yoursite/*_layouts/ViewType.aspx?List=longUniqueIdForYourList

Finding the list's unique ID is the challenge here, but is fairly easy as all you have to do is find another page for the survey with a similar URL. One page that has what we need is the Settings page. In the survey's menu bar click **Settings** and **Survey Settings** and you will see a URL similar to this:

http://*yourserver/sites/yoursite/*_layouts/survedit.aspx?List=%7B28939D89%2DB9D4%2D4679%2DBBDC%2D6195E438D79D%7D

Don't worry about the ID, just edit the URL and change "**survedit.aspx**" to "**ViewType.aspx**" and press Enter.

http://yourserver/sites/yoursite/_layouts/**ViewType.aspx**?List=%7B28939D89%2DB9D4%2D4679%2DBBDC%2D6195E438D79D%7D

You will then see the standard Create View page:

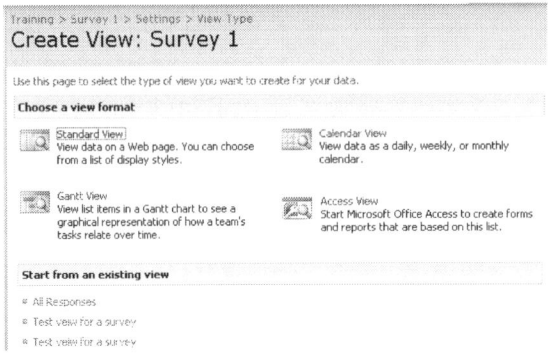

Create your view as normal but add one extra step. In the view settings expand "Style" and pick any style except for "Default". "Basic Table" is a good choice. If you forget to do this you will get a standard survey "Overview" page.

Edit your custom view (2007 only)

Editing the view will be a bit more work as you need two unique IDs, one for the list and one for the view. You already know how to find the ID for the list. In the survey's menu bar click **Settings** and **Survey Settings** and you will see a URL with the unique ID for the list.

To get the ID for the view you will need to display your custom view and then use your browser's "view source" feature (For Internet Explorer click the "View" menu then "Source" or right-click the page and select "View source"). Search the page source for "View=%7B". The ID you need starts with "%7B" and ends with "%7D".

Your edit page URL will then look like this:

http://*yourserver/sites/yoursite*/_layouts/ViewEdit.aspx?List=***listIDhere***&View=***viewIDhere***

or with some real IDs (mine, not yours!) it would look like this:

http://*yourservername/sites/yoursite*/_layouts/**ViewEdit.aspx?List=**%7BFAA1F75F%2D8A91%2D4FFE%2DB17F%2D4C44CF3EEC60%7D**&View=**%7BBA52C2A7%2DC8E4%2D4688%2D95CB%2D968C341B8D16%7D

> The IDs used here are called GUIDs or Globally Unique IDs. In the example above, it does not matter if the letters are uppercase or lowercase. While it does not matter here, some of your SharePoint work may require these IDs to be all uppercase or all lowercase.

Here are the final steps to edit a custom survey view:

1. Display the survey and the view
2. View the source of the page using the browser's view source feature
3. Search for: View=%7
4. Copy everything from "%7B" to "%7d" (for the my example this might be: **%7b***4F95AB02%2d29A5%2d4873%2dB310%2d42744D8C483D***%7d**)
5. In the survey click **Settings** and **Survey Settings** (just to get a URL similar to what we need that includes the list ID)
6. Edit the URL
   a. Change **survedit.aspx** to **viewedit.aspx**
   b. At the end of the URL add &View= and your view ID copied in step 4

Before:

http://yourserver/sites/yoursite/_layouts/**survedit.aspx**?List={28939D89-B9D4-4679-BBDC-6195E438D79D}

After:

http://yourserver/sites/yoursite/_layouts/**viewedit.aspx**?List=%7B28939D89%2DB9D4%2D4679%2DBBDC%2D6195E438D79D%7D**&View=**%7b*4F95AB02%2d29A5%2d4873%2dB310%2d42744D8C483D*%7d

333

Surveys

How to delete a view

Nothing new here, just edit the view and click the Delete button.

A better Yes/No field for surveys and lists

This one requires no coding at all! The out of the box Yes / No column type in SharePoint just displays a checkbox with no text next to it. If you are using it in a survey then you have biased the results as the field is either pre-un-checked or pre-checked, and it defaults to "Yes"! The workaround? Just use a Choice field with two choices, "Yes" and "No". When used in surveys the end result is exactly the same as the Yes/No column type and it defaults to neither choice selected.

And, as a bonus, you can be more verbose when needed: "Yes, I agree" / "No, I don't agree". The first example below is the basic Yes/No, while the second example is the Choice version.

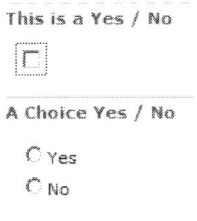

They both look the same in a survey report…

334

Adding a Welcome or Instructions Message to the Overview page

Add a Message to the Overview Page

The starting page (overview.aspx) for a survey has little value for our users. It shows the name and description of the survey, and the current number of responses.

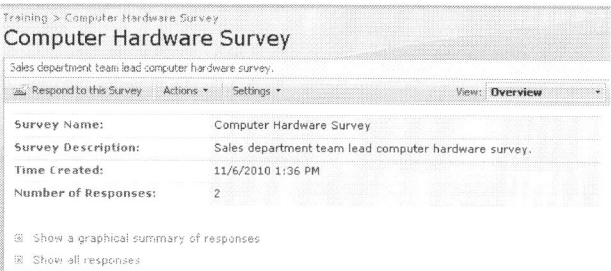

If you click the Site Actions menu you will see that this page has an "Edit Page" option, and therefore is a web part page. So to improve this page, just edit the page, add a Content Editor Web Part and add some custom text.

Is this a little better then the default? It's got a picture and formatted text and user instructions.

2007 Steps:

1. Display the survey (the overview.aspx page) and click **Site Actions** and **Edit Page**
2. Click **Add a web part** and add a Content Editor Web Part

Surveys

3. Edit the web part and add your text, hyperlinks and images

2010 Steps:

The Survey list is not yet fully integrated into SharePoint 2010. It does not have a ribbon and still uses the SharePoint 2007 toolbar. Because of this, the Content Editor Web Part does not have any editing controls! (no ribbon!) You can still add a welcome message in 2010, but you will have to create your HTML in some editor (Notepad, etc), save it to a text file, upload to a site library, edit the Content Editor Web Part and enter the path to the file in the Content Link box.

Adding a web part to a list page causes 2010 to hide the view dropdown in the title area. This is not currently a problem with the Survey page as the ribbon is not supported. If a future update brings the Survey list up to 2010 standards (ribbon, view menu only in the title area), then the following steps would break the view menu. Here's the view dropdown in the 2010 title area:

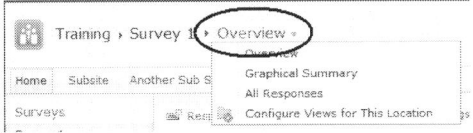

1. Create a text file with the HTML for the welcome message
2. Save the file and upload to a library in the same site as the survey (make sure the users filling out the survey have at least Read rights to this file)
3. Right-click the file in the library, click **Properties** and copy the URL to the file
4. Display the survey (the overview.aspx page) and click **Site Actions** and **Edit Page**
5. Click **Add a web part** and add a Content Editor Web Part
6. Click the web part's dropdown and click Edit Web Part
7. Past the link to your text file uploaded in step 2
8. Click OK and then reload the survey page

Adding a Welcome, Thank You or Instructions Message to a Survey

Surveys often need instructions or opening text inside of the survey. The previous example added a welcome message to the overview page. Your users will not see that message if they go directly to the "Respond to this survey" link. Here is a trick that converts a "Single line of text" question into just text so that you can add instructions anywhere within a survey.

There is one side effect; your "instructions question" will show up in the results as a question that everyone answered as "HIDDEN". (But you could change the word if you like.)

Note: See the next tip to also add colors and fonts.

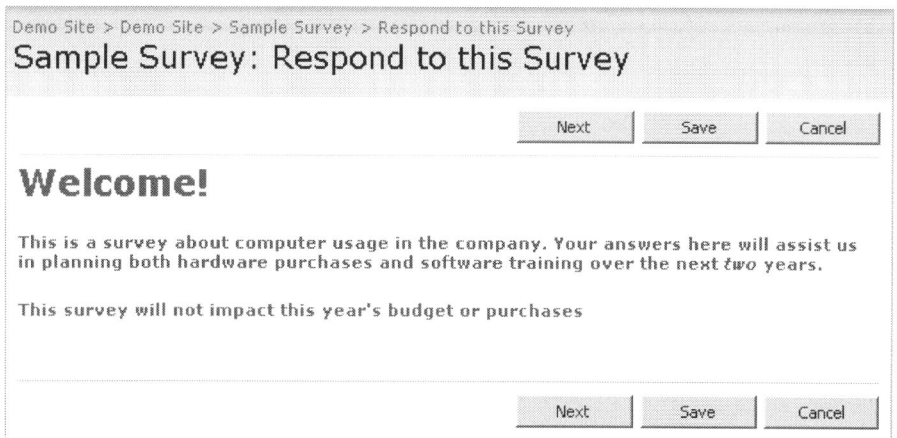

Steps:

1. For each "Instructions item" needed in the survey, add a question to the survey of type "Single line of text", add your text as the question, and set a default value of "HIDDEN"
2. If you want the instructions on their own page, then add a Page Separator after the instructions item
3. After creating your survey, click "Respond to this Survey" to display the Newform.aspx page
4. **For SharePoint 2007:**
   Edit the URL to allow access to the web parts:
      append this to the end of the URL for the NewForm.aspx URL:
         &ToolPaneView=2
      and press Enter

   `http://yourserver/sites/yoursite/Lists/SurveyTest/NewForm.aspx?Source=...overview.aspx`**`&ToolPaneView=2`**

   For SharePoint 2010 you will need to find the URL to the NewForm.aspx page.
   a. In the survey's overview page click Respond to this survey
   b. Right-click in a blank area of the dialog box and select Properties
   c. Copy the address URL up to, but not including "?IsDlg=1"
   d. Paste the URL into the address bar of the browser
   e. Add to the end of the URL this text: "?ToolPaneView=2"
      .../NewForm.aspx**?toolpaneview=2**
   f. Press Enter
5. Click **Add a Web Part** and add a Content Editor Web Part (Note: you could also edit this page in SharePoint Designer and add the code at the bottom of the PlaceHolderMain section.)
6. Move the Content Editor Web Part below the list web part (important!)

337

7. **In SharePoint 2007**, edit the web part and click the **Source Editor** button and add the JavaScript from below
   In SharePoint 2010 or as an option for 2007, add the JavaScript below to a text file using Notepad or your favorite JavaScript editor, upload the file to a site library and then edit the Content Editor Web Part and add the URL to the text file to the **Content Link** box

8. Save your changes and go test the survey!

9. **Note:** If you have a multipage form (you added page separators or branching logic) then you will need to add a web part with the same code as above in the EditForm.aspx page. If you linked to a file with the code using **Content Link**, then this will link to the same file as used in NewForm.aspx.
   SharePoint 2007:
      a. To get to this page just respond to the survey and click **Next**
      b. Then to add the web part add **&ToolPaneView=2** to the end of the URL
      c. Add the web part using the steps above for the NewForm.aspx page
   SharePoint 2010:
      a. To get to this page just respond to the survey and click **Next**
      b. Right-click in the dialog box and select **Properties**
      c. Copy the URL up to, but not including **&IsDlg=1**
      d. Add to the end of the URL this text: **&ToolPaneView=2**
          .../EditForm.aspx... ....&toolpaneview=2
      e. Press Enter
      f. Add the web part using the steps above for the NewForm.aspx page

The JavaScript to hide the text box: (color and fonts can also be added - see next section)

```
<script type="text/javascript">
// hide the input textbox for the "description" text
var x = document.getElementsByTagName("INPUT");
var i=0;
for (i=0;i<x.length;i++)
{
 if (x[i].value=="HIDDEN")
 {
   x[i].style.display="none";
 }
}
</script>
```

Adding Color, Fonts and HTML to Surveys

To add color, fonts and other HTML to any survey question just follow the steps above, but use the following JavaScript instead. You can then manually embed your HTML in the text of the question. Here's a sample question with additional HTML:

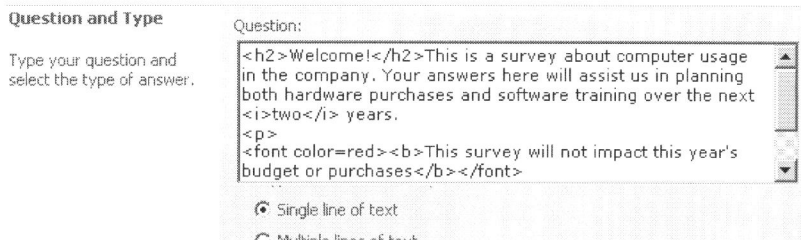

The JavaScript to make the added HTML work:

```
<script type="text/javascript">
// Fix tags to allow HTML
var t = document.getElementsByTagName('table');
for (var i=0;i<t.length;i++)
{
  if (t[i].className == 'ms-formtable')
  {
    var td = t[i].getElementsByTagName('td');
    for (var j=0; j<td.length; j++)
    {
      if (td[j].innerHTML.indexOf('&lt;') > -1)
      {
        td[j].innerHTML = td[j].innerHTML.replace(/&lt;/g,'<').replace(/&gt;/g,'>');
      }
    }
  }
}
</script>
```

Add Instructions and Color!

Want both instructions and nicely formatted HTML? Use both JavaScript routines together:

```
<script type="text/javascript">
```

```
// hide the input textbox for the "description" text
var x = document.getElementsByTagName("INPUT");
var i=0;
for (i=0; i<x.length; i++)
{
 if (x[i].value == "HIDDEN")
 {
   x[i].style.display="none";
 }
}

// Fix tags to allow HTML
var t = document.getElementsByTagName('table');
for (var i=0;i<t.length;i++)
{
  if (t[i].className == 'ms-formtable')
  {
    var td = t[i].getElementsByTagName('td');
    for (var j=0; j<td.length; j++)
    {
      if (td[j].innerHTML.indexOf('&lt;') > -1)
      {
        td[j].innerHTML = td[j].innerHTML.replace(/&lt;/g,'<').replace(/&gt;/g,'>');
      }
    }
  }
}
</script>
```

Adding Color, Fonts and HTML to Rating Sub Questions

Ratings are built from a series of sub questions that use a different HTML layout than other survey questions. If you just add HTML tags to the question, the survey will just display the text and the tags. To format this text requires two steps:

1. Add HTML to the questions
2. Add a JavaScript routine to replace the displayed HTML with functional HTML

As an example, you might have a question with embedded instructions like this one:

What is important in selecting a new laptop computer?			
	Low		Average
	1	2	3
Quality - Please consider the following: screen, keyboard, mouse pointer	○	○	○
Price	○	○	○
Screen size	○	○	○
Included software	○	○	○
Brand name	○	○	○

In order to add formatting these sub questions you might add some inline HTML like this example:

```
<span style='color:blue'>Quality</span><br/>Please consider the following:<br/> - screen<br/> - keyboard<br/> - mouse pointer
```

But without any additional work it looks like this:

What is important in selecting a new laptop computer?		
	Low	
	1	2
`<span style='color:blue'>Quality</span> Please consider the following:  - screen  - keyboard  - mouse pointer`	○	○
Price	○	○
Screen size	○	○
Included software	○	○
Brand name	○	○

While what you wanted was this:

What is important in selecting a new laptop computer?			
	Low		Average
	1	2	3
Quality Please consider the following: - screen - keyboard - mouse pointer	○	○	○
Price	○	○	○
Screen size	○	○	○
Included software	○	○	○
Brand name	○	○	○

Steps:

Follow the steps earlier in this chapter for "Adding a Welcome, Thank You or Instructions Message to a Survey", but use the JavaScript below.

The JavaScript:

```
<script type="text/javascript">
var x = document.getElementsByTagName("TH");
for (var i=0;i<x.length;i++)
{
 if (x[i].className=="msx-gridT1")
 {
  x[i].innerHTML= x[i].innerHTML.replace(/&lt;/g,'<').replace(/&gt;/g,'>');
 }
}
</script>
```

The jQuery version:

```
<script type="text/javascript" src="http://yourserver/sites/yoursite/Shared%20Documents/jquery-1.4.min.js"></script>

<script type="text/javascript">
   $('.ms-gridT1').html(function(index,oldhtml) {
     return oldhtml.replace(/&lt;/g,'<').replace(/&gt;/g,'>')
   })
</script>
```

Hide the "Save" button

When you add a Page Separator to a survey you also get a Save button ("Save and Close" in 2010) on each page.

SharePoint 2007 immediately returns the user to the survey overview page. SharePoint 2010 displays the following pop-up and then returns to the overview page:

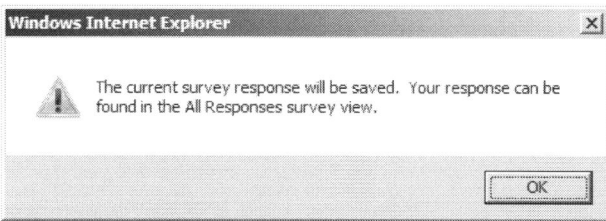

To complete their survey, the user must return to the survey list's overview page, click **"Show all responses"** and click their survey. They are directed to the survey's dispform.aspx page where they then need to click **"Edit Response"**. If your users are like mine, they will never remember to return to complete the survey.

So how do you deal with the Save button?

1. You might want to create a workflow to send a reminder... but... according to http://support.microsoft.com/kb/926370, "you cannot start a workflow from a survey response".
2. You can review the list of responses once a day and manually send an email reminder to owner of each incomplete survey. (not fun!)
3. Or just hide the "Save" button!

To hide the Save button

Write a little JavaScript to hunt down the buttons and hide them...

```
<script type="text/javascript">

var buttons = document.getElementsByTagName("INPUT");
for (var i=0; i<buttons.length; i++)
{
  if (buttons[i].value == "Save")
  {
    buttons[i].style.display = "none";
  }
}
</script>
```

Here's the result:

343

Surveys

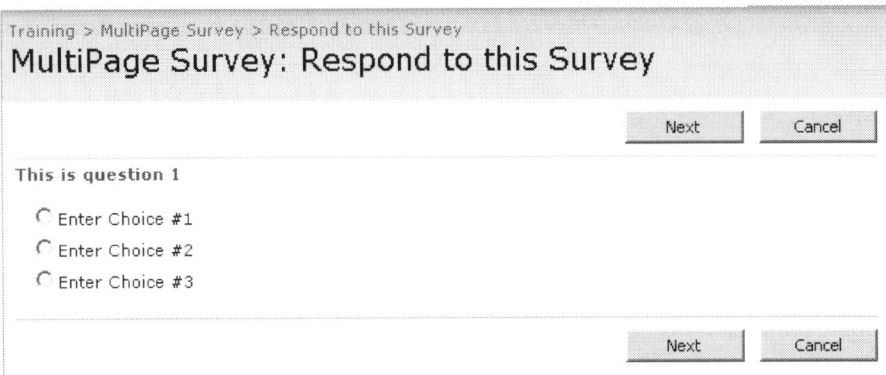

Now I know that someone will say, "there's a little too much white space between the two buttons", so here's how to deal with that:

Replace this line:

```
buttons[i].style.display = "none";
```

With these lines:

```
var theNode = buttons[i].parentNode.parentNode.parentNode.parentNode.parentNode;
theNode.style.display = "none";
theNode.previousSibling.style.display = "none";
```

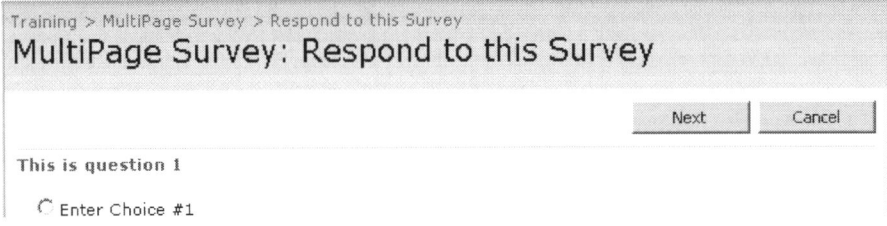

jQuery Sample

If you are using jQuery you can accomplish the above with three lines of jQuery. (See chapter 4)

```
var buttons = $("input[value=Save]").parent().parent().parent().parent().parent()
buttons.css("display","none")
buttons.prev().css("display","none");
```

Hoes does the jQuery work? The jQuery selector "**input[value=Save]**" picks all of the INPUT tags with a value of "Save". The rest of the line selects the TD that contains the TABLE, TR, TD and finally our

344

INPUT tag. The second line hides the TD found by the previous line. The third line hides the TD (used as a blank space) just before our button area.

The full jQuery version would look like this:

```
<script src="http://yourserver/sites/yoursite/Shared%20Documents/jquery-1.4.min.js"></script>

<script type="text/javascript">
  var buttons = $("input[value=Save]").parent().parent().parent().parent().parent()
  buttons.css("display","none")
  buttons.prev().css("display","none")
</script>
```

Steps:

You will need to modify both the NewForm.aspx page and the EditForm.aspx page. This can be done using the web part approach below, or by editing these two pages using SharePoint Designer and adding the code at the bottom of the **PlaceHolderMain** section.

1. Click "Respond to this Survey" to display the Newform.aspx page
2. **For SharePoint 2007:**
   Edit the URL to allow access to the web parts:
      append this to the end of the URL for the NewForm.aspx URL:
         &ToolPaneView=2
   and press Enter

   ```
   http://yourserver/sites/yoursite/Lists/SurveyTest/NewForm.aspx?Source=...overview.aspx&ToolPaneView=2
   ```

   For SharePoint 2010 you will need to find the URL to the NewForm.aspx page.
   a. In the survey click **Respond to this survey**
   b. Right-click in the **New Item** dialog box and select **Properties**
   c. Copy the address URL up to, but not including "?IsDlg=1"
   d. Paste the URL into the address bar of the browser
   e. Add to the end of the URL this text: ?ToolPaneView=2
      i.e.: .../NewForm.aspx**?toolpaneview=2**
   f. Press Enter
3. Click **Add a Web Part** and add a Content Editor Web Part
4. Move the Content Editor Web Part below the list web part
5. **In SharePoint 2007**, edit the web part and click the **Source Editor** button and add the JavaScript from below
   In SharePoint 2010 or as an option for 2007, add the JavaScript below to a text file using Notepad or your favorite JavaScript editor, upload the file to a site library and then edit the Content Editor Web Part and add the URL of the text file to the **Content Link** box

6. Save your changes and go test the survey!
7. Because we have a multipage form (you added page separators or branching logic) then you will need to add a web part with the same code as above in the EditForm.aspx page. If you linked to a file with the code using **Content Link**, then this will link to the same file as used in NewForm.aspx.

   SharePoint 2007:
   a. To get to this page just respond to the survey and click **Next**
   b. Then to add the web part add &ToolPaneView=2 to the end of the URL
   c. Add the web part using the steps above for the NewForm.aspx page

   SharePoint 2010:
   a. To get to this page just respond to the survey and click **Next**
   b. Right-click in the dialog box and select **Properties**
   c. Copy the URL up to, but not including &IsDlg=1
   d. Add to the end of the URL this text: &ToolPaneView=2
      .../EditForm.aspx... ....**&toolpaneview=2**
   e. Press Enter
   f. Add the web part using the steps above for the NewForm.aspx page

Hide survey bars where not needed!

This next customization is the result of a pet peeve of mine... the summary page displays a bar chart for each text question, even though it is very unlikely that any two people will type in the exact same text.

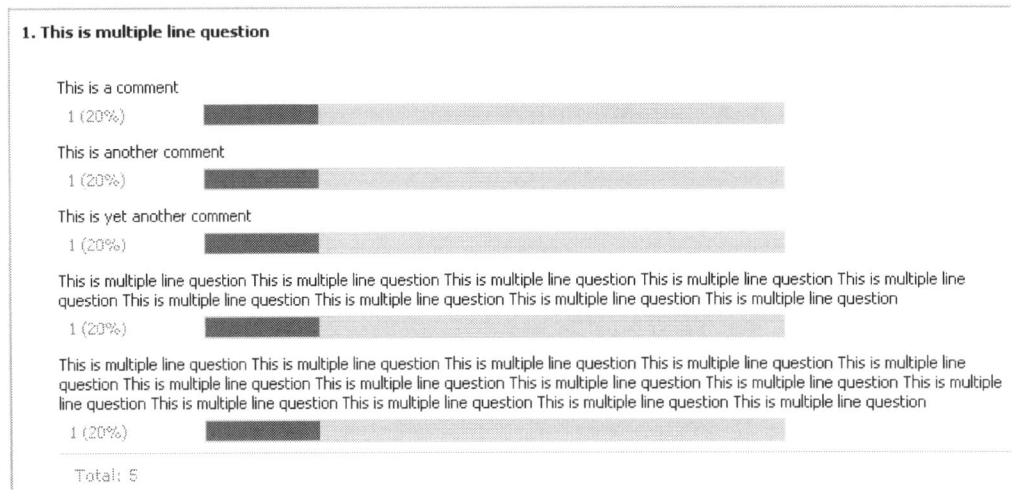

All I want to see is a list of the comments, not the useless bar charts! Something like this:

How does it work?

The HTML for the survey page is pretty basic. There are no unique IDs or class names to key off of. So for this trick you will need to list the question numbers you want to remove the bars from. The JavaScript then searches to find all of the <B> tags that contain what looks like a question number ("3. ") and then drills down to find the table containing the bar chart. It then hides the bar chart ("tbl.rows[r].style.display="none";") and adds back optional <HR> separator lines.

The JavaScript:

```
<script type="text/javascript">

// list the questions numbers here:
var hideBars = [1,3,5,6];

var Bs = document.getElementsByTagName("B");

for (var i=0; i<Bs.length; i++)
{
  for (var j=0; j<hideBars.length; j++)
  {
    // look B's that start with the number followed by a dot and a space  i.e.: "10. "
    if (Bs[i].innerHTML.indexOf(hideBars[j]+". ",0) == 0 )
    {
      var tbl = Bs[i].parentNode.nextSibling
      for (var r=2; r<tbl.rows.length; r=r+3)
      {
        // hide the bar chart
        tbl.rows[r].style.display = "none";
```

Surveys

```
      // add a separator line (optional)
      var newTD = document.createElement("td");
      newTD.innerHTML="<hr size='1' class='ms-surveyHR'>"
      tbl.rows[r-2].appendChild( newTD );
    }
   }
  }
 }
</script>
```

Modifying the "Respond to this Survey" prompt

Let's use this one as an example of how you might do some detective work… Go to your survey page (overview.aspx). Right-click the page and select your browser's "View Source" option. Search the displayed text for "Respond to this Survey".

SharePoint 2010 HTML: (*I replaced parts of the JavaScript with "…" for brevity*)

```
<a
id="ctl00_m_g_e2a6c7f0_8d5e_46a4_985f_8d175bfc5b24_ctl01_ctl00_toolBarTbl_RptControls_ctl00_diidIONewItem"
accesskey="N" title="Respond to this Survey"
onclick="javascript:NewItem2(event, ' ... ');return false;"
href="javascript:__doPostBack(' ... ','");">
  <img align='absmiddle' alt="Respond to this Survey"
       src="/_layouts/images/NewItem.gif" style='border-width:0px;' />
   
  <span class="ms-splinkbutton-text">Respond to this Survey</span>
</a>
```

SharePoint 2007:

```
<a
id="ctl00_m_g_bcf319ff_0b26_4f28_b8d3_70cbf4e8152a_ctl00_ctl00_toolBarTbl_RptControls_
ctl00_diidIONewItem"
accesskey="N" title="Respond to this Survey"
onclick="javascript:NewItem(' ... ');return false;"
href="javascript:__doPostBack(' ... ','");">
  <img align='absmiddle' alt="Respond to this Survey"
```

```
          src="/_layouts/images/NewItem.gif" style='border-width:0px;'>
    Respond to this Survey
</a>
```

There is just enough difference between 2007 and 2010 to be a nuisance! But note that in both that we have three copies of "Respond to this Survey" to change. One in the A tag, one in the IMG tag and one at the end of the A tag (and for 2010, inside a SPAN tag).

Now for some detective work:

So how do we find the one <A> tag out of all of the HTML on this page? I never depend on IDs with lots of strange characters (they tend to change from page to page) so that leaves out the normal best solution: document.getElementById("ctl00 ….. "). We could just loop through the <A> tags looking for one with a title of "Respond to this Survey". And that will work fine, but as a best practice we may want this to work regardless of the language settings used to create the site as "Respond to this Survey" will only display in the English version. So I see two other useful possibilities, find <A> tags with an ID that ends with "IONewItem" or find IMG tags that have 'src="/_layouts/images/NewItem.gif"'. I'm going to use the first of these two.

First let's write some JavaScript to find the <A> tag:

```
var atags = document.getElementsByTagName("A");
for (var i=0; i<atags.length; i++)
{
  if (atags[i].id.indexOf("IONewItem")>0)
  {
    // make text changes here...
  }
}
```

Then let's change the text:

The first change is easy. As we already have found the <A> tag (**atags[i]**) all we need to is change the title property:

```
var newsurveytext = "Click here for the survey!";
atags[i].title = newsurveytext;
```

The second change is not too hard… The <A> tag contains two or three child nodes and the first one is the image. All we need to do to it is change the ALT attribute:

Surveys

```
atags[i].childNodes[0].alt = newsurveytext;
```

We need to be careful with the next part as we want it to work in both 2007 and 2010. As 2007 has two nodes (IMG and the text) and 2010 has three nodes (the IMG, the " " text and the SPAN) we just need to check the count of nodes to make the correct edit for each version:

```
if (atags[i].childNodes.length == 2)
{  // must be 2007  ("\u00A0" is to replace the  )

  atags[i].childNodes[1].nodeValue = "\u00A0" + newsurveytext;

}
else
{   // must be 2010 (and we hope the next version!)

  if (document.all) // is IE
    { atags[i].childNodes[2].innerText = newsurveytext; }
  else           // is Firefox or other
    { atags[i].childNodes[2].textContent = newsurveytext; }

}
```

Here's the final solution:

```
<script type="text/javascript">
var atags = document.getElementsByTagName("A");
for (var i=0; i<atags.length; i++)
{
  if (atags[i].id.indexOf("IONewItem")>0)
  {
    var newsurveytext = "Click here for the survey!";
    atags[i].title = newsurveytext;
    atags[i].childNodes[0].alt = newsurveytext;
    if (atags[i].childNodes.length == 2)
    {
      // must be 2007  ("\u00A0" is to replace the  )
      atags[i].childNodes[1].nodeValue = "\u00A0" + newsurveytext;
    }
    else
    {
      // must be 2010 (and we hope the next version!)
```

```
    if (document.all) // is IE
     { atags[i].childNodes[2].innerText = newsurveytext; }
     else          // is Firefox or other
     { atags[i].childNodes[2].textContent = newsurveytext; }
   }
   break;  // no need to check the other A tags
  }
 }
}
</script>
```

To add the JavaScript to SharePoint 2007

1. Go to the survey page (overview.aspx)
2. Click **Site Actions** and **Edit Page**
3. Click **Add a Web Part** and select the Content Editor Web Part
4. Move the Content Editor Web Part below the existing survey web part (important!)
5. Edit the Content Editor Web Part and click the **Source Editor** button
6. Copy and Paste the JavaScript above, and change the **"newsurveytext"** to your text
7. Save and test

Or… edit the page (overview.aspx) in SharePoint Designer and add the JavaScript just befor the closing tag for the placeholder named **PlaceHolderMain**.

To add the JavaScript to SharePoint 2010

1. Open Notepad, copy and paste the JavaScript above and change the **"newsurveytext"** to your text
2. Save the file to a local drive
3. Upload the file to a SharePoint library (while Shared Documents will do, you may want a add a library just for these kinds of files)
4. Go to the library where you just uploaded the file and copy the URL to the file (right-click the file and click **Properties** to find the URL)
5. Go to the survey page (overview.aspx)
6. Click **Site Actions** and **Edit Page**
7. Click **Add a Web Part** and select the Content Editor Web Part
8. Move the Content Editor Web Part below the existing survey web part (important!)
9. Edit the Content Editor Web Part and paste the URL to the JavaScript file into the **Content Link** box
10. Save and test

Or… edit the page (overview.aspx) in SharePoint Designer and add the JavaScript just before the closing tag for the placeholder named **"PlaceHolderMain"**.

Reuse Your Custom Surveys

Surveys, like other lists, can be saved as a template that can then be used to create new surveys. The saved template will include all of your customizations and all of the questions. To create a new survey, just go through the usual steps to create a new list, select your custom template, create the survey, then add, edit or delete the questions.

To save the survey as a template:

1. From the start page of the survey (overview.aspx) click **Settings** and **Survey Settings**
2. Click **Save survey as template**
3. Enter the new template's name (twice)
4. Enter a description
5. Do not check "**Include Content**" as this will also save all of the users' responses

Notes:

- You cannot save a list as a template unless you have write permissions to the top level site of the site collection, or you have at least write permissions to the List Templates gallery.
- You can move this template to other site collections by going to the top level site in the site collection and clicking **Site Actions, Site Settings, List Templates**. From there you can click the template and download it. Go to the List Templates gallery in the other site collection and click upload.

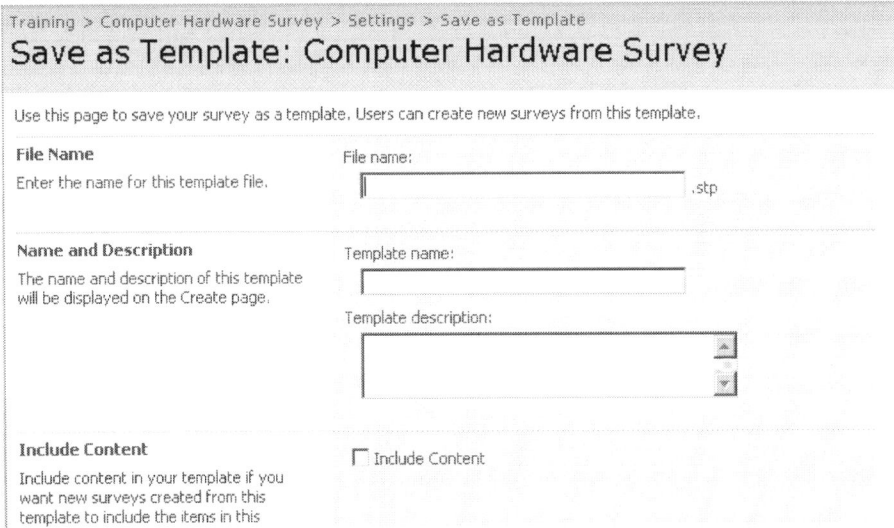

13. Links Lists

Do you need this chapter?

A Links List is just about the most basic list there is. There are only two editable columns: URL and Notes. Nice, simple, clean and prime for some JavaScript tricks!

What's in this chapter?

- Adding Pop-ups to Link lists (and open in new window)
- Add a "You are leaving this site" message to a links list
- Add a "You are leaving this site" message to a links list with confirmation
- Convert a Links list to a Dropdown list
- Convert a Links list to a Dropdown list that opens in a new window
- Convert a Links list to a Dropdown list that opens in a different web part

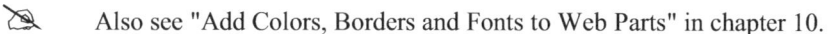   Also see "Add Colors, Borders and Fonts to Web Parts" in chapter 10.

The Links List

The Links List is the same in both 2007 and 2010, except for the default selection of columns displayed. 2007 only displays the URL while 2010 displays the check box column, file type icon, the Edit icon, the URL and the Notes.

2007:   2010:

Adding Pop-ups to Link lists (open in new window)

The links list web part is a quick and easy way to add a list of links to vendor sites, other SharePoint sites or the most popular documents in a library. The problem is that the links list web part does not have an "Open in new window" option, so when your users click the link, they navigate away from your site.

A typical links list:

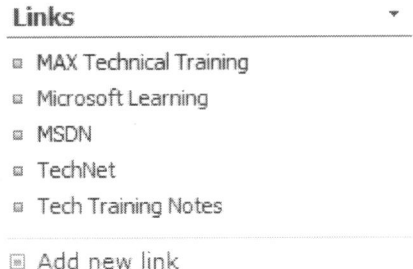

To change a links list to force "Open in new window" (or a new tab, depending on the browser):

1. Create your links list and add a links list web part to a web part or home page
2. For 2010:
   a. Open Notepad, copy and paste the JavaScript from below
   b. Edit the JavaScript to change the word **"Links"** to the name of your links list web part (Use the title of the web part, not the title of the actual list, although they may be the same)
      if (x[i].summary == "Links")   to
      if (x[i].summary == "Your Links List Title")

Links Lists

The best way to confirm this name is to right-click the web part page and search for "summary=" and copy and paste the text there
  c. Save the file to a local drive
  d. Upload the file to a SharePoint library (while **Shared Documents** will do, you may want a add a library just for these kinds of files)
  e. Go to the library where you just uploaded the file and copy the URL to the file (right-click the file and click **Properties** to find the URL)
3. Add a Content Editor Web Part (CEWP) just below the Links list web part
4. Edit the CEWP
5. Add a title to the CEWP (optional)
6. In the Advanced section of the CEWP's properties change **Chrome** to **None** to hide the CEWP (don't use the **Hidden** option in the Layout section!)
7. For 2007:
  a. Click the **Source Editor** button and then copy and paste the JavaScript from below
  b. Edit the JavaScript to change the word "Links" to the name of your links list web part (title of the web part, not the title of the actual list, although they may be the same)
     if (x[i].summary == "Links")   to
     if (x[i].summary == "Your Links List Title")
     The best way to confirm this name is to right-click the web part page and search for "summary=" and copy and paste the name
8. For 2010:
  a. Paste the URL to your Notepad file uploaded in step 1 into the **Content Link** box
9. Save your changes and see if it works!

The code:

```
<script type="text/javascript">
// CEWP trick from techtrainingnotes.blogspot.com!
// Change the following to your links list name
var linksListSummaryName = "Links Use the ... (your list summary name here!) ...";

// Find the link list
var x = document.getElementsByTagName("TABLE");   // find all of the Tables
var LinkList;
for (var i=0; i<x.length; i++)
{
  if ( x[i].summary == linksListSummaryName )
  {
    LinkList = x[i];
    break;
  }
```

355

```
}
if ( LinkList )
{
  // add a target to the <A> tags
  var links = LinkList.getElementsByTagName("A");   // find all of the
  for (var i=0; i<links.length; i++)
  {
    if (links[i].onfocus)
    {
      if (links[i].onfocus.toString().indexOf("OnLink(this)") > -1)
      {
        links[i].target="_blank";
      }
    }
  }
}
else
{
  alert("Link list named '" + linksListSummaryName + "' not found");
}
</script>
```

Add a "You are leaving this site" message

This is a small addition to the above Links List trick that will notify a user that the link just clicked will take them away from your site. Just add the following where we update the <A> tag:

```
links[i].onclick=function () {   alert('you are now leaving this site')   }
```

The fragment below is from the "Open in new window" code above, but with the new line added in **bold**:

```
...
    if (links[i].onfocus.toString().indexOf("OnLink(this)") > -1)
    {
      links[i].target="_blank";
      links[i].onclick=function () { alert('you are now leaving this site') };
    }
...
```

Add a "You are leaving this site" message to a links list with confirmation!

This is just a little variation to the previous example that warns the user that they are about to leave your site, but gives them a chance to cancel. To do this we will use the JavaScript confirm function.

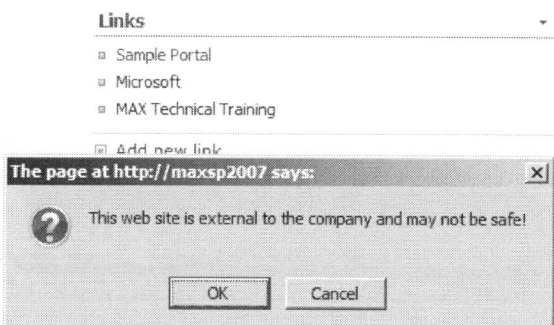

Just like the previous example, add the following where we update the <A> tag:

```
links[i].onclick=function () { if ( ! confirm('This web site is external to the company and may not be safe!')) return false }
```

The fragment below is from the "Open in new window" code above, but with the new line added in **bold**:

```
...
    if (links[i].onfocus.toString().indexOf("OnLink(this)") > -1)
    {
      links[i].target="_blank";
      links[i].onclick=function () { if ( ! confirm('This web site is external to the company and may not be safe!')) return false }
    }
...
```

Convert a Links list to a Dropdown list

Problem: There is never enough room on your SharePoint home page. So what do you do if you have a long list of vendor links you would like to display on the home page? You would usually use a Links list and add a Links list web part. But that takes up too much space. How about a simple dropdown list?

Solution: Yet another Content Editor Web Part (CEWP) trick! A CEWP and some JavaScript...

357

Links Lists

Before

Links
- MAX Technical Training
- Microsoft Learning
- MSDN
- TechNet
- Tech Training Notes

Add new link

After

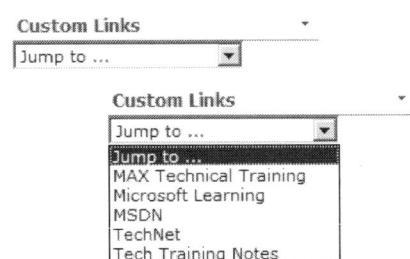

Steps:

1. Create your links list and add your links
2. Add the link list's web part to the page
3. For 2010:
   a. Open Notepad, copy and paste the JavaScript from below
   b. Edit the JavaScript to change the word "Links" to the name of your links list web part (title of the web part, not the title of the actual list, although they may be the same)
      if (x[i].summary == "Links")   to
      if (x[i].summary == "Your Links List Title")
      The best way to confirm this name is to right-click the web part page and search for "summary=" and copy and paste the name
   c. Save the file to a local drive
   d. Upload the file to a SharePoint library (while **Shared Documents** will do, you may want a add a library just for these kinds of files)
   e. Go to the library where you just uploaded the file and copy the URL to the file (right-click the file and click **Properties** to find the URL)
4. Add a Content Editor Web Part (CEWP) to the page just under the links list web part
5. Modify the CEWP and set its title to something useful
6. 2007:
   a. Click Source Editor and then copy and paste the HTML and JavaScript from below
   b. Edit the JavaScript to change the word "Links" to the name of your links list web part (title of the web part, not the title of the actual list, although they may be the same)
      if (x[i].summary == "Links")   to
      if (x[i].summary == "Your Links List Title")
      The best way to confirm this name is to right-click the web part page and search for "summary=" and copy and paste the name
7. 2010:
   a. Paste the URL to your Notepad file uploaded in step 1 into the **Conent Link** box
8. Exit the edit mode and test it

The HTML and JavaScript:

```
<!-- the dropdown list for the link items -->
<select name="JumpToList" id="JumpToList"
   onchange="javascript:JumpToUrl(JumpToList.options[JumpToList.selectedIndex].value)">
  <option>Jump to ...</option>
</select>

<script type="text/javascript">

var linksListSummaryName = "Links Use the ... (your list summary name here!) ...";

function JumpToUrl(url)
{
   location.href = url;
}

//code to hide the links list and populate the select list

//Find the link list and hide it
var x = document.getElementsByTagName("TABLE");   // find all of the Tables
var LinkList;
for ( var i=0; i<x.length; i++ )
{
  if (x[i].summary == linksListSummaryName)
  {
    //
    LinkList = x[i];

    //hide the links list web part (tables in tables in tables ...)
    // Note: while testing, you may want to comment out the next line

x[i].parentNode.parentNode.parentNode.parentNode.parentNode.parentNode.parentNode.parentNode.parentNode.style.display="none";
    break;
  }
}

if (LinkList)
{
  //Copy all of the links from the link list to the select list
```

Links Lists

```
  var ToList = document.getElementById("JumpToList");

  var links = LinkList.getElementsByTagName("A"); // find all of the links
  for ( var i=0; i<links.length; i++ )
  {
    if (links[i].onfocus)
    {
      if (links[i].onfocus.toString().indexOf("OnLink(this)") > -1)
        { ToList.options[ToList.length] = new Option(links[i].innerHTML, links[i].href); }
    }
  }
}
else
{
  alert("Link list named '" + linksListSummaryName + "' not found");
}
</script>
```

Add a confirmation:

This is just a little variation to the previous example that warns the user that they are about to leave your site, but gives them a chance to cancel.

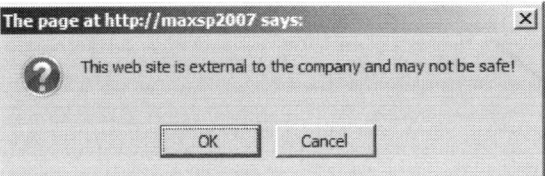

Just edit the JumpToUrl function to add the prompt:

```
function JumpToUrl(url)
{
  if ( confirm('This web site is external to the company and may not be safe!') )
  {
    location.href = url;
  }
}
```

Convert a Links list into a dropdown list that opens in a new window

1. Complete the steps for "Convert a Links list to a Dropdown list" above

2. Change the JumpToUrl function from location.href to window.open as listed below:

```
function JumpToUrl(url)
{
   //location.href = url;
   window.open(url,'mywindow','toolbar=yes,menubar=yes,location=yes,scrollbars=yes,resizable=yes')
}
```

Convert a Links list to a dropdown list that opens in a different web part

If your links list is a collection of reports that you would like to display right in the page, then all you need to do is add a Content Editor Web Part with an <IFRAME> to host the report and then make one small change to the links list JavaScript code.

1. Complete the steps for "Convert a Links list to a Dropdown list" above
2. Add a Content Editor Web Part and inside of that add an IFRAME tag and give it an ID. (i.e. ID="linkframe")
3. Set the height, width and other attributes of the IFRAME as needed.
4. In the JavaScript code change the line "document.location.href = url" to "document.getElementById('linkframe').src = url"

Example of the Content Editor Web Part HTML for an IFRAME:

```
<iframe id="mylinkframe" height="300" width="400"></iframe>
```

Code change needed:

Change this:

```
function JumpToUrl(url)
{
   location.href = url;
}
```

to this:

```
function JumpToUrl(url)
{
   document.getElementById('mylinkframe').src = url;
}
```

14. Task Lists

Do you need this chapter?

The out of the box task list does it job of tracking collaboration team member's tasks just fine, but its display can be greatly improved. So if you would like to improve the way tasks are displayed, read on…

Oh, and while you are here, study the techniques used as they can be reapplied to most other lists.

What's in this chapter?

- Color coding task lists
- Color Code Past Due / Late Tasks in a Task List
- Hide the bottom section of the Gantt chart
- Prevent editing of completed tasks

   Also see " Add Colors, Borders and Fonts to Web Parts" in chapter 10.

Color Coding Task Lists

SharePoint does not have an out of the box way to set colors based on the data in a list or library. There are both third party web parts and open source projects, such as those found at codeplex.com, that can color code lists, but these usually require installing code on the SharePoint web servers. In this article we will look at color coding lists just using the built-in Content Editor Web Part and some JavaScript.

While you can't see the colors in a black and white book, here's an example of a color coded list where the entire row is color coded based on the Status column. In Progress tasks are green, Completed tasks are blue, Deferred tasks are gray and "Blame it on someone else" (oops… I mean "Waiting on someone else") tasks are orange.

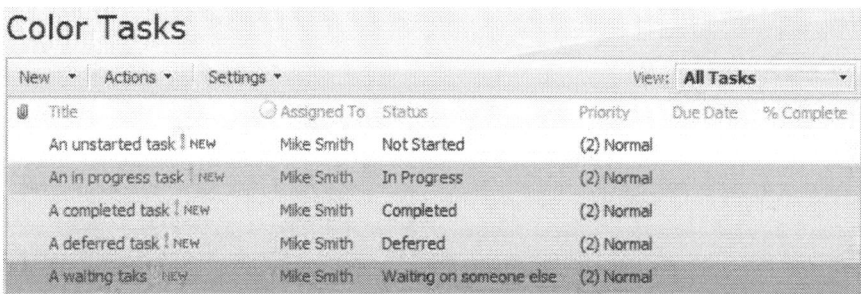

Instead of setting the background of the entire row, you could just set the text and the background for a single column. This example uses normal text on a white background for "Not Started" tasks and white text on a green, blue, gray or red background for the other status types.

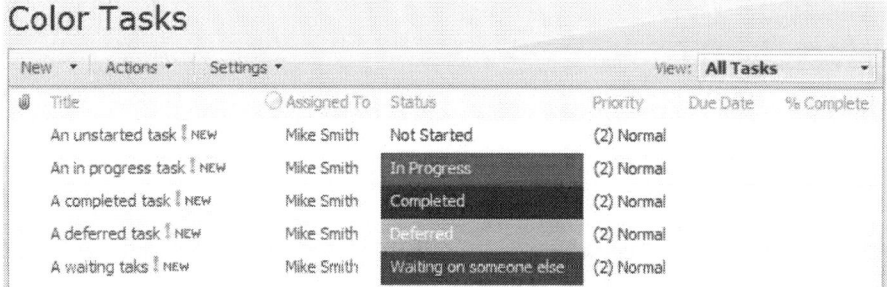

This color coding could be applied to any kind of list as the code is just looking for certain keywords in HTML table cells. This customization only requires a small JavaScript routine, and some place to store it.

Task Lists

You can either add the JavaScript using a Content Editor Web Part or add it directly to the page using SharePoint Designer.

To add the Content Editor web part and JavaScript:

Steps:

1. Display the view to color code (each view page will need its own web part and JavaScript)
2. Add a Content Editor web part:
    a. Site Actions, Site Settings, Edit Page
    b. Add a Content Editor web part
    c. Move this web part so it is below the list you are color coding
3. Click in the web part, click the edit dropdown and edit the web part
4. In the **Appearance** section change **Chrome** to **None**.
5. Add the JavaScript:
    a. SharePoint 2007:
        i. Click the **Source Editor** button
        ii. Type or paste the JavaScript (examples below)
    b. SharePoint 2010:
        i. Open Windows Notepad
        ii. Paste in the JavaScript from below
        iii. Save the file and then upload it to a SharePoint library in the site
        iv. In the library where you uploaded the file, right-click the file, click **Properties** and copy the URL to the file
        v. In the edit panel of the Content Editor Web Part, paste the URL into the **Content Link** box
6. Save your changes and test

Example 1: Set the background color of a row based on data in the row

To color code a row all we need is:

- A column with the key words to check (such as the Task Lists' status column)
- JavaScript to find the key words in a table TD tag
- JavaScript to assign a style to the TD's parent row (TR)
- And of course, the web part described above to hold the JavaScript

Task Lists

The Code:

```
<script type="text/javascript">
  var x = document.getElementsByTagName("TD") // find all of the TDs
  for (var i=0; i<x.length; i++)
  {

    if (x[i].className == "ms-vb2") //find the TDs styled for lists
    {

      if (x[i].innerHTML == "Not Started") //find the data to use to determine the color
      {
        x[i].parentNode.style.backgroundColor='white';   // set the color
      }

    //repeat the above for each data value

      if (x[i].innerHTML=="In Progress")
      {
        x[i].parentNode.style.backgroundColor='lightgreen'; // set the color
      }

      if (x[i].innerHTML=="Completed")
      {
        x[i].parentNode.style.backgroundColor='lightblue'; // set the color
      }

      if (x[i].innerHTML=="Deferred")
      {
        x[i].parentNode.style.backgroundColor='lightgrey'; // set the color
      }

      if (x[i].innerHTML=="Waiting on someone else")
      {
        x[i].parentNode.style.backgroundColor='orange'; // set the color
```

365

Task Lists

```
        }
      }
    }
}
</script>
```

- Color names: Note the spelling of "lightgrey ". Gray was inconsistently spelled in early browsers and continues that way for compatibility. In addition to color names you can also use color numbers.

- Colors: For a list of color names and numbers see Link 201.

Code Notes:
- x[i] is one of the table cells (TD)
- x[i].innerHTML is the contents of a cell (TD) (which may include additional HTML)
- x[i].parentNode is the row containing the cell (a TR)

Example 2: Set the color of a single field/column based on data in the field

To color code a cell all we need is:
- A column with the key words to check (such as the Task Lists' status column or a library's approval status column)
- JavaScript to find the key words in a table TD tag
- JavaScript to assign a style to the TD

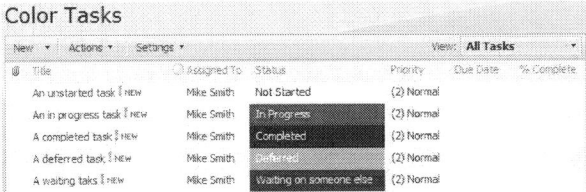

Here is the revised JavaScript fragment for color coding a single cell. Notice that the cell is referenced (**x[i]**) and not the row (**x[i].parentNode**). This example also shows how to change the font color.

```
if (x[i].innerHTML=="Completed") //find the data to use to determine the color
{
   x[i].style.backgroundColor='darkblue';    // set the background color
```

366

```
    x[i].style.color='white';    //set the font color
}
```

Project Tasks / Gantt Chart (2007 only)

How to hide the list in the bottom section of the Gantt view

Sometimes you only want to display the top part of a Gantt view, just the chart, and not the list at the bottom. It turns out that this is a simple CSS trick. This is for 2007 only as the 2010 view does not split the Gantt view into two parts.

Before:

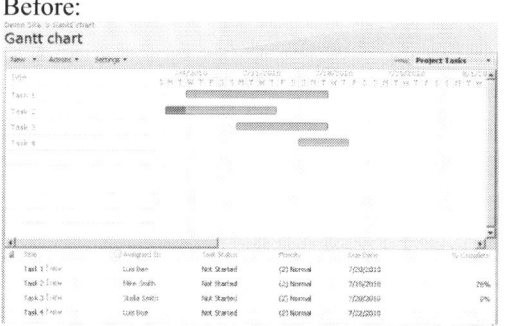

After:

How it works: Both the visibility of the bottom portion of the view, and the height of the top portion, are controlled by styles in SharePoint's CORE.CSS file. All that's needed is to override three of these styles to hide the bottom portion and change the height of the remaining section.

How would you have discovered this? If you use the "View Source" option of your browser you can explore the styles set on the DIVs and TABLEs around the HTML for the Gantt view. You might start by searching for the word "Gantt", or words from your tasks such as "Task 1" in the example above.

Steps:

1. Go to the Gantt view page
2. Add a Content Editor Web Part (see the basic steps in chapter 9) and move this below the Gantt web part
3. Decide whether to add the CSS to the **Source Editor** button or in a linked file (again see the basic steps in Chapter 9)
4. Add the following CSS to the linked file or by using the **Source Editor** button

```
<style type="text/css">
.ms-listviewtable {  display:none; }
.ms-ganttDiv {  height:800px;}
```

Task Lists

```
.ms-ganttDivNotIE { height:800px; }
</style>
```

5. Edit the "**height:**" style to adjust the display area of the Gantt chart
6. Save your changes and exit the edit mode

Prevent editing of completed tasks

You may want to "lock" a task after it has reached completed status. This solution gets you part way there, but it only removes the edit option from the normal view of a task list. The user can still select "Edit in DataSheet" to make changes or switch to another view that does not have this edit. The customization is not a form of security as a hacker can usually work around any JavaScript code you may have.

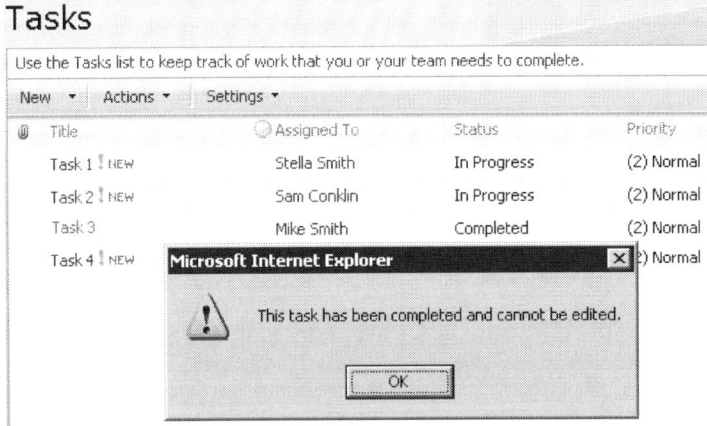

How it works: The JavaScript scans the page looking for a table cell that only contains the word "Completed". It then replaces the data in the first column, the task's dropdown list, with just the task's name and a link to a pop-up message. The 2010 version also needs to remove the checkbox.

How would you have discovered this? If you have looked at any of the other code samples, the first step is easy. Use the browser's view source option and search for the word "Completed". Then note that we need to replace the data in the cell (<TD>) with the dropdown menu in the row with just the task's name, and optionally add a hyperlink to a pop-up message.

SharePoint 2007 Steps

1. Go to the task list's view page or a web part page where you have added a task list web part
2. Add a Content Editor Web Part (see the basic steps in chapter 9) and move this below the task list web part
3. Decide whether to add the JavaScript to the **Source Editor** button or in a linked file (again see the basic steps in chapter 9)

4. Add the following JavaScript to the linked file or by using the **Source Editor** button:

```
<script type="text/javascript">
 var x = document.getElementsByTagName("TD") // find all of the TDs
 for (var i=0; i<x.length; i++)
 {
  if (x[i].className=="ms-vb2")   //find the TDs styled for lists
  {
   if (x[i].innerHTML=="Completed")
   {
    var theTargetNode = x[i].parentNode.childNodes[1];

    // The following is all one line:
    theTargetNode.innerHTML = "<a class='ms-vb2'
     href='javascript:TaskHasBeenCompleted()'>" +
     theTargetNode.getElementsByTagName("TD")[0].childNodes[0].innerHTML +
     "</a>";

   }
  }
 }
 function TaskHasBeenCompleted()
 {
  alert('This task has been completed and cannot be edited.');
 }
</script>
```

SharePoint 2010 Steps

The steps for 2010 are identical to the steps for the 2007 version, except for the column updated, and the need to hide the checkbox.

1. Go to the task list's view page or a web part page where you have added a task list web part
2. Add a Content Editor Web Part (see the basic steps in chapter 9) and move this below the task list web part (you could also edit this page in SharePoint Designer and add the code just before the end of the **PlaceHolderMain** section.)
3. Decide whether to add the JavaScript directly into the CEWP or in a linked file (again see the basic steps in chapter 9) and add the following JavaScript:

```
<script type="text/javascript">
 var x = document.getElementsByTagName("TD");    // find all of the TDs
```

```
  for (var i=0;i<x.length;i++)
  {
   if (x[i].className=="ms-vb2")   //find the TDs styled for lists
   {
    if (x[i].innerHTML=="Completed")
    {
      var theTargetNode = x[i].parentNode.childNodes[3];

      // remove the checkbox
      x[i].parentNode.childNodes[0].innerHTML="";

      // remove the dropdown menu
      // The following is all one line:
      theTargetNode.innerHTML = "<a class='ms-vb2'
        href='javascript:TaskHasBeenCompleted()'>" +
        theTargetNode.childNodes[0].childNodes[0].innerHTML + "</a>";

    }
   }
  }

  function TaskHasBeenCompleted()
  {
    alert('This task has been completed and cannot be edited.');
  }
</script>
```

Color Code Past Due / Late Tasks in a Task List

Our goal here is simple, highlight past due tasks so our team can spot them quickly. Something like this:

Task Lists

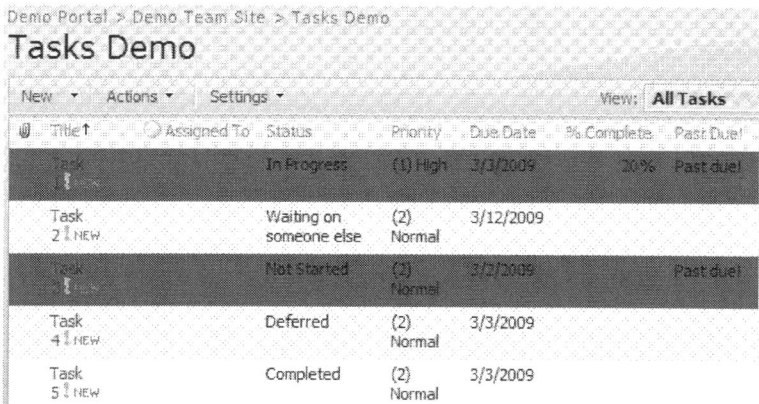

In this example we will both color code the past due tasks and add a new column to display a message such as "Past Due!".

> The steps in this customization can be used to add conditional text to any list or library.

What about a view?

If you just want a list of past due tasks, then just create a view that filters on [TODAY].

1. Create a new view for your list
2. Edit the **Filter** section to filter on **Due Date** and **Status**:

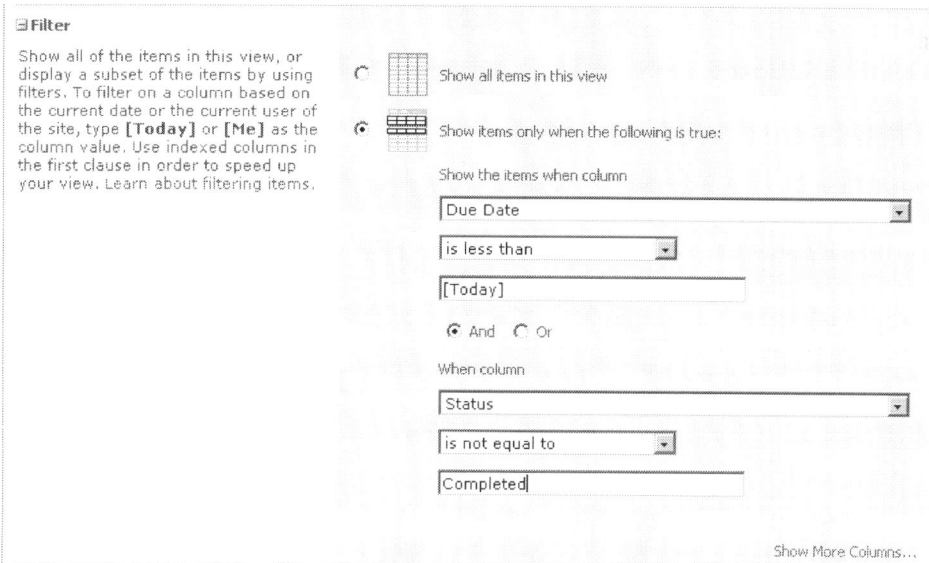

3. Click **OK** and test

Task Lists

This works, but if you want to display a complete list of all tasks, and just highlight the past due tasks, then a simple view won't work. The technique we used in "Color Coding Task Lists" would only work if we had a column with predictable text to key off of, such as "Past Due". We could try to add a calculated column to a view with a formula like "[Due Date] < [Today]" to add such as text column, but you will get this error:

> **Error**
>
> Calculated columns cannot contain volatile functions like Today and Me.
>
> Troubleshoot issues with Windows SharePoint Services.

To highlight rows of a web part using a logical comparison such as Greater Than or Less than we will need some JavaScript to do the test and to set the color.

JavaScript to the rescue

In this customization we will need to identify the column with the Due Date and test the date to see if it is before today's date. The basic date test looks like this:

```
d=new Date();    //current date/time
if (d.getTime() >= Date.parse( textFromAColumnWithADate );
```

Problem!

While the above sample appears simple and correct, it has a major flaw. The table cell (TD) with the date contains additional HTML that will confuse the JavaScript Date.parse command.

```
<TD Class="ms-vb2"><NOBR>6/13/2011</NOBR></TD>
```

The date is wrapped inside of a "No Break" tag (<NOBR>) to prevent the wrapping or splitting of the date across multiple lines in a narrow column. To read the date you will need to drill down one more child node:

```
d=new Date()    //current date/time
if (d.getTime() >=
Date.parse(x[i].parentNode.childNodes[colDueDate].childNodes[0].innerHTML) )
```

Next problem...

If you have users who have changed their SharePoint preferences (Regional Settings) to a country where they enter dates as **dd/mm/yyyy**, such as France, then JavaScript's Date.parse method will fail.

The fix for this one? Display the date in a format that Date.parse likes. JavaScript first attempts to parse the date as an ISO formatted date. It then tries other rules, but none of those support **dd/mm/yyyy**. What we need to do then is deliver a date from SharePoint that will always work with JavaScript, and one that always works is **yyyy/mm/dd**. You could just pick a locale that uses that format, but your users are not likely to be happy with that. Instead, add a calculated column to the list that generates the **yyyy/mm/dd** format, hide that column in the display (view or web part) and use that column for the JavaScript date math.

To learn more about how JavaScript works with dates see Link 1401 and Link 1402

How to deal with mixed date formats:

Note: The following is only needed if your site uses a locale with a date format other than "mm/dd/yyyy" or your users are likely to change their locale settings. The JavaScript code for the Past Due customization later in this article includes this fix.

1. Add a new column to your list and give it a name like **DueDateYYYYMMDD**
2. Add a formula:

    =YEAR([Due Date])&"/"&MONTH([Due Date])&"/"&DAY([Due Date])

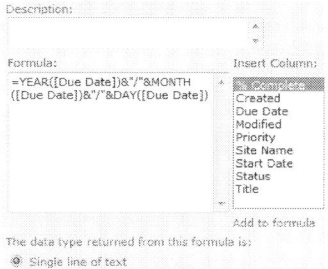

3. Save your changes
4. Add this new column to your view
5. To test this:
    a. Add some tasks with a due date and verify that both **Due Date** and **DueDateYYYYMMDD** has the same dates, just formatted differently
    b. Go to your Welcome menu, click **My Settings, My Regional Settings** and change your locale to France and confirm that while the **Due Date** column has changed, the **DueDateYYYYMMDD** is still the same
    c. Go back to your Regional Settings and reset the settings

Steps for highlighting past due tasks:

Add extra columns for the formatted due date and to display the "Past due!" message:

1. Add the "DueDateYYYYMMDD" column as described above
2. Add a new column to your task list (2007: **Settings, New Column**, 2010: Click the new column button in the ribbon)
3. Give it a title (any will do) such as "Past Due"
4. Make the column a **Calculated** column and set the formula to ="" (an equal sign followed by two quotes - we will replace the contents of this column later on using JavaScript)

Here's a sample view after adding the two new columns, but before adding the JavaScript: (a 2010 example)

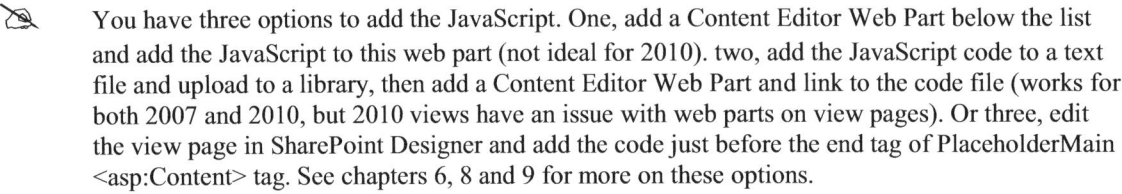

Add the JavaScript code:

- You have three options to add the JavaScript. One, add a Content Editor Web Part below the list and add the JavaScript to this web part (not ideal for 2010). two, add the JavaScript code to a text file and upload to a library, then add a Content Editor Web Part and link to the code file (works for both 2007 and 2010, but 2010 views have an issue with web parts on view pages). Or three, edit the view page in SharePoint Designer and add the code just before the end tag of PlaceholderMain <asp:Content> tag. See chapters 6, 8 and 9 for more on these options.

- **Tip for when you add code using SharePoint Designer**: You may find as you alternate between SharePoint Designer edits and view edits in the browser that the view loses your two custom columns. You effectively have two editing tools fighting each other! You may need to re-edit the view and add back the columns.

1. Display the task list view to color code (each view will need its own web part and JavaScript)
2. In SharePoint 2007: Add a Content Editor web part
   a. Click **Site Actions, Edit Page**
   b. Add a Content Editor Web Part and move it below the web part
   c. In the web part, click **Edit, Modify Shared Web Part**, and in the **Appearance** section change **Chrome** to **None**
   d. Click the **Source Editor** button
3. In SharePoint 2010:
   a. Edit the page in SharePoint Designer
   b. Switch to the Code view of the page and find the **<asp:Content>** tag for **PlaceHolderMain** and scroll down to find the matching end tag (**</asp:Content>**)
   c. Add the JavaScript code just above this end tag
4. For both versions:
   a. Type or paste the JavaScript code (examples below)
   b. Edit the **TableName** variable to set the name of the list to update - to find this, view the source of the page from the browser and search for "**summary=**" and find the task list (In 2010 this might look like summary="Tasks Use the Tasks list to keep track of work that you or your team needs to complete.")

c. Count the columns displayed in your task list to find the "Due Date" and "Past Due" columns. The Attachments column is column zero and the Due Date is typically column five (0,1,2,3,4,5). In 2010 also count the checkbox column if it is displayed.
d. Edit the JavaScript to set these three numbers:
   var colDueDate = 8;   // column with the due date in the YYYY/MM/DD format
   var colToHide = 8;   // same column as colDueDate (if you want to hide it)
   var colPastDue = 7; // set to -1 to ignore
e. Save your changes - if using a CEWP then click **Save**, **OK** and **Exit Edit Mode** to see the results

Here's the result: (2010 example)

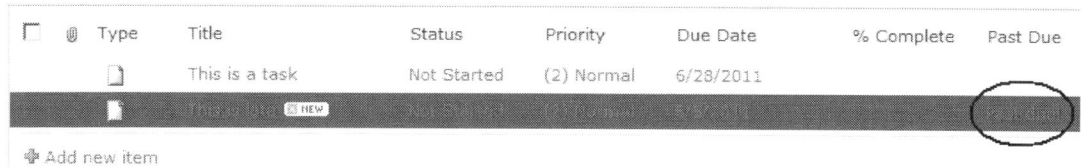

Tip: If you would like to display an image in place of the text, change this line:

x[i].parentNode.childNodes[colPastDue].innerHTML='Past due!'

to:

x[i].parentNode.childNodes[colPastDue].innerHTML='<img src="/*pathtoimage/imagename*" />'

and set your SRC to an image in your library or in the SharePoint install folder ("images").

Making this work in views other than "All Tasks"

You probably will first test this in the "All Tasks" view and then switch to one of the other task views and mumble something about Mike's hacks don't work everywhere! Well… each view page is, well… its own page. Check the URLs:

All Tasks: http://...../AllItems.aspx
Active Tasks: http://...../active.aspx
My Tasks: http://....../MyItems.aspx

Each page will need its own Content Editor Web Part (or edited page) with the JavaScript code, the extra column will need to be displayed and the column numbers in the JavaScript code adjusted.

As an example, here are the "overview" steps for the "Active Tasks" view:

- Modify the view to display the "Past Due" column and the due date column
- Determine your column numbers for the "Due Date" and "Past Due" columns
- Add the Content Editor Web Part (or edit the page in SharePoint Designer) and add the JavaScript as described above, adjusting the column numbers as needed.

Task Lists

📎 Notes:
- You cannot sort the "Past Due" column as this data is not in SharePoint. It has only been added in the user's browser. (Another plus for a workflow solution?)
- Each new view created will need the CEWP and the JavaScript added.
- Changing or reordering the columns in a view will require an update to the column numbers in the JavaScript.
- As the CEWP (or the code in the edited page) is not visible, you will probably forget that it is there, and then wonder why the color highlighting no longer works after you modify the view!
- As the CEWP (or the code in the edited page) is not visible, the next person to inherit your SharePoint site will have no idea how this works. (You do document everything you do in your site, right?)

The JavaScript for both 2007 and 2010:

```
<script type='text/javascript'>

var colDueDate = 6;  // This is the column with the due date in the YYYY/MM/DD format

var colToHide  = 6;  // This is the same column as above if you want to hide the custom date format

var colPastDue = -1; // optional column to display a custom JavaScript set message

var tableName = "Tasks"; // (from summary="")

// find the table for the list
var tables = document.getElementsByTagName("TABLE");
var table
for (x in tables)

{
  if (tables[x].summary == tableName)
  {
     table = tables[x];
     break;
  }
}
```

```
// hide the column with the special date (optional)
if (colToHide > -1)
{
  var TRs = table.getElementsByTagName("TR");
  for (x in TRs)
  {
    var toHide = colToHide;
    if (TRs[x].innerHTML)
    {

      if (TRs[x].innerHTML.toString().toLowerCase().indexOf("iframe") > -1 )
        { toHide += 1; }; // fix for 2007

      if (TRs[x].childNodes && TRs[x].childNodes.length >= toHide)
      {
        TRs[x].childNodes[toHide].style.display="none";
      }
    }
  }
}

// Color code the row based on a date calculation
var TDs = table.getElementsByTagName("TD");
var now = new Date();
for (i in TDs)
{
  if (TDs[i].className == "ms-vb2") //find the TDs styled for lists
  {
    //find a row with a key phrase
    if (TDs[i].innerHTML == "Not Started"
        | TDs[i].innerHTML == "In Progress"
        | TDs[i].innerHTML == "Waiting on someone else" )
    {
      // is this row (task) past due?
      if (now.getTime() >= Date.parse(TDs[i].parentNode.childNodes[colDueDate].innerText) )
      {
        // set the color
        TDs[i].parentNode.style.backgroundColor='red';

        // optionally display a message in another empty column
        if (colPastDue > -1)
```

```
            {
              TDs[i].parentNode.childNodes[colPastDue].innerHTML = 'Past due!';
            }
          }
        }
      }
    }
  }
</script>
```

15. Calendars

Do you need this chapter?

SharePoint calendars are pretty basic. If you would like to add some color, remove hyperlinks or show canceled events, then read on…

Oh, and while you are here, these customizations don't apply to only calendar lists. A calendar view can be added to any list or library, as long as it has at least one date of interest. As an example, if your document library has a "Review Date" column you can add a calendar view to show when documents need to be reviewed.

What's in this chapter?

- Color coded calendars
- Strike Out Canceled Events in the Calendar
- Create a Calendar View without Hyperlinks
- Using the Calendar to Schedule Meeting Rooms (multiple fields in a month view)

Calendars

Color Coded Calendars

I have been asked more than a few times if the SharePoint calendar can display items in color. It turns out this is not too hard to do. The basic steps are:

- Add a column to the calendar list to be used to pick the color
- Add a calculated column to create the HTML to display the color. This can be done with HTML or CSS. This example uses "<FONT COLOR=" or "<SPAN STYLE=".
- Add the new columns to a view
- SharePoint will convert the "<" character into "<" so we need to add a little JavaScript to convert it back. The easiest way to add the JavaScript is with a Content Editor Web Part in 2007 and with a SharePoint Designer edit in 2010.

Here's a sample with sales meetings in green, training in blue and action meetings in red. (Yes I know… colors don't show up well in a black and white book!)

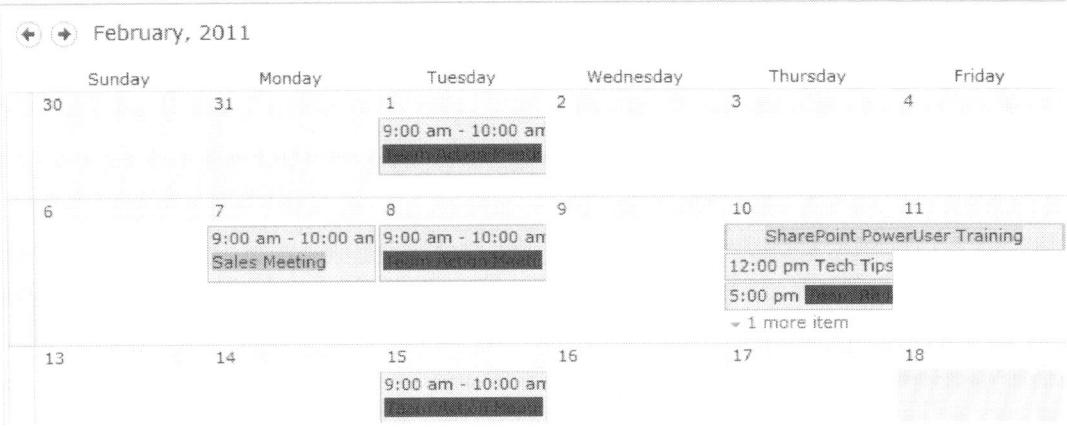

Steps:

The first few steps are the same for both 2007 and 2010.

1. Create or open a calendar
2. Add a new column named "Color" – most likely type will be Choice with choices like "Red, Green, Blue, Black", but this could be a lookup or even a single line of text
   (See here for an HTML color chart: http://www.w3schools.com/html/html_colornames.asp or see Link 1501)
3. Add a new column named "CalendarText"

a. The column type: **Calculated**
b. The Formula:

="<font color='" & Color & "'>" & Title & "</font>"

or if you prefer styles:

="" & Title & ""

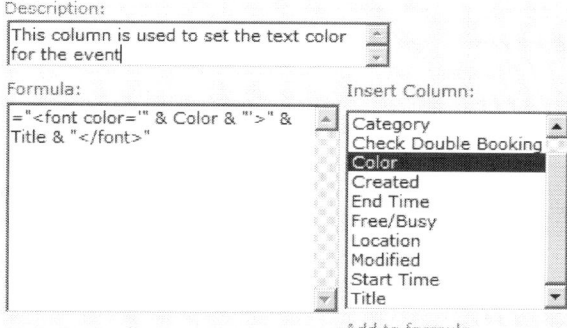

c. Set **Data type returned** as **Single line of text**
4. Modify the existing view, or create a new view such as "Color Calendar"
5. Change the field used for the **Month View Title** *and* the **Day View Title** *and* the **Week View Title** to your new calculated column ("CalendarText")

6. Save and exit (The HTML for "<FONT" or "<STYLE" will now be displayed. Some JavaScript will be needed to fix the HTML tags)

Add the JavaScript

SharePoint 2010 changed how the calendar is drawn so we need one script for 2007 and another for 2010.

Steps for 2007:

1. Add a Content Editor web part
   a. Site Actions, Site Settings, Edit Page
   b. Add a Content Editor web part and move it below the calendar web part
   c. Click the web part's dropdown menu and edit the web part
   d. Click the **Source Editor** button

381

Calendars

e. Add the following JavaScript:

The code:

```
<script type="text/javascript">
// color code calendar - 2007 version
var x = document.getElementsByTagName("TD");
for (var i=0; i<x.length; i++)
{
  if (x[i].className.substring(0,6) == "ms-cal")
  {
    x[i].innerHTML= x[i].innerHTML.replace(/&lt;/g,'<').replace(/&gt;/g,'>');
  }
}
</script>
```

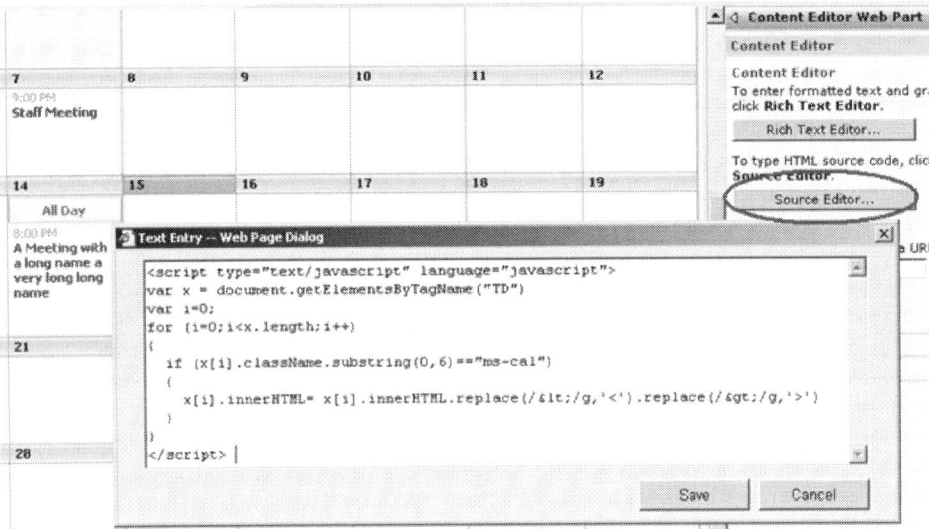

2. Click Save, OK, Exit Edit Mode
3. Add a new calendar item and select a color... Color calendars!

Steps for 2010:

In 2010 the data for the calendar is asynchronously loaded using a SharePoint built-in JavaScript function called *after* the page is loaded. That means that the data we want to change is not yet in the browser when the JavaScript is run from within the Content Editor Web Part. To get our code to run at the right time we need to hook into the SharePoint function that loads the calendar items. This is a function named

"SP.UI.ApplicationPages.CalendarNotify.$4a". We also need to delay the load of our code, and we can do that with a SharePoint feature named "_spBodyOnLoadFunctionNames.push".

This example will use a SharePoint Designer edit to add the script. For an example of how you might use a Content Editor Web Part see "Create a Calendar View without Hyperlinks (2010)" later in this chapter.

1. Open your site in SharePoint Designer 2010
2. Click **Lists and Libraries** in the **Site Objects** pane
3. Click your calendar list and click the new view
4. In the ribbon click the **Advanced Mode** link (so you can edit the entire page)
5. Search for "</WebPartPages:WebPartZone>" and insert a new line just after this tag
       </WebPartPages:WebPartZone>
         your customization goes here (don't type this ☺)
       </asp:Content>
6. Add the JavaScript from below
7. Save your changes in SharePoint Designer - you may be asked about "customizing" - answer **Yes**

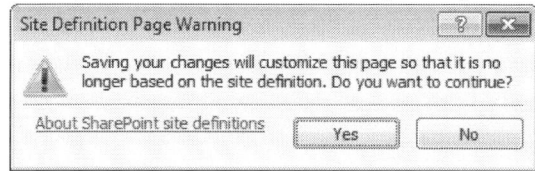

8. Go to the calendar, add a new event, select a color, and check to see if the color is displayed

The Code:

```
<script type="text/javascript">
// color code calendar - 2010 version
// load our function to the delayed load list
_spBodyOnLoadFunctionNames.push('colorCalendarEventLinkIntercept');

// hook into the existing SharePoint calendar load function
function colorCalendarEventLinkIntercept()
{
  var OldCalendarNotify4a = SP.UI.ApplicationPages.CalendarNotify.$4a;
  SP.UI.ApplicationPages.CalendarNotify.$4a = function ()
    {
      OldCalendarNotify4a();
      colorCalendarEventLinks();
    }
}

// hide the hyperlinks
function colorCalendarEventLinks()
```

383

```
{
  // find all DIVs
  var divs = document.getElementsByTagName("DIV");
  for (var i=0; i<divs.length; i++)
  {
    // find calendar item DIVs
    if (divs[i].className.toLowerCase() == "ms-acal-item")
    {
      divs[i].innerHTML = divs[i].innerHTML.replace(/&lt;/g,'<').replace(/&gt;/g,'>');
    }

    // find "x more items" links and re-apply color on Expand/Contract
    if (divs[i].className.toLowerCase() == "ms-acal-ctrlitem")
    {
      var links = divs[i].getElementsByTagName("A");
      if (links.length == 1)
      {
        links[0].href="javascript:colorCalendarEventLinks();void(0);";
      }
    }
  }
}
</script>
```

Strike Out Canceled Events in the Calendar

Moving or deleting an event in a calendar is not always the best way to make sure people notice the change. Sometimes it's better to "cancel" a meeting and then create a new meeting than just moving it in the calendar. The SharePoint calendar list does not have a built in way to do this. So... yet another JavaScript trick! Here's what we want to see when we cancel an event:

Monday	Tuesday
1	2
2:00 PM ~~Sales Team Meeting~~	10:00 AM Sales Team Meeting

The following is just a variation on how to color code a calendar. The "big change" is an IF statement that checks a "Canceled" column to make the formatting conditional. By expanding the calculated column's formula a bit you can have both color coded and canceled events.

The basic steps are:

- Add a column to the calendar list to indicate that the event has been canceled
- Add a calculated column to create the HTML to display the formatted cancelation message. This can be done with HTML or CSS. This example just uses "<s> *text* </s>" to "strike out" the text
- Add the new column to the calendar view
- SharePoint will convert the "<" character into "<" so we need to add a little JavaScript to convert it back. The easiest way to add the JavaScript is with a Content Editor Web Part.

Steps:

1. Create or open a calendar
2. Add a new column named "Canceled" (**Settings, List Settings**) – most likely type will be "Choice" with choices like "No" and "Yes" with a default of "No"
3. Add a new column named "**CalendarText**"
    a. Column Type: **Calculated**
    b. Equation: =IF(Canceled="Yes", "<s>" & Title & "</s>", Title)
    c. Data type returned: **Single line of text**
4. If you want to also change the color, then add a FONT or SPAN tag:
    =IF(Canceled="Yes", "<font color='gray'><s>" & Title & "</s></font>", Title)
5. Modify the existing view, or create a new view such as "**Calendar with cancel**"
6. Change the field used for the **Month View Title** *and* the **Day View Title** *and* the **Week View Title** to "CalendarText"

7. Save and exit (The HTML for "<s> *text* </s>" will now be displayed. The JavaScript below will be needed to fix the HTML tags.)

Add the JavaScript

SharePoint 2010 changed how the calendar is drawn so we need one script for 2007 and another for 2010.

Steps for 2007:

Calendars

1. Add a Content Editor web part
    a. Site Actions, Site Settings, Edit Page
    b. Add a Content Editor web part and move it below the calendar web part
    c. Click in the web part click Edit, Modify Shared Web Part
    d. Click the Source Editor button
    e. Add this JavaScript:

The code:

```
<script type="text/javascript">
// calendar strike out - 2007 version
var x = document.getElementsByTagName("TD");
for (var i=0; i<x.length; i++)
{
  if (x[i].className.substring(0,6) == "ms-cal")
  {
    x[i].innerHTML= x[i].innerHTML.replace(/&lt;/g,'<').replace(/&gt;/g,'>');
  }
}
</script>
```

2. Click Save, OK, Exit Edit Mode
3. Test: Add a new calendar item and select a your cancel option

Steps for 2010:

In 2010 the data for the calendar is asynchronously loaded using a SharePoint built-in JavaScript function called *after* the page is loaded. That means that the data we want to change is not yet in the browser when the JavaScript is loaded from within the Content Editor Web Part. To get our code to run at the right time we need to hook into the SharePoint function that loads the calendar items. It is a function named "SP.UI.ApplicationPages.CalendarNotify.$4a". We also need to delay the load of our code, and we can do that with a SharePoint feature named "_spBodyOnLoadFunctionNames.push".

1. Open your site in SharePoint Designer 2010
2. Click Lists and Libraries in the Site Objects pane
3. Click your calendar list and click the new view
4. In the ribbon click the Advanced Mode link (so you can edit the entire page)
5. Search for "</WebPartPages:WebPartZone>" and insert a new line just after this tag
    </WebPartPages:WebPartZone>
    your customization goes here (don't type this ☺)
    </asp:Content>
6. Add the JavaScript from below

7. Save your changes in SharePoint Designer - you may see a message about "customizing" - answer Yes

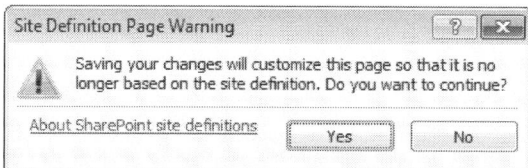

8. Test: Add a new calendar item and select a your cancel option

The Code:

```
<script type="text/javascript">
// calendar strike out - 2010 version
// load our function to the delayed load list
_spBodyOnLoadFunctionNames.push('strikeoutCalendarEventLinkIntercept');

// hook into the existing SharePoint calendar load function
function strikeoutCalendarEventLinkIntercept()
{
  var OldCalendarNotify4a = SP.UI.ApplicationPages.CalendarNotify.$4a;
  SP.UI.ApplicationPages.CalendarNotify.$4a = function ()
   {
     OldCalendarNotify4a();
     colorCalendarEventLinks();
   }
}

// hide the hyperlinks
function colorCalendarEventLinks()
{

  // find all DIVs
  var divs = document.getElementsByTagName("DIV");
  for (var i=0; i<divs.length; i++)
  {
    // find calendar item DIVs
    if (divs[i].className.toLowerCase() == "ms-acal-item")
    {
      divs[i].innerHTML = divs[i].innerHTML.replace(/&lt;/g,'<').replace(/&gt;/g,'>');
    }

    // find "x more items" links and re-apply color on Expand/Contract
```

Calendars

```
    if (divs[i].className.toLowerCase() == "ms-acal-ctrlitem")
    {
      var links = divs[i].getElementsByTagName("A");
      if (links.length == 1)
      {
        links[0].href="javascript:strikeoutCalendarEventLinks();void(0);"
      }
    }
  }
}
</script>
```

Create a Calendar View without Hyperlinks (2007)

If you just need a calendar that's just a display of events and you don't need or want hyperlinks, then a little JavaScript will do what you need. This example works for the Month view and would have to be modified a bit for the Week and Day views.

If you want to remove all links for a view:

1. Go to the calendar and create a new Calendar view
2. Go the Monthly view of the calendar
3. Click **Site Actions, Edit Page**
4. Add a Content Editor Web Part
5. Move the new web part below the calendar web part
6. Edit the web part and use the **Source Editor** button to add the following JavaScript
7. Save your changes and test

The JavaScript:

```
<script type="text/javascript">

var tables = document.getElementsByTagName("TABLE");
for (var i=0; i<tables.length; i++)
{

  if (tables[i].summary == "Monthly graphical Calendar View")
  {
```

```
  var TDs = tables[i].getElementsByTagName("TD");
  for (var j=0;j<TDs.length;j++)
  {

   if (TDs[j].className == "ms-cal-monthitem")
   {
    var As = TDs[j].getElementsByTagName("A");
    if (As.length>0)
    {
     if (document.all)    // is IE
      { TDs[j].innerText = As[0].innerText; }
     else                 // is Firefox or other
      { TDs[j].textContent = As[0].textContent; }
    }

   }

  }
  break;
 }
}
</script>
```

Create a Calendar View without Hyperlinks (2010)

In 2010 the data for the calendar is asynchronously loaded using a SharePoint built-in JavaScript function called *after* the page is loaded. That means that the data we want to change is not yet in the browser when the JavaScript is loaded from within the Content Editor Web Part. To get our code to run at the right time we need to hook into the SharePoint function that loads the calendar items. This is a function named "SP.UI.ApplicationPages.CalendarNotify.$4a". We also need to delay the load of our code, and we can do that with a SharePoint feature named "_spBodyOnLoadFunctionNames.push".

Two Solutions!

1) Add a Content Editor Web Part as we have done in many of the other customizations. The problem with this approach is that SharePoint 2010 will no longer treat this page as a view. When this page is displayed you will see two changes:

- The View dropdown list in the site title area is missing

Calendars

- The ribbon will not be displayed when the page is first loaded, but will be displayed when any event item is clicked.

2) Add the custom JavaScript using SharePoint Designer. The page will then display as an ordinary view with no odd behavior.

I recommend #2.

Steps - Using SharePoint Designer

1. Go to the calendar in the browser and create a new view (maybe "Calendar - No Links")
2. Open your site in SharePoint Designer 2010
3. Click **Lists and Libraries** in the **Site Objects** pane
4. Click your calendar list and click the new view
5. In the ribbon click the **Advanced Mode** link (so you can edit the entire page)
6. Search for "</WebPartPages:WebPartZone>" and insert a new line just after this tag

    </WebPartPages:WebPartZone>
    your customization goes here   (don't type this ☺)
    </asp:Content>

7. Add the JavaScript from below
8. Save your changes in SharePoint Designer
9. Go to the calendar in a browser, select the new view and confirm that the hyperlinks have been removed

Steps - Using a Content Editor Web part

1. Open Notepad and add the JavaScript from below and save the file (maybe "HideCalendarLinks.txt")
2. Upload the file to a library (I use a library named CustomziationFiles)
3. Right-click the new library file, click **Properties** and copy the URL to the file
4. Go to the calendar in the browser and create a new view (maybe "Calendar - No Links")
5. After the new calendar view has been displayed click **Site Actions, Edit Page**
6. Add a Content Editor Web Part
7. Move the new web part below the calendar web part
8. Edit the web part and paste the URL to the text file uploaded earlier into the **Content Link** box
9. Click **OK** to save the change, then in the **Page** tab of the ribbon click **Stop Editing**
10. Go to the calendar, select the new view and confirm that the hyperlinks have been removed

Code to hide the links

```
<script type="text/javascript">

// load our function to the delayed load list
```

```javascript
_spBodyOnLoadFunctionNames.push('hideCalendarEventLinkIntercept');

// hook into the existing SharePoint calendar load function
function hideCalendarEventLinkIntercept()
{
  var OldCalendarNotify4a = SP.UI.ApplicationPages.CalendarNotify.$4a;
  SP.UI.ApplicationPages.CalendarNotify.$4a = function ()
    {
      OldCalendarNotify4a();
      hideCalendarEventLinks();
    }
}

// hide the hyperlinks
function hideCalendarEventLinks()
{

  // find all DIVs
  var divs = document.getElementsByTagName("DIV");
  for (var i=0; i<divs.length; i++)
  {
   // find calendar item DIVs
   if (divs[i].className.toLowerCase() == "ms-acal-item")
   {
     // find the hyperlink
     var links = divs[i].getElementsByTagName("A");
     if (links.length == 1)
     {
      // replace the hyperlink with text
      links[0].parentNode.innerHTML = links[0].innerHTML
     }
   }

    // find "x more items" links and re-remove links on Expand/Contract
    if (divs[i].className.toLowerCase() == "ms-acal-ctrlitem")
    {
      var links = divs[i].getElementsByTagName("A");
      if (links.length == 1)
      {
        links[0].href = "javascript:hideCalendarEventLinks();void(0);"
      }
```

Calendars

```
    }
   }
  }
</script>
```

Using the Calendar to Schedule Meeting Rooms (multiple fields in a month view)

This customization is not a complete way to manage meeting rooms, only a tip on displaying multiple fields in a SharePoint calendar view. In particular, you might want to see both the location (Room 6B) and the meeting title (Staff Meeting) in the month view of the calendar. When displaying a calendar in Month view you can only display the time (unchangeable) and a single field (your choice). To display more than one field you will need to add a calculated column to merge the two (or more) fields.

Steps:

1. Display the calendar, click **Settings, Create a column**
2. Add a calculated column (I'll call it **MonthData**) with an equation to join the columns you want to display. Example: **Location & " - " & Title** (If you return to modify this equation it will have been reformatted as: =Location&" - "&Title)
3. Uncheckmark **Add to default view** and the click **OK**
4. Click the **View** menu and select **Modify this view**
5. In the **Calendar Columns** section of the page change "Month View Title:" to your new column (MonthData)
6. Click **OK** and check the results in the month view of the calendar

You could also add a new column named "reserved by" and use that in your calculated column to display the room and who has it reserved: =Location&" - "&[Reserved By]

Sorry, there are no tips here on how to find an available room or other to create "scheduling features"! Search the web and you will find a few interesting articles on using the calendar for scheduling.

16. Bonus Content

This is not the last chapter… this book does not have an end. Although this book will very likely have a Volume Two in a year or so, this book is a dynamic document and is being updated on a regular basis on its web site. Go to the book's web site, register and subscribe to the RSS feed or create alerts on lists and libraries of interest.

What's on the web site

- A bonus chapter!   Sound, Video, Silverlight and Flash!
- All of the source code from the book, ready for copy and paste
- All of the resource links from the book
- Working examples of many of the book's customizations
- A forum where you can post questions to the author

Index

$

$ · *See* jQuery

%

%$Resources · 200

&

&IsDlg=1 · 247, 250, 329, 337, 338, 345
&Source= · 246
&ToolPaneView · 120

_

_fV4UI · 84
_LAYOUTS · *See* Pages, _LAYOUTS
_spBodyOnLoadFunctionNames · 82
_spBodyOnLoadFunctionNames.push · 81
_spUserId · 106

A

Accordion menus · 175
Active Directory groups · 108
ASP.Net
    controls · 29
    tags · 29
ASP.Net Controls
    Asp:Menu · 169, 212
Audience · 108

B

Basic pages
    adding Quick Launch (2007) · 179
    cleaning up (2007) · 181
    cleaning up (2010) · 187
    remove Quick Launch (2010) · 188
Branding · 14, 138, 236
Browser detection
    using JavaScript · 52
Browser developer toolbars · 77

C

Calculated columns · 373
    and dates · 73
Calendar control (ASP.Net) · 29
Calendars · 379
    add new event · 292
    adding color coding · 380
    create view without hyperlinks · 388
    delayed loading of · 82
    SP.UI.ApplicationPages.CalendarNotify · 83
    strike out canceled events · 384
    to schedule meeting rooms · 392
    views · 392
Cascading Style Sheets · 33
    !important · 40
    @media print · 42
    2010 title area CSS style names · 149
    adding to SharePoint · 41
    classes · 38
    comments · 39
    Content Edtior Web Part · 42
    defined · 34
    display:none · 39
    example
        Quick Launch · 40
    for printing · 42
    inline · 35, 40
    jQuery · 69
    link media=print · 42
    linked files · 35
    linking to · 44

Index

masterpage, adding to · 41
overriding inline styles · 40
position DIVs · 39
position:absolute · 39
selectors · 37
SharePoint Designer, adding with · 41
style attribute · 35
syntax · 37
visibility · 39
CDN · *See* Content Delivery Networks
CEWP · *See* Content Editor Web Part
childNodes · 60
Color
   calendars · 380
   HTML colors · 21
   libraries · 240
   past due tasks · 370
   site title · 148
   surveys · 339
   task lists · 57, 363
   web parts · 218
Color coded lists · 237
Configuration · 12
Confirm site exit · 167
Content Delivery Networks
   source for jQuery libaries · 66
Content Editor Web Part · **128**
   2007 · 131
   2010 · 132
   best practices · 136
   broken 2010 views · 122
   Cascading Style Sheets · 42
   hide title bar (chrome) · 132
   JavaScript · 81
   jQuery · 67
   linking to code stored in a library · 135
   list and library customization · 236
   overview · 129
   reusing in other pages · 135
CORE.css · 43, 44
corev4.css · 18, 41, 43, 44
Crumb trail · 124, 146, 152, 186, 241, 324
CSS · *See* Cascading Style Sheets

Custom Development · 12
Customization · 12
   What can be customized · 13

D

DataViewWebPart · 252
   display pictures or thumbnails · 269
default.aspx
   change or replace the home page · 216
DHTML · 30
Dialog boxes
   &IsDlg=1 · 247, 250, 329, 337, 338, 345
Discussion list
   change the "No Items" message in a discussion web part · 289
Document libraries
   add hyperlinks in libraries for special URLs · 296
   adding hyperlinks to document libraries · 295
   One library, multiple sites · 305
Document Object Model · 52
document.all · 52, 53
DOM · *See* Document Object Model

E

ECMAScript Class Library Object Method · 91
Error messages
   Warning: The HTML source you entered might have been modified · 134
ExecuteOrDelayUntilScriptLoaded · 92

F

Firefox · 32, 52
   browser detection · 52
   developer toolbar add-ins · 77
   view source · 76
Flash · 393
Folders

Index

how to add columns (metadata) to SharePoint folders · 302
Form Web Part · 129

G

Gantt chart · 367
getElementById · 52
getElementsByClassName · 55
getElementsByClassName function · 56
getElementsByName · 54
getElementsByTagName · 55
Ghosted page · 95
GUIDs · 307

H

home.aspx
    change or replace the home page · 216
HTML · 17
    <a> · 27
    <body> · 20

 · 23
    <div> · 28
    <head> · 20
    <html> · 20
    <iframe> · 361
    <link> (CSS example) · 44
    <p> · 23
    <script> · 47
    <script> - for jQuery · 66
    <span> · 28
    <title> · 20
    anchor · 27
    ASP.Net tags · 29
    attributes · 21
    colors · 21
    DHTML · 30
    entities · 25
    hyperlinks · 27
    ID attribute · 23
    in SharePoint · 18
    innerText attribute · 52
    JavaScript · 47
    lists, <ul>, <ol>, <li> · 24
    name attribute · 23
    name vs id · 24, 54
    non-breaking space -   · 23
    page tags · 20
    SharePoint controls · 29
    SharePoint tags · 29
    tables <table>, <tr>, <td> · 26
    tags · 19
    text formatting · 22
    URL character encoding · 246
HTML editors · 77
Hypertext Markup Language · 17

I

ie:menuitem · 160
innerText
    and browser compatibility · 52
Internet Explorer
    browser detection · 52
    developer toolbar · 77
    view source · 76

J

JavaScript · 45
    _spBodyOnLoadFunctionNames.push · 81
    added to a master page · 71
    added to a site page · 71
    alert statement · 167
    array · 50
    as used in SharePoint · 46
    blocks - IF and FOR · 61
    browser detection · 52
    case sensitive · 47
    childNodes · 60
    comments · 48
    comparison operators · 63
    confirm statement · 168

Content Editor Web Part · 46, 71
controlling with code runs · 81
Date.parse · 72
dates - SharePoint issues · 72, 372
finding web part table cells · 238
for loop example · 48
FOR statement · 61
functions · 51
getElementById · 52
getElementsByClassName · 55
getElementsByName · 54
getElementsByTagName · 55
how to find an image web part · 80
IF statement · 62
name vs id to find tags · 54
nextSibling · 60
onclick event example · 47
parentNode · 57
previousSibling · 60
Query String - accessing · 64
setTimeout (timer) · 81
SharePoint tips · 71
syntax · 47
URL - accessing · 64
variables · 50
when will scripts run in SharePoint · 71
jQuery · 65
    $(document).ready · 82
    an example of · 67
    attr (attribute) selector · 160
    before selector · 142
    change the "No Items" message in a discussion board · 291
    contains selector · 291
    Content Editor Web Part · 67
    CSS - Cascading Style Sheets · 69
    downloading · 65
    example - add a message at the top bottom of a page - 2007 · 140
    example - add a message at the top bottom of a page - 2010 · 142
    example - hide menu options (2007) · 160
    functions · 70
    hide the "Save" button in a survey · 344
    linking to · 66
    linking to libraries on the web · 66
    resources · 70
    selecting HTML elements / tags · 69
    table
        first selector · 140
    tr
        first selector · 140
    wild cards in selectors · 160

L

LAYOUTS pages · *See* Pages, _LAYOUTS
Library customizations · 235
Link to a Document · 295
Links lists · **353**
    add a "You are leaving this site" message · 356
    add a "You are leaving this site" message with confirmation · 357
    adding pop ups (open in new window) · 354
    convert a links list into a dropdown list that opens in a new window · 360
    convert a links list to a dropdown list · 357
    for navigation · 234
List and Library Customization
    add a web part to display a library folder · 281
    add hyperlinks in libraries for special URLs · 296
    adding hyperlinks to document libraries · 295
    change the "Add New" message for a web part · 292
    change the "No Items" message in a discussion web part · 289
    color code a library · 240
    color coded lists · 237
    create a "What's New" web part · 280
    customizing the New button · 244
    Group By on more than two columns · 250
    Group By on more than two columns (2007) · 253
    Group By on more than two columns (2010) · 261
    hide a web part with zero rows · 283

Index

hiding the Checked Out icon from anonymous users · 303
how to add columns (metadata) to SharePoint folders · 302
how to truncate a Multiline column and add a "More" link · 298
one library, multiple sites · 305
printing a list or library · 321
quote or the day / tip of the day · 270
redirect after clicking Cancel · 248, 249
redirecting after adding a new item · 245, 248
removing view group headings and counts · 276
rotating pictures, random pictures · 309
List customizations · 235
Lists
    calculated columns · 73
ListViewWebPart · 252

M

Master pages
    defined · **97**
    versioning · 98
    where stored · 98
MSOImageWebPart_*xxx* · 80
MSOZoneCell_WebPartWPQ · 220

N

NewItem.aspx
    example customization · 110
nextSibling · 60

O

Office 365 · 15

P

Page Viewer Web Part · 130
    add a web part to display a library folder · 281

security issues · 130
Pages
    _LAYOUTS · 13, 29, 170
parentNode · 57
Permission levels · 113
    for Visitors, Contributors, Designers and Owners · 113
Permission Levels · 110
Permissions
    table of · 113
PermissionsString · 29, 111
Picture libraries
    rotating pictures, random pictures · 309
previousSibling · 60

Q

Quick Launch
    accordion menus · 175
    add a "Create New" link · 244, 246
    adding to Basic pages (2007) · 179
    confirm site exit · 167
    CSS styles (2007) · 172
    CSS styles (2010) · 173
    hide bullets (2007) · 194
    JavaScript tricks · 166
    pop out menus · 169
    removing from Basic pages (2010) · 188

R

Ribbon
    hide disabled ribbon options (2010) · 165
    how to hide · 156
Run me last rountine · 83

S

Security
    customizing People and Groups views · 115

Index

Security Trimmed Control · *See* SharePoint Controls, SPSecurityTrimmedControl
SharePoint
    calculated columns · 73
    Configuration · 12
    controls · 29
    Custom Development · 12
    Customization · 12
    dates - JavaScript issues · 72
    editions · 15
    error messages · *See* Error messages
    locale - My Regional Settings · 72
    menu IDs - 2007 · 160
    menu IDs - 2010 · 162
    permission levels · 110
    regional settings · 72
    security · 105
    Themes · 13
    tools needed · 14
    trivia · 16
    version detection · 15, 84
    version detection - _fV4UI variable · 85
    version detection - from ECMAScript Class Library · 91
    version detection - from HTTP header · 87
    version detection - from style names · 86
    versions · 15
    Welcome menu · 72
SharePoint "in the cloud" · 15
SharePoint Controls
    SharePoint:AspMenu · 169, 213
    SharePoint:SPLinkButton · 115
    SharePoint:SPSecurityTrimmedControl · 29, 110, 115, 164
SharePoint Designer · 93
    advanced mode editing · 103
    Cascading Style Sheets · 41
    customizing / un-ghosting a page · 95
    finding custmoized pages · 96
    list and library customization · 236
    master pages - editing - 2007 · 99
    master pages - editing - 2010 · 99
    online resources · 94
    resetting / undoing customizations · 96
    security restrictions · 94
    site pages - editing - 2007 · 101
    site pages - editing - 2010 · 102
    XSLT Data View · 122
SharePoint Permissions · 113
    permission levels · 113
Silverlight · 18, 129, 393
Site Collection Administrator · 13, 14, 115
    defined · 14
Site Owner · 12, 13, 14, 104, 111
    defined · 13
Site pages
    advanced mode editing · 103
    editing - 2007 · 101
    editing - 2010 · 102
    editing examples · 100
    example customization · 110
    finding custmoized pages · 96
    resetting / undoing customizations · 96
    site page edits vs. using the Content Edtior Web Part · 130
Site Templates · 15
Sound · 393
source code from the book · *See* Chapter 1
SP.ClientSchemaVersions.currentVersion · 91
SP.UI.ApplicationPages.CalendarNotify · 83
Static web parts · 122
Surveys · **327**
    a better yes/no field · 334
    add a message to the Overview page · 335
    add a Welcome, Thank You or Instruction message · 336
    add instructions and color · 339
    adding color, fonts and HTML · 339
    create custom view (2007) · 331
    hide the "Save" button · 342
    modify the "Respond to this Survey" prompt · 348
    overview · 328
    reuse your custom surveys · 352
    survey pages · 328
    survey tips · 329
    use a direct URL to a survey · 329

Index

T

Task List
    color - JavaScript example · 57
Task lists · **362**
    color code past due / late tasks · 370
    color coding task lists · 363
    hide the bottom section of a Gantt chart · 367
    prevent editing of completed tasks · 368
textContent
    and browser compatibility · 52
Themes · 13
Three C's of SharePoint Customization · 12
Top Link Bar
    add dropdown menus (2007) · 203
    add dropdown menus (2010) · 211
    confirm site exit · 167
    JavaScript tricks · 166
Tree View
    adding lines · 199
    change Site Hierarchy / Site Content text · 200
    CSS / styles · 198
    customization · 115
    customizations · 196
    hide the icons · 200
    pre-expanded · 198
    sub sites only · 197
Trivia
    Cascading Style Sheets · 44
    HTML · 32
    JavaScript · 74
    SharePoint · 16

U

Un-ghosted page · 95, 241
URL character encoding · 246
URLs
    absolute vs. relative · 245
    add hyperlinks in libraries for special URLs · 296
    URL character encoding · 246
User

    current logged in · 106
    identifing by group membership · 108
    indentify by permissions · 110
User Interface Customization · 137
    add a message at the top bottom of a page · 139
    add a message at the top of every page · 142
    add a page footer · 145
    add colors, borders and fonts to web parts · 218
    add dropdown menus to the Top Link bar (2007) · 203
    basic pages · 179
    change or replace the home page · 216
    custom menus · 212
    hide disabled ribbon options (2010) · 165
    hide menu options (2007) · 158
    hide menu options (2010) · 162
    hide menu options for selected users · 164
    hide Quick Launch bullets (2007) · 194
    hide the SharePoint 2010 ribbon from visitors and anonymous users · 156
    hide web part columns · 189
    Quick Launch accordion menus · 175
    Quick Launch and Top Link Bar tricks · 166
    Quick Launch pop outs · 169
    redesign the SharePoint 2010 site tile and crumb trail · 152
    site title and icon (2007) · 145
    site title and icon (2010) · 148
    Tree View customizations · 196
    web part pages · 179

V

Version detection
    _fV4UI variable · 85
    from ECMAScript Class Library · 91
    from HTTP header · 87
    from style names · 86
    SharePoint · 15
Video · 393
View All Site Content
    how to hide for selected users · 114

View source · 76
Views
    broken 2010 views (Content Editor Web Part) · 122
    broken 2010 views (DataFormWebPart) · 261
    calendar · 392
    color coding · 240
    create a "What's New" web part · 280
    create a calendar view without hyperlinks · 388
    create custom survey views (2007) · 331
    customizing People and Groups views · 115
    Group By on more than two columns · 250
    move totals the bottom of each group · 250
    past due tasks · 371
    remove unwanted group headings · 250
    removing group headings and counts · 276
Visual Studio · 13, 77

W

Web part pages
    add / remove web part zones · 192
    adding Quick Launch (2007) · 179
    changing column widths · 191
    hide web part columns · 189
Web part zones
    add / remove · 192
Web parts
    "Add New" message IDs · 292, 293
    &ToolPaneView · 120
    ?Contents=1 · 120
    add colors, borders and fonts · 218
    change the "Add New" message · 292
    chrome · 80

Content Editor Web Part · *See* Content Editor Web Part
DataViewWebPart · *See* DataViewWebPart
disable or hide "Close" · 127
does page have web parts · 120
exporting, importing and reusing · 121
Form Web Part · 129
hide a web part with zero rows · 283
how to delete "bad" web parts · 120
How to find a web part in code · 78
image web part · 80
ListViewWebPart · 252
MSOImageWebPart_*xxx* - web part ID · 80
no "Edit Page" in Site Actions · 120
Page Viewer Web Part · *See* Page Viewer Web Part
prevent closing · 125
prevent closing and display a popup · 126
round corners (link) · 234
static web parts · 122
styles · 218
summary attribute · 78
title attribute · 78
web part "must knows" · 119
XSLT Data View · 122
XsltListViewWebPart · 252
Welcome menu · 72
    get current logged in user · 107
    relocate (2010) · 157
Welcome page · 217

X

XSLT Data View · 122
XsltListViewWebPart · 252

Printed in Great Britain
by Amazon.co.uk, Ltd.,
Marston Gate.